PROFESSIONAL HEROKU® PROGRAMMING

PROFESSIONAL

Heroku® Programming

PROFESSIONAL

Heroku® Programming

Chris Kemp
Brad Gyger

John Wiley & Sons, Ltd.

To my fiancée, Fiona, whose support and inspiration made writing this book possible; and my parents, Don and Vlasta, who gave me the opportunities throughout my life that made this and all of my achievements possible.

—CHRIS

To my wife, Nabila; my son, Cameron; and my parents, Roger and Judy. Without you all this wouldn't have been possible.

—BRAD

ABOUT THE AUTHORS

CHRIS KEMP is a cloud architect, innovator, and entrepreneur with experience developing software in a number of languages. The bulk of his development experience is with PHP, Java, and the Salesforce Platform. He started a software development consultancy, Vandelay Enterprises, at the age of 15, developing applications, mostly on the LAMP stack, for customers around the world. Chris then moved to the fast-growing Toronto start-up, I Love Rewards (now Achievers), where he developed rewards and recognition software in PHP and Java, before joining Salesforce.com.

Chris currently works out of Salesforce.com's Toronto office, as a Senior Solution Engineer on the Advanced Technical Solutions team, an international team of trusted pre-sales advisors and architects. He is the worldwide leader of the Heroku Ambassador group, a team of leading Heroku experts in the company. Chris has developed a number of open source projects in Apex and Visualforce, including the wildly popular Cloud Swarm application. He is a named inventor on seven patent applications for innovations developed at Salesforce.com.

Chris holds a B.Sc. in Computer Science (Software Engineering specialist, 0T4) from the University of Toronto.

BRAD GYGER has extensive experience with various development platforms, including Heroku. Early in his career, he focused on Java application stacks at Sun Microsystems and then Oracle, and later migrated to the cloud, first working at platform provider Engine Yard, and then Heroku.

Brad currently leads the Customer Advocacy team at Heroku, where he is tasked with the success of customer applications running on the platform. This requires working knowledge of all supported application architectures, languages, frameworks, and tools within the Heroku universe. He works with customers on a daily basis to ensure that their applications are implemented optimally on the platform. During his career, Brad has worked with thousands of customer applications and made sure each one was as successful as possible.

Brad holds a Bachelor of Science degree from Indiana University. He and his family currently reside in the San Francisco Bay Area.

ABOUT THE TECHNICAL EDITOR

GREG NOKES has more than 20 years of experience in systems engineering, ranging from designing wide area networks to helping high-traffic web applications scale successfully. He has successfully lead customer-facing as well as highly technical teams on a variety of projects. He is fluent in several technologies, including cutting-edge web application servers and deployment tools.

Currently, Greg is the Lead Technical Account Manager at Heroku, the premier PaaS provider. In this role, he helps a large and dynamic group of companies learn the best practices for optimizing their applications, as well as assists with technical and architectural advice.

Greg enjoys hiking, paintball, and soaking up the surroundings in the beautiful Puget Sound area of the Pacific Northwest.

CREDITS

VP CONSUMER AND TECHNOLOGY PUBLISHING DIRECTOR
Michelle Leete

ASSOCIATE DIRECTOR—BOOK CONTENT MANAGEMENT
Martin Tribe

ASSOCIATE PUBLISHER
Chris Webb

ASSISTANT EDITOR
Ellie Scott

ASSOCIATE MARKETING DIRECTOR
Louise Breinholt

MARKETING MANAGER
Lorna Mein

SENIOR MARKETING EXECUTIVE
Kate Parrett

EDITORIAL MANAGER
Jodi Jensen

SENIOR PROJECT EDITOR
Sara Shlaer

PROJECT EDITOR
John Sleeva

COPY EDITOR
Luann Rouff

TECHNICAL EDITOR
Greg Nokes

PRODUCTION EDITOR
Kathleen Wisor

PROOFREADER
Nancy Carrasco

INDEXER
Jack Lewis

COVER DESIGNER
LeAndra Young

COVER IMAGE
© boboling / iStockphoto

ACKNOWLEDGMENTS

THIS BOOK COULD NOT HAVE BEEN POSSIBLE without the vision and incredible dedication from the uber-smart founders and team at Heroku in developing such an amazing technology and making it better every day. Salesforce.com's senior leadership team, especially Marc Benioff, must be thanked for bringing Heroku into the Salesforce.com family.

The team at Wiley, including Chris Webb, John Sleeva, Luann Rouff, Kate Parrett, Lorna Mein, and Ellie Scott, have done an outstanding job with all the hard work behind the scenes to make this book the best it can be. Greg Nokes has also done an incredible job in ensuring this book's technical accuracy.

My co-author, Brad, deserves huge thanks for being so patient in teaching me the ins and outs of Heroku. You are truly an outstanding individual to work with. Your great efforts are massively appreciated. And we're both crossing one item off of our bucket lists together!

I would not have had the opportunity to write this book were it not for the foresight of my manager, Richard Ho, and the support of the Sales Engineering management team at Salesforce.com, including Dominic Dinardo, Pat McQueen, Anne DelSanto, and Sandy Jones. Your leadership continues to inspire me to do great things every day. My colleagues have been so supportive throughout my career at Salesforce.com and deserve big thanks for that.

I also want to thank Will Tran and Craig Kerstiens for lending their Java and Heroku Postgres wisdom. A big thanks to my cousin, Adam Kemp, for lending me the family cottage and keeping me company while I wrote the bulk of this book; and to his dad, George, for his valuable legal advice. And thanks to all my friends for your encouragement and kind words.

The biggest thanks goes to Fiona, for your support and patience while I wrote this book; and to my family, who raised me and taught me just about everything I know. I can never thank you enough for all you've done for me throughout my life. This book is for you.

—CHRIS

A BIG THANK YOU TO MY TEAMMATES at Heroku. It has been an inspiration to watch you create amazing things and empower our community with truly revolutionary technology. Your support and encouragement have been instrumental in the creation of this book. I hope we do Heroku proud.

I must thank my co-author, Chris. We met soon after Heroku joined the Salesforce.com family and clicked immediately. It's been a lot of fun creating with you, Chris, both within this book and on all those apps!

A quick thank you to our Technical Editor, Greg Nokes. He's been a colleague for several years now, keeping me honest the whole time.

I also want to thank the people at Wiley, especially Chris Webb, John Sleeva, Luann Rouff, Kate Parrett, Lorna Mein, and Ellie Scott. You have all done a great job supporting Chris and me.

Most of all, I must thank my family. Your love and support has been instrumental in completing this book.

—BRAD

CONTENTS

INTRODUCTION

APPS ARE EVERYWHERE! Whether bookmarked in web browsers or downloaded to mobile devices, apps of all sorts are pervasive in everyday life. With cloud computing now on the forefront of technology, creating and delivering such apps is easier than ever. Anyone from a senior research fellow to an aspiring web developer can create amazing apps for people to enjoy at record pace.

Enabling such creation is the concept of cloud platform-as-a-service (PaaS). PaaS enables architects, developers, and even hobbyists to take their ideas, write some code locally, and then deploy an app in a matter of moments. No longer are people saddled with the burden of managing servers, operating systems, databases, language run times, framework libraries, or additional tools. In the PaaS world, all of the mundane is taken care of, enabling "creators" to focus on their great ideas.

Leading this innovative new approach to creating, developing and deploying apps is Heroku. Now part of the Salesforce.com family of companies, Heroku is considered by many to be the leading PaaS for multi-language, cloud-based app deployment. With more than a million users, and more than two-and-a-half million deployed apps, Heroku also supports more languages and third-party tools than any other PaaS in the market today.

Professional Heroku Programming is a hands-on guide to creating apps on Heroku. We walk you through the core concepts in PaaS and Heroku, introducing you to a new way of thinking about developing and deploying your apps. We address the core concepts of architecture, application stack components, scaling and management — but in a whole new light, via the Heroku platform.

Wherever possible, this book provides step-by-step instructions on carrying out tasks that may be new or foreign when compared to how most people go about building and deploying apps. Stick with it! It's a brave new world for app creators, and Heroku is the path of least resistance to rapidly create apps and easily manage them.

WHO THIS BOOK IS FOR

This book is for anyone who wants to learn how to create and deploy apps on the Heroku platform. The book's main audience may be targeted towards the professional application developer or architect, as many of the concepts are geared towards professional application delivery. However, anyone, including hobbyists, is welcome to enjoy this book in order to become proficient in Heroku.

It is recommended that you are versed in at least one open development language and/or framework (Ruby/Rails, Python/Django, Java/Spring), as many of the concepts and code snippets follow along with those types of apps and conventions. An understanding of object-oriented programming is also advised, as most languages we will be developing with are object-oriented.

It is also helpful to have some knowledge of development platforms — in particular, cloud platforms — though it's not a requirement in order to follow this book's content.

Chapter by chapter, we walk you through all the core concepts, starting with defining PaaS and Heroku, gradually diving deeper into platform. While the first section details the basics, more advanced developers or architects may wish to skip ahead to sections of greater interest.

WHAT THIS BOOK COVERS

This book is divided into five unique parts. You can progress through the chapters sequentially, or you can consume a specific Part or Chapter alone.

➤ **Part I, "An Overview of Heroku,"** provides you with an understanding of the core concepts of Heroku. Those concepts are then applied to both brand new or existing apps you'd like to run on the platform.

  ➤ Chapter 1, "How Heroku Works," details the basics behind the platform and its unique approach to application deployment.

  ➤ Chapter 2, "Architectural Considerations," goes into the concepts you need to consider when architecting new apps for the Heroku platform.

  ➤ Chapter 3, "Porting Your Applications to Heroku," outlines the tasks and considerations when deciding to port apps to Heroku.

➤ **Part II, "Creating and Managing Heroku Applications,"** provides the fundamentals of daily life with Heroku. After reading this Part, you should be able to grasp any aspect of managing your apps on Heroku.

  ➤ Chapter 4, "Deploying Your Applications to Heroku," walks you through how to deploy your apps to the platform, including the pre-work required to configure your local machine(s) properly.

  ➤ Chapter 5, "Managing Releases with Heroku," describes how you can manage releases across the apps you've successfully deployed, and how you can build out your development workflow within Heroku.

  ➤ Chapter 6, "Working with Add-Ons," shows you how to extend your app using add-ons, third-party services that provide core architectural components you'd otherwise curate on your own.

  ➤ Chapter 7, "Managing, Monitoring, and Scaling Your Heroku Applications," teaches you how to manage, monitor, and scale your apps on Heroku. As soon as significant volumes of traffic start hitting your apps, it's important to know how to properly support apps running in a live state on Heroku.

➤ **Part III, "Using a Data Store with Your Heroku Applications,"** examines where to put your data on Heroku. You learn about the several options the platform provides for storing and interacting with your data. Each app is unique; so, too, are the data service requirements. Heroku can help address that with a choice of alternatives to best fit your unique use case.

➤ Chapter 8, "Using Heroku Postgres as a Data Store for Your Heroku Applications," details the most commonly used data store option, Heroku Postgres. While delivered by the same company, Heroku Postgres is its own unique data-as-a-service (DaaS) that can be consumed either with a Heroku app or as a standalone product.

➤ Chapter 9, "Using Database.com as a Data Store for Your Heroku Applications," presents a compelling option from Heroku's parent company, Salesforce.com, with its Database.com service. Database.com provides a great mechanism for developers who must write or exchange data with any Salesforce.com implementations to drive their business needs.

➤ Chapter 10, "Using Third-Party Data Stores for Your Heroku Applications," switches gears and looks to third parties for various options. Via the add-ons ecosystem (and other DaaS providers outside of the add-ons), developers can leverage a wide array of options to fit their specific needs.

➤ **Part IV, "Programming on Heroku's Polyglot Platform,"** gets into nitty-gritty details of developing on Heroku. With its support for more open languages and frameworks than any other PaaS, Heroku empowers developers to use the best tool for the job. After completing this Part, you should recognize that you're never limited by the Heroku platform.

➤ Chapter 11, "Developing with Ruby," examines development with the first programming language available on Heroku, Ruby. You'll be presented with sample apps touching on both the Rack and Sinatra frameworks.

➤ Chapter 12, "Developing with Java," focuses on the most widely adopted open language, Java. Deploying Java apps on Heroku can be a very different workflow than most people are used to in traditional Java development. Spring and Play, two very popular Java frameworks, are available for development and deployment on Heroku.

➤ Chapter 13, "Developing with Other Supported Languages," touches on the remaining languages available within Heroku: Python, Scala, Clojure, Node.js, Grails, and PHP.

➤ Chapter 14, "Understanding Buildpacks," details the concept of buildpacks and how they empower you to extend the power of Heroku to nearly any language you choose. You will see examples using existing buildpacks for .NET apps on Mono and Perl, and then create your own buildpack.

➤ **Part V, "Creating a New Generation of Heroku Applications,"** wraps up the book by demonstrating how to build next-generation apps. In today's application landscape, a large portion of what's being built is meant to engage and delight users. The most common ways to do that are via mobile devices and social networks.

➤ Chapter 15, "Building Mobile Applications with Heroku," demonstrates how to build mobile apps on Heroku using both native and HTML5-style client front ends.

➤ Chapter 16, "Building Social Applications with Heroku," details the ways in which you can easily build social apps for the web.

HOW THIS BOOK IS STRUCTURED

This book is structured so that it may be consumed from start to finish for the true Heroku novice, or as a tactical reference at the Part or Chapter level for more seasoned developers and architects. Each Part covers a unique aspect of the Heroku experience, with the individual chapters providing specific reference material, where required.

The final Part may not be required if you're already building apps in the mobile or social genres. However, a quick skim may provide some insight into how building those sorts of apps on Heroku is much more efficient.

WHAT YOU NEED TO USE THIS BOOK

To develop with the Heroku platform, you will need a local machine (laptop or desktop) running Windows, Mac OS, or Linux. Administrator or Super User rights are preferred to install various developer tools, but not strictly required in most cases. On your local machine, you'll need to have created a Heroku user account and have the Heroku Toolbelt installed on your machine.

You can create your Heroku account at any time by visiting `https://api.heroku.com/signup`.

You can download the Heroku Toolbelt from `https://toolbelt.heroku.com`.

You will also need to have your local machine configured for development in your preferred language (Ruby, Python, Java, etc.). We outline the steps needed to do this in the respective chapters where these languages are used.

CONVENTIONS

To help you get the most from the text and keep track of what's happening, we've used a number of conventions throughout the book.

> **WARNING** *Warnings hold important, not-to-be-forgotten information that is directly relevant to the surrounding text.*

> **NOTE** *Notes indicates notes, tips, hints, tricks, or and asides to the current discussion.*

As for styles in the text:

➤ We *highlight* new terms and important words when we introduce them.

➤ We show keyboard strokes like this: Ctrl+A.

➤ We show file names, URLs, and code within the text like so: `persistence.properties`.

➤ We present code in two different ways:

```
We use a monofont type with no highlighting for most code examples.
```

```
We use bold to emphasize code that's particularly important in the present context.
```

SOURCE CODE

As you work through the examples in this book, you may choose either to type in all the code manually or to use the source code files that accompany the book. All the source code used in this book is available for download at `http://www.wrox.com`. You will find that the code snippets from the source code are accompanied by a download icon and note indicating the name of the program, so you know it's available for download and can easily locate it in the download file. Once at the site, simply locate the book's title (either by using the Search box or by using one of the title lists) and click the Download Code link on the book's detail page to obtain all the source code for the book.

> **NOTE** *Because many books have similar titles, you may find it easiest to search by ISBN; this book's ISBN is 978-1-118-50899-2.*

Once you download the code, just decompress it with your favorite compression tool. Alternately, you can go to the main Wrox code download page at `www.wrox.com/dynamic/books/download.aspx` to see the code available for this book and all other Wrox books.

There is also a GitHub repository available at `https://github.com/ProfessionalHerokuProgramming` where code can be downloaded locally using:

```
$ git clone git@github.com:ProfessionalHerokuProgramming
/ch<chapter number>-<example name>.git
```

where `<chapter number>` is the number of the chapter that the code appears in, and `<example name>` is the name of the example application.

ERRATA

We make every effort to ensure that there are no errors in the text or in the code. However, no one is perfect, and mistakes do occur. If you find an error in one of our books, like a spelling mistake or faulty piece of code, we would be very grateful for your feedback. By sending in errata you may save another reader hours of frustration and at the same time you will be helping us provide even higher quality information.

To find the errata page for this book, go to `http://www.wrox.com` and locate the title using the Search box or one of the title lists. Then, on the book details page, click the Book Errata link. On this page you can view all errata that has been submitted for this book and posted by Wrox editors. A complete book list including links to each book's errata is also available at `www.wrox.com/misc-pages/booklist.shtml`.

If you don't spot "your" error on the Book Errata page, go to `www.wrox.com/contact/techsupport.shtml` and complete the form there to send us the error you have found. We'll check the information and, if appropriate, post a message to the book's errata page and fix the problem in subsequent editions of the book.

P2P.WROX.COM

For author and peer discussion, join the P2P forums at `p2p.wrox.com`. The forums are a web-based system for you to post messages relating to Wrox books and related technologies and interact with other readers and technology users. The forums offer a subscription feature to e-mail you topics of interest of your choosing when new posts are made to the forums. Wrox authors, editors, other industry experts, and your fellow readers are present on these forums.

At `http://p2p.wrox.com` you will find a number of different forums that will help you not only as you read this book, but also as you develop your own apps. To join the forums, just follow these steps:

1. Go to `p2p.wrox.com` and click the Register link.

2. Read the terms of use and click Agree.

3. Complete the required information to join as well as any optional information you wish to provide and click Submit.

4. You will receive an e-mail with information describing how to verify your account and complete the joining process.

> **NOTE** *You can read messages in the forums without joining P2P but in order to post your own messages, you must join.*

Once you join, you can post new messages and respond to messages other users post. You can read messages at any time on the web. If you would like to have new messages from a particular forum e-mailed to you, click the Subscribe to this Forum icon by the forum name in the forum listing.

For more information about how to use the Wrox P2P, be sure to read the P2P FAQs for answers to questions about how the forum software works as well as many common questions specific to P2P and Wrox books. To read the FAQs, click the FAQ link on any P2P page.

PROFESSIONAL

Heroku® Programming

PART I
An Overview of Heroku

1

How Heroku Works

Heroku is a polyglot, cloud-based development and application-delivery platform. It helps developers focus on building apps by removing the need for servers, system administration, and stack maintenance. The Heroku platform is a multi-tenant architecture built on virtual machines in Amazon Elastic Compute Cloud (Amazon EC2). Application management and scaling is done either through a command-line interface or online and on mobile devices, wherever you happen to be, via the API. Apps built on Heroku benefit from Heroku's managed stack and self-healing architecture, ensuring that they do not require system administrators to manage the underlying platform in order to keep them secure and reliable. Automated failover, disaster recovery, and bit rot prevention are built in to the platform.

The Heroku platform offers capabilities for near-immediate deployment for both development and production apps. Heroku greatly assists agile development methodologies and allows for seamless continuous deployment. Configurable access security enables individual members of the development or scrum team to push changes. Overhead to set up and manage software development life-cycle support environments is no longer a chore, with Git's version control system built in, automated dependency management, and system rollback available with a single command. Developers can leverage a readily available Postgres database, using either SQL or key-value data storage, or use their own external data store of choice. Add-ons for enhanced features such as monitoring and deploy hooks are readily available. This provides marked gains in developer productivity and enables an organization to both predict and reduce management costs.

The first part of this chapter discusses stacks, the deployment environment used to run the apps you develop. It then covers the dyno manifold, which is the hands-off process management environment, built on a cloud-computing platform. After outlining the dyno isolation process, which enables you to manage different process types in a rapidly scalable, fault-tolerant environment, you will learn how code is deployed to be run as a dyno, and how version control is enforced with Git. We will then take a look at the benefits that this architecture offers to prevent application erosion and to enable coding in an operations-free environment. Next, we'll discuss how version control is managed with code deployed to Heroku, and how this code is packaged and run on Heroku with the slug compiler. Finally, we will describe how HTTP requests are routed to your deployed Heroku app.

HOW THE STACKS STACK UP

Each stack is a base operating system, language execution environment, and application serving software. There are different stacks to support different operating environments provided, as detailed in the following table. The stack sits on top of a virtually isolated Linux-based machine in Amazon's managed data center. Stacks enable you to run your app in the cloud without having to consider the underlying infrastructure.

STACK	BASE TECHNOLOGY	MRI 1.8.6	REE 1.8.7	MRI 1.9.2	NODE .JS	CLOJURE	JAVA	PYTHON	SCALA
Argent Aspen	Debian Etch 4.0	X							
Badious Bamboo	Debian Lenny 5.0		X	X					
Celadon Cedar	Ubuntu 10.04		X	X	X	X	X	X	X

The only stack on which you can currently create new apps is Celadon Cedar. Cedar is a versatile polyglot stack that enables development with a supported, managed stack for apps coded with Ruby, Java, Python, Node.js, Scala, or Clojure. Cedar is flexible enough for you to architect and manage your own custom stacks with various languages, development frameworks, and libraries of your own choosing while still taking advantage of the managed infrastructure and deployment tools built in to the platform. Leveraging the stacks provided enables hands-off operations without the need for patching, and includes the latest security updates and reliability improvements for the operating system and language run times without requiring user intervention.

Prior to Cedar, the default stack was Badious Bamboo, which supports Ruby 1.8 and 1.9 app development when running on a Debian 4 OS. Both MRI (Matz's Ruby Implementation) and REE (Ruby Enterprise Edition) were supported. Argent Aspen was the original stack created for the deployment of Ruby 1.8.x apps, both run on Debian. The largest difference between these two and Cedar, beyond the polyglot capabilities in Cedar, is that both Aspen and Bamboo provide a caching layer using Varnish, a reverse proxy and HTTP accelerator, which is no longer a recommended approach. You can no longer create apps on Aspen or Bamboo. Aspen is end of life, and Bamboo is expected to be very shortly.

The Heroku command line enables you to control your local code base and remote Heroku apps in a terminal running on Windows, Mac, or Linux. After installing the Heroku command-line tool, which is included with the Heroku Toolbelt (see Chapter 4, "Deploying Your Applications to Heroku"), you can see the currently available stacks using the command line:

```
$ heroku stack
  aspen-mri-1.8.6
  bamboo-mri-1.9.2
  bamboo-ree-1.8.7
* cedar (default)
```

The command-line tool runs within the context of the current directory of your command line (Windows or Mac Terminal, bash, etc.) and interacts with Heroku's API. In the preceding example, the asterisk beside the stack name indicates which stack the current app (within the context of the current directory) is running. You can use this to create an app that will run on the stack of your choice, as follows:

```
$ heroku create
Creating young-summer-9942... done, stack is cedar
http://young-summer-9942.herokuapp.com/ | git@heroku.com:young-summer-9942.git
```

The preceding example creates an app that will run on the default Cedar stack. Simply running `heroku create` without additional flags will provision an app run time on Heroku's current default stack. At the time of writing, the default stack is Cedar. Some stack features may have beta status, meaning they are still undergoing testing and improvement and should therefore be used with caution for production-grade apps, as interfaces (APIs and versions of stack components) may change. When running apps with beta components, developers may be required to make infrequent, minor changes to ensure that their apps are compatible with the latest interfaces provided. Apps can be upgraded to run on subsequent stacks, in order to take advantage of enhancements or improvements. An automated process for this migration is documented on the Heroku Dev Center (https://devcenter.heroku.com/articles/cedar-migration).

If you have automation scripts and tools, you may choose to include the `--stack` flag, because the default stack may change in the future, resulting in deployment to the incorrect stack after the change is made.

> **NOTE** *This book focuses on the current default stack, Cedar. All the examples and discussions use this stack.*

UNDERSTANDING DYNOS AND THE DYNO MANIFOLD

Stacks and the accompanying code will run on a *dyno,* which is a single process of any type running from your app on the Heroku platform. Each dyno can run a variety of different types of processes, including but not limited to the following:

➤ Web apps that serve pages

➤ Processes that serve API requests

➤ Time-based batch or background workers

➤ One-off programs

The *dyno manifold* can be thought of as a giant, distributed, fault-tolerant, horizontally scalable computer in the sky, capable of running a nearly infinite number of diverse programs in the cloud. It offers you complete and instantaneous control over your process formation, and it is completely hands-off and maintenance-free once your processes are up and running as dynos.

Dynos offer users a number of features and advantages:

➤ **Scaling elasticity:** Processes can take advantage of the inherent elasticity of a cloud-based infrastructure, enabling developers to run as many instances of the process as needed at any given time. Different copies of each process can be scaled up and down across one or more dynos to provide near instant and nearly unlimited scalability to adapt to demand. For instance, if you have a background process that takes a very long time to complete on a single dyno, it can be run on another dyno in parallel, creating a divide-and-conquer solution to complete the task at hand in significantly less time. A running web app that begins to slow under heavy demand (perhaps an app has "gone viral" or is experiencing load spikes) can be scaled in seconds to serve more requests at once.

➤ **Intelligent routing:** The dyno manifold also provides automated load balancing that does not require complex configuration. HTTP traffic from your hostname(s) is intelligently directed to the correct web dyno inside the dyno manifold. The herokuapp.com HTTP stack offers a direct routing path to your web dynos. This allows for advanced HTTP uses, such as chunked responses, long polling, and using an asynchronous web server to handle multiple responses from a single web process. Traffic management is handled by a load balancer that offers HTTP and SSL termination. From there, requests are directly passed to the routing mesh. This shorter path enables full support of HTTP 1.1 but without offering any implicit caching capabilities.

➤ **Process management automation:** Processes that are unresponsive or misbehaving are restarted automatically. Continuous monitoring ensures that this is done without user intervention, routing future requests to available and responsive dynos while the existing dyno is restarted. Dynos typically are cycled once a day or when degradation or failure in the underlying hardware is detected and fully logged. Because of this ephemeral nature of a dyno, apps must be written in a manner that does not rely on a particular instance, in close alignment with best practices for horizontally scalable, stateless app design. (For more information, see Chapter 2, "Architectural Considerations.")

➤ **Distribution and redundancy:** Because your process can run on multiple dynos, failover and redundancy are built in. When multiple dynos are running in parallel, processes are automatically distributed onto different physical hardware, providing protection from a single point of failover on a particular server. Dynos are run in multiple Amazon data centers, providing geographical redundancy and automated backup.

➤ Isolation: Each process is run completely separately from the others. Individual processes run in a hardened container that prevents other apps from using the same memory or filesystems, which enforces fair allocation of processor resources on the server. In a multi-tenant environment, this behavior is very important to ensure security and reliability when running multiple apps on the same infrastructure.

Each dyno is allocated 512MB of memory, which is isolated from other dynos and processes to ensure that any memory leaks that occur do not affect other apps running on the same hardware. It also provides protection against violations of memory safety introduced by events such as buffer overflows, thereby minimizing security risks and vulnerabilities for apps run on the platform.

Exceeding the 512MB of memory on a dyno neither prevents an app from executing nor kills it. Instead, additional memory required over the 512MB allocation will go in to swap. This results in sub-optimal performance of apps on the system, as I/O requests are often many orders of magnitude slower than random memory access. If memory usage exceeds three times the limit $(3 \times 512MB = 1.5GB)$, the app is automatically restarted. You can also restart your entire app manually at any time, by entering the following:

```
$ heroku ps:restart
Restarting processes... done
```

You can also restart individual dynos manually by using the preceding command followed by the name of the process:

```
$ heroku ps:restart worker.12
Restarting worker.12 process... done
```

This will trigger a SIGTERM signal to all processes, allowing your app, running processes, and the underlying software stack to optionally catch the signal and do what it needs to do to shut down gracefully.

Apps that have only one web dyno will idle out after an hour of inactivity. When idling, it takes a few seconds for the dyno to wake back up and start processing requests, causing a short delay in responsiveness to your app. When your app has more than one dyno, subsequent dynos and worker dynos are never idled.

UNDERSTANDING DYNO ISOLATION

As stated earlier, each process in Heroku runs in isolation from one another, despite the fact that a number of different processes may be running on a single virtual instance. Heroku ensures that each dyno has its own independent filesystem and that memory and system resources are evenly distributed. Isolation also ensures that overloaded apps cannot compromise other apps running on the same virtual machine or server, and even isolates processes from the underlying operating system itself. Process isolation is achieved using LXC (Linux Containers) and `chroot`.

LXC is used to ensure that each dyno runs within its own container on an Amazon EC2 virtual machine. Therefore, in essence, you can think of Heroku as a virtual environment running in a virtual machine. LXC is a lightweight virtual system mechanism that its own website refers to as "chroot on steroids." LXC can emulate thousands of systems on a single server using Linux's built-in control groups (cgroups) functionality, which provides process containers. Dynos running within an LXC cannot see other processes running on other dynos because of process namespacing built in to the OS kernel.

Each dyno also has its own filesystem, which is kept completely separate from filesystems on other dynos using `chroot`. This filesystem includes the OS and stack used to execute your code, and the last deployed copy of the code itself. You can write files to this filesystem; however, because of the temporary nature of individual dynos, which are continuously brought up and down and cycled regularly, this filesystem is ephemeral and should not be used for permanent storage of any sort. Instead, for longer-term storage, you can store content to be used as assets in services such as Amazon Simple Storage Service (Amazon S3). The share-nothing nature of dynos also makes the local filesystem inappropriate for storing session information, as subsequent web requests could be routed by the load balancer to other dynos without the session information.

EXPLORING THE PROCESS MODEL

The Heroku process model is very similar to the UNIX process model, so if you are familiar with that you can consider them to work in the same way — that is, enabling diverse process types, not just simple web processes that wait for web requests. The process model also enables capabilities such as background processes that divide up the work and complete tasks in parallel on Heroku. However, because many dynos are running on a single virtual instance, the dyno manifold provides a distributed process manager.

Typically, when you start up a server, you need to do things such as start cron jobs and the web server. In traditional UNIX systems, you would add these programs to `init.d` to have them start automatically. For example, a Rails app will typically have a web server, such as Webrick, Unicorn, or Thin, as well as a library for queuing and asynchronously running worker processes, such as Resque, BackgroundJob, or ActiveMessaging. Different processes need to be run for different apps, and this information must be defined somewhere.

Therefore, using the Rails example, when you start up your web server, you want the processes defined in the following table to start automatically:

PROCESS TYPE	INVOCATION COMMAND
Web	`bundle exec rails server`
Worker	`bundle exec rake jobs:work`

Similarly, if you want that web server to run Python apps on the Django framework, the following table demonstrates the processes:

PROCESS TYPE	INVOCATION COMMAND
Web	`python manage.py runserver`
Worker	`celery -loglevel=INFO`

You can define which process invocation command you want your dyno manifold to execute on dyno creation using a file named `Procfile` that is placed in the root of your app. In the preceding example, you would set your `Procfile` as follows:

```
web: bundle exec rails server
worker: bundle exec rake jobs:work
```

Although this example uses the process type names `web` and `worker`, you could use any names you want to describe your process types. The only special process type name is `web` because this is the process type that receives HTTP traffic. The `Procfile` uses the following simple format for each line:

```
<process type>: <invocation command>
```

Note that the `Procfile` is optional; if it is not found when you push your code, the dyno manifold will detect the language automatically and launch the default web process. To see what processes are running, use `heroku ps`:

```
$ heroku ps
Process          State                Command
-----------      ------------------   -------------------------------
web.1            up for 7m            bundle exec rails server mongrel -..
web.2            up for 2s            bundle exec rails server mongrel -..
worker.1         up for 7m            env QUEUE=* bundle exec rake resque:work
worker.2         up for 3s            env QUEUE=* bundle exec rake resque:work
worker.3         up for 2s            env QUEUE=* bundle exec rake resque:work
worker.4         up for 3s            env QUEUE=* bundle exec rake resque:work
```

You can see from the first column that two web dynos and four worker dynos are currently running. This command also returns the state of the process and which command was invoked (defined in the `Procfile`, if one were found). Note that when you scale up your apps, you can scale each process type independently, providing an additional level of granularity over virtual machines. For more information on scaling, see Chapter 7, "Managing, Monitoring, and Scaling Your Heroku Applications."

You can schedule a process to run at a specified time of day or time interval (similar to cron in UNIX) using the Heroku Scheduler. See Chapter 6, "Working with Add-Ons," for more information.

Sometimes, you will need to run a one-off process such as initializing or migrating a database, or run a one-time script that sits somewhere in the committed code. You can run these one-off processes using the heroku run command. However, this is very different from running a process formation (like the previous example with web and worker processes) in a number of different ways.

When using heroku run, your local computer's terminal is attached to the dyno. This new dyno uses the naming convention run.N (instead of web.N or worker.N). Anything you type is interpreted as standard input (STDIN) on the dyno. Standard output (STDOUT) is typically pushed to the log; but when you are using heroku run, STDOUT is redirected to your terminal, unless you use the heroku run:detached command.

To terminate this session and kill the dyno, press Ctrl+C or use heroku ps:stop <process name>. Dynos are not restarted or cycled while using heroku run; and these dynos will never receive HTTP traffic like web dynos, as HTTP traffic is routed only to web dynos. (For more information, see the "Routing HTTP Requests" section.)

Using heroku run can also provide interactive console access to your app:

```
$ heroku run console
Running `console` attached to terminal... up, run.1
irb(main):001:0>
```

This is helpful for interactive run time or debug sessions against your app or to launch one-off jobs. Note that the session will remain active with an allocated dyno running until you run exit to terminate the session.

UNDERSTANDING EROSION RESISTANCE

One of the main benefits of using the Heroku platform is its built-in mechanisms to self-heal, often without the need for user intervention. When running your app on a server over time, entropy will almost certainly creep in at some point, resulting in crashes due to stack issues that have not been patched, log files filling the server's available disk space, or apps crashing or freezing, which requires killing and restarting the app or the server. This is commonly referred to as *bit rot* or *software erosion*.

The dyno manifold provides erosion resistance through a number of different techniques. First, dynos are typically cycled on a daily basis. In the background, the dyno manifold spawns a fresh dyno using the most recently pushed version of the code base and the latest version of the managed stack. Old dynos are brought down gracefully after they have finished their current work and replaced with this new dyno, with no perceived downtime to the user. This means that if any updates have been made to the underlying stack, they are automatically patched through this process, giving you the most stable and secure version of the stack to run on without the need to manually patch and restart your server. Minor revisions are used for these patches, so stack updates should not break your app.

Second, the dyno manifold also detects crashes that occur, either during startup or operation. If this happens, the dyno manifold will automatically restart the dyno. If it crashes again, another restart is attempted after a ten-minute cooldown period. If you want to restart manually during this period, you can do so using the `heroku ps:restart` command.

If an underlying hardware failure is detected by Heroku's robust app-monitoring system, the dynos running on that system are automatically restarted on different hardware. This enables Heroku users to take a no-operations approach to running their apps. Expensive monitoring software is no longer required, as fault tolerance is built into the system. Heroku's team of engineers wear the pagers, so system administrators are not needed to "keep the lights on" or continually keep on top of patches for each element of the stack and install them. This minimizes app downtime and avoids the high operational costs associated with software erosion, enabling an organization using Heroku to focus on innovation, rather than ongoing monitoring and maintenance.

MANAGING VERSION CONTROL

Heroku has a built-in version control system, so you don't have to build and configure your own. Git is an open source, distributed, revision control and source control management system. It was originally designed and created by Linus Torvalds for maintaining the source code for the Linux kernel, after Torvalds was criticized for using a proprietary solution. Git creates a `.git` directory in your local code repository that contains all the versioning and historical information for your code base. This is a paradigm shift from traditional systems that rely on a central server, often remote, to manage revision tracking. Git is also very fast and scalable, making it ideal for use with projects of any size.

In addition to providing source control management, Git is the deployment mechanism used to push code to Heroku. Deployment is done via GitHub, an online code-hosting service using Git. Though GitHub has both free and paid accounts available, a paid account is not required to use this service with Heroku.

Deploying your code takes two commands — one to commit your code and another to push it to Heroku:

```
$ git commit -am "My latest change"
[master a3f713b] My latest change
 1 files changed, 1 insertions(+), 1 deletions(-)

$ git push heroku master
Counting objects: 11, done.
Delta compression using up to 4 threads.
Compressing objects: 100% (3/3), done.
Writing objects: 100% (6/6), 432 bytes, done.
Total 6 (delta 2), reused 0 (delta 0)

-----> Heroku receiving push
```

After you have run these commands successfully, your code will be deployed in production to all dynos running your app's processes. You can also use this process to deploy your app to different development environments. For instance, if your team's deployment process requires that you first test your changes in a staging or quality assurance (QA) environment, the `git remote` command enables you to manage multiple environments for an app without having to provision and maintain multiple servers, keep the stacks identical between environments, or write scripts for deploying to each environment.

Heroku's easy deployment and built-in code management explain why developers love using it. In traditional development environments, one must install a source control management system somewhere, maintain the repository, and keep backups and provide disaster recovery if something happens. Deploying code to multiple servers also requires a lot of additional work in terms of writing and maintaining deployment scripts that keep track of the ever-changing list of servers that must be deployed to. In addition, because the code repository is centralized, developers must have access to this server, either on-site at the office where it is firewalled or via a virtual private network (VPN), which can be expensive and complex to set up. This all results in more unnecessary operational overhead and headaches for the developers, when all they want to do is deploy their code.

> **NOTE** *For more on using Git and GitHub, see Chapter 4.*

UNDERSTANDING THE SLUG COMPILER

Before pushing your code to Heroku, you first must compile and package it. During this process, your code is sent to Heroku's slug compiler, which will get the latest copy of your code from the head (the most recent commit) of the master branch of your repository, install dependencies needed to run your app, compile your code (if needed), and deploy this "slug" to each of your dynos. The slug is stored on Heroku's servers; therefore, when scaling up, the slug is reused, making scaling very fast, with no need to recompile the code.

Consider the following example push of a Ruby app:

```
$ git push heroku master
Counting objects: 11, done.
Delta compression using up to 4 threads.
Compressing objects: 100% (6/6), done.
Writing objects: 100% (6/6), 483 bytes, done.
Total 6 (delta 4), reused 0 (delta 0)

-----> Heroku receiving push
-----> Ruby/Rails app detected
-----> Installing dependencies using Bundler version 1.1.2
       Running: bundle install --without development:test --path vendor/bundle
       --binstubs bin/ --deployment
       Using rake (0.8.7)
       [...]
       Using rails (3.1.1)
       Your bundle is complete! It was installed into ./vendor/bundle
       Cleaning up the bundler cache.
-----> Writing config/database.yml to read from DATABASE_URL
-----> Preparing app for Rails asset pipeline
       Running: rake assets:precompile
       (in /tmp/build_3p1i65rctat1c)
       /usr/local/bin/ruby /tmp/build_3p1i65rctat1c/vendor/bundle/ruby/1.9.1/bin/rake
       assets:precompile:nondigest RAILS_ENV=production RAILS_GROUPS=assets
       (in /tmp/build_3p1i65rctat1c)
```

```
-----> Rails plugin injection
       Injecting rails_log_stdout
       Injecting rails3_serve_static_assets
-----> Discovering process types
       Procfile declares types      -> (none)
       Default types for Ruby/Rails -> console, rake, web, worker
-----> Compiled slug size is 17.3MB
-----> Launching... done, v13
-----> Deploy hooks scheduled, check output in your logs
       http://freezing-day-9626.herokuapp.com deployed to Heroku
```

Note that during the slug compile process, the compiler first automatically detects the app type. In this case, a Ruby on Rails app is being deployed. Next, Bundler, the Ruby app dependency manager, installs your app's dependencies. Then, configuration variables (also known as *config vars*) are used to inject environment-specific information — for instance, the database URL and login info, which might be different in staging than production; see Chapter 5, "Managing Releases in Heroku" for more details. After this, process types are discovered. Default types that are created automatically appear here, as well as any process types declared in the Procfile (refer to the "Exploring the Process Model" section). Finally, the slug is compiled and this latest version of your app is launched on each of your dynos running on Heroku.

During compilation, the .git directory and any unnecessary files (for instance, with a Ruby app, anything in the log or tmp directory and any local .gem files) are not sent to the slug compiler. A .slugignore file in the root directory can also be used to indicate any other files or directories that should be ignored by the slug compiler. For instance, unit tests, design specs, and art originals (such as Photoshop files) are good candidates for the .slugignore file. Files used in the .gitignore file are also excluded from the slug compiler.

Each file or directory is specified on a single line in the .slugignore file, as follows:

```
*.psd
*.pdf
test
spec
```

This particular .slugignore file ensures that .psd and .pdf files are not included, as well as the contents of the test and spec directories.

During the compile process, the slug file size is reported. The maximum size for any slug is 200MB. However, if your slug is over 50MB, you should consider minimizing it. This can typically be done by using the .slugignore file to remove unnecessary files and/or moving your static assets (PDFs, images, etc.) to an external file storage service such as Amazon S3. Large slugs take the dyno manifold longer to deploy, resulting in slower scaling.

ROUTING HTTP REQUESTS

HTTP requests are automatically routed to your app's web dynos. These requests are sent to load balancers that provide SSL termination, and are then passed down the routing mesh to be intelligently distributed to the dyno with the least workload to serve the response. This load balancing provides optimized throughput, minimizing response time, as well as maximum reliability and redundancy when multiple dynos are available.

Load balancing is always handled automatically within Heroku. As shown in Figure 1-1, anytime you add or remove dynos from your app, Heroku will add or remove those dynos from the routing layer of the platform. Each request is routed to a randomly chosen dyno. Note that Heroku does not support sticky sessions or session affinity.

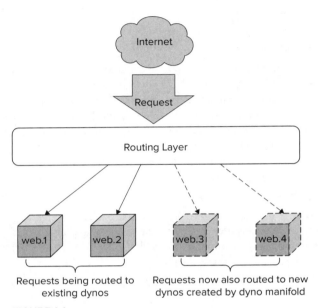

FIGURE 1-1

Apps that are deployed to the default Cedar stack offer a direct routing path to dynos through the `herokuapp.com` HTTP stack. Requests to `yourappname.herokuapp.com` use this stack, which fully supports HTTP 1.1 except for implicit caching. HTTP 1.1 allows for chunking, which transmits responses in a series of fragments, optimizing response time when large amounts of data are returned, as content can begin transmission before the entire content payload is dynamically generated.

Requests are made directly to the application server, not proxied through an HTTP server such as nginx. Therefore, response compression must be performed in your app; and because requests are being made via HTTP, WebSockets and incoming TCP connections outside of web ports are not natively supported. Third-party Heroku add-ons, such as Pusher (`https://addons.heroku.com/pusher`), enable you to add this functionality to Heroku apps.

> **NOTE** *See Chapter 6 for more information on how to leverage add-ons.*

Any requests that arrive at the Cedar stack must return a response data within 30 seconds; otherwise, the connection will time out and terminate. Once an initial response is sent, subsequent responses or requests must be made within 55 seconds to keep the connection alive. Long polling is supported, allowing a request to be held if no information is immediately available. When information is available, or the connection subsequently times out, a response can be transmitted.

Multi-threaded apps can be utilized to enable apps to maintain multiple connections simultaneously and do asynchronous processing. For instance, Ruby web servers such as Goliath and Thin (with a suitable web framework such as Async Sinatra) can take advantage of multi-threading in a single process. You can also spawn and control your own threads if, for instance, you write a Java app or Node.js app built with the Express framework that uses this functionality.

The Aspen and Bamboo stacks provide built-in HTTP acceleration using Varnish. Cedar apps do not provide this, in order to support advanced HTTP features that Varnish does not support. Couchbase's Memcache add-on provides scalable, in-memory object caching, based on the popular memcached system. Using this add-on with `Rack::Cache` or `Radiant::Cache`, Ruby developers can speed up delivery by reducing database load, often the biggest bottleneck to an app's performance. (For more information, see the "Caching with Ruby" section of Chapter 11, "Developing with Ruby.") Content delivery networks (CDNs), such as Amazon S3 and CloudFront, can be leveraged to speed up page load times through distributed local delivery of static assets.

SUMMARY

This chapter provided a high-level overview of Heroku. We explored Heroku's stacks, including the current default, Celadon Cedar. You should also have an understanding of dynos and how they fit into the platform architecture via the dyno manifold, as well as what dyno isolation means to your app and how to leverage it. You should comprehend how versioning in Heroku works and how the platform ensures your app remains erosion resistant as the platform evolves over time. Digging deeper, you saw how app delivery is possible via app slugs and the slug compiler, which builds apps when they are ready to be fired off into dynos. You also gained insight into the unique HTTP routing that Heroku provides, regardless of wherever in the platform your app resides, or whichever dynos you may leverage. Heroku's routing will always funnel requests properly to ensure your app is serving requests with optimal performance. This emphasis on performance is also at the core of Chapter 2, which explores the architectural considerations you'll need to keep in mind as you design, build, and deploy apps on the Heroku platform.

Architectural Considerations

WHAT'S IN THIS CHAPTER?

➤ Building twelve-factor apps

➤ Managing your app portfolio with pace layering

➤ Ensuring security and compliance

➤ Understanding redundancy and reliability

➤ Securing your Heroku app

➤ Encrypting communications

➤ Storing static assets and using content delivery networks

Although developing on Heroku is not very different from developing on any scalable architecture, some architectural considerations should be taken into account.
Heroku's architecture is stateless and temporary, which makes it highly scalable. Dynos are ephemeral, so they should be considered temporary. This means that apps need to be written to be scaled horizontally, which enables them to be easily architected to solve big problems and load faster. However, because of its temporary nature, Heroku is not well suited for apps that are stateful on the server level or for apps for which sessions are stored locally on each server.

You must carefully consider the overall architecture of the system you want to build, which typically is broken down into the following three parts:

➤ **Language and framework:** Skilled craftspeople have a selection of tools in their toolbelt, allowing them to choose the best one for the job. Heroku's polyglot nature enables a broad choice of languages and frameworks to choose from, allowing you to select whichever best fit the job at hand. You can use one of Heroku's many pre-built, readily available, and fully supported languages and framework stacks, such as Play on Java. If you require more specialized configuration under the hood,

Heroku provides a lot of value aside from the managed stack with respect to ease of development and scaling.

➤ **Data store:** Most web apps need a back end, and Heroku provides a number of options for storage. Without any configuration required, Heroku apps are pre-built with a development database suitable for test and development programming. For production apps, a fully managed database is available with Heroku Postgres, offering different packages primarily based on how big a data set you need to reside on the in-memory cache is. Salesforce.com offers data as a service (DaaS), through `database.com`, with built-in authentication and point-and-click, record-level security. Add-ons provide a rich choice of data stores through third-party offerings, such as MySQL, NoSQL, and other data-storage solutions. The architect has a diverse choice of data storage options to work with. For more information, see Part III, "Using a Data Store with Your Heroku Applications."

➤ **Static asset storage and content delivery networks:** Because of the ephemeral nature of dynos, assets should be stored either within the app (if they're truly static, in the app's codebase itself) or within a database blob or cloud storage, which is best suited for large amounts of user-generated content and large files, such as movies. Storing assets such as site images and JavaScript in a highly scalable site requires a content delivery network (CDN), where the assets can be distributed by a provider, such as Amazon CloudFront, and delivered locally to the visitor.

These three key architectural considerations are the basic building blocks for any Heroku app. In this chapter, we introduce advanced architectural concepts in order to share best practices for writing web-based apps and managing a portfolio of apps; the twelve-factor app; and pace layering. We then do a deep dive into security and compliance considerations for apps written on the Heroku platform, followed by a discussion of the reliability and redundancy of the underlying infrastructure. You will then see how an app can use Secure Sockets Layer (SSL) for secure transactions. Finally, this chapter outlines how you can upload and store static assets with Amazon's Simple Storage Service (Amazon S3).

BUILDING TWELVE-FACTOR APPLICATIONS

After writing and overseeing the development and deployment of hundreds of web apps, Adam Wiggins, one of the co-founders of Heroku, developed the first draft of a methodology for writing apps that maximize automation, offer maximum portability, can be deployed on modern cloud platforms (whether Heroku or others), allow for continuous deployment, and scale quickly. By following these twelve best practices when designing and developing apps, you can realize these benefits in your organization.

An app that follows Wiggins' methodology is called a *twelve-factor app*. The criteria for this is defined as follows:

1. **One codebase, multiple deploys:** A twelve-factor app is tracked in a single repository in a version-control system. There is a one-to-one relationship between the codebase and the repository. There should not be multiple versions of the same codebase (this is a distributed system), nor should multiple apps share the same code (this should be a dependent library).

This single codebase can then be deployed in multiple environments, typically production, staging, and local development environments in a simple example. They all share the same root codebase but may be slightly different versions as changes propagate through the software development life cycle, from development to production.

2. **Dependency declaration and isolation:** Twelve-factor apps use explicit dependency declaration and isolation. Using a dependency declaration manifest, such as the Gem Bundler for Ruby or Pip for Python, enables dependencies to be swapped in and out easily when new, more stable versions are introduced. Dependency isolation requires that all tools necessary to run the app are included in the codebase, and no special environment setup is needed outside of the language run time and dependency manager. For instance, an app should not have to shell out to cURL to execute, thereby requiring that cURL be installed on all systems on which code will run. This ensures that new developers can be up and running as quickly as possible, with minimal environment setup needed.

3. **Store configuration in the environment:** When developing an app in multiple environments, configuration must differ between these environments to ensure that, for instance, the deployment you use for testing is not making changes to your production database. Environment variables are both language and operating system agnostic, maximizing portability. These configuration variables (config vars) should not be checked in to the codebase, as you could potentially compromise the security of your app if you open source the code. Instead, environment variables can be used to cleanly define environment differences without running the risk of accidentally checking in credentials to the codebase.

4. **Treat backing services as attached resources:** Many different kinds of backing services are typically used to make an app operate, such as data stores, messaging/queuing systems, and SMTP systems for sending e-mail. The code for a twelve-factor app does not distinguish between local and third-party services. You should be able to swap out a local service with a remote service simply by changing the configuration — for instance, by changing the resource handle or URL with the credentials. Code changes should not be needed if a database misbehaves and needs to be replaced with a recent working copy.

5. **Strictly separate build and run stages:** Each time a change is made to the code, dependencies are gathered and binaries and assets compiled. This produces a unique release that, once combined with config vars, will be executed in the run time environment. Releases can be archived to provide a record of what the running app looked like at any point in time. Changes must not be allowed to the run time, as this will neither create a release record nor allow you to propagate the change backward to your codebase easily. This would also restrict your ability to easily roll back the run time to the previous release if the change introduces a bug or breaks the running app.

6. **Execute the app as one or more stateless processes:** Your app runs as one or more processes, which should be completely independent and self-sufficient. Only backing services should be used to share anything between these nodes. It should be assumed that the filesystem and memory are temporary to a single execution transaction, and noncentralized session information (such as sticky sessions) must be avoided.

7. **Export services via port binding:** Whereas traditional apps are often run inside a container, such as Tomcat for Java or Apache HTTPD for PHP, twelve-factor apps are entirely self-contained. Dependency declaration is used to add a web server as a library to the app instead of relying on those built into the container. Twelve-factor apps bind to a port and wait for incoming requests on that port, typically returning an HTTP response or whatever other response type that particular protocol defines. This architecture enables the app to run as a true software as a service (SaaS), allowing it to be a backing service for other apps.

8. **Scale out the process model:** In twelve-factor apps, the UNIX process model is mirrored to divide each type of work the app needs to do into different process types. For instance, a web process can serve web requests, while a worker process may run batch processes in the background. These processes collectively form the process formation of the app. Each process may have it own threads and should not daemonize. This approach makes concurrency easily repeatable and reliable.

9. **Maximize robustness with fast startup and graceful shutdown:** Each process running is disposable, meaning it can be stopped and restarted without affecting the app's operation in the long term. Web processes should easily shut down when signaled to do so. Worker processes should put a job back on the work queue when receiving a shutdown signal. This enables you to safely scale up apps and redeploy when code changes are made. It also makes apps more durable when processes crash and must be suddenly restarted.

10. **Keep development, staging, and production as similar as possible:** Historically, there have been three types of gaps between development and production environments. Without a continuous development methodology, there is a *time gap* when developers work on code that won't be in production for weeks or months while waiting for a release. There is a *personnel gap* because operations teams deploy the code, not the coders themselves. Finally, there is a *tools gap* because developers often use lightweight stacks that differ from the tools used in production. With a twelve-factor app, developers deploy code nearly immediately, deploy code themselves, and use tools as similar as possible in both development and production environments, minimizing the risk of introducing bugs in production that are not easily repeatable in test environments.

11. **Treat logs as event streams:** On traditional platforms, logs are written to a log file that sits on the server's hard drive. This can result in catastrophe when the app fails because it can no longer write to the local drive, which has been filled with logs. Twelve-factor apps do not concern themselves with writing logs or how they are output. Logs are treated as a stream, where developers can observe them in real time. The archival method for these logs is determined by the developer; and backing services, such as Loggly, are often used to provide robust log analysis tools and alerting.

12. **Run admin/management tasks as one-off processes:** Often developers need to do maintenance tasks, such as run database migration scripts to change the data model or other one-off scripts. In twelve-factor apps, these are run against a release and executed as a process, much like any web or worker processes that may be associated with an app. Because the script is included in the codebase, it is easily replicated across developer and production environments.

Heroku adheres strictly to these twelve factors. You should understand and apply them when developing on the Heroku platform to get the most out of it.

MANAGING YOUR APPLICATION PORTFOLIO WITH PACE LAYERING

Pace layering is an app portfolio management approach, adapted from an old concept used in the architecture of buildings. Architect Frank Duffy introduced the idea, which was made famous in Stewart Brand's book *How Buildings Learn: What Happens After They're Built* (Penguin Books, 1995). Brand views a building as a set of components (*shearing layers*) that can be subdivided into layers with varying levels of longevity. For instance, the building's site is eternal and will almost never change, except in the extreme circumstance — for example, when a historical building is relocated. However, the service layer, composed of components such as the electrical wiring and HVAC, will change, but only every 7–15 years, when efficiencies can be gained. On the other extreme, the "stuff" in the house — tables, lamps, and paintings — may change weekly or monthly.

Architects use pace layering to ensure that the correct choices are made when designing slower-changing layers in order to facilitate the faster level of change in layers for which change is expected more often. The outside of your house will be made of something durable, such as bricks, that will last for hundreds of years because this isn't something that will likely change in that time span. However, when choosing paint, you do not need paint that will last that long because repainting is typically done every 5–10 years. The choice of materials must be appropriate for the rate of change of that particular shearing layer.

The concept of pace layering can be applied to software app portfolio management. The technology research company Gartner describes pace layering as "a new methodology for categorizing apps and developing a differentiated management and governance process that reflects how the applications are used and their rate of change" (www.gartner.com/it/page.jsp?id=1923014). Some business processes change often and require software that is easy to change quickly, whereas other processes are more static, requiring fewer changes to accommodate the slower pace of process change. Gartner categorizes systems into the following three distinct layers:

➤ Systems of record

➤ Systems of differentiation

➤ Systems of innovation

Systems of Record

Systems of record expect little or no change over their useful lifetime. Classic examples of these systems include accounting software packages and enterprise resource planning (ERP) systems, which are typically set up once, with only minor, infrequent tweaks made as supported processes change. These systems are not greatly differentiated between companies in the same industry (accounting practices are heavily regulated, which necessitates this) and lay a stable foundation for other pace layers.

Systems of Differentiation

Systems of differentiation change more often than systems of record and must be designed as such. They typically support processes that are unique to a particular organization within its industry, and are updated often when business processes are adjusted to support novel ideas or efficiency improvements. These systems are less durable than systems of record and are often re-architected and rewritten every three to five years to better align with the current state of underlying business processes.

Systems of Innovation

Systems of innovation are typically experimental, ad hoc, and rapidly developed in order to support new ideas of competitive differentiation for the organization. They have a very short usable lifetime compared with the other two types of systems, often lasting less than one year. An example of this would be a Facebook app that supports a new marketing campaign. Marketers need to develop supporting apps quickly to get to market faster than competitors, and often must use minimal resources because the success of the campaign may be difficult to gauge accurately in the planning and development stages.

Classification

Apps can be classified according to the dominant pace within that app, even though each individual app may be categorized into one or more of these layers. For instance, a customer relationship management (CRM) system can provide a system of record for a company by storing account and contact information for existing and prospective customers. However, if the company uses a unique methodology for prospecting that helps to better identify prospective customers and stores this data in the CRM, that functionality could be categorized as a system of differentiation. Even within a single software system, many different pace layers can be identified among its different functions.

Note that these different pace layers among apps and functions are not static. Over time, systems may move between the layers in tandem with the changing importance of the business process that each system supports. For instance, what may at one time be a system of innovation may become a system of differentiation, after competitors have had a chance to replicate the base functionality but are still playing catch-up on innovations built since then. The opposite is also true: Functionality in a system of record may be identified to produce a competitive advantage, thereby becoming a system of innovation or differentiation. It is important to keep in mind that the classification of pace layers is constantly in flux, evolving with the needs of the business and the competitive landscape.

Security and Reliability

Each layer also requires very different considerations for security and reliability. If systems of record break, the fallout for the organization could be disastrous, resulting in disruption and lost business. When an ERP system goes down, products cannot be shipped, potentially delaying the collection of payment for the goods. If systems of innovation break, the result often has less impact. For example, if a company's Facebook app is unresponsive, lost opportunities may be incurred, but general business is not disrupted. However, if this Facebook app is part of an expensive campaign supporting an ad run during a major sporting event, this system may be considered a system of differentiation because the loss in potential revenue is much larger, so the system's importance and the company's investment in it would be much higher.

The different levels of security and reliability required by these layers directly impact the amount of time it takes to create and maintain these systems. Systems of record often take years to be put into place. They require the highest level of security, which means using hardened systems that take a long time to develop. Patching and penetration testing must be done frequently to ensure ongoing protection of these systems and their precious data. Redundancy must also be built into these systems to ensure that there is no single point of failure because of the importance of their continuous availability.

Governance

Different layers require different levels of governance. Though systems of record don't change as often as other layers, change introduces a risk to the stability and security of any system, with the potential to create bugs and security holes that can be exploited. These systems also have complex development processes, often involving deployment and testing in multiple environments, such as integration, quality assurance (QA), and staging/user acceptance testing (UAT), before code is promoted live to production. This means that the time from concept to release in a live production environment for a system of record is longer than for systems of differentiation, and is orders of magnitude slower than systems of innovation. Heroku significantly helps reduce the burden involved in setting up these multiple environments by making it quick and easy to both manage and push changes to environments, and by eliminating the need to manage multiple servers or virtual machines for each purpose. Single command rollback also minimizes the risk of a bad or accidental code release causing lasting disruption. The capability to deploy a new version of your app without service disruption eliminates downtime in high-availability systems.

Conversely, systems of innovation require a much lower level of governance than systems of record. For these systems, a "test in production" approach is often acceptable, as these systems are not mission critical. Systems of innovation typically use agile processes to release changes and improvements often and in smaller increments than systems of record. Rapid deployment using a platform like Heroku significantly reduces the overhead involved in releasing code, making the platform highly beneficial for such a system. Coders can also enjoy spending less time with app setup overhead such as writing deploy scripts, and instead simply start coding.

Application Portfolio Management

Organizations often take a "one size fits all" approach to their app portfolio. However, this approach fails to match the most appropriate platform to the app's rate of change and its functions. Using systems and platforms that require huge amounts of setup and maintenance for systems of innovation will slow the pace at which the app can be delivered and incur high change and setup costs. Similarly, untested but agile platforms used for systems of record result in insecure or unreliable systems for which these characteristics are most important. In any app portfolio, different platform strategies are required for apps with different rates of change.

Similar to an investment portfolio, an app portfolio must consist of apps with varying levels of risk and reward. Systems of record are those for which the risk of delivering an app that does not meet requirements is low, as specifications are typically well defined and change is not needed often if plans are followed rigidly. The potential for reward is low, but very predictable. In systems of innovation, risk is often high, as experimentation may be needed to "get the formula right," with specifications being murky at best or determined using educated guesses. However, reward can be very high because if the app becomes popular, it could be a huge hit. For example, a Facebook app supporting a marketing campaign that goes viral can have enormous benefits for a business from a brand-visibility perspective. With a balanced portfolio consisting of few underlying systems of record and many systems of innovation, risk and reward can be optimized to maximize potential returns.

Heroku can greatly help the architect build an app portfolio geared to best fit the rate of change required by all three pace layers. The greatest advantages are brought to systems of innovation, for which Heroku's quick setup enables minimal operational overhead in getting apps up and running. This provides a "fail fast" approach in which innovative apps can be built in a way such that minimal costs are sunk into experimental projects. Instant deployment also ensures that innovations are delivered as quickly as possible, before competitors launch similar initiatives. This also enables resources to deliver the most variety of apps in the shortest period of time, allowing the organization to hedge its bets on the success of any single initiative.

On the opposite end of the pace layering spectrum, systems of record also gain significant advantages on the Heroku platform. System operations teams often spend much of their time building redundancy into the system to meet reliability requirements. Because mechanisms for redundancy are baked into the dyno manifold, system operations no longer has to deploy and manage copies of the codebase to multiple locations. In addition, with a managed stack, maximum security and reliability are ensured with continuous, managed patching. These systems also typically last many years, making erosion resistance important.

In conclusion, Heroku brings advantages to apps in any category of the pace-layering model (as shown in the following table) and can help you maintain a healthy portfolio of apps, from foundational systems of record to systems of innovation that provide competitive advantages, and everything in between.

CHARACTERISTIC	SYSTEMS OF RECORD	SYSTEMS OF DIFFERENTIATION	SYSTEMS OF INNOVATION
Frequency of change	Low	Medium	High
Time to create	Years or months	Months or weeks	Days or hours
Tolerance for risk	Low	Medium	High
Change governance	Strict change process	Some change process in place	Little process needed
Potential for reward with success	Low	Medium	High
Clarity of requirements	Deep understanding	Known but possibly changing	Unclear or experimental
Competitive differentiation	Low	Medium	High
Agility to change	Very slow	Medium	Very rapid
Support needed	High	Medium	Low

ENSURING SECURITY AND COMPLIANCE

When considering any platform, two of the most important selection criteria are generally the level of security needed for the use case and the platform's ability to meet the regulatory compliance needs of your specific business or organization. Heroku takes security very seriously. Salesforce's executive vice president of technology, Parker Harris, has stated that "nothing is more important to our company than the privacy of our customer's data" (http://trust.salesforce.com/). However, multi-tenant platforms still tend to be misunderstood, and uninformed architects and IT managers often dismiss such a platform as being insecure because of the shared nature of its underlying infrastructure.

Dismissing a multi-tenant infrastructure as insecure by design essentially ignores the shared security and isolation controls built into the platform. This argument is similar to the argument made by those who do not trust banks with their money and prefer to put it under their mattress: If your money is being controlled by someone other than you, it can't possibly be as safe. What if the bank manager decides to transfer your money into his friend's account? Or what if a bug in the bank's software resets your account's balance to zero?

Although these are real (though extremely unlikely) possibilities, they completely ignore the fact that the bank has spent millions of dollars investing in physical security, software security, monitoring, and auditing to ensure that the aforementioned scenarios, and many others, do not happen. Clearly, few people choose to hide their money under their mattress instead of keeping it in a bank. Similarly, Heroku and other shared platforms have also invested millions of dollars in making their platforms secure, certainly more secure than most organizations could reasonably afford to spend for their infrastructure.

Physical Security and Safeguards

The servers on which your Heroku apps are run are hosted in Amazon's data centers. Only a few people within Amazon who need such knowledge know exactly where these nondescript data centers physically reside. As one would expect in a high-security data center, physical access to these facilities is controlled by security staff and automated surveillance and intrusion-detection systems. Staff who have legitimate business purposes for physical access are required to pass two-factor authorization multiple times before entry is permitted, and all entry is logged and audited routinely.

In addition to physical security to prevent intruders, Amazon's data centers are equipped to minimize impact in case of unexpected events. Data centers are climate-controlled to ensure optimal operating conditions for servers, including a fully redundant power supply with uninterrupted power supply (UPS) units and generators to ensure true 24x7 operations, even in the case of extended power interruption. Automated fire-detection equipment is installed with sprinkler systems to minimize the impact of a fire. These safeguards ensure the operation of servers even when the unexpected happens.

Network Security

Network security is provided by state-of-the-art firewall equipment that allows only permitted ports and services to pass through, mitigating risk. Host-based firewalls are utilized to isolate servers from each other within the network. IP, MAC, and ARP spoofing is prevented on the network by managed firewalls. The network's infrastructure and virtual machine's hypervisor prevent network sniffing by allowing packets to be delivered only to the addressed interface. Port scanning is actively monitored and blocked by Amazon.

Distributed Denial of Service (DDoS) mitigation techniques employed include TCP SYN cookies and connection rate limiting, in addition to maintaining multiple backbone connections and internal bandwidth capacity that exceeds the Internet carrier-supplied bandwidth. However, because of the massive bandwidth that Heroku's cloud consumes, an incident in the past that monitoring systems picked up as a suspected DDoS attack did not even have a noticeable impact on other customers. The incident turned out to be an app that went viral, and it only consumed a nearly unnoticeable percentage of Heroku's overall bandwidth.

Data resides on secure, access-controlled systems with redundancy built in to mitigate the risk of data loss. Heroku employees who are given such levels of permission may have access to this data, though not as a part of routine operations. Employees are subject to rigorous background checks, and all of their activities are logged and may be audited. With millions of apps on the Heroku platform, the likelihood of your app or database being targeted would be on a par with winning the lottery. For apps that require high levels of data security, data should be encrypted at rest on Heroku databases as a best practice.

Routine audits and automated penetration testing are conducted, but Heroku customers are welcome to do their own white-hat security testing on their own apps. All that Heroku asks is that you inform them of your intention to do such testing first. This ensures that Heroku's security operations personnel do not block what their detection systems will perceive as an attack from an intruder.

Apps that require virtual private network (VPN) or Secure Shell (SSH) tunnel access with other systems or IP whitelisting are not appropriate candidates for Heroku. Heroku does not allow incoming TCP connections (only HTTP), making VPN or SSH tunneling impossible; and because Heroku runs in the Amazon cloud, the IP range for Heroku apps could be part of a pool of millions of IPs. This makes whitelisting Heroku IPs ineffective. Instead, use SSL for these apps to establish a connection securely between Heroku and outside systems, or use the Proximo add-on (`https://addons.heroku.com/proximo`) to route outbound traffic through a single, static IP address.

Dyno- and Stack-Layer Security

Below the infrastructure, apps running on Heroku are isolated in such a way that they cannot interact with one another in malicious ways or cause stability issues for other apps on the same physical hardware (see the "Understanding Dyno Isolation" section in Chapter 1, "How Heroku Works"). All communications with Heroku and other systems is done over secure connections. Heroku staff can gain operating system access only through closely guarded username and key-based authentication. Passwords are not used, to minimize the risk of brute-force attacks.

Heroku is notified of patches and updates for the software it runs on, and the importance of each update is assessed and ranked for resolution based on risk. Updates to the stack that dynos run on are performed automatically once patches are pushed out and without interruption or perceived downtime to the end user. Penetration tests, vulnerability assessments, and source code reviews, both internal and external, are utilized to identify possible security risks to all aspects of the platform.

Data Retention

Data-retention best practices are employed on Heroku to ensure that deleted data is not recovered by malicious parties. When an app or database is deprovisioned, the data is kept for one week, and then the storage volume on which the data resides is wiped before reuse. When physical storage devices are decommissioned, Amazon adheres to the processes described in DoD 5220.22-M ("National Industrial Security Program Operating Manual") or NIST 800-88 ("Guidelines for Media Sanitization") to ensure that data is securely erased and unrecoverable.

Dealing with Security Issues

No organization is immune to incidents that compromise security. Even the CIA, one of the world's most secretive organizations, had its website hacked by a notorious hacker group, Lulz Security, in 2001. However, much can be learned about how organizations respond to such a breach.

On January 16, 2011, long-time Heroku customer David E. Chen found a security vulnerability in the platform. Heroku was storing the slug with the compressed code and config vars of the app in a directory name that was seemingly randomly generated and locked down so that you could not access it unless you could guess this random ID. Mr. Chen found that the ID in this unique name was also used elsewhere, allowing him to access other customers' slugs by guessing the directory name, and to view their source code and credentials to databases and other services.

Mr. Chen immediately notified Heroku, and Heroku began remediating the issue by closing this security gap, which they found was introduced just three weeks earlier. Logs were checked to ensure that this code was not exploited by anyone other than Mr. Chen. It wasn't, but appropriate precautions were taken nonetheless. Credentials for Heroku Postgres were rolled. Within five days of the incident, in accordance with zero-day exploit best practices, third-party providers were notified so that they could roll their credentials, and customers were advised to change outside credentials stored in config vars.

This incident demonstrated that exploits can appear on any platform, even Heroku. However, Heroku's swift actions ensured that minimal damage was done. Log auditing enabled Heroku to assess the extent of the exploit, and measures were taken above and beyond those needed, just in case. Flaws like this are found in commercial-grade software all the time, and even companies that specialize in security software have had major security incidents. However, unlike some of these companies, Heroku's transparency and swift actions to remedy the issues enabled it to retain its customers' trust.

Certifications, Accreditations, and Compliance

The Amazon infrastructure that supports Heroku apps has a number of accreditations, including ISO 2700 certification, SOC 1 report publishing with auditing in accordance with SSAE 16 and ISAE 3402 standards (previously SAS 70 Type II), Level 1 PCI compliance, and FISMA Moderate compliance — and customers have built HIPAA-compliant apps on it. However, this does not mean that because Heroku is built on Amazon's infrastructure it inherits any or all of these certifications; and it makes no claims to these certifications or accreditations. Heroku's parent company, Salesforce.com, is a publicly traded company in the United States and is audited annually to remain in compliance with the Sarbanes-Oxley (SOX) Act of 2002.

Because Heroku offers 24x7 support, it employs staff in countries such as Canada and Australia, who may have access to customer data. Therefore, Heroku is not appropriate for apps that require International Traffic in Arms Regulations (ITAR) compliance. Any apps that require this should be built directly on the Amazon Elastic Compute Cloud (Amazon EC2) web service (`http://aws.amazon.com/ec2/`) in the GovCloud (US) region.

> **NOTE** *The GovCloud region is a physically and logically segmented infrastructure of Amazon Web Services available for government agencies and contractors. It is designed and operated to meet the stringent compliance needs for these organizations.*

Heroku may also not be an appropriate platform when an app must follow Health Insurance Portability and Accountability Act (HIPAA) security and privacy rules. In addition, Heroku does not currently enter into business associate agreements (BAAs) with customers. BAAs are required for compliance by any services involving the use and/or disclosure of protected health information (PHI) in order for an app to be HIPAA compliant.

Those using Heroku for running financial services apps should also be cautious. Such apps typically require more stringent security and processes, which may or may not be supported by Heroku. These needs often can be addressed by encrypting data in the database, ensuring it is secure at rest, and encrypting data in transit with SSL. However, you should contact a Heroku representative for specific requirements that may not be met with these methods.

UNDERSTANDING REDUNDANCY AND RELIABILITY

Heroku has several processes in place to ensure the system's continued reliability and redundancy in the event of failover of a single node within the system. Automated backups are routinely executed during deploys for app source code, and data backup is achieved with a write-ahead log for databases and configuration. These backups can be used to retrieve a fresh copy of the app for deployment if a dyno fails; and malfunctioning databases can be restarted with minimal data loss. In this section, you will learn about how disaster recovery and continued reliability is achieved on the Heroku platform, and how transparency is used to address issues that arise in the course of Heroku's operation.

> **NOTE** *For more information on architecting your database for redundancy and failover, see Chapter 8, "Using Heroku Postgres as a Data Store for Your Heroku Applications."*

Disaster Recovery and Availability Zones

Disaster recovery and redundancy are provided using multiple data centers. All Heroku data resides on servers located within Amazon's data centers in the US East (Northern Virginia) region. This region contains multiple availability zones (four at the time of writing), which are distinct locations designed to be isolated from failure from other availability zones by eliminating single points of failure within those zones.

Each time a dyno is created, it is spawned in a random availability zone. This means that an app with two running dynos may not be absolutely shielded from failure in a single availability zone, as it is possible that the same availability zone may be selected for both dynos. However, given enough dynos running, it is statistically unlikely that all dynos will be placed in the same availability zone. Routinely, as part of dyno cycling, dynos will respawn, making it unlikely that dynos reside in the same availability zone for very long.

Heroku's system provides built-in monitoring and self-healing mechanisms that ensure that apps and databases are restored in case of an outage, either locally for the dyno or in case of a major outage. Core apps in the data centers are engineered in an N+1 redundancy configuration, ensuring that in case of disaster at one data center, remaining sites have the available capacity to handle the additional load.

However, these systems are not absolutely infallible. On April 21, 2011, Amazon suffered a failure in its Elastic Block Store (EBS) system (their persistent block storage mechanism) in a single availability zone because a routine network traffic rerouting operation was done incorrectly. This issue manifested itself in a major outage, as automated systems unexpectedly cascaded the effect of the issue to multiple availability zones within the region. Heroku suffered its largest outage to date, with some non-production apps using development-grade databases experiencing up to 60 hours of operational downtime. Despite the fact that the problem was clearly caused by a major outage with Amazon, Heroku took full responsibility for it and has taken steps to ensure that such an outage does not occur again.

Availability and Transparency

When something goes wrong on the platform on which your production app resides, nothing is worse than not knowing what is going on or when the issue will be resolved. Heroku does not readily offer customers a service-level agreement (SLA) guaranteeing uptime or availability. However, it does want to earn its users' trust, and the only way to do that is through complete operational transparency. Heroku's status site, status.heroku.com, provides the current status of system performance and security, offering public accountability for the platform's availability.

As shown in Figure 2-1, the Heroku status site provides status and incident reports for both production and development systems; and it is updated in real time, obviating the need to refresh the page using the Pusher Heroku add-on (see Chapter 6, "Working with Add-Ons"). Although not shown here, the color of each circle's perimeter indicates the current system's status. Green means that all systems are operating optimally; yellow indicates that something is currently degrading performance or causing intermittent issues; and red indicates a major outage of one or more parts of the Heroku system. The timeline below the circles outlines all known incidents in chronological order, and each incident is clickable to access a full incident report.

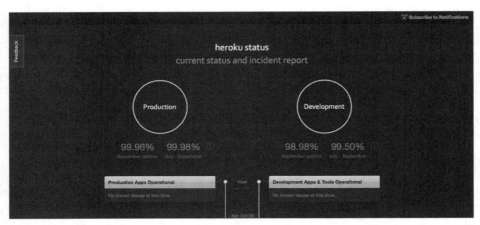

FIGURE 2-1

Also included are uptime percentages for the previous month of service, as well as the aggregated uptime from the previous three months. Taken together, it is clear that Heroku takes availability very seriously, believing that what is measured is improved. They take a hardline approach to uptime, considering any interruption to any customer impacting this number. Therefore, if Git pushes to Heroku are performing more slowly than usual, downtime will be recorded even though systems may still be operational, though not optimally functioning. This number is recorded for both production and development apps. What is considered a "production" app versus a "development" app?

Heroku considers a production app to be one that is currently running two or more dynos and is attached to a production-grade (i.e., nondevelopment) database. Heroku has always prioritized incident response for production apps over development apps. If a production app is down, this could be catastrophic for a business that relies on the Heroku platform for continuous service. If a development app is down, this may delay the deployment of code temporarily or cause developers to have to wait to test the latest version of their app. The impact is very different for issues that arise with these two types of systems.

You can also consume alerts in a number of different ways, besides going to the Heroku status site. Alternatively, you can subscribe to receive alerts using e-mail (new issues and updates) or SMS (new issues only); by following @herokustatus on Twitter; by subscribing to the Heroku Status RSS feed (at `https://status.heroku.com/feed`); or via the public API.

From the command line, you can check the current status at any time as follows:

```
$ heroku status
=== Heroku Status
Development: No known issues at this time.
Production:  No known issues at this time.
```

You can also call the REST API to get the current status:

```
$ curl "https://status.heroku.com/api/v3/current-status"
{"status":{"Production":"green","Development":"green"},"issues":[]}
```

The API can also be used to get a list of incidents. The `since` flag is used to get incidents since a specific date, and the `limit` flag is used to get a maximum number of results. The following code uses cURL to simulate an API request to get the current status:

```
$ curl "https://status.heroku.com/api/v3/issues?since=2012-05-25&limit=1"
[{"created_at":"2012-05-26T07:15:43Z","id":364,"resolved":true,"title":"Shared
  Database Server
Offline","updated_at":"2012-05-26T07:37:43Z","href":"https://status.heroku.com/
api/v3/issues/364","updates":[{"contents":"The database server is back online
with no data
loss.","created_at":"2012-05-26T07:37:43Z","id":1057,"incident_id":364,"
status_dev":"green","status_prod":"green","update_type":"resolved","updated_at":
"2012-05-26T07:37:46Z"},{"contents":"A shared database server has gone offline.
We are in the process of restarting
it.","created_at":"2012-05-26T07:15:43Z","id":1056,"incident_id":364,"status_dev
":"yellow","status_prod":"green","update_type":"issue","updated_at":"2012-05-
26T07:15:46Z"}]}]
```

For additional details about a specific incident number (in this case, incident #364), use the following:

```
$ curl "https://status.heroku.com/api/v3/issues/364"
{"created_at":"2012-05-26T07:15:43Z","id":364,"resolved":true,"title":"Shared
Database Server
Offline","updated_at":"2012-05-26T07:37:43Z","href":"https://status.heroku.com/
api/v3/issues/364","updates":[{"contents":"The database server is back online
with no data
loss.","created_at":"2012-05-26T07:37:43Z","id":1057,"incident_id":364,"
status_dev":"green","status_prod":"green","update_type":"resolved","updated_at":
"2012-05-26T07:37:46Z"},{"contents":"A shared database server has gone offline.
We are in the process of restarting
it.","created_at":"2012-05-26T07:15:43Z","id":1056,"incident_id":364,"status_dev
":"yellow","status_prod":"green","update_type":"issue","updated_at":"2012-05-
26T07:15:46Z"}]}
```

SECURING YOUR HEROKU APPLICATION

Although Heroku provides a strong foundation for security, developers are responsible for the security of both the app layer and their Heroku account. This section describes a few basic principles that Heroku recommends following to ensure the security of your apps.

Use a Strong Password for Your Heroku Account

A difficult to guess password is your top defense against having your Heroku account hacked by a malicious party. In addition, of course, you should not share this account with anyone. Use the contributors functionality to share code (see Chapter 7, "Managing, Monitoring, and Scaling Your Heroku Applications"), rather than share credentials. You should also store SSH keys in a safe place. In accordance with security best practices, change your password and SSH keys frequently. Heroku does not force you to change these, so you must remember to do so on your own.

Encrypt All Data in Transit

Any data that will be leaving the Heroku system, whether a connection to web services or a database, should be encrypted in transit. Using transport-level encryption such as SSL between secure endpoints ensures that data is not intercepted in transit. Authentication and sensitive data that is presented to the end user should be shown via HTTPS (see the section "Encrypting Communications with SSL" later in this chapter) to prevent disclosure and man-in-the-middle attacks.

Encrypt Sensitive Data at Rest

Your database should be secured with a password, and all data transmitted between your app and database should be done over an SSL connection to prevent eavesdropping. However, an attacker could still gain access to any database, possibly by exploiting a zero-day attack or social engineering someone with access. Adding another layer of security by encrypting sensitive data sitting in the database is recommended for maximum data privacy, rendering stolen data useless without the key to decrypt.

Use Best Practices for Secure Development

Attackers who exploit security holes in your app introduced by developers can gain access to your web app's data or compromise your end users' security by injecting malicious code into your site. Developers should familiarize themselves with best practices for their particular programming language and framework to minimize common exploits such as SQL injection and cross-site scripting (XSS).

> **NOTE** *For general information on common web app security risks and how to prevent them, see the Open Web Application Security Project's Top Ten Project, at* `https://www.owasp.org/index.php/Category:OWASP_Top_Ten_Project.`

Don't Reinvent the Wheel

Although most developers are talented enough to rewrite the login code used for web frameworks, most of them do not. This is because most mature frameworks have authentication procedures that were written and/or reviewed by security experts and have been patched and hardened over many releases when possible exploits were discovered. Unless they are experts in web app security, developers should resist the do-it-yourself mentality whenever possible, especially with respect to authentication and encryption functionality provided in frameworks.

Verify Security and Compliance Needs with Third-Party Providers

Any services used by your Heroku app should be considered untrusted until you have verified their security. Heroku does not review or guarantee the security of third-party add-on providers.

Consumers of these services should independently verify that these providers meet the security and compliance requirements for their use case with the appropriate vendors before using them.

Monitor Your Application's Logs

If you suspect your app has been compromised, the best way to investigate is through your app's logs. Heroku's logs are rolling, so configuring an external syslog drain or leveraging a third-party log-management solution, such as Loggly, is highly recommended for later investigation. A frequent review of these logs for suspicious activity is also strongly advised.

ENCRYPTING COMMUNICATIONS WITH SSL

SSL enables you to provide end-to-end encryption for data transmitted to and from your Heroku app. This can be used in conjunction with the Hypertext Transfer Protocol (HTTP) to allow private communication between the user's browser and your web app and to prevent third parties from tampering with HTTPS. This can be accomplished either by piggybacking on Heroku's SSL certificate or by using Heroku's SSL Endpoint add-on.

When transmitting sensitive information from the user's browser to your app and vice versa, it is best to do so over a secured connection with SSL. For instance, it is recommended that usernames and passwords be sent over HTTPS to ensure that prying eyes cannot see this information traveling from browser to website in plain text.

Piggybacking on Heroku's SSL Certificate

Heroku has installed a wildcard certificate for all apps to use, free of cost. By accessing your app with the URL `myappname.herokuapp.com` for apps on the Cedar stack or `myappname.heroku .com` for apps on the Aspen or Bamboo stacks (where `myappname` is the name of your app), you can piggyback on Heroku's certificate available for all apps.

> **NOTE** *Adding SSL functionality does not require installing any add-ons, as the deprecated Piggyback SSL add-on did in the past.*

You can also use SSL with a custom domain by visiting `https://www.yourcustomdomain.com`; however, this produces an error in the browser, as the domain being accessed will not match the domain indicated on the SSL certificate (`*.herokuapp.com`). This can be used for internal apps, where you can tell users to ignore the message, but is not suitable for external apps.

> **NOTE** *If you require a specific form on your site or require that all traffic to be sent over a secure connection, you should verify in your app's code that the page(s) is being accessed via the HTTPS protocol, and reroute traffic from* `http://` *to* `https://`*.*

Using SSL Endpoint

SSL Endpoint is a commercial add-on that allows websites to use HTTPS with their custom domains, enabling customers to access their web apps securely with either `https://www.yourdomainname.com` or `https://secure.yourdomainname.com`.

If you are wondering why Heroku charges for this add-on, there is a good reason why this feature is available for an additional cost. When SSL was designed, it assumed that web servers would be located at a dedicated, static IP address. Amazon does not allow multiple IP addresses to connect to a single Amazon EC2 instance, so Heroku must have an instance available for each domain. Installing the Endpoint SSL add-on provisions this Amazon EC2 instance for the dedicated, static IP address needed to provide SSL termination.

> **NOTE** *SSL Endpoint replaces a number of deprecated SSL add-ons, including SNI SSL, Hostname-Based SSL, and IP-Based Custom SSL, and simplifies the selection and configuration of features relative to these add-ons.*

You can set up SSL Endpoint for your app either by going to `https://addons.heroku.com/ssl` and following the instructions there or by issuing the following command in your app's directory:

```
$ heroku addons:add ssl:endpoint
Adding ssl:endpoint to heroku-ninja... done, v3 ($20/mo)
Next add your certificate with: heroku certs:add PEM KEY
ssl:endpoint documentation available at: https://devcenter.heroku.com/articles/ssl
```

After adding the SSL Endpoint add-on to your app, you should set up a custom domain name, as described in the "Adding Custom Domains" section of Chapter 7. In this example, we are going to set up `secure.mydomainname.com`. Naked domains (domains without a subdomain, such as `mydomainname.com`) are not supported. With your custom domain now added, the next step to get SSL working with your custom domain is to purchase and set up your certificate.

> **NOTE** *It is not necessary to purchase an SSL certificate to transmit information securely. You can also use a self-signed certificate that you can generate on your computer. However, generating your own certificate will cause a browser warning page to appear because your certificate is not considered trusted by a certificate authority (CA). For your certificate to be trusted, it must be signed by one of the trusted providers (such as Verisign) whose root certificate is built in to the browser and establishes a chain of trust. Purchasing a certificate from a trusted provider or installing your certificate explicitly in users' browsers prevents this message from appearing. For instructions on generating your own self-signed certificate, see* `https://devcenter.heroku.com/articles/ssl-certificate-self`.

When you purchase or self-generate a certificate, you will end up with two files: a certificate file and a certificate key file. (You may also have a bundle of chained certificates, a scenario we can ignore in the context of this section.) This certificate must be uploaded to Heroku using the following command in your app's directory, which assumes that you have saved the certificate file to `server` `.crt` and the certificate key file to `server.key` in the current local directory:

```
$ heroku certs:add final.crt site.key Adding SSL endpoint to heroku-ninja...done

heroku-ninja now served by miyagi-1554.herokussl.com

Certificate details:

    subject: /C=CA/ST=Ontario/L=Toronto/O=Vandelay
    Enterprises/CN=secure.herokuninja.com/emailAddress=ckemp@salesforce.com

    start date: 2012-06-09 10:43:58 EDT

    expire date: 2013-06-09 10:43:58 EDT

    common name(s): secure.herokuninja.com

    issuer: /C=CA/ST=Ontario/L=Toronto/O=Vandelay
    Enterprises/CN=secure.herokuninja.com/emailAddress=ckemp@salesforce.com

    SSL certificate is self signed.
```

The preceding example uses a self-signed certificate, so your output may differ.

Finally, add a Canonical Name (CNAME) record entry to your DNS provider, using `secure` `.mydomainname.com` as an alias for the SSL endpoint — in the preceding example, `miyagi-1554` `.herokussl.com`. As long as you are not still waiting for the DNS changes to propagate, which might take a while, you should be able to access your website via `https://www.yourdomainname` `.com` without security warnings.

You can view information on the SSL endpoints set up for your app using the following command:

```
$ heroku certs
Endpoint                    Common Name(s)         Expires                  Trusted
------------------------     ----------------------  -----------------------  -------
miyagi-1554.herokussl.com   secure.herokuninja.com  2013-06-09 10:43:58 EDT  False
```

Detailed certificate information for an SSL endpoint can be retrieved using the following command in an app's directory:

```
$ heroku certs:info
Fetching information on SSL endpoint miyagi-1554.herokussl.com... done
Certificate details:
        subject: /C=CA/ST=Ontario/L=Toronto/O=Vandelay
          Enterprises/CN=secure.herokuninja.com/emailAddress=ckemp@salesforce.com
        start date: 2012-06-09 10:43:58 EDT
        expire date: 2013-06-09 10:43:58 EDT
        common name(s): secure.herokuninja.com
        issuer: /C=CA/ST=Ontario/L=Toronto/O=Vandelay
          Enterprises/CN=secure.herokuninja.com/emailAddress=ckemp@salesforce.com
        SSL certificate is self signed.
```

Finally, you can remove an SSL endpoint by using the following command in an app's directory:

```
$ heroku certs:remove
Removing SSL endpoint miyagi-1554.herokussl.com from heroku-ninja... done
De-provisioned endpoint miyagi-1554.herokussl.com.
NOTE: Billing is still active. Remove SSL endpoint add-on to stop billing.
```

The preceding warning alerts you to remove the associated add-on as well, to avoid being charged for SSL that you are not using, which you can do with the following command:

```
heroku addons:remove ssl:endpoint
```

STORING STATIC ASSETS AND USING CDNS

Static assets are files that your web app relies upon to look and function correctly; they do not contain code or configuration. Some examples of assets include the following:

➤ Your user interface's images (GIFs, JPGs, PNGs, etc.)

➤ Downloadable documents (DOCs, PDFs, etc.)

➤ Videos and audio files (AVIs, MP3s, etc.)

➤ Client-side multimedia apps (Flash SWFs, Silverlight XAPs, etc.)

> **NOTE** *Presentation assets for the view layer (CSS files, JavaScript libraries, etc.) may also be included, if they do not change often or are not modified directly by coders other than to upgrade occasionally (for example, outside libraries such as JQuery), and they do not need to be tracked by version control.*

Traditionally, static assets sit in the codebase as part of the app; however, there are a few advantages to storing them outside of the codebase.

First, storing assets in the codebase bloats slug size, which may result in scrambling to pull assets out later when the 200MB limit is suddenly reached. Second, storing assets in the codebase slows down deployment and dyno provisioning done by the dyno manifold when restarting an app or scaling up dynos, as larger slug sizes take longer. Finally, there are usability improvements to be gained by moving static assets to a CDN or storage solution closer to your user base, especially when your app will be accessed internationally. For instance, Japanese users can download videos from a server in Japan instead of from a dyno located in eastern USA, resulting in less latency. Leveraging cloud storage solutions such as Amazon S3 for asset storage and Amazon CloudFront as a CDN can help keep your codebase lean, your deployment snappy, and your app pages loading swiftly for international visitors.

Storing Static Assets on Amazon S3

Amazon S3 provides online storage as a service (STaaS) that is available through web services. It is a high scalability, durability, and reliability solution, offering an SLA of 99.99% availability for objects stored on its service. According to Amazon, one trillion objects were stored in Amazon S3 as of June 2012 (http://aws.typepad.com/aws/2012/06/amazon-s3-the-first-trillion-objects.html); and it routinely handles more than 650,000 requests per second for objects within the service (`http://aws.typepad.com/aws/2012/04/amazon-s3-905-billion-objects-and-650000-requestssecond.html`). Though there are other cloud-based storage offerings, Amazon S3 has established itself as the de facto standard by offering excellent service at a reasonable price.

Because Amazon S3 makes it easy and affordable to store static assets, it is an ideal alternative to storing them in the Heroku app's codebase. Files are organized within a user's Amazon S3 account in what Amazon refers to as *buckets*. Every object stored on Amazon S3 must be stored in a bucket, which is simply a uniquely named file container that is located in a specific region. The capability to change the region of buckets enables you to minimize latency by storing assets as close as possible to the largest number of users.

> **NOTE** *Amazon S3 pricing differs per region, so architects must weigh the additional costs for storage, request volumes, and bandwidth when deciding in which Amazon S3 region assets should be stored.*

The objects contained in the buckets are simply any sort of file — a document, video, or image. Each bucket and object stored on Amazon includes metadata that defines things such as the access control list for the bucket or object, and who has permissions to do what with the object. Objects are available by accessing `http://s3.amazonaws.com/bucket/key`, where `bucket` refers to the bucket in which the object is stored, and `key` is the user-defined key for the object.

Objects are added and buckets managed using either a REST or Web Services API. Access to these APIs is controlled by an Access Key ID and a Secret Access Key. Together, these are similar to a username and password; you must protect these because unauthorized access could result in unwanted charges or changes being made to your account. To retrieve your Access Key ID and Secret Access Key, select My Account/Console from the Amazon Web Services home page (`http://aws.amazon.com`), and then select Security Credentials from the drop-down menu. Under the Access Credentials heading, you will find your Access Key ID. Clicking the Show link will display your Secret Access Key, as shown in Figure 2-2.

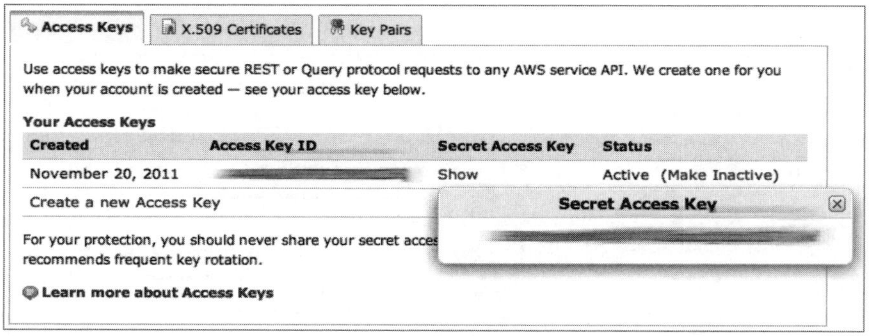

FIGURE 2-2

You should store your Access Key ID and Secret Access Key credentials in your app's config vars if you are planning to upload files to Amazon S3. You should *not* store the credentials in the codebase, per the third factor in building twelve-factor apps. If you are only storing files that will be accessed publicly as part of the website, they can simply be accessed directly through the URL in your app's presentation layer, and you will likely not need to store these credentials. You can add these to your app's config vars, using the following command within an app's directory:

```
$ heroku config:add AWS_ACCESS_KEY_ID=abc123 AWS_SECRET_KEY=xyz789
Adding config vars and restarting my-app-accessing-s3... done, v2
AWS_ACCESS_KEY_ID: abc123
AWS_SECRET_KEY: xyz789
```

You can access Amazon S3 with a number of different tools built on top of the Amazon Web Services (AWS) API. Amazon provides its own GUI for services, called the *AWS Management Console*. However, several popular alternatives are available:

➤ **S3Fox Organizer:** This is a Firefox plug-in that enables you to upload and download files, synchronize with local folders, and change access to objects and buckets. It looks and behaves like traditional FTP clients, where you can use drag and drop, and allows you to manage Amazon CloudFront content distribution. It is cross-platform and will work wherever Firefox works.

➤ **CloudBerry Explorer:** This is a freemium product for Windows that offers a user interface similar to S3Fox Organizer. However, CloudBerry provides more functionality, with features such as Windows PowerShell support for automation, scheduling, and copying files across Amazon S3 accounts. The professional version provides even more advanced functionality, with compression, encryption, multi-threading, and support for files over 5GB.

➤ **Cyberduck:** This is a Mac-based FTP client on steroids. It provides not only basic functionality like most other clients, but also advanced features such as Amazon CloudFront support, versioning support, multi-factor authentication (MFA) delete, and encryption. The best part? It's free.

To set up an Amazon S3 bucket and add objects, perform the following steps:

1. Open the AWS Management Console by going to My Account/Console and selecting AWS Management Console from the drop-down menu. This provides a GUI on top of the API for Amazon S3 and other Amazon Web Services (see Figure 2-3).

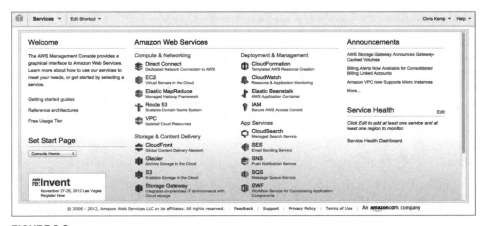

FIGURE 2-3

2. Select the Amazon S3 tab and click the Create Bucket button to create your first bucket. Name it something meaningful (it has to be unique across all users, so be creative), and set the region to either US Standard or whatever region will be closest to the bulk of your user base, as shown in Figure 2-4, and then click Create.

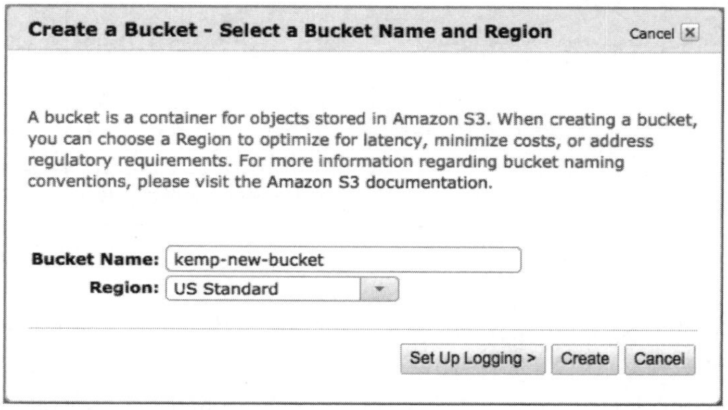

Create a Bucket - Select a Bucket Name and Region   Cancel ☒

A bucket is a container for objects stored in Amazon S3. When creating a bucket, you can choose a Region to optimize for latency, minimize costs, or address regulatory requirements. For more information regarding bucket naming conventions, please visit the Amazon S3 documentation.

Bucket Name: kemp-new-bucket
Region: US Standard ▾

Set Up Logging >   Create   Cancel

FIGURE 2-4

When selecting a region, keep in mind that transfers between your Heroku app and any Amazon S3 region other than US Standard are metered and chargeable.

> **NOTE** *Specifying the US Standard region will route traffic either to the eastern US (Northern Virginia) or to the Pacific northwest, based on proximity. To ensure that data you store resides in the US East, use a named endpoint such as* `http://s3.amazonaws.com/your-bucket-name/somefile.txt` *instead of* `http://s3-external-1.amazonaws.com/your-bucket-name/somefile.txt`*. The* "`s3-external-1`" *part tells Amazon to force the upload to a particular Amazon S3 region.*

3. To add a file, click Upload, and then click the Add Files button. You can add one or more files by holding down the Ctrl (Windows) or Command (Mac) button in the file selector dialog.

4. Click Open to verify your file list (see Figure 2-5).

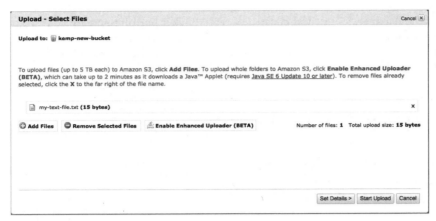

FIGURE 2-5

5. Click the Start Upload button to begin the file transfer. A Transfers pane will open, updating you on the progress of your file transfer(s).

6. To make your newly uploaded file public, click the filename to highlight the file, and then click the Properties button.

7. From the Permissions tab, click the Add More Permissions button. Select Everyone from the drop-down to indicate that you want to set permissions for the general public.

8. Check the Open/Download checkbox to indicate that access to this object should be public, as shown in Figure 2-6.

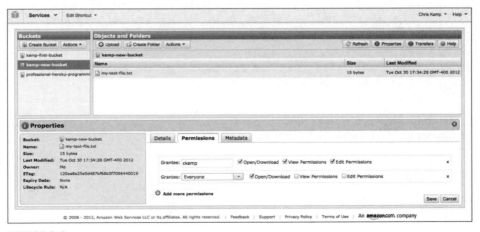

FIGURE 2-6

9. Click Save. You should be able to access your file at `http://s3.amazonaws.com/`
`[bucket name]/[filename]`.

Speeding Up International Applications with Amazon CloudFront

Heroku apps are run in a data center in the US East region. This means that apps may appear less responsive to users accessing them from more geographically removed locations. According to the cloud consulting group Cedexis, a user in Singapore would experience nearly half a second longer average response time to Amazon EC2's US East region than someone accessing the same file in the eastern United States. Using a CDN enables such users to obtain faster web page loading, especially when pages contain many images and other resource-intensive assets. A CDN such as Amazon's CloudFront service or Akamai can be leveraged to deliver web content locally, regardless of where the user is located. This significantly reduces page load times and provides a more favorable experience for international users.

Because you have already set up a bucket on Amazon S3, you can now set up an Amazon CloudFront distribution for the objects within that bucket. Follow these steps:

1. Go to aws.amazon.com, click My Accounts/Console, and choose AWS Management Console from the top-right. Log in, if needed.

2. Select the Amazon CloudFront tab in the AWS Management Console.

3. Create a new distribution by clicking the Create Distribution button, as shown in Figure 2-7.

FIGURE 2-7

4. Select a delivery method, as shown in Figure 2-8. Typically, you will use the Download delivery method unless you are streaming a video file you have created using Adobe Flash Media Server's RTMP protocol. Click the Continue button.

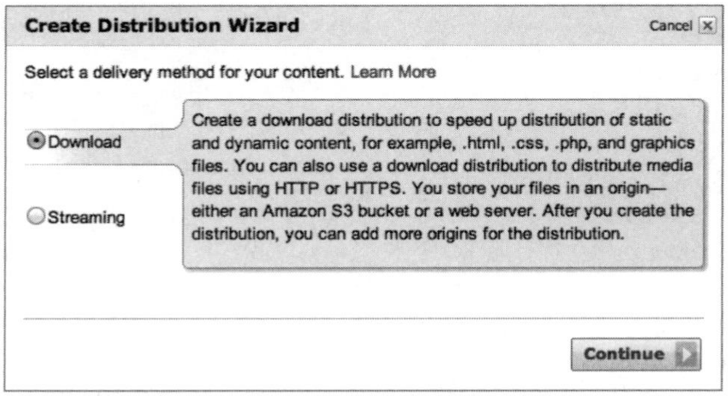

Create Distribution Wizard   Cancel ✕

Select a delivery method for your content. Learn More

⦿ Download

○ Streaming

Create a download distribution to speed up distribution of static and dynamic content, for example, .html, .css, .php, and graphics files. You can also use a download distribution to distribute media files using HTTP or HTTPS. You store your files in an origin— either an Amazon S3 bucket or a web server. After you create the distribution, you can add more origins for the distribution.

Continue ▶

FIGURE 2-8

5. Choose your origin, which is simply the Amazon S3 bucket in which the file(s) that you want to be a part of your distribution are located. Click on the textbox beside Origin Domain Name, as shown in Figure 2-9, to see a list of the buckets you have set up. Choose the appropriate bucket. The origin will be filled in for you automatically. Click Continue.

6. On the Create Default Behavior screen, you can customize options such as which protocols your content can be distributed on (see Figure 2-10). You can leave these settings at their defaults unless content must be sent over HTTPS. Click Continue.

7. In the Distribution Details screen, shown in Figure 2-11, you can customize your distribution's URL. If you would rather use `image .yourdomainname.com` instead of something like `abc123.cloudfront .net`, you can alter your domain's CNAME settings in your DNS provider's configuration and add the domain(s) here. You can also add access logging and set a default root object to serve up if someone goes to your naked URL. Click Continue.

8. Review your settings and click Create Distribution.

You should now see your new distribution, with the status InProgress while it is being distributed. When the status of your distribution changes to Deployed (it will probably take a few minutes), you can test it by going to `https://d1str0nam3.cloudfront .net/somefilename.txt`, where `d1str0nam3` is the value in the Domain Name column for your distribution, and `somefilename.txt` is the name of one of the publicly available files in your Amazon S3 bucket. If that worked and you can see your file, your distribution is deployed and ready to go. The final step is to change the URLs

FIGURE 2-9

FIGURE 2-10

FIGURE 2-11

for all the assets in your codebase that you are delivering using the CDN to point to your Amazon CloudFront URL.

SUMMARY

You should now understand how to optimally architect apps that will be run on the Heroku platform. Using the twelve-factor app methodology, your organization can build portable and scalable web-based apps. Pace layering provides a methodology that can assist in categorizing your app portfolio, and Heroku provides advantages for apps within each of the layers of the pace-layering model. As with any platform, security and compliance are an important consideration and must be understood fully. Heroku provides built-in mechanisms to ensure the reliability and availability of your apps, as well as transparency into past incidents. The security of your apps is paramount and can be ensured by following best practices, such as encrypting communications with SSL. Rapid scaling and app performance can be achieved by storing assets with an asset storage service, such as Amazon S3, and a CDN, such as Amazon CloudFront. In Chapter 3, we will discuss best practices in porting existing apps to Heroku.

3

Porting Your Applications to Heroku

WHAT'S IN THIS CHAPTER?

➤ Understanding differences from traditional filesystems

➤ Choosing a data store

➤ Managing sessions

➤ Understanding caching

➤ Storing static assets

➤ Managing configuration variables

➤ Replacing web servers and containers

➤ Managing dependencies

➤ E-mailing from your application

➤ Running cron jobs

➤ Understanding logging

➤ Relying on external programs

➤ Scaling up versus scaling out

➤ Binding to ports

➤ Managing long-running processes

➤ Shutting down gracefully

➤ Moving your domain

Porting your existing apps to the Heroku platform seems like a no-brainer. After all, it enables you to take advantage of the many efficiency gains that you can realize by developing on and deploying with the Heroku platform. Nevertheless, you must consider the cost involved in porting an app to the Heroku system. Though apps can be easily moved off of the Heroku platform and onto your platform of choice with little or no change, the reverse is not necessarily true.

Timing is important. Is this the right time to move an app to Heroku? It is often difficult for IT to convince business owners or management that spending developer time to move the app to a new platform is a valuable use of resources. In most organizations, IT departments are considered a cost center, so any activities that do not deliver new features that can help the business side sell more or charge more money for the product or service is difficult to justify. Although you can present a ROI analysis of developer time spent on noncoding activities and system operations costs and labor saved with Heroku, this calculation is complex and difficult to coordinate, and its accuracy may be met with skepticism from those who do not fully understand the development process.

Enterprise apps are typically rewritten every three to five years, when refactoring becomes cumbersome. At this point, the development team is generally working with design decisions made before new technologies were released, or it is working to optimize parts of the app that are causing issues, rather than attacking the problem's source. This app rewrite period is often the best window of opportunity for replatforming apps to Heroku, as they are going to be rewritten regardless, and no additional perceived cost is spent on the process. Your organization must decide whether rewriting the app on the Heroku platform makes more sense than porting it, and weigh the risks and reward of each option accordingly.

This chapter outlines general architectural considerations you should keep in mind before moving apps to Heroku. It will help you understand the many moving parts involved in porting an app to the Heroku platform and identify parts of your existing app that may need to be modified or re-architected. With this knowledge in hand, you should be able to decide whether this is a good time to port your app to Heroku and understand what needs to be done to do so.

Note that this chapter is not an extensive language- or framework-specific checklist. Nor does it present an exhaustive list of issues that may arise when moving apps to Heroku. In some cases, dependencies that your app relies on or language- and framework-specific functions may not work as expected because they may not be architected for use on a platform like Heroku. Although this chapter touches on many of these issues, it is safe to assume that unexpected hiccups may still need to be overcome in the porting process.

This chapter provides general best practices that should be followed when porting any app. For supported apps and frameworks, later chapters address language- or framework-specific considerations. If you are using buildpacks to run apps on unsupported languages or implementing frameworks that are not covered in this book, this chapter provides important considerations to keep in mind.

UNDERSTANDING DIFFERENCES FROM TRADITIONAL FILESYSTEMS

When using Heroku or porting over apps, some key considerations should be kept in mind regarding the filesystem, as Heroku's filesystem is quite different from traditional filesystems. Its ephemeral nature means that it cannot be relied on for long-term storage and for apps running on more than one dyno. You should consider Heroku's filesystem as read-only.

Ephemeral Filesystems

The current state of the Heroku filesystem can be assumed to last only as long as a single request. Therefore, relying on the local filesystem any longer than the duration of a request may result in unexpected consequences. For instance, consider a scenario in which you have a program to which users upload files, which are stored in the filesystem. In order to retrieve these files later (even if it is very soon after, but not in the same request transaction), the dyno may have reset or respawned since the previous request, wiping out any files added to the filesystem earlier during the file upload.

Each time a dyno is restarted or scaled up, a copy of the app is retrieved from the slug created during the last code push and deployed on the dyno. This includes a fresh copy of the filesystem, which is why files cannot be relied upon for more than one request. With dynos cycled as much as once a day, one cannot reliably predict how long files stored on the Heroku filesystem will last.

Multi-Dyno Applications

For a multi-dyno app, you cannot guarantee that the load balancer will redirect subsequent requests from the same user to the same dyno onto which the file was originally uploaded, even if it is still there. For instance, you may save an uploaded file to the local filesystem of a dyno. When the user makes a subsequent request to view the file, Heroku's load balancing will randomly route the request to any one of the available dynos. This means that the subsequent requests may be redirected to a different dyno from the original one, where the file does not exist. All local filesystem access, unless temporary and isolated to a single request, should be refactored out of the app and stored in persistent storage elsewhere.

Considerations for Porting Existing Applications

When porting an app to Heroku from a traditional architecture, you should look for file uploads, places where saved or temporary files are created on the filesystem, and embedded databases.

File Uploads

You should look for code where your web app accepts file uploads and ensure that uploads are not being stored on the local filesystem for longer than the request. If you do find parts of your web app where files are being uploaded, you typically have two alternatives: move the file upload to a file storage service, like Amazon Simple Storage Service (Amazon S3) or store the file in the database.

Amazon S3 is well suited for persistent file storage. However, it can be expensive if a lot of large files are being stored with both storage and transfer costs. Refactoring your app to use Amazon S3 will require more complex code to store and retrieve these files through the Amazon S3 API. For large files, it is important that you use the direct upload technique, as described in the section "Managing Long-Running Processes," to ensure that long-running uploads do not time-out and close the connection.

Database storage can be used as an alternative. In most modern database systems, files can be kept as binary large objects (BLOBs), which are are well suited for this purpose. However, adding files to your database may significantly increase its size. For instance, if you are using a production-grade Heroku Postgres database, you may hit the 1TB database size limit much faster if you are storing videos in the database alongside the rest of your existing data. This will also make backups much larger in size and result in backup and restore activities taking longer to complete.

Saved or Temporary Files

Often programs and libraries save temporary files, for things like caching or indexing. For instance, Ferret can be used for full-text indexing for Ruby apps. However, this app creates a local file that caches the indexed information. You must look for places in your app and its libraries where local files may be saved, and then either refactor your code to store this information in a data store or choose alternative libraries that do not rely on saving local files (e.g., using the Flying Sphinx add-on instead of Ferret).

Embedded Databases

Some databases, especially embedded databases, store their data in a file on the local filesystem. In fact, this is how most databases work. However, embedded databases typically are supposed to be used for standalone, single-instance apps. Examples of such databases include SQLite, GDBM, and SQL Anywhere. These databases are not suitable for use with scalable platforms like Heroku because each dyno will have a different copy of the database stored locally. Apps that use embedded databases should be refactored to use a centralized database that does not reside in a local file on each dyno, choosing alternatives like Heroku Postgres or a data store from the Heroku add-ons.

CHOOSING A DATA STORE

Most traditional apps use a database that is running on either the same server as the app or one or more servers within the same local network as the app. In theory, you can still run your Heroku app with a backing database on the same database server within your organization's four walls (but exposed externally as a service). However, this typically is not practical because of the latency involved in making requests.

On Heroku, several options are available for data stores, depending on the use case. The following are the most common options:

- ➤ The Heroku Postgres database
- ➤ Database.com, Salesforce's data as a service (DaaS)
- ➤ An add-on provider, such as Redis to Go for key-value stores or Xeround for MySQL
- ➤ A third-party DaaS outside the add-on ecosystem, such as Amazon DynamoDB

Using Heroku Postgres as a Data Store

The most common choice for Heroku apps backed by a relational database is to leverage the Heroku Postgres database. It is simple to set up, easy to add redundancy, and has continuous protection built in to safeguard your data. Because it is built on the same Amazon Web Services (AWS) network as your Heroku app, the latency is on a par with a traditional setup (i.e., the database on the same LAN as the web app). Heroku Postgres databases also support schema-less data storage, making them a flexible option for both structured and unstructured data.

Heroku Postgres database production plans include 1TB of data, making them an affordable choice for storing large amounts of data, especially for high-volume transactional data. Sharing can be used to expand your total storage above and beyond the single database limit. However, if a massive amount of data (e.g., hundreds of terabytes) is being stored, it may become impractical to maintain so many databases. In this case, using a solution like the Treasure Data add-on to store the data and Hadoop to run analytics on it is advisable.

If you are moving from a non-Postgres database, additional work might be required to convert your database. The syntax is also different from other databases, like MySQL. This may make the transition more challenging for developers who are familiar with a particular syntax for database operations. Though some additional effort is required to learn a new database system, the benefits typically outweigh the short-term inconveniences.

> **NOTE** *For more information on how Heroku Postgres works, see Chapter 8, "Using Heroku Postgres as a Data Store for Your Heroku Applications."*
>
> *For more information on converting from other databases to PostgreSQL, see the PostgreSQL Wiki (*`http://wiki.postgresql.org/wiki/Converting_from_other_Databases_to_PostgreSQL`*).*

Using Database.com as a Data Store

Salesforce.com's DaaS solution is a secure, scalable data store that provides a number of conveniences for users on top of data storage. Database.com provides user and identity management services on top of data storage that leverage standard-based authentication methods, like OAuth. The built-in sharing and security model also allows for object-, field-, and record-based security that can be configured using point and click instead of code. This suits moderately complex security models, like role hierarchies, where complex code no longer has to be written and maintained.

Database.com has a number of built-in conveniences, like a data-modeling tool that makes data modeling an easy and quick process that does not require SQL, coding, or downloading separate apps. Apps built with Database.com are inherently social, can use the Chatter API, and are well suited for collaboration. For instance, if you are writing a project-management app, discussions can happen on each project's record in the data store, and news feeds can be used for any given user to get real-time updates on only projects they are interested in. The security model ensures that only users who have access to those records will have visibility into discussions on those records.

Though Database.com is a good choice as a back-end for building social apps, it is not always a good fit for all use cases. It is financially impractical to store large amounts of data on Database.com because the costs get high when getting into the hundreds of millions of records ($10 per 100,000 records). This makes it a poor choice for high-volume transactional databases.

Database.com uses SOQL, a proprietary querying language similar to SQL that will require some learning for developers to adapt to. The complex security layer built on top of a multi-tenant database makes database transactions take longer than traditional databases — usually about a quarter of a second. This, in addition to the transmission time between Database.com's servers and Heroku, which are on different infrastructures, makes it suboptimal for uses where very fast transaction times are needed between database and app.

> **NOTE** *For more information on how Database.com works, see Chapter 9, "Using Database.com As a Data Store for Your Heroku Applications."*

Using Add-On Data Stores

Heroku's add-on ecosystem offers a plethora of choices for developers who want to use a particular type of database with which they are familiar. Developers who prefer to use MySQL can use Amazon Relational Database Service (RDS), ClearDB, or Xeround. Those who have a large number of transactions that are short-lived and touch a small subset of the same pieces of data frequently will be best served using JustOneDB. When storing data that is connected through relationships, a graph-based database like Neo4J is optimally suited. Big data apps should use Treasure Data for warehousing and analysis.

Sometimes databases are too heavyweight and slow for either simple storage needs, like session storage, or apps where large volumes of transactions happen in a short amount of time. In these cases a NoSQL store may be more appropriate. Heroku add-ons are available for Redis, CouchDB, Memcachier, or MongoDB. General-use key value stores, like IronCache, can also be leveraged.

When using add-on data stores, you must conduct due diligence to ensure that you choose the correct one. Third-party companies provide data stores in Heroku's Add-on library. Security, reliability, and compliance for these solutions should be investigated separately from Heroku. Most Add-ons include a free plan that can be used for testing and ensuring that the Add-on fits your use case through building a small proof of concept.

> **NOTE** *For more information on using third-party add-ons as a data store, including an in-depth comparison, see Chapter 10, "Using Third-Party Data Stores for Your Heroku Applications."*

Using a Third-Party Data-as-a-Service Provider

Third-party DaaS providers should be used with care and caution. Though a particular DaaS provider may seem ideally suited for use with your app, it may suffer similar latency issues as using a remotely located database within the four walls of your organization. Unless the DaaS service is running within Amazon AWS's US East region, requests may take significantly longer between your app and database. Testing should be conducted to ensure adequate performance before selecting a third-party DaaS provider.

Third-party DaaS services, such as Amazon DynamoDB, are well suited for use with Heroku apps. When provisioning your DynamoDB, you should select the US East region. This will ensure minimal latency between your app and the database. You must also perform due diligence to ensure that any third-party DaaS provider meets the security, reliability, and compliance needs of your app.

Using Multiple Data Stores

Often, it is best to use a combination of different types of data stores within an app. For instance, a common architecture uses a Heroku Postgres database for storing an app's data while also using a Redis data store for storing session data. This approach leverages the advantages of both, with the Redis data store providing quick and lightweight access to session information. The Heroku Postgres database is better suited for transactional data storage and access.

Considerations for Porting Existing Applications

A best practice for porting existing apps to Heroku is using the same type of database when available. For instance, if you are porting a PHP app that runs on an in-house MySQL app, it would be best to use an add-on provider who offers MySQL databases, such as Xeround or ClearDB. This type of change typically only requires exporting your data from your old database and re-importing it in your new database. Little change in code is required, unless you are moving between different major versions of the database (e.g., moving from MySQL 4.1 to 5.5, where some functionality might have changed).

If you are using a database where no similar add-on provider exists, porting your app requires more significant effort, as you have to switch database types. For instance, if your app uses a Microsoft SQL Server database, you need to refactor your app significantly to accommodate a different database type throughout your code. Though ANSI SQL-compliant databases theoretically are portable, differences in certain databases make porting more difficult in reality. This may require changing code for handling transactions or rewriting and optimizing complex queries that behave or perform differently on different databases.

The complete effort of moving databases should be weighed when deciding to move data to a different database, though it may be difficult to accurately predict. If a significant effort is required to port your app to a new database, this may present an opportunity to rearchitect your app entirely. If you are looking to get your existing app up and running on Heroku quickly, you may want to estimate the level of effort required to port your app by moving a small portion of it to gauge the level of effort required to move the app in its entirety.

MANAGING SESSIONS

Web apps can manage sessions in a number of different ways, only some of which are safe for use with Heroku. Storing session information on the local filesystem or in memory is obviously not recommended. Distributed memory sharing and memory virtualization are not supported on Heroku. Nor are stateful sessions supported with Heroku's share-nothing model. With load balancing happening transparently, persistent sessions, such as sticky sessions, cannot be used.

You must either store session information client-side in cookies or use a persistent method to share session information across dynos. Storing information client-side introduces issues of confidentiality and integrity that must be overcome with encryption. However, this technique is practical only when the session information size is small, due to browser limits and the fact that the cookie must be transmitted during each request. Storing information in a data store shared by dynos can be done either with a traditional relational database or, more appropriately, with a key-value pair store such as memcached or Redis. You must consider your need for session durability when deciding between these alternatives.

When porting an app, you will need to investigate how your app stores session data. Often, this is taken care of transparently by the framework that you are using. Most frameworks use memory-based session storage out-of-the-box for simplicity. When porting your app, you have to refactor your app or reconfigure your framework to ensure that a backing data store is used instead. This could be as easy as changing a configuration setting, or it may require a more significant effort. You should explore what is necessary to port your app and understand the level of effort involved before making the decision to do so.

Some frameworks that use client-side session storage use an encryption key to ensure that session data is stored securely. Sometimes, these frameworks will generate a random key when the app is first run (if none is already found in the configuration) and store the key locally on the filesystem. This method does not work well with apps on Heroku, as the filesystem is different across different dynos. Apps running on multiple dynos will not be able to decrypt information generated by different dynos because the keys will be different, so a new session is spawned on each different dyno the app is run on. In this case, you should generate your own key and store it in configuration variables (config vars), which will persist across different dynos.

> **NOTE** *For examples of using key-value data stores with your app, see Chapter 10.*

UNDERSTANDING CACHING

Because of Heroku's distributed nature and its ephemeral filesystem, built-in caching mechanisms for many languages, such as Ruby, do not work properly; therefore, application-layer caching must be used. A number of different methods can be used to improve performance through caching, each suited to a specific use case.

Common caching methods include page caching, data caching, and HTTP caching. Page caching can be done by caching entire web pages requested or partial pages. This is best suited for pages or sections within pages that don't contain dynamic data.

Data caching saves data, typically in-memory, when it would normally have to be retrieved by accessing a database or third-party service. This can be done with add-ons like Memcachier for memcached data storage or Redis to Go for Redis-based storage. Each time you need to query the database, a unique key is used to check if the data is already cached. For instance, Ruby implements this using a built-in method, `Rails.cache.fetch`:

```
>> Rails.cache.fetch('my_query_key')
==> "nil"
>> Rails.cache.fetch('my_query_key') { // do real database query here }
==> 42
Rails.cache.fetch('my_query_key')
==> 42
```

In the first attempt to receive a value from the cache with our key, we get a cache miss because the query has not been run yet, so we do not have the cached results. In the second attempt, we provide an alternative method to get the data if is not cached inside the curly braces. Subsequent requests, like that in the third attempt, return the cached data. Care should be taken not to return stale data that has changed in the database since the result was cached.

HTTP caching either uses distributed methods to serve pages or assets, caches content locally in the user's browser, or caches with an external proxy server. Content distribution networks (CDNs) are well suited for serving static assets (see the next section for more details). HTTP cache headers can be used for browser-based caching. (See `https://devcenter.heroku.com/articles/` `increasing-application-performance-with-http-cache-headers` for details and examples.) Proxy servers can be used, although they typically are not well suited for Heroku apps, as they add another layer of complexity and maintenance and cannot be used with features like HTTP polling.

> **NOTE** *For language-specific details on caching techniques, see Chapter 11, "Developing with Ruby," Chapter 12, "Developing with Java," and Chapter 13, "Developing with Other Supported Languages."*

Page and data caching can be used for Heroku apps, but cached pages must be stored in a data store, such as a database or key-value store, to ensure that it is available and consistent across multiple dynos. This may require simple configuration changes (as with the Play framework, shown in the example in Chapter 12). However, this may involve refactoring to switch to a central data store, especially if the caching mechanism saves static information in the filesystem. Before porting your app, you should explore how the caching mechanism works to make sure a central data store is used, and gauge the level of effort needed to port your app to a scalable platform like Heroku.

HTTP caching involves little or no additional effort if done through browser caching. Typically, CDNs can be used in the same way that your app is using them today if your app simply points your static assets to the CDN server, as described in Chapter 2, "Architectural Considerations." Proxy-based servers can be replaced using a middleware layer specific to your framework of choice that typically provides comparable performance.

STORING STATIC ASSETS

Most codebases for traditional web apps contain the static assets, such as images, videos, documents, music files, and so on. Generally, these assets can still be included if they don't take up an inordinate amount of space. Some sites that are heavy on static assets will need to move these elsewhere to avoid hitting the 200MB slug size limit. Using a solution such as Amazon S3 as high-availability storage for such assets is advisable.

When porting an app to Heroku, you need to change the codebase to point to the new home for the assets. Typically, this is a simple search-and-replace operation, mostly in the view layer, looking for the relevant file extensions, like .css, .js, and .pdf, and refactoring to use the fully-qualified domain name (FQDN) provided by the CDN provider instead.

For example, a CSS file referred to in the view layer may look like this:

```
<link rel="stylesheet" type="text/css" href="mystyle.css">
```

When moving this CSS file to Amazon S3, it will need to be changed to look like this:

```
<link rel="stylesheet" type="text/css" href=" http://s3.amazonaws.com/
your-bucket-name/mystyle.css">
```

> **NOTE** *For detailed instructions on how to upload files to Amazon S3, see the "Storing Static Assets and Using CDNs" section in Chapter 2.*

MANAGING CONFIGURATION VARIABLES

Traditionally, developers put environment-specific config vars, such as database credentials, under source control. Developers often have these in configuration or properties files somewhere specific to that particular development environment (staging, integration, production, etc.). This can be error prone and have disastrous results if the incorrect properties file is used in the wrong environment. No one wants to clean up the mess after a testing environment is accidentally pointed to a production database, overwriting mission-critical data.

In Heroku, config vars are stored as environment variables in each of the different environments. All credentials for databases and backing services (for example, credentials for Amazon S3) should be moved to config vars to differentiate credentials that should be used for the environment-specific configuration.

> **NOTE** *For more information on how to manage config vars, see the section "Managing Configuration Variables" in Chapter 5, "Managing Releases in Heroku."*

Finding and moving credentials to config vars is an exercise that takes a relatively low amount of effort. Traditional web apps often store these credentials in configuration files as hardcoded strings, which may make them easier to find. For instance, in a Java Bean, you may refer to your backing database using the following configuration:

```
<bean class="java.net.URI" id="dbUrl">
    <constructor-arg value="postgres://username:password@yourdomain.com:5432/dbname"/>
</bean>
```

When refactoring your app, this should be changed to a config var — for instance, using DATABASE_URL when using a Heroku Postgres database:

```
<bean class="java.net.URI" id="dbUrl">
    <constructor-arg value="${DATABASE_URL}"/>
</bean>
```

If you need to make these config vars available during the build of your app, you may need to use Heroku Labs' user-env-compile tool to make these parameters available before your dyno is deployed. (See https://devcenter.heroku.com/articles/labs-user-env-compile for more information on enabling this feature for your apps.) For instance, when using a continuous integration tool that runs before deployment and runs tests that require database access, you will need to inject your database credentials, stored in configuration variables, during build time using user-env-compile.

> **NOTE** *Heroku Labs features are experimental and may change or may be removed without notice. See* https://devcenter.heroku.com/articles/labs *for more information on using Heroku Labs features.*

REPLACING WEB SERVERS AND CONTAINERS

The classic methodology for running web apps is to use a web server, such as Apache HTTP or Tomcat, to service web requests from clients. With Heroku, web servers are no longer needed in their traditional form. All the developer needs to worry about is writing code. However, this means that some services that may have been handled by the web server configuration will have to be moved to the application layer (for example, basic authentication, HTTP compression, etc.).

Java developers often rely on web containers (also called *servlet containers*), such as WebSphere, JBoss, and GlassFish, to deliver their apps. Web containers may provide not only a runtime environment for servlets, but also other services, such as security, concurrency, life-cycle management, transaction management, and deployment management. Heroku apps are entirely self-contained and do not rely on functionality provided by outside systems. Apps bootstrap themselves, and services are provided with the apps' code and dependencies. Functionality that relies on container-specific functionality must be refactored from the code or provided by a declared dependency.

Jetty and Tomcat are embeddable and called upon as dependencies, like any other library that provides Java Platform, Enterprise Edition (Java EE) APIs. These dependencies enable you to run servlets or JavaServer Pages (JSP). Mojarra or Apache MyFaces can be used to provide JavaServer Faces (JSF) and other rendering frameworks.

Hibernate or DataNucleus JPA can provide an ORM persistence layer on top of your data store of choice. Other features that web containers typically provide — such as deployment, clustering, load balancing, and logging — are superfluous, as they are provided as part of the Heroku platform.

Porting apps that use containers is often a time-consuming endeavor and may require considerable refactoring for existing apps. Often, alternative libraries can be used to replace specific functionality provided by containers by declaring each library as a dependency in your app. (See more in the next section.) However, this approach may require significant effort in identifying libraries needed, evaluating alternatives, and testing existing functionality to ensure that it works as expected.

Often, it is best to port your app when a re-architecture is planned because of the significant amount of changes required. Embracing the containerless approach to web app development is a significant paradigm shift. Your organization should weigh the benefits gained in using this approach (like portability) with the amount of effort required to refactor your app when deciding to port your app to Heroku.

MANAGING DEPENDENCIES

Most apps include libraries they rely on within their source code. This can be problematic if some enterprising developer decides to modify the dependent library; the next time the dependency is upgraded to the latest version, things can break. Whenever possible, you should use dependencies available in public repositories; Heroku will fetch them and compile them into the slug upon deployment. Before porting your app, you should remove libraries from the codebase and move dependencies to the appropriate location for your language.

If the library is not available in a public repository, you can use a local repository to store the file. If the dependency is available only as a binary, you can compile it, store it in an external location (like Amazon S3), and include it with your buildpack.

> **NOTE** *For more information on packaging external dependencies, see Chapter 14, "Understanding Buildpacks."*

If you are using standard, publicly available libraries in your app and are already using the dependency managers used in standard buildpacks for your language or framework, the effort required to port your app would be low. If you have altered standard libraries, you may have to refactor your code to override specific functionality in the standard libraries that has been custom coded. If you are not using public repositories, you will need to explicitly declare these libraries in your build configuration.

If your existing app does not use the same dependency manager and build tool that Heroku uses for your language or framework, you will need to refactor your code. You will need to switch your dependency manager to the Heroku-supported program. If you are using a different build tool from the standard tool Heroku uses, you may have to bootstrap your build script using your preferred build tool (e.g., for Java apps, have Maven kick-off the Ant script that builds your app). Alternatively, you can use a custom buildpack that uses your preferred built tool or dependency manager instead (e.g., use `https://github.com/dennisg/heroku-buildpack-ant` for building Java apps with a custom buildpack that uses Ant).

> **NOTE** *See Chapter 14 for instructions on using and creating custom buildpacks, as well as the tradeoffs between custom buildpacks and standard buildpacks.*

E-MAILING FROM YOUR APPLICATION

Most web apps send e-mails to users. For instance, when a user creates an account on your web app, you may want to send them a welcome message. Heroku itself does not offer a reliable outgoing mail service, as it runs on Amazon Elastic Compute Cloud (Amazon EC2). Because just about anyone can run a mail server on Amazon EC2 to send spam, this IP range is blacklisted and nearly guarantees that your e-mail will be classified as spam and not reach the intended recipient.

To send e-mail from your app, you must use either an external SMTP server or an e-mail service add-on. Heroku offers two add-ons for e-mail services: SendGrid and Mailgun. Mailgun also offers incoming e-mail services to push incoming e-mails to your app via HTTP. Note that if you are not already using external SMTP, you will have to refactor your code to use one of these methods. If you are using SMTP, your e-mails are already being sent through a third-party e-mail service, so it will work in the same way on Heroku, assuming your SMTP server is not behind a firewall.

If you are not already using an external SMTP server or third-party e-mail server, you will need to evaluate the level of effort required to use one of these services to send e-mail. This may be as easy as altering configuration (e.g., changing SMTP settings in a configuration file), or it may require refactoring your app to use the tool's provided API to send e-mail, depending on the tool you are using to send e-mail and its compatibility with your framework or language of choice for your app.

> **NOTE** *Check SendGrid (*`http://sendgrid.com/docs/Integrate/index.html`*) and Mailgun's (*`http://documentation.mailgun.net/wrappers.html`*) documentation to see language- and framework-specific examples and toolkits to gauge the level of effort needed to integrate these tools in to your codebase.*

RUNNING CRON JOBS

In many cases, apps need to perform actions at pre-set intervals. Traditional apps accomplish this with the operating system's cron service, which runs an app at scheduled times. Because Heroku's filesystem is read-only, cron jobs cannot be added. Instead, you can use the Heroku Scheduler add-on to run tasks either hourly, daily, or every 10 minutes. You can install the add-on by running the following command within the app's directory:

```
$ heroku addons:add scheduler:standard
```

After adding the Scheduler add-on to your app, you can access its administration panel, shown in Figure 3-1, by first clicking the Add-on Resources icon and then clicking Heroku Scheduler Standard.

FIGURE 3-1

From the administration panel you can view all the currently scheduled jobs and add new ones. Jobs are added and will run with the command specified here, starting at the time you indicate. For instance, if you want to run the command `ping myapp.herokuapp.com` every hour, 20 minutes after the hour, you would do so as shown in Figure 3-2 (assuming that your dyno has the `ping` utility installed, which it is not by default).

FIGURE 3-2

Each job will run as a one-off process, which appears in the process formation with the name scheduler.N. If you have only one scheduled process running, you can view the logs for the scheduled process using the following command in your app's directory:

```
heroku logs --ps scheduler.1
```

You can test a job by using heroku run. Using the previous example, run the following command in the app's directory:

```
heroku run ping myapp.herokuapp.com
```

> **NOTE** *It is recommended that you use the Heroku Scheduler only for short-running jobs, less than a couple of minutes. You can use worker processes for longer-running jobs.*

You must ensure that any cron jobs set up for your existing app in the server's crontab are migrated to the Heroku Scheduler. If you need to run a process more frequently than every 10 minutes, you can use the Clockwork app to define more frequently running tasks (see https://github.com/ tomykaira/clockwork). This will continually run a process that will execute at the specified times.

> **NOTE** *If very frequent runs are required (for instance, every minute or less), it is recommended that you run two dynos for this process to ensure that the first dyno does not idle, delaying the process from running immediately, as it will take time to restart. Note that having this second dyno running all the time will consume dyno hours, even while it sits waiting, which may result in additional costs.*

Sometimes you need to run a process not every single hour, but on every fourth hour instead. In this case, you can simply add logic to your scheduled process. For instance, in a Ruby script used to run scheduled tasks, the following code runs the task each four hours:

```
if ([0,4,8,12,16,20].include?(Time.now.hour)) {
    // run scheduled task
}
```

If you configure the Heroku Scheduler to run this script every hour, your job will be run every hour, but your scheduled task will only be executed at 12:00 A.M., 4:00 A.M., 8:00 A.M., 12:00 P.M., 4:00 P.M., and 8:00 P.M.

UNDERSTANDING LOGGING

Logs on the Heroku platform work a bit differently from traditional apps. Classic logs are text files with massive amounts of data, tracking everything that has happened since the app was first run. With Logplex, Heroku's built-in logging functionality, logs are simply a stream of the events happening in your app. This is a very different way of thinking, as logs are no longer archived forever unless something is done with this log stream.

You can decide to do many things with logs. Firstly, you can simply leave them as a temporary stream and not archive them. However, this may be problematic when something goes wrong and no archived logs are available.

Another option is to run a server elsewhere that will collect this log stream and store the logs in a more durable manner. If you don't want to run your own log server somewhere else, Heroku's add-ons library offers a number of third-party solutions. Providers such as Loggly, Logentries, and Papertrail deliver logging with a lot of other useful functionality for things like log analysis. These services enable you to store logs coming from a Heroku log stream, receive alerts, or automatically perform actions when certain types of errors occur, and analyze your archived logs.

Adapting to Heroku's logging typically is a welcome change with relatively little effort required. With a third-party logging service, you no longer need to maintain log-rotation scripts or monitor log size, removing this administrative burden. For adding popular logging add-ons, such as Loggly and Paperclip, the add-on simply needs to be added to your app; no code changes or refactoring is necessary.

An easy solution for collecting the log stream on a dedicated log server without third-party add-ons is to run an Amazon EC2 instance. Amazon EC2 has an Amazon Machine Image (AMI) with a 64-bit Ubuntu 10.04 LTS (Lucid Lynx) Server installed that can be used for log collection. To create a micro instance of Amazon EC2 with this AMI pre-installed, enter the following command:

```
$ ec2-run-instances -t t1.micro ami-1234abcd
```

You must also create a firewall rule to allow Heroku to send the logs to `syslog`, the standard Unix logging program, on port 514, the standard TCP port on which `syslog` sends remote log messages:

```
$ ec2-authorize default -P tcp -p 514 -u 012345678901 -o logplex
```

Once the system is up and running, SSH in to the instance and edit `/etc/rsyslog.conf`, adding the following lines to allow `syslog` to receive the logs on port 514:

```
$ ModLoad imtcp
$ InputTCPServerRun 514
```

Then restart the instance to make the changes take effect:

```
$ restart rsyslog
```

You can add one or more log drains on Heroku by entering the following command, replacing `ec2-XXX-XXX-XXX-XXX.compute-1.amazonaws.com` with your Amazon EC2 instance's hostname:

```
$ heroku drains:add syslog://ec2-XXX-XXX-XXX-XXX.compute-1.amazonaws.com:514
Drain syslog://ec2-XXX-XXX-XXX-XXX.compute-1.amazonaws.com:514 added to myapp
```

You can also list existing drains with `heroku drains`:

```
$ heroku drains
syslog://ec2-XXX-XXX-XXX-XXX.compute-1.amazonaws.com:514
syslog://ec2-YYY-YYY-YYY-YYY.compute-1.amazonaws.com:9999
```

To remove drains, use the following:

```
$ heroku drains:remove syslog://ec2-YYY-YYY-YYY-YYY.compute-1.amazonaws.com:9999
Removing syslog drain... done
```

RELYING ON EXTERNAL PROGRAMS

Many apps implicitly rely on programs that are external to the libraries in the codebase that they rely on to run. This can cause major issues if an app needs to be installed on a new server and the implicit step to download and install the missing program is skipped. Relying on external programs is more error-prone for developers to set up their own development environments because they may not have the same program installed on their computer. For example, many apps rely on shelling out to the program cURL on the command line to do URL transfer tasks.

When porting your app, you must ensure that any programs on which the app relies are either declared as dependencies or packaged as buildpack dependencies. This means that you must either find an embeddable library for your respective language (which may be difficult to find) or compile the app on a Heroku instance, fetch the binary during build time, and package it as part of the slug.

You must verify that your code is not using methods like Java's `Runtime.getRuntime().exec()` or Ruby's `%x` notation, backticks, `exec()`, or `system()` to shell out to external apps. If you are using one of these methods, you need to check that the external dependency you are using is available on your Heroku dyno. This can be done by running `heroku run bash` in your app directory and running the command(s), as demonstrated in the following example:

```
$ heroku run bash
Running 'bash' attached to terminal... up, run.1
~ $ curl http://www.heroku.com


<!DOCTYPE html>
...
    <title>Heroku | Cloud Application Platform</title>
...
```

You should make sure that the version of the external program on your dynos is comparable to the version of the external program running on your old server. It is good practice to verify that you are getting the same results with both versions of the external program, especially if they are drastically different versions running on both environments. If you do not get the same results on the two systems, you will have to either refactor your code to adapt to the new version (if possible) or package the old version of the program as a binary buildpack dependency (see Chapter 14).

SCALING UP VERSUS SCALING OUT

One traditional approach to managing apps that start to slow is to throw more hardware at the problem. After all, hardware is usually cheaper than developer time. However, this treats the symptoms, not the problem, and soon hardware upgrades are needed again.

For instance, suppose you are porting over an app that processes a lot of records in batches. If you run all the records at one time, Heroku may start to slow if memory usage exceeds the 512 MB limit, and throw R14 (Memory Quota Exceeded) errors. With Heroku, upgrading the hardware is not an option, so you may need to parallelize the processing to take advantage of the platform's concurrent nature. In terms of dividing and conquering tasks, Heroku excels at scaling out to solve the problem quickly and without hitting limitations.

Memory management is an important practice when porting apps to Heroku. Apps that have a large memory footprint may need to be refactored to operate properly on Heroku or may not be good candidates for porting over if they require very large amounts of memory even after refactoring. When testing your app on Heroku, you can use a general-purpose performance-management tool, like the New Relic add-on (`https://addons.heroku.com/newrelic`), to report on average memory usage across dynos. However, New Relic only tells you how much memory you are using, not how the memory is being used. For a level of granularity where you can find out how the memory is used, you will need to use a memory profiler.

Memory profilers are language-specific because each language uses different internal mechanics to manage memory and expose this information to memory profiling tools. For instance, in Rails, you can the use popular memory-management tools Memorylogic (`https://github.com/binarylogic/memorylogic`) for understanding how memory is being used in your app. Here, you can identify which parts of your app are memory-heavy and refactor them before porting. Memory-profiling tools can also help find where memory leaks are happening in your app if memory usage grows unexpectedly as the app runs.

All the files pushed from your codebase are compiled to the slug, which must be copied each time a dyno is started or your app scales up. To ensure that scaling can be done quickly, your app's codebase should be kept as lean as possible. It is recommended that you use a `.gitignore` file to ensure that files that are not required for your app to run are excluded from the slug. Github provides a number of pre-defined, language- and framework-specific `.gitignore` files (`https://github.com/github/gitignore`). It is a best practice to include the appropriate `.gitignore` file in all projects you port to Heroku to minimize launch time.

> **NOTE** *See the "Storing Static Assets" section earlier in this chapter for tips on how storing assets externally can reduce slug size.*

BINDING TO PORTS

Each Heroku process is assigned a port for accepting requests. The routing mesh ensures that the incoming request is routed to your dyno on the correct port. If your app is doing port binding, you have to use the $PORT environment variable to bind to the correct port, which is different on each dyno. For instance, you would define your thin web server process in your Procfile as follows:

```
bundle exec thin start -R config.ru -e $RACK_ENV -p $PORT
```

This tells the thin web server to sit on the port on which the dyno is configured to accept requests, and Heroku automatically defines this environment variable for each dyno on which the process is run.

You must refactor your app if it is set to run on multiple ports or nonstandard ports (that is, anything that isn't the standard HTTP or HTTPS ports, 80 or 443). If it listens on multiple ports, it may have to be divided into separate process types, with each process listening on one port only. Bi-directional communications between running processes can be achieved with the Pusher add-on. Pusher uses WebSockets to enable you to set up a server that can communicate with browsers and push information and updates, using port 80 to work safely with Heroku.

As an example of how this works, examine the following snippet of Java code:

```
public static void main(String[] args) throws Exception{
    Server server = new Server(Integer.valueOf(System.getenv("PORT")));
    ServletContextHandler context =
        new ServletContextHandler(ServletContextHandler.SESSIONS);
    context.setContextPath("/");
    server.setHandler(context);
    context.addServlet(new ServletHolder(new JavaEmbeddedJettyExample()),"/*");
    server.start();
    server.join();
}
```

This function binds the embedded server to the standard PORT environment variable. Because the PORT environment variable is different on each dyno, it is set for the purpose of identifying the correct port to bind to.

If your app binds to an incoming e-mail port to intercept and handle e-mails, you should refactor to use an incoming e-mail service, like the CloudMailin add-on (https://devcenter.heroku.com/articles/cloudmailin).

MANAGING LONG-RUNNING PROCESSES

Heroku recommends that your app process requests in less than half a second — ideally, a fifth of a second (200 ms) or less — as a best practice. However, some apps may take much longer to process a request. Heroku allows a maximum of 30 seconds to pass between the first request and its response, and will terminate any connection that takes longer. Every subsequent communication resets a rolling 55-second window before timing out and terminating the connection. This may result in unintended behaviour, as the web process will still be running after the connection terminates, possibly blocking future requests from being served while the process finishes.

If your app takes a very long time to process requests or makes requests to external services, you may need to re-architect the requests so that they run as background processes. Because background processes run asynchronously, longer processes can run without connections being terminated. For instance, if you need to make an API request to a third-party system, you should do so as a background process, because you cannot guarantee that the external service will complete execution within the 30 seconds it needs to finish. Regardless of timeouts, using background processes for long-running requests is a best practice because otherwise your dyno will be blocked from subsequent requests during that time, impacting performance for concurrent users. Background workers pick requests off the queue and complete the work, storing any results they need in a data store, such as a database or a Memcachier add-on. The front end can continually poll the data store to see if the results are ready for use.

> **NOTE** *An example of creating an architecture where long-running tasks are queued and a background process picks them off and processes them can be found in Chapter 11, in the section "Using Delayed Job for Background Jobs."*

Note that large file uploads may result in request timeouts. Typically, if you are uploading files larger than 4MB, a best practice is to use a technique called *direct upload* to create a direct connection between the user's browser and Amazon S3, bypassing the connection to the dyno. Client-side libraries such as S3SwfUpload (`https://github.com/nathancolgate/s3-swf-upload-plugin`) can also be leveraged to upload directly to Amazon S3. The downside of this alternative is that you cannot process the file before storing it, only afterward, thereby increasing the amount of bandwidth used threefold in uploading, downloading to your app, and updating the file.

A tutorial written by James Murty on Amazon's community site (`http://aws.amazon.com/articles/1434?_encoding=UTF8&jiveRedirect=1`) gives the following example for a direct upload to Amazon S3 via a `POST`:

```html
<html>
    <head>
        <title>S3 POST Form</title>
        <meta http-equiv="Content-Type" content="text/html; charset=UTF-8" />
    </head>
    <body>
        <form action="https://s3-bucket.s3.amazonaws.com/" method="post"
            enctype="multipart/form-data">
            <input type="hidden" name="key" value="uploads/${filename}">
            <input type="hidden" name="AWSAccessKeyId"
                value="YOUR_AWS_ACCESS_KEY">
            <input type="hidden" name="acl" value="private">
            <input type="hidden" name="success_action_redirect"
                value="http://localhost/">
            <input type="hidden" name="policy"
                value="YOUR_POLICY_DOCUMENT_BASE64_ENCODED">
            <input type="hidden" name="signature"
                value="YOUR_CALCULATED_SIGNATURE">
            <input type="hidden" name="Content-Type" value="image/jpeg">
```

```
            <!-- Include any additional input fields here -->

            File to upload to S3:
            <input name="file" type="file">
            <br>
            <input type="submit" value="Upload File to S3">
        </form>
    </body>
</html>
```

This HTML code will upload the file, replacing the `${filename}` with the name of the uploaded local name (for example, `Pictures of Furry Cats.jpg`). Note that the `acl` value has been left as `private`, indicating that this file is not available to the general public. This should be changed; the newly uploaded file is supposed to be publicly available. Additional steps are also required to create a signature (`YOUR_CALCULATED_SIGNATURE`), as outlined in the article at `http://aws.amazon.com/articles/1434`.

Sometimes, you need to process the file being uploaded before storing it on Amazon S3. In this case, an upload technique called *pass-through* should be used. For instance, consider a photo-upload site where you want to reduce the resolution of images before storing them to minimize storage costs. This can be done by saving the file locally, resizing it, and then using the Amazon S3 API (`http://docs.amazonwebservices.com/AmazonS3/latest/API/Welcome.html`) to upload the file from your dyno. Libraries typically are available for your language or framework of choice to simplify Amazon S3 uploading, like the `AWS::S3` library for Ruby (`http://amazon.rubyforge.org/`) or the AWS SDK for Java (`http://aws.amazon.com/sdkforjava/`). Keep in mind that using the pass-through method is not appropriate for large files, typically over 4MB, as the request will time out and not complete successfully.

SHUTTING DOWN GRACEFULLY

Occasionally, Heroku requires that an app be restarted, typically during dyno cycling or when `heroku restart` is run from the Heroku command-line interface. All Heroku processes should be equipped to trap a `SIGTERM` signal to ensure that the app shuts down cleanly. Once the `SIGTERM` signal is sent, the dyno manifold will give the app 10 seconds to shut down. When this deadline expires, a `SIGKILL` signal is sent, terminating the app (whether it's ready or not), and an error is logged.

If your app does not already handle `SIGTERM` signals, this capability should be added to your app. Your app should not accept new requests during this time and should complete short-running requests that will finish in less than 10 seconds. We have already discussed how long-running processes can be identified and executed in a background process. This principle is also very important for handling unexpected shutdowns, as, with this approach, the job can easily be put back on the queue and completed by another background process later.

For example, consider the following snippet of Ruby code that shows how to trap a `SIGTERM` signal:

```
trap('TERM') do
    // placeholder for code to gracefully shut down
    exit
end
```

The code that would appear in this placeholder could do a number of things, such as close open connections or alert users that they must retry their requests, depending on what is most appropriate for the context of their apps. However, if the dyno running this example code were a worker that was picking jobs off a queue and processing them, then upon trapping the SIGTERM, the job the worker was processing should be put back on the queue to ensure that it is completed by another dyno.

MOVING YOUR DOMAIN

Apps that run on Heroku can be tested using the domain myappname.herokuapp.com. When porting production apps to Heroku, most developers want to refer to the app using a custom domain, such as www.mydomainname.com, instead of myappname.herokuapp.com. Heroku allows you to do this by pointing the Canonical Name (CNAME) entry on your DNS provider's settings to provide an alias for your domain name.

HTTPS over SSL

HTTPS over SSL also works differently for Heroku apps than for traditional apps. SSL connections are terminated at the load balancer on Heroku, not at the server. After the load balancer terminates the SSL, information is transferred over a non-HTTPS connection between Heroku's load balancer and your app's dyno (as shown in Figure 3-3), much like a reverse proxy. The load balancer also adds an additional HTTP header to the request:

```
X-Forwarded-Proto: https
```

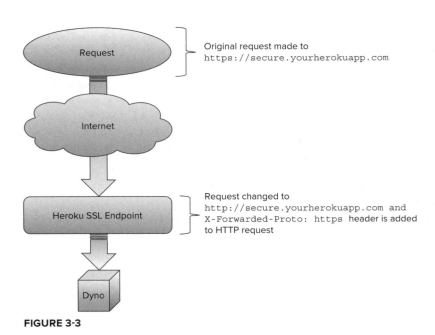

FIGURE 3-3

This header will indicate to the app that the original request from the user came in over a secured channel.

Considerations for Porting Existing Applications

If you are porting an app that uses a naked domain (also called a *bare* or *apex domain*) that looks like http://mydomainname.com, you will need to change this to ensure optimal operation of your app. When using naked domains, any time your app's users visit http://myappname.com, a look-up is done on the Domain Name Service (DNS) provider to the Address (A) record. The A record points requests to this domain to the IP address of the server. This approach works well in a traditional scenario in which a server may sit in a data center where the IP address does not change often.

The dynamic nature of Heroku dynos makes accessing a dyno using a single IP address impractical. In order for this to work, the A record would need to be updated each and every time the dyno is restarted because the IP address may have changed. Pointing to a single IP address directly also surpasses Heroku's load balancing, which is needed to route requests appropriately for apps that use more than one running dyno. Existing apps with naked domains should add a preceding www (e.g., http://www.myappname.com instead of http://myappname.com) and use CNAME records (instead of A records) to point to myappname.herokuapp.com. This will avoiding the aforementioned issues and leverage Heroku's load-balancing capacities. Wildcard domains can be set up in the same way, pointing *.myappname.com to myappname.herokuapp.com also using CNAME records. Transferring existing domains that use CNAME records can be done in a straightforward manner, by updating the record to <your-heroku-application-name>.herokuapp.com, where <your-heroku-application-name> is the name of your Heroku app.

> **NOTE** *For detailed instructions for setting up domains for your app on Heroku, see the "Adding Custom Domains" section of Chapter 7, "Managing, Monitoring, and Scaling Your Heroku Applications."*

When transferring your domain to point to your ported app on Heroku, make sure to shut down your previous app or replace it with a warning message to users. This will prevent users with cached DNS settings from accessing your old app and having their data lost later when their DNS information is updated and they access your new app. It is typically also best to make this DNS update during off-peak hours, to ensure that the changes have enough time to propagate to your users' Internet service providers (ISPs) who may cache DNS information. Typically, this will take only a couple of hours for most users, but it may take up to 72 hours in a worst-case scenario.

If the app you want to port to Heroku uses an HTTPS connection, you will have to first follow the instructions in the "Encrypting Communications with SSL" section in Chapter 2. After following these instructions, you will have added the SSL Endpoint add-on to your app and added your SSL certificates to Heroku. Next, you must verify that your app is not expecting secure communications to come in through an HTTPS port.

Secured requests will be coming from your load balancer over HTTP. When accessing a form that should be secured (like a payment processing page), some libraries and frameworks will check to ensure that the request is happening over HTTPS to prevent the user from inadvertently sending sensitive information over an insecure channel. If the request did not come in over HTTPS (as it never will with Heroku since SSL is terminated by the load balancer), the user is redirected to the same page with an `https://` prefix. On Heroku, this will cause an infinite redirection loop for the browser and throw an error.

Heroku apps must be refactored to take this behaviour into account. Instead of checking that the request came over HTTPS, your app should check the `X-Forwarded-Proto` HTTP header to verify whether requests were made securely or not. For example, the Spring Security plug-in did not check for this before version 1.2.7.2. If you are using a version older than this, you can either upgrade the plug-in to a more recent version or make some minor modifications to your codebase to fix this.

Checking for `X-Forwarded-Proto` in the headers can be done by overriding the `decide()` method in the `SecureChannelProcessor` and `InsecureChannelProcessor` classes that Spring Security uses to check if the request is happening over a secure connection:

```
@Override
public void decide(FilterInvocation invocation, Collection<ConfigAttribute>
    config) throws IOException, ServletException {

    Assert.isTrue((invocation != null) && (config != null),
                "Invocation or config cannot be null");

    for (ConfigAttribute attribute : config) {
        if (supports(attribute)) {
            if (invocation.getHttpRequest().
                getHeader("X-Forwarded-Proto").equals("http")) {
                    entryPoint.commence(invocation.getRequest(),
                        invocation.getResponse());
            }
        }
    }
}
```

A similar technique can be used for other frameworks to change the behaviour of how they verify whether sensitive communications are happening over a secured connection. This should ensure that your ported app works properly with the way that Heroku handles HTTPS over SSL.

SUMMARY

This chapter provided an overview of the key concepts that you need to write apps on Heroku and effectively port apps to the platform. Heroku's filesystem should be treated as read-only, and you should ensure that ported apps do not write to the filesystem or use embedded databases. Several varieties of data stores can be used, and you should move your data to a DaaS, like Heroku Postrges, that has the correct characteristics for your app's needs and is performant. If session management is stored in memory, you will need to reconfigure your framework or refactor your app to store session data in a database or client-side, in cookies.

Caching in apps ported to Heroku can be done using a number of different methods, each of which is best suited for particular situations. Generally speaking, your app should be refactored to store cached information in a data store, like a database or key-value store. Ported apps should be refactored so that static assets are served from a CDN, to keep dyno size below the limit and allow for rapid scaling.

Credentials in apps ported to Heroku should be moved into config vars, and apps that use containers should be refactored to be containerless. This can be done by pulling out functionality that relies upon the container to libraries that can be declared as dependencies. These dependencies should be managed using the Heroku-supported dependency manager, referencing publicly available libraries. Apps that use dependency managers or build tools that are not the same as the Heroku supported programs for that particular language will have to be refactored to do so, or buildpacks should be used to make them work with Heroku.

Any e-mails sent by your ported app should be refactored to use an external SMTP server or an e-mailing service. Cron jobs on your old app must be recreated in the Heroku Scheduler, and the app logs should be streamed to a place where they can be archived, like a logging service or external log server. Ported apps should not rely on external programs to run properly, and if they must, they will have to use buildpacks to pre-install the external binaries onto the app's dynos.

Memory management is important in ported apps, and usage should be consistently kept below the 512MB threshold through investigating memory usage and refactoring. Apps that bind to more than one port or bind to non-HTTP(S) ports must be rewritten to sit on a single, standard port. Long-running processes should be refactored to use a background process that will run these tasks asynchronously, from a queue.

Ported apps should also ensure that they can shut down gracefully, and handlers for `SIGTERM` signals should be added to ensure that apps are not left in an inconsistent state when interrupted. Your ported app's domain should be pointed to Heroku using CNAME records, and naked domains or A records should not be used. SSL is also done differently from traditional apps, so your ported app should ensure that it handles this properly.

PART II
Creating and Managing Heroku Applications

Deploying Your Applications to Heroku

➤ Installing the Heroku Toolbelt

➤ Interacting with Heroku via the command-line interface

➤ The magic of `git push`

➤ Post-deploy hooks

➤ Navigating the Heroku Dashboard

This chapter covers the basics of setting up your local machine to interact with Heroku and familiarizing yourself with both Heroku's command-line interface (CLI) and the standard Heroku Dashboard. We'll also explore a few key concepts and tools that are made much more powerful via Heroku. These steps are important as you begin deploying apps to Heroku.

INSTALLING THE HEROKU TOOLBELT

Now that you have a fundamental understanding of how Heroku works and how to properly architect your apps for the Heroku platform, and you have determined the best way to build and iterate on your apps in the context of Heroku workflow, it is time to begin the process of setting up your local environment for Heroku use so that you can begin the deployment process.

The first time you interact with the Heroku platform to create or deploy apps, you'll need to install the Heroku Toolbelt (`https://toolbelt.heroku.com/`). To install the Toolbelt, simply download the appropriate package (available for Windows, Mac OS, and Linux). Once the download completes, run the installer, and you are ready to interact with Heroku. The Heroku Toolbelt consists of the following:

➤ Git

➤ Foreman

➤ The Heroku client

It's important to note the following:

➤ Heroku has bundled these components for Windows, Mac OS, and Debian/Ubuntu Linux for easier installation; however, each component can (and may already) be installed separately, based on the local machine's configuration.

➤ Each component is entirely open source. By visiting the main project and public code repositories, users can download, modify, use, and contribute their own flavors for the tools Heroku provides.

This chapter provides a brief overview of the Git, Foreman, and the Heroku client — all the starting components you need to be dangerous on Heroku. If you would like to dive deeper into either the Git or the Foreman technologies, an abundance of resources is available online.

Git

Git is a relative newcomer as an option for source code control management. It empowers a very distributed and open development workflow, geared for maximum control and power, as close to the developer as possible. This new workflow is what most truly agile development teams are working toward, and, as a result they have adopted Git as their source control system of choice.

The core difference between Git and other version control systems, such as Concurrent Versions System (CVS) or Apache Subversion (SVN), is that Git is based fundamentally on a *distributed* model, as opposed to a *centralized* model, meaning any developer working on a project has the entire source code structure available locally. This distributed model lends itself very well to the cloud and for deployments to application platforms such as Heroku, where many developers building their own versions (or against a single version) of an app can deploy code continuously.

Git has been made popular by the growing community of web app developers and the "social coding" website GitHub (www.github.com). GitHub enables any developer to upload and share his or her code, and empowers others to "fork" their own version of a project and to build any improvements they wish via the community development process. While we won't focus here on how to use Git, you should be aware of its importance in the new developer workflow and familiarize yourself with some of the basic commands you need to master to effectively deploy and manage apps on the Heroku platform.

To create a new, empty Git repository in the local working directory structure, use the following:

```
$ cd /my_app
$ git init
```

To add all directories, subdirectories, and files within the working directory structure, use this command:

```
$ git add .
```

The following commits all changes to the repository and comments on the updates:

```
$ git commit -m "<something useful & witty>"
```

Finally, use this command to send all code to the Heroku platform and deploy the app:

```
$ git push heroku master
```

A lot of magic happens when you `git push` to Heroku. You'll explore this in more detail in the section "The Magic of git push."

Foreman

Foreman is an extremely powerful and vastly underrated tool that enables you to re-create the process model (as described in Chapter 1, "How Heroku Works") on your local machine.

Using traditional local deployment, you are usually limited by virtual machines (VMs) and server instances to run specific app process types and distributed architectures. For example, consider a current sample app architecture consisting of the following:

➤ A web component that serves requests via browsers

➤ A mobile component that services API calls from mobile devices

➤ Background processes that manipulate/render user-generated content

Successfully deploying this app locally and demonstrating its ability to horizontally scale (we are pushing to the cloud, after all) would be nearly impossible due to limitations of local configuration options. With Foreman, regardless of whether you deploy your app to Heroku or any other cloud application platform, you can deploy the app on your local machine with the fully independent processes running behind your app.

After creating your app locally and defining a Procfile (as detailed in Chapter 1), you can run the same processes that you would on Heroku.

```
$ foreman start
```

When you run `foreman` from the app's working directory, the relevant process types and count will start. Hitting Ctrl+C will terminate the processes just as easily.

Foreman is incredibly powerful when paired with Git, as it enables any developer to not only own and modify the entire app, but also run it as intended on his or her local machine. This enables unparalleled productivity and effectiveness relative to any app you would build from scratch.

Foreman is an open-source project lead by open-source contributor and Heroku engineer David Dollar. As of this writing, the Foreman project has almost 50 contributing members. The project can be found on GitHub (`https://github.com/ddollar/foreman/network`), where anyone can view the contributions or participate — if you want to take things further than installation of the Heroku Toolbelt permits.

> **NOTE** *The Forman Process Manager Project is not to be confused with the The Foreman Project, which is focused on application lifecycle management.*

The Heroku Client

The Heroku client is the local CLI component of the Heroku platform. Once the client is installed, users can create and manage apps deployed onto Heroku.

> **NOTE** *The Heroku client is the only piece of the Toolbelt that's required in order to use the Heroku platform.*

If you want to download the Heroku client directly and forego installing Git and Foreman, you can simply download the latest version from the Heroku client repository on GitHub (`https://github.com/heroku/heroku`). The GitHub repository is publicly accessible, and *forks* (your own branches of the code) and *pull* requests (review/approval for merging changes into the main branch) are strongly encouraged to support the community efforts and contributions. Alternatively, the Heroku client can be installed as a Ruby gem:

```
gem install heroku
```

> **NOTE** *Heroku does not recommend that you install the client separately, as the Heroku Toolbelt installer handles all system dependency checks for all supported operating systems (Windows, Mac, and Linux).*

After installing the Heroku client, log in to Heroku using your e-mail and password credentials created during signup on `www.heroku.com`:

```
heroku login
```

This creates an API token that enables all other commands against the Heroku platform from the CLI. By default, your API tokens will be stored in `~/.netrc`.

Next, you need to generate and add a Secure Shell (SSH) key to Heroku in order to deploy code to the platform, as shown in the following example (if you already have an SSH key, you can simply add it):

```
ssh-keygen -t rsa
heroku keys:add
```

Now you are ready to start interacting with Heroku directly from your local machine.

INTERACTING WITH HEROKU VIA THE COMMAND-LINE INTERFACE

The Heroku CLI is where most interaction with the platform takes place. For help on any topic or to generally understand what your command-line options are, running `heroku help <optional_ topic>` will provide a view similar to UNIX-style man pages for each topic and command available via the CLI.

Some commands act at the account level and provide information or modification for the user account as a whole. Examples include the following:

➤ `heroku auth`: Logs in/out

➤ `heroku account`: Displays user credentials

➤ `heroku apps`: Displays all user apps

➤ `heroku update`: Updates your client to the latest version

Other commands are geared toward app-level interactions. Commands focusing on app-level behavior can be run from the top-level working directory of the app, or the app can be specified:

➤ `heroku apps:info`: Top-level app directory

➤ `heroku apps:info --app my-first-heroku-application`: Anywhere on the local machine

Some additional examples include the following:

➤ `heroku config <--app appname>`: Provides all the configuration data for an app

➤ `heroku ps`: Returns a UNIX-style listing of all processes for a given app

➤ `heroku run`: Starts an interactive app session to run one-off commands

That covers the basics. Let's get to the fun stuff and create an app.

The following command will create a new app in the Heroku namespace and add a remote git repository (also called a *git remote*) for your app of the same name within the platform, ready to accept your code:

```
heroku create <appname>
```

The output should look something like this:

```
$ heroku create my-first-heroku-application
Creating my-first-heroku-application... done, stack is cedar
http://my-first-heroku-application.herokuapp.com/ |
git@heroku.com:my-first-heroku-application.git
```

Congratulations! Through the magic of Heroku, you now have your first app running on the platform, which you can confirm with a quick check in the browser (see Figure 4-1). True, there is currently not much to see, but you'll change that soon enough!

Heroku | Welcome to your new app!

Refer to the documentation if you need help deploying.

FIGURE 4-1

As soon as you have code to deploy (ignoring languages for now), you can run through the following standard Git commands to add code to the repository, commit the changes, and deploy to Heroku.:

➤ `git init`: Initializes the Git repository

➤ `git add`: Adds all files from the local directory into the repository

➤ `git commit -m "first time!"`: Commits your code to the repository

➤ `git push heroku master`: Sends your code to Heroku and deploys the app

Be sure you are running through each step within your app's top working directory.

Once you `git push`, you should see output similar to what is shown in Figure 4-2.

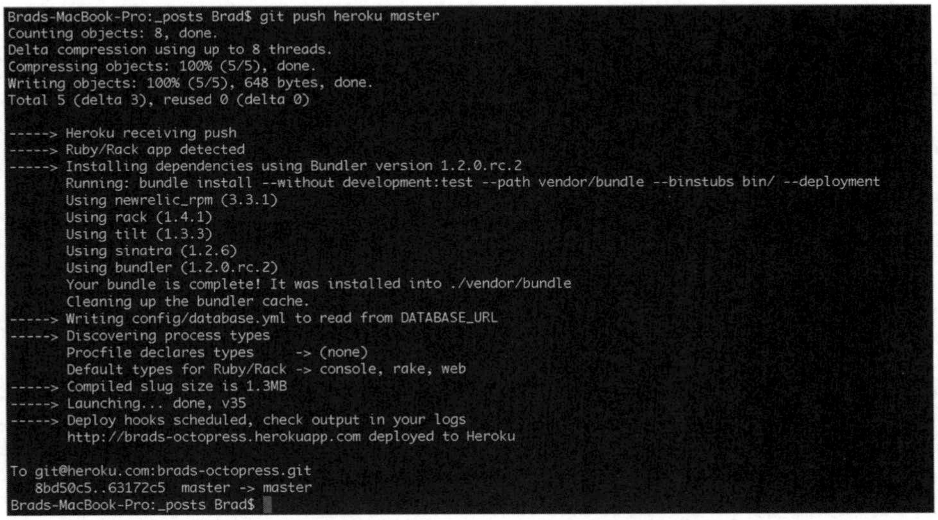

```
Brads-MacBook-Pro:_posts Brad$ git push heroku master
Counting objects: 8, done.
Delta compression using up to 8 threads.
Compressing objects: 100% (5/5), done.
Writing objects: 100% (5/5), 648 bytes, done.
Total 5 (delta 3), reused 0 (delta 0)

-----> Heroku receiving push
-----> Ruby/Rack app detected
-----> Installing dependencies using Bundler version 1.2.0.rc.2
       Running: bundle install --without development:test --path vendor/bundle --binstubs bin/ --deployment
       Using newrelic_rpm (3.3.1)
       Using rack (1.4.1)
       Using tilt (1.3.3)
       Using sinatra (1.2.6)
       Using bundler (1.2.0.rc.2)
       Your bundle is complete! It was installed into ./vendor/bundle
       Cleaning up the bundler cache.
-----> Writing config/database.yml to read from DATABASE_URL
-----> Discovering process types
       Procfile declares types      -> (none)
       Default types for Ruby/Rack -> console, rake, web
-----> Compiled slug size is 1.3MB
-----> Launching... done, v35
-----> Deploy hooks scheduled, check output in your logs
       http://brads-octopress.herokuapp.com deployed to Heroku

To git@heroku.com:brads-octopress.git
   8bd50c5..63172c5  master -> master
Brads-MacBook-Pro:_posts Brad$
```

FIGURE 4-2

Many things are taking place within a small amount of time on Heroku, so let's examine each step:

1. Git examines your app code, compresses up the code, and runs a `diff` to identify changes from the last deployment.

2. Heroku receives the app code from your local working git repository into the git remote on Heroku.

3. Heroku identifies the type of app you've written and installs all dependencies on your behalf.

4. Heroku updates and configures your database (if one is present).

5. Heroku starts all the different processes you defined using a procfile.

6. The app is now stored as a fully bundled, ready-to-run app on Heroku called a *slug*.

7. The Heroku slug is launched successfully and your app is available via the URL.

Congratulations! You've successfully deployed your first app to Heroku.

THE MAGIC OF GIT PUSH

Now that you have an app with your own code up on Heroku, let's examine what's going on when you run the `git push heroku master` command. In effect, all you're doing from a Git workflow perspective is simply sending your Git repository to a specified git remote. Upon quick inspection, you'll see where the app and git remote point to. Running the following command:

```
git remote -v
```

should generate output similar to the following:

```
heroku      git@heroku.com:brads-octopress.git (fetch)
heroku      git@heroku.com:brads-octopress.git (push)
```

This output demonstrates that the remote Git server with which you both push and fetch your source code is in fact Heroku. This is shown by the `git@heroku.com` piece. Your Heroku application repository (git remote) is described right after — in this example, `brads-octopress.git`.

Recall from earlier in the chapter that when you configured Heroku, you generated your own SSH key pair, and Git itself operates over the standard SSH port 22. This port often is blocked by company firewalls, and there are mechanisms to configure SSH to operate on a nonstandard port. Other options include configuring Git to operate over the SSL port (443) or in unauthenticated read-only mode (port 9418), which enables only fetch capability. Google is your friend for more information in both cases; we won't explore those configuration details here.

Focusing on the output from the `git push heroku master` command, you can see that a few things happened here:

1. Heroku receives and acknowledges a `git push` to the remote Git server. There's really no magic here other than the Internet at work.

2. Upon receiving the code repository, Heroku automatically detects the type of app that's being deployed. This does a few things in the background that are worth noting:

➤ The appropriate language runtime (buildpack) is being prepped and readied for code.

➤ The associated dependency management system is being readied to read the dependency file (in this case, a Ruby gemfile) for installation.

3. All dependencies are automatically detected and installed to the application build. This is compelling in that Heroku doesn't require anything beyond the language's native configuration or dependency mapping to begin installing everything the app needs to run successfully. That's pretty cool!

4. Heroku deploys the defined number of dynos for each process type that the app will run. If it doesn't find any, it will execute a single default runtime process. This provides instant scale and extra configurability to any app that runs on the Heroku platform. Try doing that with servers in a data center!

5. The finalized, ready-to-boot app is encapsulated into a slug. No more having to wrap code in tarballs, wars, and binaries. Heroku handles the bundling and safekeeping of your app for you.

6. The slug is sent off to the dyno manifold and booted up, ready to serve requests. In one fell swoop Heroku has also versioned your app, making rollbacks easy by simply calling the requisite version number.

7. Deploy hooks tied to other systems for follow-up jobs or tasks that are kicked off (completion e-mails, IRC notifications, etc.). This gives developers and operations staff the heads-up that the app is up and running. (More on this in the next section.)

8. Finally, Heroku provides the URL for your deployed app and the Git repository details.

POST DEPLOY HOOKS

Post deploy hooks are a simple service that can be attached to your apps via the Heroku add-ons library. (More about add-ons in Chapter 6, "Working with Add-Ons.") Conceptually, they are simply notification mechanisms for various communication channels, but they can serve to notify you, your team, supporting teams, or your bots that Heroku has successfully done its job and now other tasks can commence. You can also customize the content of the hook. The following command enables you to e-mail your boss, customer, or team that the app is live:

```
heroku Add-ons:add deployhooks:email \
  receipient=me@mydomain.com myteam@mydomain.com \
  subject="App Deployed" \
  body="{{user}} completed a deploy of {{app}}"
```

This capability also provides a useful failsafe to ensure a bit of lightweight change control or send security notifications. Anytime the app changes or new code is deployed, you can notify all the application stakeholders.

If you are connecting your app to monitoring, alerting, or logging services, use the HTTPS hook to send data to the appropriate URL:

```
heroku Add-ons:add deployhooks:http \
  url= https://mymonitoring.mydomain.com \
```

NAVIGATING THE HEROKU DASHBOARD

Now that your apps are deployed and running well, let's gain some visibility using the Heroku Dashboard, your main graphical user interface (GUI) for the platform.

Oftentimes you won't require the depth of administration provided by the Heroku CLI, or perhaps you are feeling a bit lazy. For tasks that don't require code manipulation or more involved interaction with the Heroku system, you can use the Dashboard, shown in Figure 4-3.

FIGURE 4-3

When you first log in, you'll notice a list of all your apps and the same navigation visible from the Heroku website. You'll also notice that the My Apps | My Account | Login link is displayed. The My Apps link brings you back to the main page shown in Figure 4-3. The My Account link, highlighted in Figure 4-4, provides access to all configuration data for your login (e-mail address, password, API key, and billing data). On the far right is the Logout link.

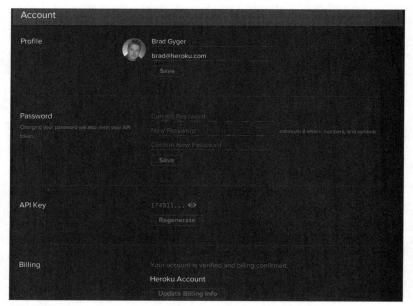

FIGURE 4-4

Let's dig into an app's details. When you click an app name from the My Apps page, you're immediately taken to the app's main page, as shown in Figure 4-5.

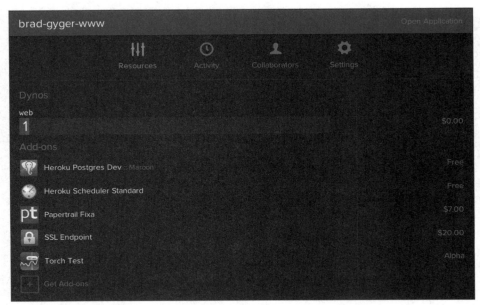

FIGURE 4-5

Here you can view your app's name and change it if desired. You can also add custom domains or collaborators to the app itself, as well as view source detail for both the git repo and slug size.

The following sections describe the available fields you can edit or update.

Changing Your Application's Name

By default, as demonstrated earlier, Heroku will automatically generate an application name if you do not specify one. Via the UI, the given name (or the name you specified) can be changed from this field at any time. Alternatively, you can run the following from the command line:

```
heroku apps:rename <bettername>
```

or, if you're outside the working directory:

```
heroku apps:rename <bettername> -app <currentname>
```

In either case, renaming from the UI or CLI requires that you also update your Heroku git remote:

```
git rm heroku
git remote add heroku git@heroku.com:bettername.git
```

Adding Custom Domains

Any custom domains or subdomains you wish to use with your Heroku app can be added here. Note that you can map a single app to multiple domains or subdomains. This can be done via the UI by simply adding the fully qualified domain name (FQDN) or via the command line:

```
heroku domains:add <www.sweetdomainname.com>
```

You should also ensure that you map your DNS properly, using either a Heroku add-on or your DNS provider of choice.

Among one of the Heroku best practices for custom domains is to avoid using naked, bare, or apex domains (such as domain.com); instead, always point to a subdomain for an additional level of routing configurability and scalability — for instance:

➤ www.domain.com

➤ app.domain.com

➤ secure.domain.com

In effect you are creating a CNAME alias that performs a permanent 301 redirect from your standard Heroku URL:

➤ app.heroku.com (for Aspen and Bamboo apps)

➤ app.herokuapp.com (for Cedar apps)

> **NOTE** *Some DNS providers, such as DNSimple, are starting to offer "alias" records, which allow you to point an apex domain at your* app.herokuapp.com *record. If you need a naked or apex domain pointed at your app, you should investigate these options*

Adding Custom Collaborators

Situations often arise when additional Heroku users must be added to your apps. Perhaps a teammate, business partner, or third-party user needs access to your app(s) in order to deploy changes and keep the development efforts moving forward. To do this, Heroku provides collaborator functationality. A *collaborator* is any user that currently exists in Heroku that you have explicitly granted access to an app. With collaborators you can add a Heroku user's e-mail address to the "Collaborators" page within your Heroku app's details, and the recipients will be able to both clone from and push to the Heroku remote Git repository. This enables them to participate as active developers or contributors to the app. Figure 4-6 shows the Collaborators page within Heroku Dashboard.

FIGURE 4-6

If the e-mail address owners are already Heroku users, they will receive an e-mail notification similar to Figure 4-7. Once received, the collaborating users can simply log into their Heroku Dashboard and the app will be listed. Then, to access and contribute code, they will need to run the specified `git clone` command. Individuals who are not already Heroku users need to create an account and follow the instructions for the Heroku Toolbelt installation.

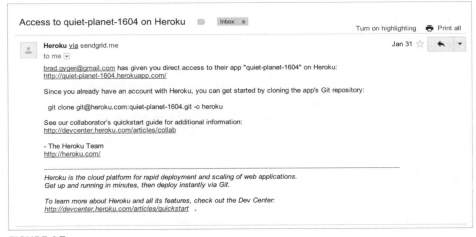

FIGURE 4-7

Scaling Resources

From the Resources page within Heroku Dashboard, you will see two moving pieces that can be manipulated up or down based on the demands of your app and user base: dynos and add-ons.

> **NOTE** *To scale any of these areas, you need to have a verified Heroku user account with a valid credit card entered.*

We've already described dynos in previous chapters. Depending on your process model, as defined in your Procfile, you can scale your specific dynos via the CLI, as follows:

```
heroku scale <dyno_type>=N
```

For example:

```
heroku scale web=2
heroku scale api=5
```

Your dyno usage, translated in estimated monthly dollars, will appear in the Dyno Resources and Total windows (refer to Figure 4-5).

The second moving part, add-ons, refers to any component or service that you want to connect to your app running within dynos. The Heroku add-on ecosystem can be viewed any time at `https://addons.heroku.com`. We'll dive into add-ons in Chapter 6. For now, here's a quick rundown on how the Dashboard exposes add-ons and attaches them to your app.

By default, no add-ons are attached to your apps. Services such as databases, DNS management, and logging/performance management are just a few examples of services that you can attach to the apps you run on Heroku.

The Heroku Postgres database service is among the most popular tools you can attach to your app. From Heroku Dashboard, on the app's Resources page (again per Figure 4-5), you will see the "Get Add-ons" button. When you click it, you will be dropped into the add-ons library. Navigate to Heroku Postgres, select the plan you desire (see Figure 4-8), and then hit "add." To finish the process, click "Install Heroku-postgresql," and you'll see Heroku provision the service automatically.

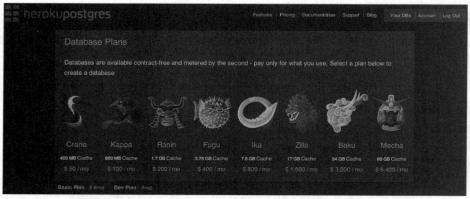

FIGURE 4-8

Postgres databases can also be enabled via the command line, as follows:

```
heroku Add-ons:add heroku-postgresql:<instance_size>
```

For example:

```
heroku Add-ons:add heroku-postgresql:zilla
```

Once enabled, the database instance will be highlighted via the UI, and details are viewable via the CLI by using the following command:

```
heroku pg:info
```

This returns the following:

```
=== HEROKU_POSTGRESQL_BLACK
Plan          Zilla
Status        available
Data Size     5.1 MB
Tables        0
PG Version    9.0.5
Created       2012-06-25 17:59 UTC
Conn Info     "host=ec2-107-22-255-215.compute-1.amazonaws.com
              port=5432 dbname=dk2sf5va742n3rd
              user=uy5gymvzvyast6ee sslmode=require
              password=psdf12dfa2yzx1q8g48dp1mo3a"
```

> **NOTE** *See Chapter 8, "Using Heroku Postgres as a Data Store for Your Heroku Applications," for an in-depth look at the Heroku Postgres service.*

If you have installed several add-ons, they will be displayed within the Resources page (see Figure 4-9). For more details about a service you are considering, click the "Get Add-ons" button, and then browse the marketplace.

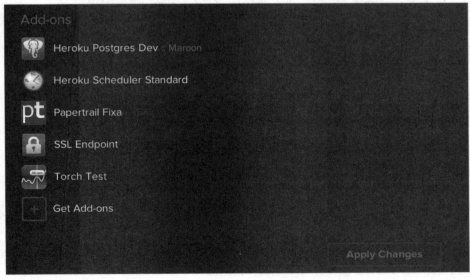

FIGURE 4-9

Let's switch gears slightly and add SendGrid, a popular e-mail service, as an another example. If you just want to try it out, you can simply click the Starter link, and you'll see the dialog to choose the associated app for the SendGrid service. After clicking Select, as shown in Figure 4-10, the Heroku platform will automatically add the service to your app.

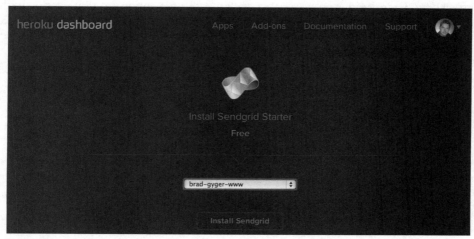

FIGURE 4-10

For those of you who prefer the command line, every option has the syntax available from the Add-ons detail page:

```
heroku Add-ons:add sendgrid:starter
```

To view your add-ons, simply return to the Resources page to see a current list, or make the call via the CLI, as follows:

```
heroku info
```

The following shows example output:

```
=== brad-gyger-www
Add-ons:        Chargify Developer
                MongoHQ MongoHQ Free
                New Relic Standard
                Piggyback SSL
                Zerigo DNS
 . . .
```

SUMMARY

Now you have successfully navigated the Heroku deployment workflow from start to finish. Although the Toolbelt installation is required only once, it is important to understand how Git, Foreman, and the Heroku client help drive the different parts of your development and deployment

workflow on Heroku. Digging deeper, remember everything that happens when you
`git push heroku master`, where previously all those steps would be your responsibility and could
potentially be optimized and scripted, now happens with a single command. For those apps that you
have deployed initially and want to build out, it's of paramount importance to properly use add-ons
to create a robust application architecture deployed to Heroku. If you need to be made more aware
of the events attached to your deployments, use post deploy hooks for notification/integration with
other systems. Everything non-development related that you do to your apps can be carried out via
the Heroku Dashboard. You will see much more of this throughout the remainder of the book. To
take the conversation further, now that you have an app deployed, you will want to set up a true
development workflow with multiple environments, release processes, deployment methodologies
inline with how you want to work. We'll dive into this in Chapter 5, "Managing Releases with
Heroku."

Managing Releases with Heroku

WHAT'S IN THIS CHAPTER?

➤ Managing multiple environments

➤ Managing configuration variables

➤ Securing Development environments

➤ Versioning and rolling back releases

➤ Using deploy hooks

➤ Managing planned downtime and custom error pages

➤ Implementing continuous integration

WROX.COM CODE DOWNLOADS FOR THIS CHAPTER

The wrox.com code downloads for this chapter are found at www.wrox.com/remtitle .cgi?isbn= 1118508998 on the Download Code tab. The code is in the Chapter 5 download and individually named according to the names throughout the chapter.

When writing apps, development shops often design a process outlining what activities need to be performed to take code from an idea to a live, end user–facing app. This process is designed to maximize developer productivity, while ensuring that checks are in place to reduce the risk of introducing bugs into production systems, and that all the initial requirements for the software are met. The goal of such a system is to provide a repeatable process for releasing high-quality software.

The software development life cycle encapsulates all activities in software development, from the early planning stages to implementing the software and all the way to deployment and post-deployment maintenance. Several models exist for these stages, such as the waterfall model and agile development methodologies. Discussing the pros and cons of each of these is beyond the scope of this book, but they share some aspects in common, such as release management and collaborative development, that Heroku can streamline — and those topics are the focus of this chapter.

MANAGING MULTIPLE ENVIRONMENTS

For some teams, release management is a complex process involving many intermediate steps in order to move the code from a developer's computer to the live app. In larger development shops, many members of the team (and sometimes an independent DevOps team) are responsible for ensuring that the code is acceptably error free, and to approve movement to the next stage of the process. In other, usually smaller, organizations, this is a simpler process that often uses a staging environment to mirror the production environment for pre-release testing to ensure that the app behaves as it should, sometimes with the same person who wrote the code testing it. In the most simple case, it includes only the developer's machine and the production environment (see Figure 5-1).

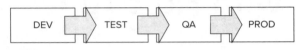

FIGURE 5-1

In the typical release management life cycle, developers begin by developing and running code on their local machines. However, this isn't always the case; sometimes developers use a nonlocal environment to do their initial testing. After the developer is reasonably sure that the code compiles and runs as expected, it is merged into code from other developers that has reached the same stage of readiness and is then deployed on an integration server. Here, the code from all (or a subset of) developers is tested together to ensure harmonious functioning and discover where one developer's code makes another's break.

Once integration testing is complete, the code is ready for quality assurance (QA). Sometimes the QA environment and integration environment is the same, but it is a best practice to keep these isolated so that the QA environment is stable enough to not slow down QA's testing if a developer pushes code that breaks the build. Once QA has run their tests, user acceptance testing (UAT) is often done to ensure that the end user is happy with the result. Finally, code is pushed to production, where it is live for the end users.

In all but the simplest process, multiple environments must to be set up that isolate the branch(es) of code being tested. However, these environments are often very different. Developers may be developing on a Windows machine, whereas the production environment may be a Linux box. In this case, the differences between the environments may cause the app to behave very differently. Therefore, it is important that the closer you get to production, the more similar that environment should be to the production environment, so that test runs behave as similarly as possible as in production.

Heroku makes it easy to match your pre-production environments with your production environment, which helps to mitigate the risk of inconsistent behavior. With traditional in-house hosting, setting up multiple environments involves setting up either multiple servers or virtual machines, which is time-intensive. Keeping these environments as similar as possible also provides a unique challenge and is often very error prone. This could result in bugs being identified in production environments that are not replicable in staging as a result of these differences, making debugging difficult for developers.

Heroku apps are deployed using Git. Git remotes are used to tell Git where code will be deployed. Remotes are simply references to remote repositories, such as development or production environments. Whenever you create a Heroku app, a default remote is created as part of the process. To create multiple environments, we must create two remotes: one for our staging environment and one for your production environment.

1. Create your Git repository, as follows, in your app's directory:

```
$ git init
Initialized empty Git repository in
  /Users/ckemp/Documents/Sites/multi-environment-app/.git/
```

2. Create your Heroku app:

```
$ heroku create
Creating furious-robot-7619... done, stack is cedar
http://furious-robot-7619.herokuapp.com/ | git@heroku.com:furious-robot-7619.git
Git remote heroku added
```

The last line of the preceding example indicates that the Git remote has been added. The Git URL for the app is `git@heroku.com:furious-robot-7619.git`.

3. Check what your Git remote configurations look like with the following command:

```
$ git remote -v
heroku     git@heroku.com:furious-robot-7619.git (fetch)
heroku     git@heroku.com:furious-robot-7619.git (push)
```

At this point, you have defined a remote named "heroku" that can be used to fetch the latest copy of code from GitHub or push the code to Heroku from the GitHub repository.

> **WARNING** *If you have accidentally created your Heroku app before initializing a Git repository, you will get the following error when you try to deploy your app:*
>
> ```
> $ git push heroku master
> fatal: 'heroku' does not appear to be a git repository
> fatal: The remote end hung up unexpectedly
> ```
>
> *To add a remote for Heroku after you have created your Heroku app, simply use the following command:*
>
> ```
> $ git remote add heroku git@heroku.com:furious-robot-7619.git
> ```
>
> *Here, you have added a remote, called "heroku" to your app, furious-robot-7619. You should substitute furious-robot-7619 with the name of the app you created in the previous steps.*

4. Change your remote to "staging" in order to define a remote for your staging environment, where your app is to be tested before pushing it to your production environment:

```
$ git remote rename heroku staging
$ git remote -v
staging    git@heroku.com:furious-robot-7619.git (fetch)
staging    git@heroku.com:furious-robot-7619.git (push)
```

Now your remote is renamed. If you hadn't already created a remote, you could have used the following command when creating your Heroku app:

```
$ heroku create --remote staging
```

5. Create a simple PHP app (probably the simplest you'll ever see) by opening a text editor and creating a file called index.php in the app's directory:

```
<p>My multi-environment app</p>
```

6. Add this file to your Git repository and commit it as follows:

```
$ git add .
$ git commit -am "first commit"
[master (root-commit) 86432b4] first commit
1 files changed, 1 insertions(+), 0 deletions(-)
create mode 100644 index.php
```

7. Push your local repository to your staging environment:

```
$ git push staging master
Counting objects: 7, done.
Delta compression using up to 4 threads.
Compressing objects: 100% (4/4), done.
Writing objects: 100% (7/7), 580 bytes, done.
Total 7 (delta 1), reused 0 (delta 0)
  Heroku receiving push
  PHP app detected
  Bundling Apache version 2.2.22
  Bundling PHP version 5.3.10
  Discovering process types
      Procfile declares types -> (none)
Default types for PHP -> web
  Compiled slug size is 9.5MB
  Launching... done, v3
    http://furious-robot-7619.herokuapp.com deployed to Heroku
To git@heroku.com:furious-robot-7619.git
* [new branch] master -> master
```

Now your staging app is running. Note that you use "staging" instead of "heroku" in the git push command. This indicates the Git remote to which you want to push the code. You can test your code in this environment to ensure that it's working here as expected before pushing it to production.

> **WARNING** *You can use whatever name you want for the Git remote, but there is one special remote name that Git uses:* origin. *This defines the default remote repository, where you can simply use* git push *to deploy. You can use this if you like, but it is a best practice to explicitly define a remote name that clearly describes to where you are pushing the code — to minimize the risk of pushing it to unintended environments.*

8. Create a production environment by creating a new app with the remote name "production." (If you're doing this at home, you might want to use another unique name instead of my-production-app, as Heroku application names have to be unique.)

```
$ heroku create my-production-app --remote production
Creating my-production-app... done, stack is cedar
http://my-production-app.herokuapp.com/ | git@heroku.com:my-production-app.git
Git remote production added
```

9. Check your Git remotes one last time:

```
$ git remote -v
production    git@heroku.com:my-production-app.git (fetch)
production    git@heroku.com:my-production-app.git (push)
staging       git@heroku.com:furious-robot-7619.git (fetch)
staging       git@heroku.com:furious-robot-7619.git (push)
```

10. Push your code to production:

```
$ git push production master
Counting objects: 7, done.
Delta compression using up to 4 threads.
Compressing objects: 100% (4/4), done.
Writing objects: 100% (7/7), 580 bytes, done.
Total 7 (delta 1), reused 0 (delta 0)
  Heroku receiving push
  PHP app detected
  Bundling Apache version 2.2.22
  Bundling PHP version 5.3.10
  Discovering process types
  Procfile declares types -> (none)
Default types for PHP -> web
Compiled slug size is 9.5MB
  Launching... done, v3
    http://my-production-app.herokuapp.com deployed to Heroku
To git@heroku.com:my-production-app.git
* [new branch]  master -> master
```

You now have two identical environments, and you can easily push to either one from the same code base. As this simple example demonstrates, you no longer have to strive to keep your two environments as similar as possible to avoid production bugs that are difficult to reproduce in your test environments. Heroku eliminates that extra effort.

MANAGING CONFIGURATION VARIABLES

All the code in this section can be found in `ch5-managing-configuration-variables.zip`.

Though you want your testing and production environments to be as similar as possible, you don't want them to be exactly the same, of course. If they were, you would have major problems with both environments pointing to the same database! You need to manage their differences with environment-specific configurations.

Most traditional apps store environment-specific information in configuration files, using one of two methods. The first method is to have multiple, environment-specific configuration files and swap the files in and out depending on the specific deployment endpoint. However, this method is error prone if the incorrect configuration file is deployed to the wrong location. The second (and often preferred) method is to store configuration in a central configuration file, such as the YAML file in Ruby, which is checked in to the source code. This is less error prone than the former approach but it can be disastrous in the case of an open-source project if credentials are accidentally checked in with the rest of the code base.

On Heroku, the preferred approach is to use environment variables for setting an environment-specific configuration. Using this approach, each app has its own set of configuration variables (config vars) specific to that environment. In addition, eliminating the configuration from the code base mitigates the risk of exposing your credentials to outside parties that shouldn't see them. Heroku also has built-in controls; so when you deploy your app, Heroku takes care of installing your config vars on each dyno on which your app runs.

To demonstrate how config vars work, the following example creates a very simple Ruby program with three files: `web.rb`, `Gemfile`, and `Procfile`.

> **NOTE** *You must have Ruby and Bundler set up on your computer for this example to work. See* https://devcenter.heroku.com/articles/ruby *for information on how you can set up your workstation to create Ruby apps on Heroku.*

1. Create a file called `web.rb`:

```
# web.rb:
require 'sinatra'
get '/' do
    "Hello, " << ENV['NAME']
end
```

The `ENV['NAME']` variable is what retrieves the environment variables in Ruby.

2. Define a `Gemfile` for your app's dependencies:

```
# Gemfile:
source :rubygems
gem 'sinatra', '1.1.0'
gem 'thin'
```

A real-world app would have more dependencies than this simple program, of course.

3. Create your `Procfile` with a single line:

```
web: bundle exec ruby web.rb -p $PORT
```

This tells Heroku to create a process with `web.rb` running.

4. Bundle your app:

```
$ bundle install
Fetching source index for http://rubygems.org/
Installing daemons (1.1.8)
Using eventmachine (0.12.10)
Installing rack (1.4.1)
Using tilt (1.3.3)
Installing sinatra (1.1.0)
Installing thin (1.3.1) with native extensions
Using bundler (1.0.21)
Your bundle is complete! Use `bundle show [gemname]`
   to see where a bundled gem is installed.
```

5. Initialize your Git repository:

```
$ git init
Initialized empty Git repository in
   /Users/ckemp/Documents/Sites/config-var-test/.git/
```

6. Create a Heroku app (using a different app name than "config-var-test"):

```
$ heroku create config-var-test
Creating config-var-test... done, stack is cedar
http://config-var-test.herokuapp.com/ | git@heroku.com:config-var-test.git
Git remote heroku added
```

7. Add your app's files to your Git repository:

```
$ git add .
```

8. Commit your changes:

```
$ git commit -am "Initial push"
[master (root-commit) 8f141ca] init
4 files changed, 30 insertions(+), 0 deletions(-)
create mode 100644 Gemfile
create mode 100644 Gemfile.lock
create mode 100644 Procfile
create mode 100644 web.rb
```

9. Push to Heroku:

```
$ git push heroku master
Counting objects: 6, done.
Delta compression using up to 4 threads.
Compressing objects: 100% (5/5), done.
Writing objects: 100% (6/6), 665 bytes, done.
Total 6 (delta 0), reused 0 (delta 0)
-----> Heroku receiving push
-----> Ruby app detected
-----> Installing dependencies using Bundler version 1.2.0.pre
       Running: bundle install --without development:test
```

```
        --path vendor/bundle --binstubs bin/ --deployment
        Fetching gem metadata from http://rubygems.org/.....
        Installing daemons (1.1.8)
        Installing eventmachine (0.12.10) with native extensions
        Installing rack (1.4.1)
        Installing tilt (1.3.3)
        Installing sinatra (1.1.0)
        Installing thin (1.3.1) with native extensions
        Using bundler (1.2.0.pre)
        Your bundle is complete! It was installed into ./vendor/bundle
        Cleaning up the bundler cache.
-----> Discovering process types
        Procfile declares types -> web
        Default types for Ruby  -> console, rake
-----> Compiled slug size is 2.0MB
-----> Launching... done, v3
        http://config-var-test.herokuapp.com deployed to Heroku
To git@heroku.com:config-var-test.git
* [new branch]        master -> master
```

You now have a web app running; however, you will get an error because you have not yet added any config vars to it.

10.   Add the config var to your Heroku app:

```
$ heroku config:add NAME="World"
Adding config vars and restarting config-var-test... done, v4
NAME: World
```

If you run the app again, you can see "Hello, World" displayed as expected because your app replaced ENV['NAME'] with the value you designated in the previous command — in this case, the word "World."

11.   Change your config var's value to "Joe":

```
$ heroku config:add NAME="Joe"
Adding config vars and restarting config-var-test... done, v5
NAME: Joe
```

If you return to your app and refresh, you will see "Hello, Joe" displayed instead.

12.   To see your current config vars for an app, use the following command:

```
$ heroku config
=== Config Vars for config-var-test
GEM_PATH: vendor/bundle/ruby/1.9.1
LANG:      en_US.UTF-8
NAME:      Joe
PATH:      bin:vendor/bundle/ruby/1.9.1/bin:/usr/local/bin:/usr/bin:/bin
```

In the preceding example, you can see the config var that you added, NAME, along with other config vars that have been automatically added to the app — namely, GEM_PATH, LANG, and PATH.

> **NOTE** *The config vars returned by the preceding command may also include variables from add-ons to your app, such as credentials for backing services.*

You can also add multiple config vars at once:

```
$ heroku config:add KEY1="value 1" KEY2="value 2"
Adding config vars and restarting config-var-test... done, v6
KEY1: value 1
KEY2: value 2
$ heroku config
=== Config Vars for config-var-test
GEM_PATH: vendor/bundle/ruby/1.9.1
KEY1:     value 1
KEY2:     value 2
LANG:     en_US.UTF-8
NAME:     Joe
PATH:     bin:vendor/bundle/ruby/1.9.1/bin:/usr/local/bin:/usr/bin:/bin
```

As you can see, your config vars have been added successfully. You can also remove one or more config vars:

```
$ heroku config:remove KEY1 KEY2
Removing KEY1 and restarting config-var-test... done, v7
Removing KEY2 and restarting config-var-test... done, v8
$ heroku config
=== Config Vars for config-var-test
GEM_PATH: vendor/bundle/ruby/1.9.1
LANG:     en_US.UTF-8
NAME:     Joe
PATH:     bin:vendor/bundle/ruby/1.9.1/bin:/usr/local/bin:/usr/bin:/bin
```

> **NOTE** *When developing locally, you can either set environment variables locally or use Foreman, which is installed with the Heroku Toolbelt, to load the variables set in the* `.env` *file, and use* `.gitignore` *to ensure that this file is not pushed to Heroku. For more information on setting up local environment variables and synchronizing your local config vars with your app's, see* `https://devcenter.heroku.com/articles/config-vars#local_setup`.

You have created an app that uses config vars, demonstrating how environmental differences can be managed in Heroku and how config vars are managed. In Heroku, this is done without the hassle of swapping configuration files, and you do not run the risk of accidentally exposing sensitive credentials if you open source your app.

SECURING DEVELOPMENT ENVIRONMENTS

All the code in this section can be found in `ch5-securing-development-environments.zip`.

When developing your app, you will likely be testing your code in a staging environment, as described previously. However, most organizations do not want their test environments to be publicly available for a number of reasons, including alerting competitors about new features under development or soon to be released. Heroku does not support techniques such as using VPNs to restrict who can access your development environment, so you are responsible for ensuring that your development environment is secured.

One way to do this is using HTTP Basic authentication, which ensures that anyone accessing your app on test environments is authorized to do so. This is accomplished by challenging them to enter the correct username and password. Regardless of your development language and framework of choice, it is typically easy to add this form of authentication to your app.

> **WARNING** *Though Basic authentication does not send credentials in strictly plain text (it is Base64 encoded), the credentials are not sent in a secure way and are open to man-in-the-middle attacks. To ensure that credentials are secured, it is recommended that you force your app to use HTTPS only.*

Using the app that you created to test adding config vars, the next example adds some code to instruct the Sinatra framework to perform Basic authentication:

1. Edit the `web.rb` file from the example in the previous section and replace it with the following code:

    ```ruby
    # web.rb
    require 'sinatra'
    helpers do
            def protected!
            unless ENV['RACK_ENV'] != 'staging' || authorized?
                    response['WWW-Authenticate'] = %(Basic realm="Restricted Area")
                    throw(:halt, [401, "Not authorized\n"])
            end
            end
            def authorized?
            @auth ||=  Rack::Auth::Basic::Request.new(request.env)
            @auth.provided? && @auth.basic? && @auth.credentials &&
              @auth.credentials == ['alladin', 'opensesame']
            end
    end

    get '/' do
            protected!
            "Hello, " << ENV['NAME']
    end
    ```

    Note that on line 5 (bolded), you are checking the config vars to determine whether this is your staging environment.

2. Commit your changes and push them to Heroku:

    ```
    $ git add .

    $ git commit -am "Adding basic authentication"
    [master 1d6ca07] Adding basic authentication
    ```

```
   1 file changed, 17 insertions(+), 3 deletions(-)

$ git push heroku master
Counting objects: 5, done.
Delta compression using up to 4 threads.
Compressing objects: 100% (3/3), done.
Writing objects: 100% (3/3), 576 bytes, done.
Total 3 (delta 1), reused 0 (delta 0)

-----> Heroku receiving push
-----> Ruby app detected
-----> Installing dependencies using Bundler version 1.2.1
       Running: bundle install --without development:test -path
       vendor/bundle --binstubs bin/ --deployment
       Using daemons (1.1.9)
       Using eventmachine (1.0.0)
       Using rack (1.4.1)
       Using tilt (1.3.3)
       Using sinatra (1.1.0)
       Using thin (1.5.0)
       Using bundler (1.2.1)
       Your bundle is complete! It was installed into ./vendor/bundle
       Cleaning up the bundler cache.
-----> Discovering process types
       Procfile declares types -> web
       Default types for Ruby  -> console, rake
-----> Compiled slug size: 1.8MB
-----> Launching... done, v7
       http://config-var-test.herokuapp.com deployed to Heroku

To git@heroku.com:config-var-test.git
   d7cd562..1d6ca07  master -> master
```

3. Add the config var to your Heroku app to indicate that it is running in your staging environment:

```
$ heroku config:add RACK_ENV="staging"
Adding config vars and restarting config-var-test... done, v6
RACK_ENV: staging
```

Now, when your app is selected in a web browser, users are prompted for a username and password before access is allowed. When you deploy this app to production, you can change your config vars in that environment to eliminate the need for authentication:

```
$ heroku config:add RACK_ENV="production"
Adding config vars and restarting config-var-test... done, v8
RACK_ENV: production
```

Your development environment is now secured and you have leveraged config vars to ensure that authentication does not affect your production environment.

VERSIONING AND ROLLING BACK RELEASES

Heroku maintains a history of releases that it updates every time you deploy an app or change its configuration. As a built-in fail-safe, this release history enables you to roll back an app to a working release if someone deploys code that does not work properly. See a list of your app's available releases with the following command:

```
$ heroku releases
=== afternoon-snow-6237 Releases
v3    Deploy 5828ec9    ckemp@salesforce.com    1m ago
v2    Add config        ckemp@salesforce.com    1m ago
v1    Initial release   ckemp@salesforce.com    1m ago
```

The first column of output indicates the version number of the most current app, which is incremented with each new release. The second column specifies the reason for the change, including the Git commit number with which this deploy is associated — in this case, 5828ec9. The third column indicates which team member triggered the release, showing his or her Heroku username. Finally, the last column specifies when each release occurred.

Note what happens when you make a change to your app and push it:

```
$ heroku releases
=== afternoon-snow-6237 Releases
v4    Deploy 73e5ac5    ckemp@salesforce.com    9s ago
v3    Deploy 5828ec9    ckemp@salesforce.com    40m ago
v2    Add config        ckemp@salesforce.com    40m ago
v1    Initial release   ckemp@salesforce.com    41m ago
```

The preceding output indicates that your latest release, v4, has been added to the list and is associated with commit number 73e5ac5. Configuration changes also trigger a release, as shown here:

```
$ heroku config:add KEY="value"
Adding config vars and restarting afternoon-snow-6237... done, v5
KEY: value
$ heroku releases
=== afternoon-snow-6237 Releases
v5    Add KEY config    ckemp@salesforce.com    18s ago
v4    Deploy 73e5ac5    ckemp@salesforce.com    1m ago
v3    Deploy 5828ec9    ckemp@salesforce.com    42m ago
v2    Add config        ckemp@salesforce.com    42m ago
v1    Initial release   ckemp@salesforce.com    43m ago
```

Adding or removing add-ons also triggers a new deployment:

```
$ heroku addons:add scheduler:standard
Adding scheduler:standard to afternoon-snow-6237... done, v6 (free)
[...]
$ heroku releases
=== afternoon-snow-6237 Releases
v6    Add scheduler:standard add-on    ckemp@salesforce.com    11s ago
v5    Add KEY config                   ckemp@salesforce.com    3m ago
```

```
v4    Deploy 73e5ac5              ckemp@salesforce.com    5m ago
v3    Deploy 5828ec9              ckemp@salesforce.com    45m ago
v2    Add  config                 ckemp@salesforce.com    45m ago
v1    Initial release             ckemp@salesforce.com    46m ago
```

Now v6 appears in the list of releases, confirming that the Heroku Scheduler add-on was added to the app.

To see detailed information about a particular release, run the following command:

```
$ heroku releases:info v5
=== Release v5
By: ckemp@salesforce.com
Change: Add KEY config
When:   8m ago
=== v5 Config Vars
KEY: value
```

Suppose you have made a change to your app and pushed it, but something went wrong. You can quickly and easily roll back to the last release as follows:

```
$ heroku rollback
Rolling back afternoon-snow-6237... done, v6
```

> **WARNING** *Keep in mind that after you have rolled back, if someone accidentally does a* `git push heroku master` *on your code, you will push the same bad code from which you rolled back! Changes in add-ons or config vars also result in the latest version being pushed. Rollbacks should be used as a temporary measure to make emergency fixes for bad pushes; to maintain app integrity, you should ensure that no add-on or config var changes are made during this time.*

The following shows that the rollback also adds another release, v8, which was a rollback to release v7:

```
$ heroku releases
=== afternoon-snow-6237 Releases
v8    Rollback to v6               ckemp@salesforce.com    21s ago
v7    Deploy 004436d               ckemp@salesforce.com    50s ago
v6    Add scheduler:standard add-on ckemp@salesforce.com  10m ago
v5    Add KEY config               ckemp@salesforce.com    14m ago
v4    Deploy 73e5ac5               ckemp@salesforce.com    16m ago
v3    Deploy 5828ec9               ckemp@salesforce.com    56m ago
v2    Add  config                  ckemp@salesforce.com    56m ago
v1    Initial release              ckemp@salesforce.com    57m ago
```

Finally, you can roll back to a specific release number, which enables you to step back any number of releases at once:

```
$ heroku rollback v7
Rolling back afternoon-snow-6237 to v7... done
```

> **WARNING** *If you add or remove add-ons, you cannot roll back to a previous release with a different set of add-ons as the current release. If you try to do a rollback, you will get an error message:*
>
> ```
> $ heroku rollback
> Rolling back afternoon-snow-6237... failed
> !    Cannot rollback to a release that had
>      a different set of addons installed
> ```
>
> *Rollbacks only switch deployed code and config vars back to those that were present in the previous release. If structural database changes were made since the release you rolled back to, the previous code may not work properly with your new database structure. You must also ensure that the external state of add-ons, such as Memcachier, does not adversely affect your rolled-back app.*

USING DEPLOY HOOKS

Often, you need to notify members of the development team, and development life-cycle tools, when new code is pushed to Heroku. Heroku provides a number of automated *deploy hooks* that are built into the platform and can be accessed via the Deploy Hooks add-on (`https://addons.heroku.com/deployhooks`). Each time your app is deployed, you can have Heroku send an e-mail; perform an HTTP POST to a URL; or post a message in an IRC room, on your project in the popular project-management tool Basecamp (`http://basecamp.com/`), or in the collaboration tool Campfire (`http://campfirenow.com/`).

For example, the following sets up a deploy hook to send a message to me when my code is deployed:

```
$ heroku addons:add deployhooks:email \
    --recipient="ckemp@salesforce.com" \
    --subject="The Application Has Been Deployed" \
    --body="{{user}} deployed the application to {{url}}"
Adding deployhooks:email to app-with-deploy-hooks... done, v11 (free)
```

Replace the e-mail address in this code with your own. Now when you push your app, you get an additional message, indicating that your deploy hook has been scheduled:

```
$ git push heroku master
Counting objects: 5, done.
Delta compression using up to 4 threads.
Compressing objects: 100% (3/3), done.
Writing objects: 100% (3/3), 326 bytes, done.
Total 3 (delta 1), reused 0 (delta 0)
-----> Heroku receiving push
[...]
-----> Launching... done, v12
-----> Deploy hooks scheduled, check output in your logs
       http://app-with-deploy-hooks.herokuapp.com deployed to Heroku
```

The deploy hook execution is also noted in your app's logs:

```
2012-06-27T03:16:26+00:00 heroku[deployhooks]:
    Sent email notification to ckemp@salesforce.com
```

Shortly after your deploy, you should receive a message alerting you to the deployment:

```
Date: Tue, 26 Jun 2012 20:16:26 -0700
From: <noreply@heroku.com>
To: ckemp@salesforce.com
Subject: The Application Has Been Deployed
ckemp@salesforce.com deployed the application to
    http://app-with-deploy-hooks.herokuapp.com
```

E-mail can simply alert a single person or distribution group of a push, but using deploy hooks to make an HTTP POST to a URL, you can define pretty much any custom behavior you like. This might be an app that you have written on Heroku that will accept the POST, parse its contents, and push the results into an online project management tool's API. Deploy hooks enable you to integrate with any third-party app that has an online API in order to send notifications when you deploy code to Heroku.

> **NOTE** *For a listing of the deploy hook commands and examples using each, see* `https://devcenter.heroku.com/articles/deploy-hooks`.

MANAGING PLANNED DOWNTIME AND CUSTOM ERROR PAGES

One of Heroku's advantages is being able to release new deploys without any perceived downtime for the user. However, sometimes downtime is required — for instance, if you need to run a database migration, which means the old code won't work until you push the new code. In this case, you want to display some sort of user-friendly message that lets your users know that the app is in the middle of expected downtime and will be available again shortly.

Heroku enables you to put your app into *maintenance mode*, during which time all requests to your app are redirected to a predetermined page during planned downtime. Unless you indicate otherwise, enabling maintenance mode for your app redirects users to `http://s3.amazonaws.com/heroku_pages/maintenance.html`, Heroku's default maintenance mode page. If you want to define your own page, you can host your maintenance mode custom page on another server, such Amazon S3.

To put your app into maintenance mode during planned downtime, perform the following steps:

1. Create an HTML file with your maintenance mode page (code name: `maintenance_page.html`):

```
<html>
    <body>
        <h1>App Temporarily Unavailable</h1>

        <p>
```

```
          Sorry, but this application is temporarily offline while we work to
          make it better.<br />
          Wait a couple of minutes and try again.
      </p>

    </body>
</html>
```

2.   Upload this file to Amazon S3 and make it publicly viewable.

> **NOTE** *If you don't recall how to create a bucket, upload a file to Amazon S3,*
> *and make it public, refer to the instructions in the section "Storing Static Assets*
> *on Amazon S3" in Chapter 2, "Architectural Considerations."*

Figure 5-2 shows an example where the `maintenance_page.html` file has been added to a bucket called "kemp-first-bucket" on Amazon S3.

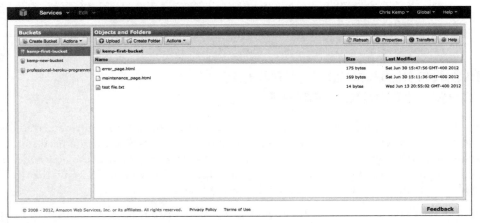

FIGURE 5-2

3.   Test this page by visiting `http://s3.amazonaws.com/kemp-first-bucket/maintenance_page.html`, substituting `kemp-first-bucket` with the name of the bucket in which you stored the `maintenance_page.html` file.

Now you must instruct Heroku to serve up this URL when you are in maintenance mode. There are two ways to do this: either via the Heroku user interface or via the command line.

4. To set your maintenance mode custom page via the Heroku UI, open your app and click the Settings icon in the top-right corner. Near the bottom of the page, under Custom Error Pages, you can change the value of "Maintenance URL" to the URL of the page you created and put on Amazon S3, and then click Save (see Figure 5-3).

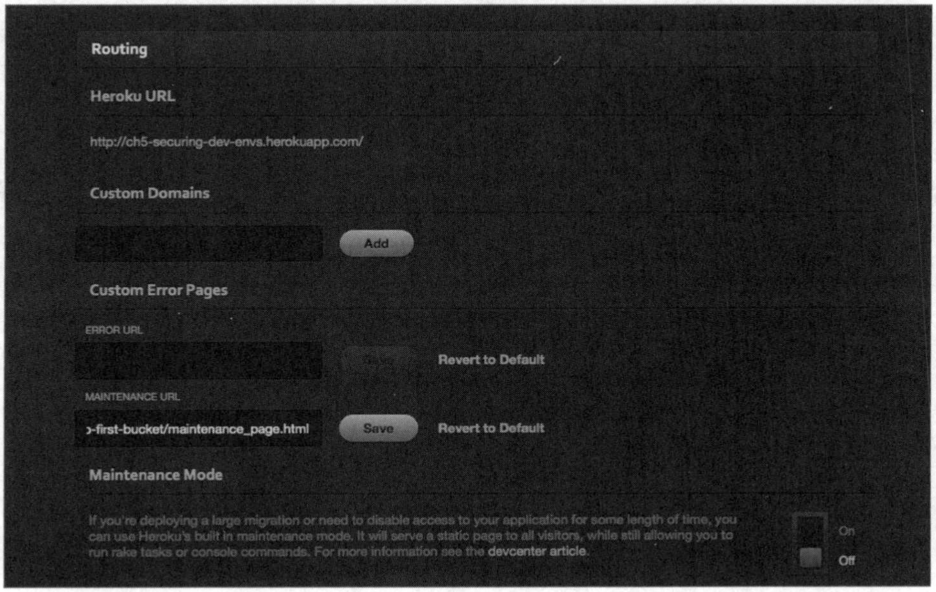

FIGURE 5-3

To do the same thing via the command line, add a config var called MAINTENANCE_PAGE_URL to your Heroku app:

```
$ heroku config:add \
MAINTENANCE_PAGE_URL=http://s3.amazonaws.com/kemp-first-bucket/maintenance_page.html
Adding config vars and restarting config-var-test... done, v34
MAINTENANCE_PAGE_URL: http://s3.amazonaws.com/kemp-first-bucket/maintenance_page.html
```

Changing this config var will override the default maintenance page for your app.

5. Test the new maintenance page by enabling maintenance mode for the app. There are two ways to do this. One way is to use the Heroku UI from within your app. Click the Settings icon in the top-right corner. Then, at the bottom of the page, move the slider under the Maintenance Mode section to On, as shown in Figure 5-4. Now, when users visit your app, they will see the custom page set earlier.

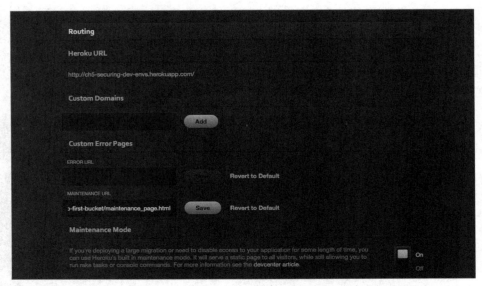

FIGURE 5-4

The alternative method for enabling maintenance mode is via the command line. Simply run the following:

```
$ heroku maintenance:on
Enabling maintenance mode for config-var-test... done
```

6. You can easily turn off maintenance mode from the command line as follows:

```
$ heroku maintenance:off
Disabling maintenance mode for config-var-test... done
```

By redirecting visitors to your maintenance page, you can run your migration scripts and do whatever else you need to do while maintenance mode is on. In a similar way, you can also define a custom error page for your app. This is the page that is displayed when your app encounters a system-level error, such as the app crashing entirely (not something like a 404 error, which is handled by your app). By default, Heroku displays the error page at `http://s3.amazonaws.com/heroku_pages/error.html`.

You can customize your error page in the Heroku UI by changing the value of "Error URL." Alternatively, you can simply add a config var named `ERROR_PAGE_URL` to your app. You can test this easily by adding a syntax error to your code and pushing the code. When users visit your app, they will now see the custom error page. The 503 error code that resulted in redirection to this error page produces the following output in the log:

```
2012-06-30T19:50:34+00:00 heroku[router]: Error H10 (App crashed)
-> GET config-var-test.herokuapp.com/
   dyno= queue= wait= service= status=503 bytes=
```

IMPLEMENTING CONTINUOUS INTEGRATION

All the code in this section can be found in `ch5-implementing-continuous-integration.zip`.

In a typical development project, a developer checks out a copy of the code, makes some changes, and then commits the code back to the source control and deploys it. This is easy enough if he or she is working alone, but when multiple developers are working on the same project, these changes often conflict with one another and break the codebase. It takes significant effort for a developer to fix the conflicts and get both changes working properly. This becomes more difficult as the number of changes that need to be integrated increases.

A best practice for minimizing the amount of time needed to integrate changes is to use a technique called *continuous integration*, whereby changes are merged into the team's master copy as frequently as possible. Frequent check-ins reduce the amount of work needed to resolve conflicts between all the teams' changes. Continuous integration typically also involves running regression tests with every commit to the code base or push of the code, or at set intervals to ensure that the sets of changes being integrated do not unintentionally break the existing code base for all coders. Often, teams do not employ continuous integration because of the overhead of the scripting setup required and the additional servers and maintenance needed to keep the servers running.

Heroku provides an add-on, called Tddium, that provides Ruby developers with continuous integration as a service. (Python, Node.js, and PHP support is coming soon.) This makes it much easier for a team to employ continuous integration without the aforementioned drawbacks, because Heroku provides the build scripts and Tddium takes care of servers for you.

The following steps show how to set up Tddium with a simple app:

1. Create an app and add the Tddium add-on:

```
$ git init
Initialized empty Git repository in /Users/ckemp/Documents/Sites/ci-with-tddium/.git/
$ heroku create ci-with-tddium
Creating ci-with-tddium... done, stack is cedar
http://ci-with-tddium.herokuapp.com/ | git@heroku.com:ci-with-tddium.git
Git remote heroku added
$ heroku addons:add tddium
Adding tddium to ci-with-tddium... done, v2 ($7/mo)
tddium documentation available at: https://devcenter.heroku.com/articles/tddium
```

> **NOTE** *In this example, you are adding the Tddium Starter package. Visit* `https://addons.heroku.com/tddium` *to see the different packages available and choose the one best suited for your team's use case.*

Now that your add-on is running, you need to install the Tddium gem:

2. Run the following command:

```
$ gem install tddium
[...]
5 gems installed
[...]
```

3. With the gem installed on your workstation, create a `Gemfile` with Tddium's gem declared as a dependency only for development and testing:

```
source :rubygems
gem 'sinatra', '1.1.0'
gem 'thin'
gem 'rake'
gem 'rack-test'group :development, :test do
  gem 'tddium'
end
```

4. Add your `web.rb` file, which contains your simple Sinatra app:

```
# web.rb
require 'sinatra'
get '/' do
    "Hello, #{params[:name]}"
end
```

This app appends a single parameter, `name`, to the string `Hello,`.

5. Create the `Procfile` to run this app:

```
web: bundle exec ruby web.rb -p $PORT
```

6. Install the `Rack::Test` gem for your testing framework:

```
$ gem install rack-test
Successfully installed rack-test-0.6.1
1 gem installed
[...]
```

7. Create a test script called `test/web_test.rb`:

```
require './web.rb'
require 'test/unit'
require 'rack/test'
set :environment, :test
class MySimpleTest < Test::Unit::TestCase
    def test_basic
    browser = Rack::Test::Session.new(Rack::MockSession.
        new(Sinatra::Application))
    browser.get '/', :name => 'Brad'
    assert_equal 'Hello, Brad', browser.last_response.body
    end
end
```

This test script simply runs the app, injecting the parameter `Brad`, and confirms that you get the expected result.

8. Run `bundle`:

```
$ bundle
Fetching source index for http://rubygems.org/
[...]
Your bundle is complete! Use 'bundle show [gemname]'
  to see where a bundled gem is installed.
```

9. Add the files you created to the repository and commit:

```
$ git add .
$ git commit -am "init"
[master (root-commit) 677833d] init
5 files changed, 58 insertions(+), 0 deletions(-)
[...]
```

10. Activate your Tddium account, create a password, set an SSH key for access, and accept Tddium's terms of service:

```
$ tddium heroku
Thanks for installing the Tddium Heroku Add-On!
Your tddium username is: app1234567@heroku.com

Next, set a password and provide an SSH key to authenticate your communication
with Tddium.
Enter password: **********
Confirm your password: **********
Enter your ssh key or press 'Return'. Using '~/.ssh/id_rsa.pub' by default:
Before you can use Tddium, you must agree to our Terms of Service.
Read them at this URL:
https://www.tddium.com/terms.html
Type 'I AGREE' to accept the Terms of Service and continue: I AGREE
Tddium is configured to work with your Heroku app.
Next, you should register your test suite and start tests by running:
$ tddium run
```

Notice that your username, app1234567@heroku.com, was generated automatically when you installed the add-on.

11. Finally, run your tests to verify everything is working properly:

```
$ tddium run
... Detected branch master
... Detected ruby ruby 1.9.2p290 (2011-07-09 revision 32553) [x86_64-darwin10.8.0]
... Detected bundle Bundler version 1.0.21
... Detected gem 1.8.10
Creating suite 'ci-with-tddium/master'. This will take a few seconds.
>>> Waiting for your repository to be prepared. Sleeping for 10 seconds...
>>> Pushing changes to Tddium...
Counting objects: 11, done.
Delta compression using up to 4 threads.
Compressing objects: 100% (5/5), done.
Writing objects: 100% (6/6), 630 bytes, done.
Total 6 (delta 3), reused 0 (delta 0)
To ssh://u614@git.tddium.com/home/users/u614/repo/ci-with-tddium/
  d988ebf..f74069b  master -> master
>>> Starting Session with 1 tests...
>>> To view results, visit: https://api.tddium.com/1/reports/12345
>>> Press Ctrl-C to stop waiting. Tests will continue running.
---> Waiting for workers to become ready...
---> Tddium Stage 2 Started (version unknown)
```

```
---> Running ci-with-tddium/master from ssh://u123@git.tddium.com/home/users/u123/
repo/~ci-with-tddium/in cli mode
[...]
---> Running setup hooks -- output from tasks is in tddium-rake.log
---> Setup hooks complete
---> Starting Subsystem: last
---> Starting tests...
---> Collecting Results
---> Posting Results
---> Worker Rendezvous
>>> To view results, visit: https://api.tddium.com/1/reports/52845
>>> Press Ctrl-C to stop waiting. Tests will continue running.
    .
>>> Tddium Warnings:
No Rakefile found in repository -- installing empty one

>>> Run `tddium web` to open the latest test results in your browser.
Finished in 57.350604 seconds
1 tests, 0 failures, 0 errors, 0 pending, 0 skipped
```

If your tests run successfully, you are ready to automate a continuous integration build every time you push code to Heroku. Ideally, you want a workflow that looks something like this:

1. Push your code to the development environment with `git push`.

2. The Heroku development environment deploy hook triggers Tddium.

3. Tddium pulls the latest copy of the code base from Heroku.

4. Tddium runs the build tests.

5. If the tests pass, Tddium pushes the code base to the Heroku staging (or production) server and e-mails the client.

However, there is no way to pull Heroku code from an external system, so you have to use another system, GitHub. The revised workflow is as follows:

1. Push your code to a GitHub repository with `git push`.

2. The GitHub repository deploy hook triggers Tddium.

3. Tddium pulls the latest copy of the code base from GitHub.

4. Tddium runs the build tests.

5. If the tests pass, Tddium pushes the code base to the Heroku staging (or production) server and e-mails the client.

To get started, create a GitHub account on GitHub's website if you don't already have one. (It's free!) Once you have an account, perform the following steps:

1. Log in and create a new repository by clicking the New Repository button. In this case, name your repository **ci-with-tddium**, as shown in Figure 5-5, and then click Create Repository.

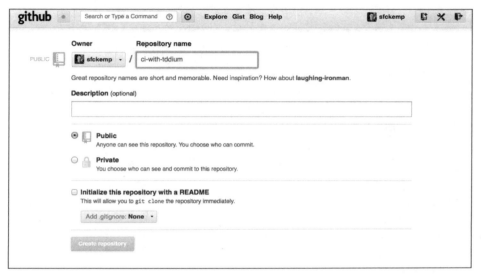

FIGURE 5-5

> **WARNING** *If you create a public repository, everyone on the web will be able to see your code. Don't do this with private (read: non-open source) code bases. GitHub charges for private repositories, so you need a paid account to keep the code private.*

2. Create a remote for your new GitHub repository:

```
$ git remote add github https://github.com/sfckemp/ci-with-tddium.git
```

3. In order to set up Tddium to pull the code repository from your new GitHub repository and push the code to Heroku, you provide Tddium with your Github URL (the repository to pull the code from) and your Heroku Git URL (the repository to push the code to). You can get your Github URL on your Github repository's home page (see Figure 5-6) and your Heroku Git URL by running `git remote -v`:

```
$ tddium suite --edit
[...]
Enter a pattern or press 'Return'. Using 'features/**.feature, spec/**_spec.rb,
  spec/features/**.feature, test/**_test.rb,
    spec/javascripts/**.js' by default:
[...]
Enter git URL to pull from (default '') or enter 'disable':
git@github.com:sfckemp/ci-with-tddium.git
Enter git URL to push to (default '') or enter 'disable':
git@heroku.com:ci-with-tddium.git
Custom Campfire room for this suite (current: '') or enter 'disable':
Custom HipChat room for this suite (current: '') or enter 'disable':
Updated suite successfully.
```

FIGURE 5-6

4. Run the following command to verify that the info you just entered was added correctly:

```
$ tddium suite
Current suite...
 Repo: ci-with-tddium/master
 Default Test Pattern: features/**.feature, spec/**_spec.rb, spec/features/**.feature,
  test/**_test.rb, spec/javascripts/**.js
 Ruby Version: ruby-1.9.2-p290
 Rubygems Version: 1.8.10
 Bundler Version: 1.0.21
Tddium Hosted CI is enabled with the following parameters:
 Pull URL: git@github.com:sfckemp/ci-with-tddium.git
 Push URL: git@heroku.com:ci-with-tddium.git
Notifications:
 Email:   ckemp@salesforce.com

>>> Tddium will pull from your Github repository.
    Visit https://github.com/sfckemp/ci-with-tddium/admin/keys
    then click "Add another deploy key" and copy and paste this key:
    ssh-rsa mY53cr3t55hK3y... ci@tddium.com
>>> Tddium will push to your Heroku application ci-with-tddium.
    To authorize the key, use the following command:
    heroku keys:add /Users/ckemp/Documents/Sites/
      ci-with-tddium/.tddium-deploy-key --app ci-with-tddium
>>> Configure Github to notify Tddium of your commits with a post-receive hook.
    Visit https://github.com/sfckemp/ci-with-tddium/admin/hooks#generic_minibucket
    then add the following URL and click "Update Settings":
    http://ci.tddium.com:888/1/builds/mYtDd1Umt0k3N
>>> See http://www.tddium.com/support for more information on Tddium CI.
>>> You can enable Campfire and HipChat notifications from your Tddium Dashboard.
>>> Run 'tddium suite --edit' to edit these settings.
>>> Run 'tddium spec' to run tests in this suite.
```

5. Go to the GitHub URL shown in the output bolded in the previous step — in this example, `https://github.com/sfckemp/ci-with-tddium/admin/keys`.

6. Add your Github deploy key to allow Tddium to access this particular repository by clicking "Add deploy key," add a title (the example uses "Tddium key"), copy and paste the SSH key from the preceding output (in this example, `ssh-rsa mY53cr3t55hK3y... ci@tddium .com`), and then click "Add deploy key" (see Figure 5-7).

FIGURE 5-7

7. Add your Tddium key to Heroku to allow Tddium to push to Heroku after your tests pass. To do this, run the `heroku keys: add` command shown in the output bolded in step 4 in the command line:

```
$ heroku keys:add /Users/ckemp/Documents/Sites/ci-with-tddium/.tddium-deploy-key
  --app ci-with-tddium
```

8. To notify Tddium of your Heroku commits with a post-receive hook, visit the URL listed in the output from step 4 — in this example, `https://github.com/sfckemp/ ci-with-tddium/admin/hooks#generic_minibucket`. Under the Available Service Hooks heading, click WebHook URLs and add your Tddium WebHook URL — in this example, `http://ci.tddium.com:888/1/builds/mYtDd1Umt0k3N`. The Github hook you created should look like Figure 5-8.

FIGURE 5-8

9. Now that the setup is complete, push your code to GitHub:

```
$ git push github master
```

This triggers your code to be tested automatically on Tddium.

If the test runs successfully, the code base is pushed to `ci-with-tddium.herokuapp.com`. After a few minutes have passed, you should get an e-mail from Tddium informing you that your build has passed, with a summary of the commits, where the code was pulled from, and the log of your push.

> **NOTE** *Tddium does not run migration scripts, so you may have to configure a post-build task to be run after successful builds by following the example at* `http://docs.tddium.com/getting-started/post-build-tasks`.

SUMMARY

Understanding how to use Heroku to manage releases of your apps is essential for getting the most from the platform, especially when working as a team. Heroku helps reduce disparity between development and production environments by making it easy to push to multiple environments using Git remotes. The difference in configuration between these environments is managed using config vars. Access to development environments is restricted using application-layer code using HTTP's Basic authentication or a similar authentication protocol.

Heroku's release history gives you a safety net to roll back your code if a deploy is made that breaks your code and the app must be restored to a usable state while a fix is being made. Deploy hooks are used to notify others and outside systems that a push of the code has occurred.

Heroku can be configured to use custom error pages in case something goes wrong with your app. When releasing a new version of your app, you can configure a maintenance page to be displayed when users access your app during this planned downtime. Continuous integration tools, like Tddium for Ruby, can be integrated with Heroku so that tests are run and must pass before being deployed to your Heroku environments. The next chapter explores the wide variety of services for which add-ons can be used to supplement your app with useful functionality.

Working with Add-Ons

WHAT'S IN THIS CHAPTER?

➤ The Heroku add-on ecosystem

➤ Architectural considerations

➤ Exploring popular add-ons

➤ Installing add-ons

➤ Creating add-ons

When building applications, you may require tools, services, or components that are intrinsic to the architecture but not part of your source code. For example, data stores, e-mail services, and search capabilities are integral pieces of a successful application; however, providing these components may take significant time away from your core focus (building the application), assuming you already have the necessary skills to create, configure, and integrate such services for your application to consume. Enter add-ons.

This chapter explores the architectural considerations that you will need to make when selecting add-ons. There may be similar options for a desired technology, each with its own attributes to consider. We'll explore those attributes and expand on what makes some add-ons popular for applications on Heroku. Then we will demonstrate installing add-ons both from the Heroku Dashboard and the command-line interface (CLI). You will see how easily you select any service your application requires and add it to the environment. The add-on will attach itself to your application automatically and be available for use, just as the service would have been if you had created it yourself. Finally, we will explain the process of creating add-ons.

THE HEROKU ADD-ON ECOSYSTEM

Add-ons are provided via an ecosystem of developers and organizations whose focus is on a specific technology or a core set of technologies for building applications. Some are individuals with a passion for a single technology who bring their talents to bear via an add-on. Some even work within the Heroku organization and enjoy dreaming up new components that users can leverage for their applications. Others are organizations whose business model is predicated on the focus of a given technology, and still others are technology portfolio firms that have a deep understanding of the Heroku platform, the services developers might need, and the ability to provide the services in an easy-to-consume offering.

All services that have been curated to run within the Heroku add-on ecosystem enable you to install, upgrade, manage, and generally consume a large variety of common tools and components you may need for your apps. Most (though not all) providers offer a complimentary tier for evaluation or development purposes, with the ability to seamlessly scale your consumption to larger tiers. Other services may be purely complimentary if they don't rely on a third party or if their use is not based on storage or compute resources (things like scheduled tasks, or deploy hooks, and triggers). Bear in mind that some services have multiple options. This chapter will help inform any decisions you make when selecting add-on services.

You can browse the entire add-ons library from `http://addons.heroku.com`, as shown in Figure 6-1. This will give you an idea of the breadth of services available, the types of teams that provide the services, and the different tiers available for each service.

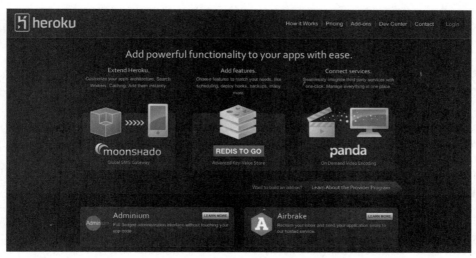

FIGURE 6-1

You can also get a complete list of all add-ons and their available packages from the command line:

```
$ heroku addons:list
```

> **NOTE** *If you are part of Heroku's beta program (*`https://beta.heroku.com/`
> `signup`*), you will see all beta status add-ons listed as well. Add-ons in the beta*
> *state typically are provided free of charge during that time; upon general avail-*
> *ability, service tiers and their associated pricing is announced. Some add-ons*
> *may incur a fee during beta (Heroku Postgres), while others may not have a fee*
> *even in general availability (deploy hooks). Also note that some Heroku curated*
> *add-ons may, over time, simply be rolled into the standard platform feature set.*
> *For example, tools such as custom error pages and release management were at*
> *one time provided only via an add-on, but now they are standard tools within*
> *Heroku. As the Heroku platform expands, expect to see other Heroku-provided*
> *add-ons rolled into the standard offering.*

ARCHITECTURAL CONSIDERATIONS

As mentioned elsewhere, the Heroku platform runs within the US-East region of Amazon Web Services (AWS). To minimize latency and maximize performance, most add-on providers also run their services from the same region. However, several providers (for example, Websolr) provision instances of their services in other AWS regions. Keep in mind, however, that doing so should be due to some requirement of the business or application. Most common reasons for this would be regulatory or compliance needs on the business side, and the need to be in closer proximity to other data (internal systems or other apps) on the technical side.

Equally important in relation to internal systems and architecture are the security and compliance standards to which your application must adhere. Whether you are addressing industry, regulatory, or internal standards, ensure that each add-on you select for your app satisfies your business requirements. Heroku cannot and does not verify the compliance posture of add-ons against each application, so be sure to vet each component carefully.

Strive for simplicity. Adding architectural components, while they may seem necessary, can add unnecessary complexity or degrade the performance/experience of your app. Be mindful of the services you include from the Heroku add-on ecosystem, ensuring that they help deliver a more robust user experience, rather than a diminished one.

EXPLORING POPULAR ADD-ONS

As we discussed in Chapter 2, "Architectural Considerations," you need to make several architectural decisions when building applications on Heroku. Many of these decisions (regarding data stores, caching mechanisms, search capabilities, etc.) directly impact which add-ons you select for your application. Although your budget should be a factor in your decisions, remember that most add-ons provide a free tier for development and evaluation purposes. If you later decide that the component is not optimal to your architecture, simply remove it and iterate on something else.

For example, when considering a component such as a data store, you have many available options. NoSQL data stores, including MongoDB, Couch, Redis, and Cassandra (to name a few), are covered in detail in Chapter 10. Even SQL-based options such as Heroku's Postgres, ClearDB, or Xeround can be considered. The point is that each has unique characteristics that make it better suited to specific use cases. Other add-ons, such as options for memcache, may behave almost (if not) identically; and the decision boils down to your experience with the provided service and available tiers or perhaps the recommendation of someone already using the add-on.

Ultimately, this myriad of options empowers Heroku users to create powerful, solution-driven applications. Many of the options make use of technologies that you, as an application/environment owner, may have previously implemented and maintained as part of your application stack. Now, with the technology integrated directly into your app environments as a service, all the headaches associated with creating such a service from scratch are eliminated. If, for example, you have ever tried to stand up a Solr search server on your own, you can appreciate the amount of work this saves you.

Most applications running on the Heroku platform leverage a set of popular add-ons that perform typical tasks or provide frequently called upon services. Although some add-ons are provided by third parties, many others, such as Heroku Postgres, Scheduler, Logging, and deploy hooks, are built by Heroku. The following sections review a few common categories and highlight some examples of each.

SQL-Based Data Stores

Part III of this book provides details about data stores. For the purposes of this section, a brief overview will give you an idea of the options available. Earlier in the chapter, you were introduced to Heroku Postgres as a data store option, so we'll start there. Postgres is one of the last true open-source SQL-based databases. Heroku curates its Postgres Service directly from the PostgreSQL Project source code, so if you decide to run Postgres locally (or via any other provider), you'll have a consistent experience across all deployments, regardless of where the databases reside.

If MySQL is more your flavor, both ClearDB and Xeround provide excellent options via the Heroku add-ons library. Be sure to note the different sizing mechanism each uses. Whereas ClearDB measures its DBs by data volume on disk and concurrent connections, Xeround scales its DBs based on throughput, connection, and support requirements.

Amazon Relational Database Service (Amazon RDS) is another option you can choose if running your database in the Heroku universe is not possible or you are already invested in getting your MySQL database running on AWS directly. The Heroku RDS add-on enables you to connect your Heroku app directly to a running MySQL database on Amazon RDS.

NoSQL-Based Data Stores

Using NoSQL-based data stores for unstructured or read-heavy data sets has become commonplace in most modern web application and services architectures. As described in the following sections, the Heroku add-ons library provides solutions for almost all of the common NoSQL options.

MongoDB

The Heroku add-ons library provides two MongoDB options: MongoHQ and MongoLab.

Both add-ons provide a free tier to get started, as well as 24×7 support, logging, monitoring, backup tools, and complete usability of the MongoDB technology. They differ mainly in tiering and pricing. MongoHQ's free tier includes 16MB of storage, whereas MongoLab's free tier provides 240MB. From there, the tiers differ in terms of additional steps up in size and price. MongoHQ also lists master/slave replica sets as part of its offering, although MongoLab may be able to provide something similar in a custom format via its relationship with Heroku.

CouchDB

Cloudant is the CouchDB provider within the Heroku add-ons library. As with the MongoDB offerings, Cloudant includes a completely free option to get started. We'll spend a fair amount of time in Part III comparing the various NoSQL data stores (and other options), but at a high level most users will choose CouchDB over MongoDB when their data set and queries don't often change and performance is critical. CouchDB is generally preferred because it can leverage HTTP caching, versus in-memory caching for Mongo DB, and being closer to the browser typically means faster response times.

Redis

Redis is another popular NoSQL key/value data store option available via the Heroku add-ons library. As of this printing, several Redis providers are available within the Heroku add-ons ecosystem. If you are considering Redis as a data store for you apps, make sure that you evaluate each to determine which product is most appropriate for your app.

Cassandra

Originally built by Facebook to power its Inbox Search functionality, the underlying source code on which Cassandra is based was later turned into an Apache Software Foundation project and open sourced. Now the Cassandra service is available as a public beta offering in the Heroku add-ons library, from `Cassandra.io`.

Neo4j

Neo4j is a cool NoSQL technology that enables you to easily persist data — hence, its popular use for building social networks and services that require a lot of querying and modeling. Neo4j is a *graph database* that enables you to create a representation of an entity (person), and then create relationships between them to model a graphical representation of your data. This becomes compelling in the social web as each person's network can be stored, queried, and visualized as a "graph." We'll explore the ramifications of this in both Chapter 10, "Using Third-Party Data Stores for Your Heroku Applications," and Chapter 16, "Building Social Applications with Heroku." As of this book's writing, Neo4j is in beta status, but it's one of the more promising new NoSQL options available.

Search

The capability to search in an application is one of the most rudimentary requirements of common web application architectures. However, rather than employ additional tools or services to adequately provide this, you can choose from among several options in the Heroku add-ons library. Many architects and developers use one of these as their go-to option, such as a Lucene-based Solr or the slightly newer and nearly as popular Sphinx. The following sections describe several of the available options.

Solr

WebSolr, available from the Heroku add-ons library, provides a search service powered by Solr, the Apache Lucene project's Java-based search engine library. However, just because it is Java does npt mean it cannot work for an application written in another language. It can do that and much more. WebSolr has service plans that scale from two managed indexes (250,000 documents) to 80 indexes (more than 25 million documents). Need more than that? The WebSolr team has been able to build solutions for more than that via the Heroku ecosystem as well. If your business requires something above and beyond the standard offering, contact the good folks at Heroku and let them help you architect a solution with the WebSolr team.

Sphinx

Flying Sphinx is the provider of choice if Sphinx, the open-source search engine, is your preferred option. If you're looking for a lightweight yet powerful search alternative that doesn't require all the features and tools that Solr makes available, take a serious look at Sphinx and Flying Sphinx.

IndexTank

IndexTank was provided as its own service via the Heroku add-ons library. In late 2011, LinkedIn acquired the firm to help bolster the product's search capability and stated its commitment to open sourcing the project when the time was right. As promised, in 2012, IndexTank was open sourced under the Apache 2.0 license. Now, rather than having to curate your own IndexTank instance, Searchify provides it for you via the Heroku add-ons library.

ElasticSearch

ElasticSearch is based on Compass, which itself is built on top of Apache Lucene. It is developed in Java. The idea was to create a RESTful, distributed search tool that was better suited to polyglot programming. The success of ElasticSearch as a core technology has resulted in three separate providers within the Heroku add-on ecosystem: Found, Bonsai, and SearchBox. These are all viable options if leveraging ElasticSearch is your preferred approach.

Logging and Monitoring

Although building your application and attaching core services are the key focus for any application development effort, the importance of effective tools to log, monitor, and tune their performance cannot be underscored enough. Unfortunately, the overhead of properly implementing tools such as these often prevents an organization from putting anything more than rudimentary solutions in place. You can find detailed information about the end-to-end process of managing apps and environments in Chapter 7, "Managing, Monitoring, and Scaling Your Heroku Applications." This section describes some recommended tools in the Heroku add-on ecosystem to make these tasks easier.

Logging

Logs may be one of the least sexy parts of the application architecture and environment, but in order to identify, understand, and fix the root cause of an issue, logs are typically the first place you look. You might recall from Chapter 3, "Porting Your Applications to Heroku," which explored logging on Heroku, the availability of Logplex to provide real-time information about your application's events. Although it provides an unparalleled level of granularity in terms of gaining visibility into your apps, Logplex does not provide any intelligence, introspection, or analysis against the continual streams of data your app will generate on Heroku.

Several log management providers are worth a look:

➤ **Loggly:** Founded by former Splunk employees, Loggly offers several tiers of service based on log volume per day and retention period.

➤ **LogEntries:** This service takes an interesting approach by providing unlimited storage and charging based on data you actually need/want to index or store for usage.

➤ **Papertrail:** This service provides a very clean, lightweight way to manage, aggregate, search, and analyze all Heroku log data.

Monitoring

Knowing that an app is alive, kicking, and behaving as expected provides application owners with serious peace of mind. The tools that provide heartbeat and status information about a running app may not be the most complex, but they are among the most important. You can expose exception tracking and downtime notifications with a potential combination of a few recommended tools:

➤ **Exceptional:** This is the standard for exception tracking in your app when deployed to the Heroku platform.

➤ **Sentry:** This tool focuses on exception tracking and error logging for Python, PHP, Node.js, and Java.

➤ **Ranger:** This very lightweight monitoring tool reports on any HTTP status other than 200.

➤ **StillAlive:** This tool enables you to confirm that your app is working properly by monitoring it via custom recipes that mimic real user behavior.

> **NOTE** *These add-ons are highlighted as recommended options for deep understanding of your apps; none are required for running your apps.*

INSTALLING ADD-ONS

You can install add-ons in one of two ways: via the Heroku Dashboard or via the CLI. The following sections demonstrate how to install Heroku Postgres, the add-on most commonly leveraged by applications.

To provide a little background, Heroku Postgres is a fully curated and managed PostgreSQL (Postgres) database service. It is one of the most commonly used open-source SQL databases and can be run locally by developers or on large-scale production grade systems. We'll explore Heroku Postgres in greater detail later in this book, but for now it will serve as an example add-on.

Installing Add-Ons from the Heroku Dashboard

To install an add on (here, Heroku Postgres) from the Heroku Dashboard, perform the following steps:

1. From your application's main page within the Heroku Dashboard (see Figure 6-2), click the "Get Add-ons" button.

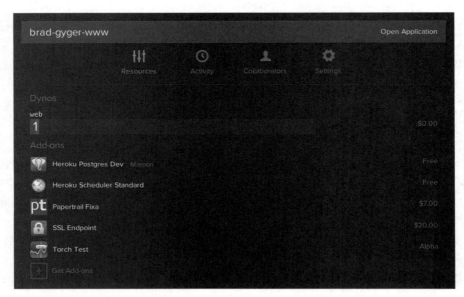

FIGURE 6-2

2. From the main Add-ons dialog that appears, navigate to the Heroku Postgres add-on and click Learn More (see Figure 6-3).

FIGURE 6-3

3. As shown in Figure 6-4, the add-on's detail page displays several tiers of service available for installation and use. Select the appropriate tier and click Add.

FIGURE 6-4

4. The confirmation screen shown in Figure 6-5 will then appear. Note that the application you started from is auto-selected; however, you can apply the add-on to a different app. Click the Install button below the app name to begin installation.

Following installation, you will be able to see the new app in the list of installed apps on the Heroku Dashboard, as shown in Figure 6-6.

FIGURE 6-5

FIGURE 6-6

5. Clicking directly on the add-on's name from Heroku Dashboard will provide you with the add-on's main console — in this case, Heroku Postgres (see Figure 6-7), this includes all management capabilities for the add-on itself.

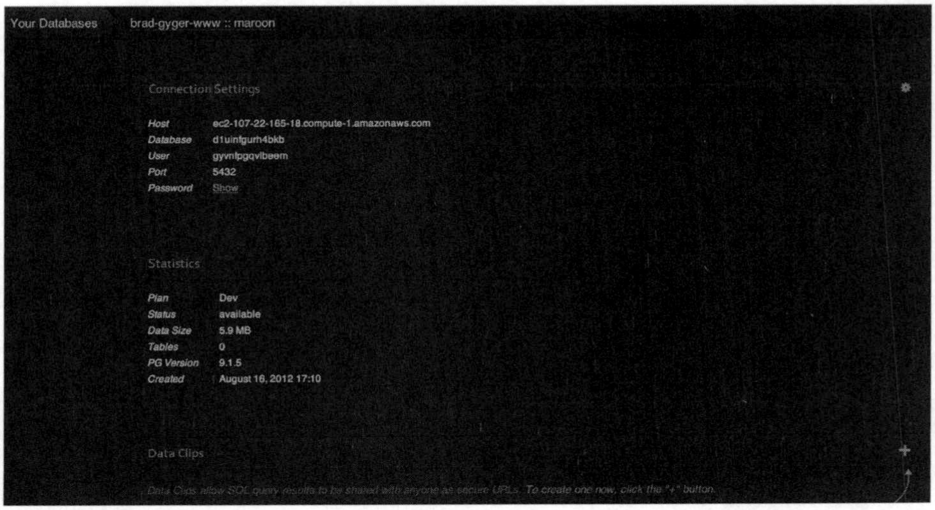

FIGURE 6-7

Congratulations, you've successfully added a new add-on service to your application! In the next section you will achieve the same goal from the CLI.

Installing Add-Ons from the Command-Line Interface

Remember that everything you are able to do from the Heroku Dashboard can also be done via the CLI, and then some! Recall that you can view the complete list of add-ons at any time with the following command:

```
$ heroku addons:list
```

This command will return a list of the add-ons currently installed:

```
$ heroku addons --app <appname>
```

The app flag is optional if you're within the working directory structure of the target application.

To install an add-on, use the following command. (Again, if you are already in the working directory, the app flag is optional.)

```
$ heroku addons:add <addon_name:tier> --app <appname>
```

For example, the following command installs the add-on used in the example from the preceding section:

```
$ heroku addons:add heroku-postgresql:fugu
```

This simply adds a Heroku Postgres database, of size "Fugu." Again, we'll dive deeper into the details of Heroku Postgres in Part III. For now, just be aware that "Fugu" is simply a tier that's available for usage, and we're creating it just as we might for any other addon_name:tier we have added instead.

```
Adding heroku-postgresql:fugu to brad-gyger-www... done, v45 ($400/mo)
Attached as HEROKU_POSTGRESQL_PINK
The database should be available in 3-5 minutes
Use 'heroku pg:wait' to track status
Use 'heroku add-ons:docs heroku-postgresql:fugu' to view documentation
```

To verify the installation, use this command:

```
$ heroku addons
=== brad-gyger-www Configured Add-ons
heroku-postgresql:fugu    HEROKU_POSTGRESQL_PINK
newrelic:standard
torch:test
```

To remove an add-on, use this command:

```
$ heroku addons:remove <addon_name> (optional) --confirm <app_name>
```

For example, the following command removes the Heroku Postgres add-on installed earlier:

```
$ heroku add-ons:remove HEROKU_POSTGRESQL_PINK --confirm brad-gyger-www
Removing HEROKU_POSTGRESQL_PINK from brad-gyger-www... done, v46 ($400/mo)
```

If you would like to change the service tier of your add-on, you may upgrade or downgrade, respectively, at any time with the following commands:

```
heroku add-ons:upgrade <addon_name:tier>
heroku add-ons:downgrade <addon_name:tier>
```

As an example, if you want to have your application send e-mail, you can leverage SendGrid, a service made available as a Heroku add-on. When getting started, you can simply add the add-on as follows:

```
$ heroku addons:add sendgrid
Adding sendgrid on brad-gyger-www... done, v74 (free)
Use 'heroku addons:docs sendgrid' to view documentation.
```

Then, if your app grows and you need to send more e-mail, you can upgrade at any time:

```
$ heroku addons:upgrade sendgrid:bronze
Upgrading to sendgrid:bronze on brad-gyger-www... done, v74 ($9.95/mo)
You have successfully upgraded or downgraded your plan
Use 'heroku addons:docs sendgrid:bronze' to view documentation.
```

Conversely, if you ever find that you need less of any resources, you can just as easily downgrade:

```
$ heroku addons:downgrade sendgrid:starter
Downgrading to sendgrid:starter on brad-gyger-www... done, v74 (free)
You have successfully upgraded or downgraded your plan
Use 'heroku addons:docs sendgrid:starter' to view documentation.
```

> **WARNING** *Most add-ons (like Sendgrid) enable you to provision a single instance per application, and then upgrade or downgrade as needed. Heroku Postgres allows you to provision multiple instances (because many applications may need more than one database instance). Be careful when adding, removing, or modifying these sorts of add-ons, as usage costs may change significantly.*

This section provides a brief primer on how to create add-ons. Anyone with the desire to create services for the Heroku platform, the expertise to deliver the service, and an understanding of the Heroku add-on provider APIs can participate. Although the experience of building, integrating, and monetizing a service via the Heroku add-on ecosystem warrants a book of its own, for the purposes of this chapter we'll cover the basic process to create a simple add-on.

CREATING ADD-ONS

To set the stage, the idea behind building an add-on within Heroku is that you already have (or will build) a service for the web development community to consume via the Heroku ecosystem. As such, this section assumes several things:

➤ That you already have created, or will create, a component to provide "as-a-service."

➤ The service is deployed in the same AWS region (US-East) as the Heroku platform.

➤ The entire service can be fully managed and manipulated using REST APIs.

➤ The service can be metered according to an on-demand, pay-for-what-you-use model.

Before following the steps to create an add-on and connect it to Heroku for exposure to end users, make sure that you familiarize yourself with the Add-on Provider Program, along with all the supporting materials and documentation, by visiting `https://addons.heroku.com/provider`.

When you are ready to proceed, sign on as a provider via the preceding link and reach out to Heroku to get listed as a provider.

Not covered in this section (or this book, for that matter) are commercial aspects of the Add-on Provider Program. Any service tiers and associated pricing should be discussed with Heroku directly as part of the process of making the add-on available within the add-ons library. To take the first step in making your add-on commercially available, contact the the Heroku add-ons team, at `addons@heroku.com`.

Our focus here is purely on the technical aspects of connecting your service to Heroku via API calls. This is done via a custom Ruby gem, called *Kensa*, created by the Heroku add-ons team.

Once installed, the Kensa gem (see `http://rubygems.org/gems/kensa`) provides a CLI to test services and build manifests, and offers an easy way to develop and test your service before launching within the Heroku ecosystem.

You need to first decide whether you want to tie a standalone, custom app to Heroku to provide the service via HTTP or leverage one of Heroku's add-on template apps. If you have already built an app and an API that can interact with Heroku, many of the first steps described below will not apply to your service. If you are not sure where to begin, start with a template app, as described below, and proceed from there.

Now let's walk through the process of using the Heroku Kensa gem to create, deploy, and manage an add-on. Note that this approach requires Ruby to be installed locally, with the capability to execute binary gems.

The first step is to run `kensa create`. This will create your template application, which ultimately enables the service to interact with the Heroku platform. From the command prompt, enter the following command:

```
$ kensa create <addon_name> --template <template-type>
```

Currently, you can specify either a Sinatra, Node.js, or Clojure template, as shown in the following example:

```
$ kensa create my-awesome-addon --template sinatra
git clone git://github.com/heroku/kensa-create-sinatra my-awesome-addon
Cloning into 'my-awesome-addon'...
remote: Counting objects: 120, done.
remote: Compressing objects: 100% (49/49), done.
remote: Total 120 (delta 63), reused 117 (delta 60)
Receiving objects: 100% (120/120), 14.12 KiB, done.
Resolving deltas: 100% (63/63), done.
Created my-awesome-addon from sinatra template
Initialized new addon manifest in addon-manifest.json
Initialized new .env file for foreman
```

Now that you've created a new template add-on, note that most of the command-line outputs are standard git and Heroku responses. The only totally new concepts are the add-on manifest and the creation of the `.env` file to run Foreman locally. The manifest file is a JSON document that describes how your service and Heroku will interact and be tested via the Kensa gem. Foreman enables you to run the add-on application locally and to connect a consuming app to your provided service as a test bed. Following is a brief example of the manifest:

```
#my-awesome-addon
{
  "id": "myaddon",
  "api": {
    "config_vars": [ "MYADDON_URL" ],
    "password": "hjbgG5bE84L1xRIt",
    "sso_salt": "ZVF5KiPP7pX8SmVL",
    "production": {
      "base_url": "https://yourapp.com/heroku/resources",
      "sso_url": "https://yourapp.com/sso/login"
    },
    "test": {
      "base_url": "http://localhost:5000/heroku/resources",
      "sso_url": "http://localhost:5000/sso/login"
    }
  }
}
```

Now install Foreman in your working template app directory and start an instance to test against:

```
$ gem install foreman
...
$ bundle install
...
$ foreman start
09:14:03 web.1  |  started with pid 81992
09:14:04 web.1  |  >> Using rack adapter
```

```
09:14:04 web.1  |  >> Thin web server (v1.2.11 codename Bat-Shit Crazy)
09:14:04 web.1  |  >> Maximum connections set to 1024
09:14:04 web.1  |  >> Listening on 0.0.0.0:5000, CTRL+C to stop
```

At this point you have a local version of your add-on running on port 5000. Next, you'll want to test your add-on using the Kensa gem. First, run a test provision:

```
$ kensa test provision

Testing manifest id key
  Check if exists [PASS]
  Check is a string [PASS]
  Check is not blank [PASS]

Testing manifest api key
  Check if exists [PASS]
  Check is a hash [PASS]
  Check contains password [PASS]
  Check contains test url [PASS]
  Check contains production url [PASS]
  Check production url uses SSL [PASS]
  Check sso url uses SSL [PASS]
  Check contains config_vars array [PASS]
  Check containst at least one config var [PASS]
  Check all config vars are uppercase strings [PASS]
  Check all config vars are prefixed with the addon id [PASS]
  Check deprecated fields [PASS]

done.


Testing POST /heroku/resources
  Check response [PASS]
  Check valid JSON [PASS]
  Check authentication [PASS]

Testing response
  Check contains an id [PASS] (id 1)

Testing config data
  Check is a hash [PASS]
  Check all config keys were previously defined in the manifest [PASS]
  Check all keys in the manifest are present [PASS]
  Check all config values are strings [PASS]
  Check URL configs vars [PASS]

done.
```

Next, you can run a simple deprovision of the same resource, pulling the id that was assigned from the previous command:

```
$ kensa test deprovision 1
```

This should return much the same output as earlier, but in this case you have mimicked removing the add-on (via either the CLI or the UI) as a user. Use the following command to initiate a complete end-to-end test run:

```
$ kensa test all
```

This will run through an entire set of requests that are carried out from the add-on (specifically, provision, change plans, and deprovision). You can also mimic a single sign-on (SSO) or manifest change, as follows:

```
$ kensa test sso <id>
$ kensa test manifest
```

The manifest validation is run automatically on all other tests, as well. This is *not* an extra step that you need to perform on your own. During each of these commands, you can also see Foreman in action. From your original terminal session, you should see the add-on instance serving requests and rendering responses. A few lines of sample output look similar to the following:

```
09:22:03 web.1  | request body:
09:22:03 web.1  | "plan"=>"foo", "heroku_id"=>app4614@kensa.heroku.com
09:22:03 web.1  | params: {"id"=>"1"}
```

That's all it takes to create an add-on that will connect your service to the Heroku user community. Now you simply need to modify the add-on-manifest.json and any.env files for your requirements. The .env files will be any configuration files that you need to provision your service. The manifest file will be the configuration file that describes how your service and Heroku will interact. As soon as you run kensa init, your manifest template will be created. Here's a sample:

```
$ kensa init
Initialized new addon manifest in addon-manifest.json

$ cat addon-manifest.json
{
  "id": "myaddon",
  "api": {
    "config_vars": [ "MYADDON_URL" ],
    "password": "xbuFztJM6paCYAqN",
    "sso_salt": "7jctJG8eSk1BNko9",
    "production": {
      "base_url": "https://yourapp.com/heroku/resources",
      "sso_url": "https://yourapp.com/sso/login"
    },
    "test": {
      "base_url": "http://localhost:4567/heroku/resources",
      "sso_url": "http://localhost:4567/sso/login"
    }
  }
}
```

Once these are defined, you can finish building your app and prepare it for distribution, at which point it will be ready for prime time via the Heroku add-on ecosystem.

SUMMARY

In this chapter you learned the nuts and bolts of add-ons, including the ecosystem in which they exist and the rationale behind their use. We started out by providing a brief primer into what an add-on is. Remember that these are fully curated services meant to eliminate the need to ever provision these types of resources (databases, monitoring, etc.) on your own ever again. Then we explored a few types of add-ons and popular services. Bear in mind that each application is different, as are the requirements, so while it's always good to have an understanding of what is available, make sure the service fits your needs. We then ran through the process of installing, upgrading/downgrading, and managing your add-ons. The unparalleled ease with which you can manage these services is a huge win when developing your apps. We then provided an introduction to creating add-ons. Although most users will never venture into this realm, it's important to understand the underpinnings of add-ons and recognize that anyone can curate an add-on for Heroku. In Chapter 7, you'll see a good portion of these add-ons in action as we dig into the process of managing, monitoring, and scaling your Heroku apps.

Managing, Monitoring, and Scaling Your Heroku Applications

WHAT'S IN THIS CHAPTER?

➤ Adding custom domains

➤ Viewing logs and associated tools

➤ Managing and tuning performance

➤ Leveraging the Heroku API

➤ Administration options

Your apps are now alive and well on the Heroku platform. All your git repos are configured; your deploys are happening at a lightning pace; and you are ready for prime time! In order to do that, however, you need to ensure that you have all the right processes and tools to go live, iterate, and scale under normal production and peak loads. Now that you have explored how to deploy apps, manage code and releases for each deploy, and attach additional services, this chapter covers how to apply these concepts to your apps at scale.

ADDING CUSTOM DOMAINS

One of the first things any production web app requires is a custom, or vanity, domain. You've already been exposed to the Heroku subdomains that are assigned as part of the deployment process (either `haiku-name-##.herokuapp.com` or `mycoolapp.heroku.com`). However, most apps will require either a custom, fully qualified domain (`www.mycompanyapp.com`) or subdomain (`coolapp1.mycompany.com`). You can easily add or remove domains from the

Heroku Dashboard. Simply enter into the application's detail view and click SettingsZ. Scroll down to the Domains section and enter in your custom domain as shown in Figure 7-1.

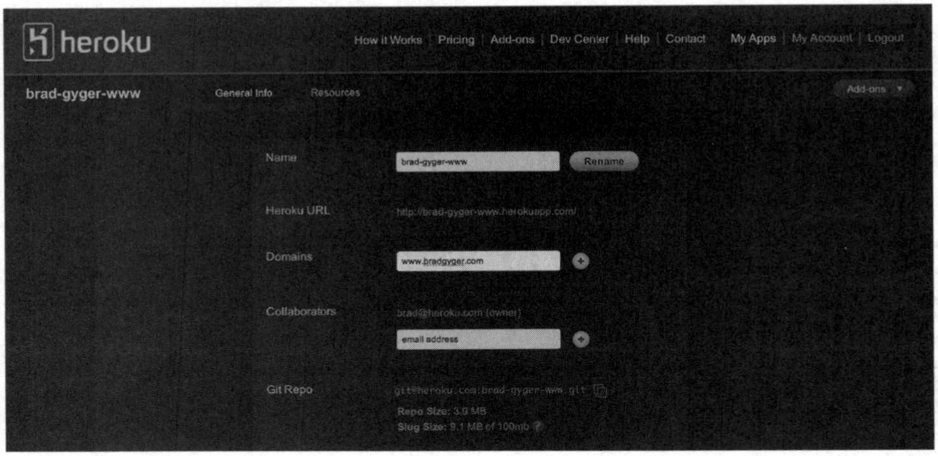

FIGURE 7-1

You can also add and remove domains via the command line, as follows:

```
heroku domains:add www.mycompanyapp.com
heroku domains:remove www.mycompanyapp.com
```

> **NOTE** *To immediately clear all domains at once, use the following command:*
>
> ```
> heroku domains:clear
> ```
>
> *However, be careful with this command, as using this can be dangerous with multiple in-use domains pointing to the same Heroku app.*

Adding a domain to your app gets you only halfway there. You also must update your Domain Name Service (DNS) to point to the app running on Heroku, now listed with your Heroku app. There are several ways to do this. You can either leverage your existing DNS provider or toolset or you can go to the Heroku Add-ons library and leverage a service such as Dyn or Zerigo DNS. The following example highlights Zerigo, both from the Heroku Dashboard and via the command line.

First, install the add-on, as follows:

```
heroku addons:add zerigo_dns:tier1
```

Alternately, you can use the Heroku Dashboard with the add-ons console, as shown in Figure 7-2, to enable Zerigo DNS. Once again, starting in the application's detail page, within the Resources view, navigate to the add-ons section towards the bottom and click the Get Add-ons button. Once you're in the add-ons menu, navigate to Zerigo and select the appropriate tier for your needs. Click Add, confirm the application name and service tier, and then click Install.

FIGURE 7-2

After you add your domains, they will be visible within the Settings tab for your application's detail page. You will need to configure the DNS add-on, so note the servers you'll need to point your registrar toward. The final step is to visit your registrar (perhaps something like GoDaddy.com or similar) and point that service to the following servers:

➤ a.ns.zerigo.net

➤ b.ns.zerigo.net

➤ c.ns.zerigo.net

➤ d.ns.zerigo.net

➤ e.ns.zerigo.net

This will tell your registrar service to send traffic for your domain name to the application running on Heroku. Each domain registrar will have a slightly different process to add these entries to their service. Consult their documentation to ensure correctness. Once completed you should now be able to visit your custom domains, along with your happy users!

> **NOTE** *Entering a new domain for your app in Heroku will actually create two separate entries: a canonical name (CNAME) to* www.mydomain.com *from* myapp.heroku.com *and a permanent 302 redirect from* mydomain.com *to* http://www.mydomain.com. *Heroku does not recommend using bare domains (those without* www.*), as doing so does not take full advantage of Heroku's load-balancing services.*

VIEWING LOGS AND ASSOCIATED TOOLS

Logging is one of the most underrated components of any app. When you want to benchmark performance, understand user heuristics, or debug issues, logs are often the first place you look for introspection. Unfortunately, logging every aspect of a system properly takes significant time and effort in order to implement the level of visibility necessary. Thankfully, Heroku provides a service, called *Logplex*, that addresses this. Logplex is provided within the platform, and it logs every piece of the architecture — from the inbound load balancer all the way back to any data store you hit. Each piece is treated as a constant stream of data that can be viewed in aggregate or as separate feeds. These feeds can then be routed to your favorite log-management solution, such as Splunk or one of the Heroku add-on providers. We'll highlight one (Papertrail) later in this section.

First, let's dive into the Heroku logging system itself. From the Heroku command line, either working within an app directory or by flagging an app, you can see the Heroku log stream by running the following command:

```
$ heroku logs
```

For example:

```
$ heroku logs –app brad-gyger-www
```

This will provide a large output of data, a small snippet of which might look similar to the following:

```
2012-08-31T19:43:21+00:00 heroku[router]: GET www.bradgyger.com/atom.xml dyno=web.1
queue=0 wait=0ms service=6ms status=200 bytes=3983
2012-08-31T19:43:21+00:00 heroku[nginx]: 74.125.19.210 - - [31/Aug/2012:19:43:21 +0000]
"GET /atom.xml HTTP/1.1" 200 1208 "-" "Feedfetcher-Google;
(+http://www.google.com/feedfetcher.html; feed-id=9383651251844576295)"
www.bradgyger.com
```

While the output looks a bit cryptic at first, on closer inspection it's no different from most system or application log outputs, and it is relatively human readable. The first entry states that an inbound GET request hit the Heroku routing layer. The web.1 dyno served the request, with no additional users waiting in the queue. (And those additional users, in turn, didn't wait any extra time for their request to complete.) Serving the response took six milliseconds (or .006 seconds), with status=200 indicating that a successful HTTP request was completed, serving up 3,983 bytes. The second entry provides a deeper level of detail for the same request. Routing passed the request to the running web server (in this case, nginx). Also shown is the source IP, in this case a Google IP address for Feedfetcher; pulling the atom.xml file for www.bradgyger.com; and that the request was served successfully.

Note another line of output that's worth examining:

```
2012-08-09T21:40:23+00:00 app[postgres]: [5-1] postgres [PINK] NOTICE: pg_stop_backup
complete, all required WAL segments have been archived
```

In this log entry you can see that the Heroku platform, even without any user or application requests, has completed a backup and synchronized all the data from the Postgres database service. It is comforting to know that even if the application is not serving requests, the Heroku platform is still hard at work and, within the context of this chapter, still actively logging entries to Logplex.

Now that you have an understanding of Logplex and the level of visibility it provides, how do you harness the power of the data? For that you can leverage the Heroku Add-ons library again. Papertrail is a wonderful solution for cloud-based log management when leveraged alongside Heroku Logplex.

To install the Papertrail add-on via the command line, run the following command, with --app flag required only when working outside the application directory structure:

```
$ heroku addons:add papertrail:fixa <--app myapp>
```

You can also install the Papertrail add-on via the Heroku Dashboard, as shown in Figures 7-3 and 7-4. Starting from your application's detail page, scroll down within the Resources tab to find the add-ons section and select Get Add-ons." Once you are viewing the add-ons library, navigate down to Papertrail and click Learn More. Select the tier that is appropriate for your logging needs, which is typically just the storage requirements. Click Add and confirm the application and tier. If everything looks good, click Install to add the service to your application.

FIGURE 7-3

FIGURE 7-4

To start using Papertrail, click on it within the Add-ons section of the Resources page for your application. Once Papertrail's dashboard loads, navigating its user interface, shown in Figure 7-5, is fairly straightforward:

➤ **Dashboard:** This provides a quick overview of events, including pre-defined searches, as well as available archives, transfer usage, and account settings.

➤ **Events:** This is the first page you see upon opening the tool. It displays your log stream in a similar fashion to output from the `heroku logs` command. It also provides a standard text search for any specific term, code, or string that you enter. These searches can also be saved for later use.

➤ **Account:** This link provides the typical administration view you'll want to use for data transfer, retention, and archiving.

➤ **Help:** This link provides access to a QuickStart guide, various command-line and usability tools, and documentation. It also enables you to get direct support from the Papertrail team.

➤ **Profile:** This link allows you to make small tweaks to your account, such as adding your name and preferred time zone, as well as to access your API token should you require it for other services.

FIGURE 7-5

Now let's walk through a quick example scenario to demonstrate how to use Papertrail effectively. Users receiving a 404 error can be the bane of any application owner's existence. However, with the right visibility, you can solve that problem quickly. Within the Papertrail Events, you can search for any requests that include `status=404` (refer to Figure 7-5). You can then save that search and refer to it at any point.

To provide an even greater level of interaction with these log entries, you can create various alerts to provide notification via several different mechanisms. Monitoring, alerting, and notification solutions, such as Boundary, Campfire, Emails, GeckoBoard, HipChat, Librato, PagerDuty, and Webhooks, can all be configured to receive an alert as soon as a new log entry meets the criteria you define — very powerful stuff, indeed.

To do this, within the search window at the bottom of the Events tab, enter your search criteria and click the Save & Setup an Alert button in the bottom search bar, as shown in Figure 7-6. You will enter the Alert detail page (see Figure 7-7). Select the alert option you prefer, complete the details required, and click Update.

FIGURE 7-6

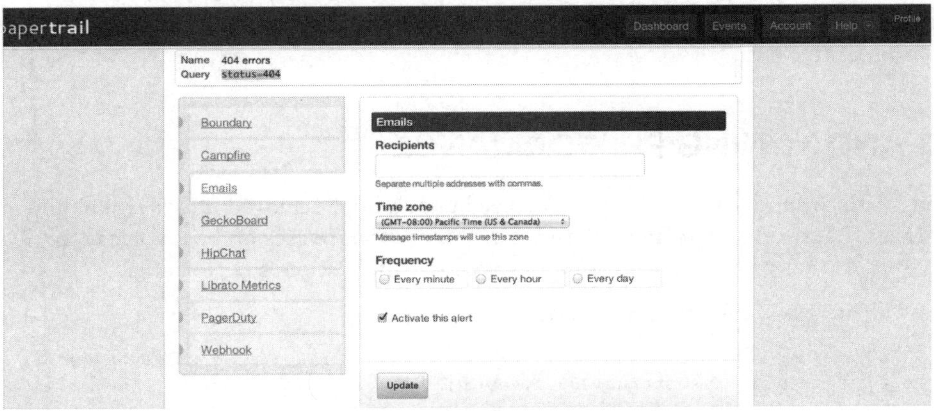

FIGURE 7-7

Once the alert is in place, you'll receive notifications at the interval specified. Figure 7-8 shows a sample e-mail you should receive.

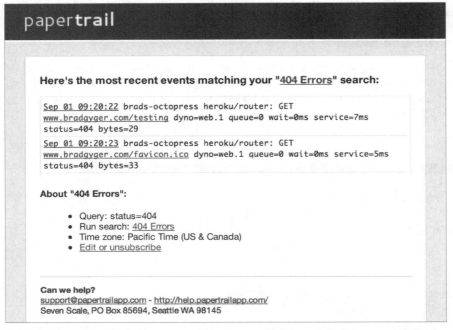

FIGURE 7-8

Now that you understand the Heroku Logplex and how to harness its vast amount of data, tying it to powerful management tools like Papertrail, you can gain visibility into your apps like never before. The next step is to parlay that visibility into improvements in your application, as discussed in the next section.

MANAGING AND TUNING PERFORMANCE

Following along with the application life cycle: You've built an app, deployed it to Heroku, and identified key areas that need refactoring and tuning. This section focuses on how you can apply the data you have to tools that provide insight into how well the application is performing.

To begin, consider the following log snippet shown earlier:

```
2012-08-31T19:43:21+00:00 heroku[router]: GET www.bradgyger.com/atom.xml dyno=web.1
queue=0 wait=0ms service=6ms status=200 bytes=3983
```

This entry alone provides a fair amount of insight into the performance of the application:

➤ `queue`: How many users are waiting

➤ `wait`: How long they waited until their request was served

➤ `service`: How long it took to complete the request

➤ `status`: The HTTP exit code

➤ `bytes`: Size of the response

The first two metrics can provide a quick way to assess the performance of your application. Are users waiting for something to happen? If so, for how long? Although you can apply a quick-and-dirty fix to this issue by increasing your application dynos (as described in the next section), it may only provide temporary relief; or, worse, it might move the bottleneck to a more critical or already strained part of the application architecture. What you really need is deep introspection into the application itself, to determine the root cause and refactor any issues that you find.

Performance Management with New Relic

New Relic is the solution we'll highlight for conducting deep introspection and analysis of your application's performance. New Relic is a cloud-based application performance management (APM) solution for most open languages and frameworks, as well as databases. It can provide visibility into your application's performance characteristics down to the SQL query level. Two options are available via the Heroku add-ons library:

➤ **Standard:** Provides deep introspection into application performance, health, and user satisfaction, with the ability to examine both application- and database-level calls. The Standard tier provides 8 days of data retention.

➤ **Professional:** Provides everything that comes with Standard plus the ability to do page-by-page analysis of your app, as well as optimization data for scaling, forecasting, capacity planning and SLA deliveries along with proactive alerting. The Professional tier provides 90 days of data retention.

New Relic is available via the Heroku Add-ons library (`https://addons.heroku.com/newrelic`) and can be installed and configured in a few brief steps:

1. Install the add-on via the command line (as follows, with the `--app` flag required only if you're working outside the app's directory structure) or by using the Heroku Dashboard (see Figure 7-9):

```
$ heroku addons:add newrelic:professional < --app myapp >
```

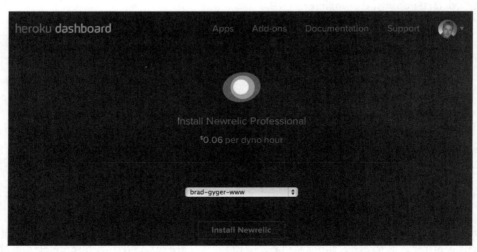

FIGURE 7-9

2. Configure your application with the New Relic libraries. The process varies according to your app's language. The Heroku DevCenter (`https://devcenter.heroku.com/articles/newrelic`) provides an excellent tutorial on the appropriate installation paths for each language.

3. Let some data populate in the tool for a few hours, with traffic (real or test) hitting your application. Alternately, apply some request or load tests against your app.

As soon as you have data available in New Relic, you can log into the Heroku Dashboard and start to look around. Figure 7-10 shows New Relic's initial screen when you open it. It contains three main sections:

➤ **Average response time, broken down by tier (ms):** This section highlights how long, at any point in time, it takes your application to respond to a request, and where in the application stack (core app, database, web external[API], etc.) the time is actively being spent. Average response time is a pretty simple way to assess application performance. If your application takes more than 500ms to complete, then segmenting or offloading work to queues or background processes usually will help. Any request that takes longer than 30 seconds to send its first byte of data will timeout on Heroku. Once the initial byte is sent, timeouts occur after 55 seconds of zero bytes sent.

➤ **Apdex score:** Here you will see your application's Application Performance Index (Apdex). Apdex is an open software industry standard developed to measure application performance in terms of user satisfaction. The idea is that a user is either satisfied (request succeeds) or not satisfied (request fails or performs poorly). In New Relic terms, this is translated into three scores: Satisfied (request served optimally), Tolerated (served sub-optimally) or Frustrated (not served or poorly served).

➤ **Throughput (rpm):** This section demonstrates how many requests per minute (RPM) your application is handling at any given time. For single-threaded languages, such as Ruby or Python, keep in mind that a dyno on Heroku can handle only one request at a time. Therefore, if a request is actively using a dyno, Heroku will block other requests from using that dyno until it completes.

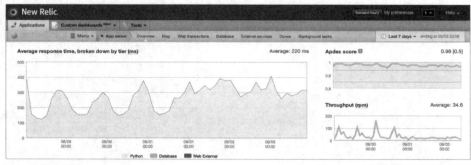

FIGURE 7-10

Now let's dig deeper into the main window and see what information can be extracted. When you click into the "Average response time..." graph, you are presented with more details about the requests your application is handling. Figure 7-11 shows an example of transactions that had the most impact on the system. To display the requests based on different criteria, select an option from the "Sort by" drop-down, shown in Figure 7-12.

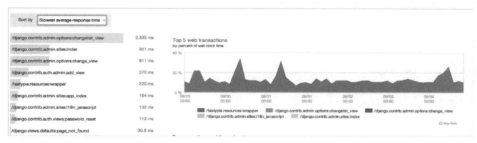

FIGURE 7-11

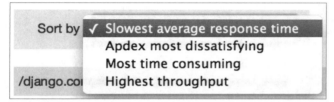

FIGURE 7-12

For the purposes of performance tuning, let's sort the output by requests with the slowest average response time. By Heroku standards, only a few of the slowest requests are worrisome, taking longer than 500ms to complete. Figure 7-13 provides details about the slowest request, including average response, throughput, and Apdex for this particular request.

FIGURE 7-13

Note a few details about this graph. First, this request is not called very frequently, so it may not require any optimization. Second, because it's called infrequently, an optimization such as caching (which we touched on in Chapter 3 and will revisit throughout Part IV) might not help, which may also explain the consistently slow response time. You can get a different view of the request profile by clicking the "Performance breakdown" tab, shown in Figure 7-14.

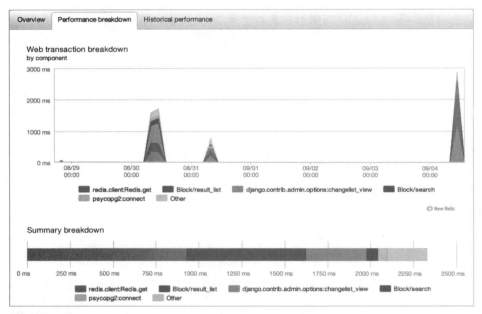

FIGURE 7-14

The "Summary breakdown" section shows that the requests take more than 1.5 seconds in Redis and returns the result set. A couple of things could be happening here. If Redis is being hammered across the app (beyond this request), then a simple bump in resources will help. Alternately, the Redis call might be poorly written, which would explain the sluggish query and poor results display time.

You can also explore other areas of the application beyond web transactions. New Relic enables you to inspect database (store) performance characteristics to the query level, external services such as Amazons S3 or other services accessed via API, dyno-level utilization, as well as any background task. Another neat view is the page render, which can be brought up directly from the Monitoring tab under the Browsers section. It shows how each browser loads your application and the performance of each.

Performance Tuning Guidelines

There are a few general performance-tuning guidelines that you should adhere to on Heroku. First, leverage horizontal scaling wherever possible by defining processes that will handle unique workloads throughout the application: front-end work (web dynos), back-end processes (worker dynos), API calls (api dynos), and so on. This will enable you to set scaling policies that ensure that you scale only what is required, and any refactoring will be isolated to those dynos if issues arise. Second, create a caching strategy. By properly caching results, your application can avoid a lot of expensive round-trips to serve a response. Using a Heroku add-on such as Memcached or Memcachier makes the chore of caching much easier. Lastly, leverage a content delivery network (CDN) where possible. Try to put things like static content or JavaScript as close to the requestor as possible. There are myriad providers out there to look at. In addition, ensure that you don't serve those sorts of payloads from Heroku, which can also contribute to a sluggish app. If the slow performance persists, you can always scale up your app as needed. One way to do that is via the API, as described in the next section.

LEVERAGING THE HEROKU API

Behind every part of the Heroku platform that you access runs an extremely powerful API. It is this API that enables all calls from the Heroku Dashboard as well as the command line. You may have noticed that the admin domain is `https://api.heroku.com` or that an API key is available via your Account page. It is this API and associated key that you can leverage for any task you want to handle programmatically.

The Heroku API is particularly relevant to this chapter, as we discuss application management, logging, and scaling, which can be done by leveraging the Heroku API. Using your API key, you can carry out any task you could do interactively via the command line or the Heroku Dashboard.

The Heroku API allows HTTP and cURL requests to be sent, and can return either JSON or XML results. From your terminal window, try the following command:

```
$ curl -H "Accept: application/json" -u :<yourapikey> https://api.heroku.com/apps
```

This command returns a JSON result set directly to your shell. It is really just a cURL command that passes a custom header (the -H flag), which Heroku expects. It then instructs Heroku to use JSON, and the user is null because the Heroku-generated API key for basic authentication is being used. This is followed by the URL suffix for the specific API call — in this case apps, to list all your apps. You can slightly modify this command for a single app, which returns output containing details for that app:

```
$ curl -H "Accept: application/json" -u :<your_api_key>
https://api.heroku.com/apps/<app_name>
```

The API call returns JSON describing the app specified. These are just a few simple examples to get you warmed up. Where API calls to Heroku become very powerful is in the context of logging, environment load, and scaling. Here's an example:

```
GET /apps/<your_app_name>/logs
logplex=true&num=5&ps=router&tail=1
```

This command returns all the router entries for a given app, including depth of your request queue, wait time for users, and response service time. You could pipe that result into a small Ruby app or even a shell script, and then based on criteria you define (queue=X, wait=Y, or service=Z), you could programmatically change your application using something like this:

```
POST /apps/<your_app_name>/ps/scale
type=web&qty=<qty>
```

You can also get creative with API interactions against your app when you incorporate calls from tools like New Relic's API, as described previously. For instance, once certain attributes or criteria are hit within Heroku logs and/or New Relic data — for example, an HTTP error code occurs or response time slows to a desired level — you could scale your application resources up to automatically remedy the issue.

If you're ready to play around more with the Heroku API, visit the Heroku API docs website (`https://api-docs.heroku.com`) and navigate through all the available calls you can make. This is one of the least leveraged and most powerful aspects of the Heroku platform, a robust and well-documented API that any user can consume.

ADMINISTRATION OPTIONS

Heroku provides multiple access points to its platform, whether it be via the web-based Dashboard, the command-line interface (CLI), or the API, as described earlier in this chapter. The platform takes these direct interaction points a bit further with mobile accessibility, both from Heroku and via third-party tools, as well as several roles to interact with applications running on Heroku. It's important to note that all these options should be considered; however, based on personal preference, company standards, or business/technical limitations, all the options outlined may not be viable for your applications.

Mobile

One of the most compelling aspects of the Heroku platform is the capability it provides to manage and scale in real time. Given the growing number of mobile device users, it is fortunate that you have several ways to manage your apps via mobile options.

The Heroku Dashboard has been designed so that the user interface will render the same on your mobile device or tablet as on a standard browser. Figure 7-15 shows an iPhone 4S running Safari. Other mobile browsers, such as Google Chrome, allow for username/password saves and can make recurring access of Dashboard via a mobile device even easier (so long as storing credentials on your mobile device doesn't pose a security risk). Even a simple bookmark to the MyApps page will enable you to interact with the Heroku Dashboard, just as you would from a standard browser.

FIGURE 7-15

Admin

If you prefer a native mobile client experience and would like to interact with Heroku in a similar fashion to the Heroku Dashboard and CLI, consider Nezumi.

Nezumi is a Heroku management application available for both iOS and Android devices, with an iPad-optimized version in the works. Nezumi is a native client built directly on top of the Heroku API (described earlier in this chapter) that enables full management of your Heroku apps, including a few things that are not available using mobile browsers — specifically, viewing Heroku logs and running interactive processes. Both of these are very powerful tools within the Nezumi app.

Although Nezumi is very handy and recommended by many users already intimately familiar with Heroku, because it is a third-party tool, any issues you may encounter need to be raised directly with the developer.

You can find more information about Nezumi on its home page (`www.nezumiapp.com`).

Status

If you like, and are comfortable using, the Heroku Dashboard via a mobile browser, the standard Heroku status page (`https://status.heroku.com`) will likely provide you with everything you need to determine the current state of the platform (see Figure 7-16).

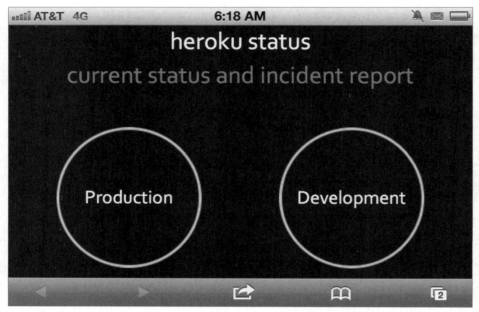

FIGURE 7-16

You can also use the Heroku status page to subscribe to notifications via e-mail, SMS, RSS, or Twitter. In the case of e-mail or SMS alerts, you can opt to be notified about all incidents or production incidents only. Of course, there's also an app for this! *Status for Heroku* is a third-party app for iOS that provides a similar look and feel to the `status.heroku.com` page, with a bit slimmer visual representation of development and production as well as a consolidated incident timeline. If you prefer the native experience on iOS and don't want to deal with a mobile browser to get status information, this app is worth checking out. Like Nezumi, this app is written by a third party, so Heroku won't be able to address any issues with the app itself; and more important, as it relates to the status of the platform, if there's an API-level issue that would limit this app's ability to function, it may provide an inaccurate view of the platform's current state.

Deploys

Another cool mobile tool that has a small piece of Heroku baked into it is *Worqbench*, a lightweight development environment for iPad. It provides a deployment mechanism for apps directly to Heroku by taking your API key (as described earlier) and running `git push` on your behalf. It will then display your Heroku platform deployment output so you can gain visibility into a successful deployment. While it doesn't appear to be meant for heavy-duty development or access to the Heroku platform, it does provide a simple IDE for folks who hack around on their iPad and want to deploy directly to their Heroku environments.

Multi-Accounts

The Heroku team frequently provides new plugins to solve problems not yet addressed either within the platform, through the Heroku Dashboard, or via the command line. One such plugin enables you to manage multiple accounts: `heroku-accounts`. With this plugin, users who have multiple accounts can tag, or name, them (e.g., "work," "personal," "play"), set their local environment up to facilitate switching, and work among several apps/accounts as needed.

To install the plugin, from your top-level development directory (or really anywhere you interact with Heroku) run the following command:

```
$ heroku plugins:install git://github.com/ddollar/heroku-accounts.git
```

This will add multi-account functionality to your local Heroku client. Once installed you can add accounts as follows:

```
$ heroku accounts:add <account_name> --auto
```

Note that the --auto flag is optional. Using `accounts:add` without it requires you to add the following snippet to your ~/.ssh/config file:

```
Host heroku.<account_name>
  HostName heroku.com
  IdentityFile "</path/to/account_ssh_key>"
  IdentitiesOnly yes
```

If you want to create a new SSH key but don't know where the original is stored, or just want a shortcut, adding the --auto flag will handle updating the config file on your behalf. To add additional accounts, simply rinse and repeat. Subsequently using the tool for viewing, removing, or changing to different accounts is just as easy:

➤ `$ heroku accounts:` Provides a list of accounts already set up

➤ `$ heroku accounts:set <account_name>`: When run from the app's top level, sets the active account

➤ `$ heroku account:default <account_name>`: Sets the system-wide default account

➤ `$ heroku account:remove <account_name>`: Removes the specified account

You can also use the Heroku account tool to clone a repository. You might do this if you're working on a different machine, vm, or other account that requires a separate working instance of the app. You can always clone the app, then set the active user account as well. Below is an example of how you may do that:

```
$ git clone git@<Host_value_from_ssh/config>:<repo_name>.git

$ heroku account:set <account_name>
```

The Heroku account tool is a simple yet powerful tool for users who live and work in multiple "worlds" associated with Heroku.

Heroku Manager

For users and organizations that require more involved administrative options or need to empower non-technical application owners with rights to their environments, Heroku recently introduced a component called *Heroku Manager*. Heroku Manager (or informally "Manager") provides another account layer on top of each individual user to provide an organizational-level view of users for a given set of apps — in essence, a Heroku Manager "organization" within which all associated applications and users can be managed. This enables a firm, or delegated users within that firm, to include all their apps and environments in a shared account, to which users can be assigned permissions to "manage" or "contribute."

Once your Manager account has been provisioned (usually for the lead Heroku user ID in your organization), you may log in via `https://manager.heroku.com`.

Upon logging in, you will see the Manager console, shown in Figure 7-17. You also need to ensure that you have installed the Heroku Manager plugin:

```
$ heroku plugins:install https://github.com/heroku/manager-cli.git
```

FIGURE 7-17

This interface highlights the organization name — in this case, `brad@heroku.com` (where the domain is the organization) and by default opens in the Applications page. The Members page is where you allocate user rights. The Activity page provides an application-level view of all activities conducted for each app in your managed organization. The Billing page is where you supply your credit card details if you haven't already secured an agreement with Heroku.

Applications

To get more details about an application, click the application name or "more-info" and you'll be presented with a drop-down menu that provides some high-level details (see Figure 7-18), similar to the Heroku Dashboard.

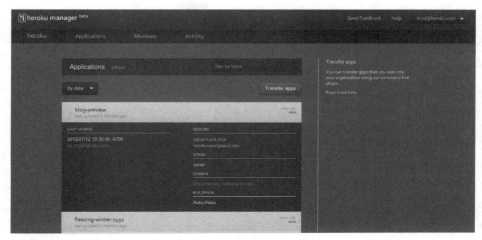

FIGURE 7-18

If you want to move any of your personal apps into the Manager organization, click the Transfer apps button. A dialog like the one shown in Figure 7-19 will appear near the bottom of the page.

Transfer your personal applications to heroku

Select from your personal applications which ones you want to transfer to the current organization.

Your personal applications	Applications in this organization
☑ brad-gyger-www	blog-preview
☐ brad-refinery	freezing-winter-7492
☐ brad-rubyurl	high-earth-6581
☐ bradhello	taps19
☐ brads-canary	taps3
☐ brads-fat-free-crm	
☐ brads-first-app	

Cancel   Confirm

FIGURE 7-19

You can select as many apps from your account as you like and send them to Manager. Once confirmed, they are available to designated users. Apps can also be added via the command line:

```
$ heroku manager:transfer –app <app_name> to <organization>
```

Note that the transfer command requires you to be the application owner; being a collaborator on an application is not sufficient. If you want to move the application back out to your standalone account, a small tweak to the `transfer` command will do the trick:

```
$ heroku manager:transfer -app <app_name> from <organization>
```

Admins vs. Members

Navigating now to the Manager screen, you'll see a place for your Heroku user list. If this is your first time logging in, you will see only the initial Manager user listed. You can add either admins or members, based on their role in the organization.

Administrators can:

➤ Add and remove admins and members

➤ Access all apps within the Manager organization

➤ Transfer apps from their personal Heroku accounts into the Heroku organization, and transfer apps from their Heroku organization back out to their personal accounts

Members can:

➤ Access apps they've been given access to within the organization

➤ Transfer apps from their personal accounts to the organization

➤ Transfer apps they've been given access to, from the organization to their personal accounts

Adding either an Admin or Member is easy. From the Members screen, scroll to the bottom of the list; enter a Heroku user's e-mail address, select Admin or Member, and then press the Invite button to confirm (see Figure 7-20). After a user is added, he or she can visit `https://manager.heroku .com` and have the same access to the Manager console as the original admin. Members, however, have access only via their standard Heroku Dashboard.

FIGURE 7-20

SUMMARY

This chapter explored all aspects of managing, monitoring, and scaling apps on the Heroku platform. You began by turning an app running on Heroku into a production-style app with a custom domain name. Remember that when apps move into production mode, typically custom domains are part of the equation, and services like Zerigo make connecting your application to your DNS registrar much simpler.

Once an app is running in a production environment and receiving real traffic, it is necessary to understand the data that's being captured and the various ways an application can be logged and consumed via the appropriate tools. Heroku Logplex provides a very unique solution to solving the consolidated logging problem. You can then extend Logplex using tools like Papertrail that give you the power when trying to manipulate, analyze and generally maximize the value of your logs.

Logging is only half the battle, however. Once you understand the issues at hand, that information needs to go into a deeper understanding of your app's performance and be applied to making your app more robust and efficient. That's where leveraging New Relic becomes instrumental to your app's success. Once your app is performant, you simply want to manage it. You learned several ways to interact with the Heroku platform via its API, exploring tools to manage your apps with third-party options that implement that API and extend the basic management capabilities you have as a user. Whether you decide to directly leverage the Heroku API or consume tools that are built on top of it, it's key to recognize the power of that underlying API and the many authenticated access points it provides.

Part III dives even deeper into the capabilities of the Heroku platform — specifically, the services you can leverage to back your application, data stores, and the options for building powerful apps on amazing services.

PART III
Using a Data Store with Your Heroku Applications

8

Using Heroku Postgres as a Data Store for Your Heroku Applications

WHAT'S IN THIS CHAPTER?

➤ Getting started with Heroku Postgres

➤ Understanding continuous protection

➤ Understanding automated health checks

➤ Creating a higher-availability database architecture

➤ Creating databases

➤ Forking databases

➤ Creating database followers

➤ Managing databases

➤ Monitoring databases

➤ Choosing the right plan

➤ Deleting databases

➤ Backing up data

➤ Importing data

➤ Using advanced features

➤ Creating a sample app

When creating a web-based app, you typically need some sort of persistent storage on the back
end. This is especially important when developing on a platform like Heroku where dynos are
ephemeral, and you cannot even rely on them to store session-based information between requests.
Heroku provides a number of options for storing your data, including several data as a service
(DaaS) providers that offer the advantage of not having to deal with hardware provisioning and
database patching.

The most common approach is to use the built-in Postgres database service provided by Heroku.
This database is durable and reliable, and leverages the highly popular PostgreSQL, which provides
advanced features for enterprise data storage. Developers who want to attach an SQL database
server to their apps and are more familiar with MySQL can utilize the ClearDB or Xeround
add-ons to attach a MySQL DaaS. These databases are excellent for general use and allow
for advanced querying and ACID (atomicity, consistency, isolation, and durability) compliance.

Salesforce.com also provides its own standalone DaaS, Database.com. This is the very same
data store that is used by Salesforce's customers when they are using the platform for customer
relationship management (CRM), customer service, or custom apps built on top of the Force.com
platform. Users can leverage the proven reliability, built-in security controls, and easy scalability
of this service, while taking advantage of other functionality provided, such as the Chatter API for
making apps social.

Often, a developer may need a database that can handle larger volumes of data than traditional
SQL-based database servers for which a fixed schema is not needed. Some of these systems also
scale out much more easily, enabling you to solve big problems faster than traditional databases.
However, these database architectures have their drawbacks; for instance, many do not offer
the guarantee of ACID compliance provided by SQL database servers. Basic store and retrieve
functionality is typically provided but little else. Advanced querying also introduces its own
challenges with unstructured data.

You can also use your own database within your organization's four walls or use a database hosted
elsewhere. However, unless this database is located in Amazon's US-East Region (like your Heroku
app), the latency in communicating between these systems and your app might make it unsuitable for
highly performant apps. Nor does this approach take advantage of DaaS' managed infrastructure.
You will still have to maintain a backup strategy for your data, upgrade and patch your database
software regularly, ensure that your database's security is configured and optimized correctly, and
"wear the pager" if something goes wrong with your database in the middle of the night.

You must look at the use case for your database to determine which is more appropriate. For
instance, if you are doing monetary transactions, you will likely want to use an SQL-based database
that ensures ACID compliance, which guarantees that transactions are recorded correctly. However,
if you are simply storing social media data, such as who has "liked" what items, ACID compliance
is less important, as it is not the end of the world if a user's action fails to be recorded or persisted
properly on occasion. Database.com provides a suitable alternative, but there is a latency penalty

with accessing this data store, and costs may become prohibitively expensive when storing very large amounts of data.

Often, these data stores can also be used together, complementing one another for your app's different data storage needs. For instance, you may decide to put your app's core data with an SQL-based data store while keeping session data within Memcache; and this app might communicate back to your organization's Salesforce.com account to push and pull information. This approach gives you the flexibility to use the tool that is best suited for the job and leverage the advantages of each approach in a safe way.

The next two chapters cover the Heroku Postgres and Database.com offerings in detail, explaining the differences between each and what you need to consider when choosing between them. You will also write a sample app in each chapter that demonstrates how to get started.

GETTING STARTED WITH HEROKU POSTGRES

The most popular data storage method for Heroku apps is Heroku's own offering, Heroku Postgres. Much like other DaaS offerings, Heroku Postgres can be thought of as a database in the cloud and nothing else — no server to manage, no software to maintain, just a database. Heroku databases run security-hardened copies of PostgreSQL 9.1 and are SQL compliant. If something goes wrong, the Heroku operations team is available around the clock to remedy any issues. Moreover, because Heroku Postgres uses an optimized instance of the open-source PostgreSQL database, your data is fully portable, not locked in.

This database is also *multi-ingress*, meaning you can use it with either Heroku apps or your own non-Heroku-based apps. Heroku Postgres databases are best suited for apps that, like those on Heroku, are located in Amazon's US-East Region. For use outside Amazon Elastic Compute Cloud (Amazon EC2), latency to servers on the east coast is about 10–30 ms, on the west coast about 60–80 ms, and across the ocean, 100 ms or more.

Two different tiers of Heroku Postgres databases are available: starter and production tiers. Starter Heroku Postgres databases are suitable for testing environments and for apps where high availability, performance, and monitoring are not of paramount importance. In terms of features, starter databases are nearly identical to the production Heroku Postgres plans, making them ideal for a staging environment.

However, starter databases do not offer the monitoring and support that are included with production database plans, in addition to more advanced features, such as forking (taking a snapshot of your database), following (making a copy of your database that is synchronized in near real-time), and automated backups. They are also limited to only 20 connections and have an upper limit on the number of rows you can store, making them suitable only for small amounts of data or a test data set. Manual backups must be performed to mitigate the possible risk of data loss with starter databases, as automated backup is not available.

UNDERSTANDING CONTINUOUS PROTECTION

Production Heroku Postgres databases offer the availability, performance, security, and automated backups required for production, public-facing apps. The database stores data by striping it across a number of Amazon Elastic Block Store (Amazon EBS) drives to ensure that the failure of one

Amazon EBS drive will not take down your database store. Continuous protection ensures multiple levels of safeguards for your data, even in catastrophic situations. Data committed to your database is pushed to the write-ahead log every minute or each time 16MB of data are written, whichever occurs first. This provides what is called *eleven nines* (99.999999999%) of designed data durability to ensure that information written to your database persists, even in the event of some failure.

Automated backups are also provided for your Heroku Postgres database. Aside from the write-ahead log, daily snapshots can be taken of your database and stored on Amazon Simple Storage Service (Amazon S3) to ensure that even in the case of accidental, user-initiated data loss (e.g., a developer dropping a database table), a recent copy of the data exists somewhere. The PG Backups add-on provides this capability with a number of manual and automatic backup options, including frequency and retention duration. Copies of data are frequently checked for integrity to minimize the risk of corruption, and data is stored in multiple data centers, ensuring maximum safety for your important data.

UNDERSTANDING AUTOMATED HEALTH CHECKS

One of the biggest advantages of using Heroku Postgres databases is that you are not relying on a database administrator to constantly monitor your database and respond if something goes wrong. Doing so would require that person to be available 24x7 in case something goes wrong. Heroku Postgres has an automated health check service built in, checking your databases every 30 seconds to ensure availability and correct operation.

The first time the automated health check detects an anomaly, your database is marked as uncertain (it could just be an isolated incident). If a second anomaly is detected, Heroku Postgres begins automated recovery. If the automated recovery fails, Heroku's on-call engineer is paged to manually investigate and resolve the issue. This enables your organization to function without on-call operations personnel to ensure the ongoing operation of your database. Heroku's team of engineers, the same engineers who built the Heroku Postgres system, takes care of that for you.

CREATING A HIGHER-AVAILABILITY DATABASE ARCHITECTURE

Though Heroku Postgres databases are designed for high durability, they do not provide extremely high availability out-of-the-box. Heroku claims an uptime of four nines (99.99%), but this can be augmented with proper system design that minimizes points of failure. To create such a system architecture, Heroku offers forking and following, which enable you to create a higher-availability architecture for your data store.

Forking creates a new database based on a snapshot of the current state of another database. This includes the structure of the database and all its data at that point in time. Forking alone does not guarantee that the new database will be synchronized with the mirrored database. For that, you must fork a database, put it in maintenance mode (not allowing writes until the new database has been created), and make the new database a follower of the original database forked. Forking databases simplifies the creation of staging databases, which will be an exact copy at that point in time of the production database. It also enables you to create a snapshot for analytics of that particular point in time.

Following a database makes a new copy of the structure and data of the original database. In addition to forking, following keeps the new copy synchronized with changes to the structure and data updates of the databases followed, less than a second behind the original. This new database is read-only, allowing for concurrency for read operations between the databases followed and following. For optimal performance of your app, read operations should be directed to the database following, and write operations should be directed to the database being followed. You can also use multiple followers if you have a very read-heavy database, to distribute the load of queries amongst several followers.

> **WARNING** *Forking can take a very long time, even hours, if your database is very large. Following can also take a very long time to set up if the followed database is very large.*

You can realize a high-availability architecture by creating a database with multiple followers. In the event that the master database fails, one of the follower databases can be hot-swapped to become the master, and new followers spawned from that database. Heroku Postgres does not offer hot failover of databases; but with automated health checks, Heroku staff can do this switchover whenever necessary on your behalf.

CREATING DATABASES

You can create a database either through the Heroku Postgres web console or using the command-line interface. Creating a database through the web interface creates a standalone database not associated with any particular app. To log in to the Heroku Postgres web console, go to `http://postgres.heroku.com`, click the Login button at the top of the screen, and log in using your regular Heroku credentials. This will take you to a screen listing all your databases. Clicking the plus (+) symbol will start the process of creating a new database. Next, choose the database plan to which you would like to subscribe by clicking on it and click Add Database (see Figure 8-1). You may have to wait three to five minutes while Heroku provisions your database.

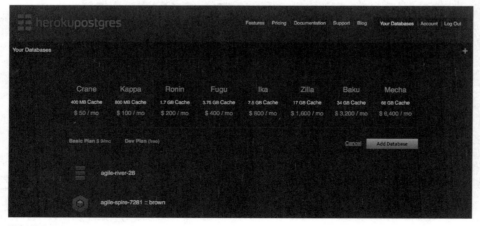

FIGURE 8-1

When your database is ready, you can click on its name to reveal details about your database. As shown in Figure 8-2, you can see the hostname, database name, username, and password needed to connect your app to your database; you can reveal the password by clicking on the Show link. The database details screen also contains statistics about your database, such as which Postgres version it is running and how much storage it is consuming. Finally, below the Statistics section, you can see the database's logs for troubleshooting.

FIGURE 8-2

Using the gear icon in the top-right corner, you can conveniently copy and paste commonly used configuration and connection strings such as PostgresSQL (PSQL), Active Record, and Java Database Connectivity (JDBC) URLs, as shown in Figure 8-3.

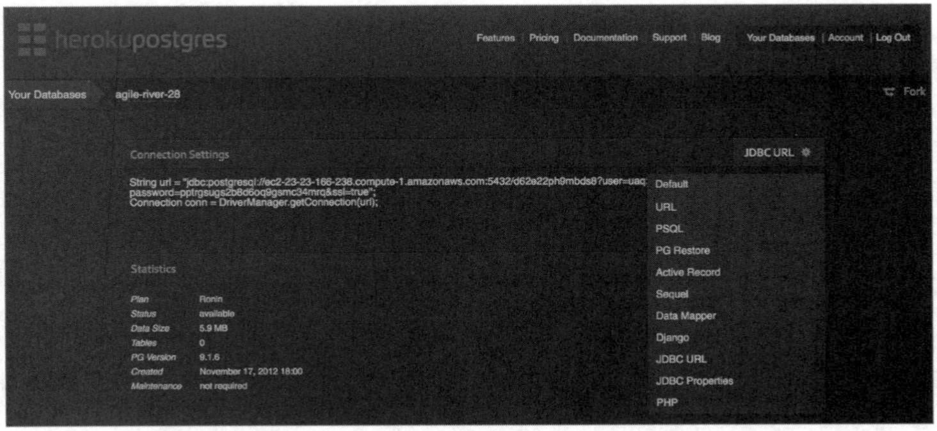

FIGURE 8-3

You can also create a database associated with a particular app via the command line, indicating which app you want to add the database to using the --app flag followed by the app name:

```
$ heroku addons:add heroku-postgresql:ronin --app test-db-app
Adding heroku-postgresql:ronin to test-db-app... done, v2 ($200/mo)
Attached as HEROKU_POSTGRESQL_YELLOW
The database should be available in 3-5 minutes
Use 'heroku pg:wait' to track status
heroku-postgresql:ronin documentation available at:
https://devcenter.heroku.com/articles/heroku-postgresql

$ heroku pg:wait
Waiting for database ... available
```

Once your new database is available, you can use the command line to see information about it:

```
$ heroku pg --app test-db-app
=== HEROKU_POSTGRESQL_YELLOW
Conn Info:
[Deprecated] Please use 'heroku pg:credentials HEROKU_POSTGRESQL_YELLOW' to
view connection info

Created:     2012-07-02 01:29 UTC
Data Size:   5.9 MB
Fork/Follow: Temporarily Unavailable
Maintenance: not required
PG Version:  9.1.4
Plan:        Ronin
Status:      available
Tables:      0

$ heroku pg:credentials HEROKU_POSTGRESQL_YELLOW
Connection info string:
"dbname=mYdaTaBa53nAm3 host=ec2-12-34-567-890.compute-1.amazonaws.com port=5432
user=mYu53rNaM3 password=mY53cr3tPa55pHrA53 sslmode=require"
```

You must also promote your database to be the default database for your app using the heroku pg:promote command:

```
$ heroku pg:promote HEROKU_POSTGRESQL_YELLOW_URL --app test-db-app
Promoting HEROKU_POSTGRESQL_YELLOW_URL to DATABASE_URL... done
```

By promoting your database, Heroku will add configuration variables (config vars) to your app containing the database's connection information, for your convenience:

```
$ heroku config --app test-db-app
=== test-db-app Config Vars
DATABASE_URL:
postgres://mYu53rNaM3:mY53cr3tPa55pHrA53@ec2-12-34-567-890.
compute-1.amazonaws.com:5432/mYdaTaBa53nAm3
HEROKU_POSTGRESQL_YELLOW_URL:
postgres://mYu53rNaM3:mY53cr3tPa55pHrA53@ec2-12-34-567-890.
compute-1.amazonaws.com:5432/mYdaTaBa53nAm3
```

The database created on the command line will also appear in the Heroku Postgres web console.

FORKING DATABASES

Creating a fork of your database makes an exact copy of it, which you can use for numerous purposes such as a staging database, to test migrations and schema changes, or to do load testing on different database plans. To fork a standalone or app database in the web console, simply click the Fork button in the top-right corner while viewing your database's details (see Figure 8-4), choose a plan for your forked database, and click the Fork Database button. Shortly, you will have an exact clone of your original database available for use.

FIGURE 8-4

You can also create a fork of your Heroku app's database using the command line:

```
$ heroku addons:add heroku-postgresql:ronin --fork HEROKU_POSTGRESQL_YELLOW
Adding heroku-postgresql:ronin to test-db-app... done, v3 ($200/mo)
Attached as HEROKU_POSTGRESQL_CRIMSON
Database will become available after it completes forking
Use 'heroku pg:wait' to track status
heroku-postgresql:ronin documentation available at:
https://devcenter.heroku.com/articles/heroku-postgresql
```

> **NOTE** *Only production databases can be forked.*

CREATING DATABASE FOLLOWERS

Followers are read-only copies of your database that are updated with database changes as they are committed to the original database they are following. These followers can be used to distribute load or run intensive queries and analytics that might slow down your production database. To create a follower of a standalone or app's database, go to the database's detail page, scroll to the bottom of the screen, and click the plus (+) beside the Followers section. Next, select the plan for your follower by clicking it, as shown in Figure 8-5, and click the Create Follower button. When the new follower is ready, you will see it listed under the Followers section of the database you are following.

FIGURE 8-5

You can also create followers for your Heroku app's database using the command line:

```
$ heroku addons:add heroku-postgresql:ronin --follow HEROKU_POSTGRESQL_YELLOW
Adding heroku-postgresql:ronin to test-db-app... done, v4 ($200/mo)
Attached as HEROKU_POSTGRESQL_VIOLET
Follower will become available for read-only queries when up-to-date
Use 'heroku pg:wait' to track status
heroku-postgresql:ronin documentation available at:
https://devcenter.heroku.com/articles/heroku-postgresql
```

Later, if you no longer want the follower database you created to keep up to date with changes made to your original database, you can unfollow. This will make your read-only follower read-write, effectively turning it into a fork of the original database at that point in time. To unfollow through the web console, simply click the Unfollow link beside the follower, type **unfollow**, and click the Unfollow button to confirm this change.

You can also unfollow an app's database from the command line after you accept the warning message:

```
$ heroku pg:unfollow HEROKU_POSTGRESQL_VIOLET
!       HEROKU_POSTGRESQL_VIOLET will become writable and no longer
!       follow HEROKU_POSTGRESQL_YELLOW. This cannot be undone.

!       WARNING: Destructive Action
!       This command will affect the app: test-db-app
!       To proceed, type "test-db-app" or re-run this command with --confirm test-db-app

> test-db-app
Unfollowing heroku_postgresql_violet... done
```

> **NOTE** *Followers can only be added to production databases.*

MANAGING DATABASES

Developers often need to log in to a specific database to run queries or change database structure manually. Heroku allows you to access a Postgres interactive terminal to your database over SSL via the command line, as follows:

```
$ heroku pg:psql HEROKU_POSTGRESQL_YELLOW
psql (9.1.4)
SSL connection (cipher: DHE-RSA-AES256-SHA, bits: 256)
Type "help" for help.

mYdaTaBa53nAm3=>
```

> **NOTE** *Using the psql terminal requires a local installation of the PostgreSQL (libpq) client. For platform-specific instructions for installing Postgres, see* `https://devcenter.heroku.com/articles/local-postgresql.`

MONITORING DATABASES

Once your Heroku Postgres database is up and running, you will want to monitor its logs. The log for Heroku Postgres databases are in the same place as your Heroku app's logs, the Logplex. To see logs specific to your Heroku Postgres databases, use this command:

```
$ heroku logs --ps postgres
2012-07-02T02:45:12+00:00 app[postgres]: [37-1]  [YELLOW] LOG:
checkpoint starting: time
2012-07-02T02:45:12+00:00 app[postgres]: [38-1]  [YELLOW] LOG:
checkpoint complete: wrote 0 buffers (0.0%); 0 transaction log file(s) added,
0 removed, 0 recycled; write=0.000 s, sync=0.000 s, total=0.419 s; sync files=0,
longest=0.000 s, average=0.000 s

[...]
```

Your database's logs are also available in the web console by going to your database and viewing recent logs in the Logs section.

> **NOTE** *For more information on how logging works on Heroku with the Logplex, see Chapter 3, "Porting Your Applications to Heroku."*
>
> *There are also a number of new and very useful Postgres administration tools as the part of the* `pg:extras` *plugin (currently in beta) for doing things like viewing database locks as well as viewing and canceling long-running queries. For more, including examples, see* `https://github.com/will/heroku-pg-extras.`

CHOOSING THE RIGHT PLAN

Heroku Postgres offers a number of different plans for production databases, suited to the particular use case for your data store. Recent trends show that the price of storage is quickly converging to zero, so unlike traditional DaaS plans, Heroku Postgres provides one terabyte of data storage regardless of which production plan you choose. Larger data sets can be accommodated using a technique like sharding to divide the data store across multiple database instances. These plans differ primarily in the amount of data that is cached in system memory for fast access. See Figure 8-6 for a list of plans available at the time of publishing from `https://postgres.heroku .com/pricing`.

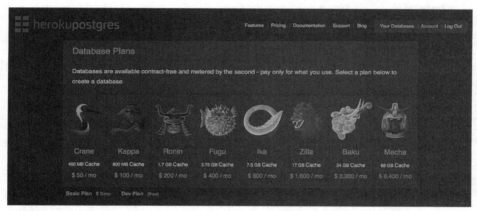

FIGURE 8-6

The traditional bottleneck in database access on spinning hard drives is I/O. Random access to the database can often take up to three orders of magnitude longer (1000x) to return data because of this bottleneck. For maximum performance, the general rule of thumb is to choose a plan that enables the most frequently accessed data in your database to be cached. However, this is not always practical with very large databases or all usage patterns. If you have a database for which some information is accessed often and other information accessed infrequently (e.g., archived or usage data), you may be fine choosing a plan with a cache only bigger than your frequently accessed data.

Unfortunately, it is very difficult to figure out beforehand which plan will best suit your app. The best way to choose the right plan is to select an initial plan, monitor performance, and then experiment with different plans to find the right one. The metric you can use to best gauge caching performance is the cache-hit ratio of database queries. This should be as close as possible to 100%. Query time is also important and can be monitored with tools such as New Relic, with common queries taking 10 ms and more infrequently made queries taking around 100 ms.

The following example uses the SQL statement that Heroku recommends for measuring your database's cache-hit ratios for tables:

```
$ heroku pg:psql HEROKU_POSTGRESQL_YELLOW
psql (9.1.4)
SSL connection (cipher: DHE-RSA-AES256-SHA, bits: 256)
Type "help" for help.

mYdaTaBa53nAm3=> SELECT
mYdaTaBa53nAm3->    sum(heap_blks_read) as heap_read,
mYdaTaBa53nAm3->    sum(heap_blks_hit)  as heap_hit,
mYdaTaBa53nAm3->    (sum(heap_blks_hit) - sum(heap_blks_read)) /
sum(heap_blks_hit) as ratio
mYdaTaBa53nAm3--> FROM pg_statio_user_tables;
 heap_read | heap_hit |          ratio
-----------+----------+------------------------
     64381 |    84408 | 0.23726424035636432566
(1 row)
```

In this case, the cache-hit ratio is only 23%. This means that you should probably experiment with a database with a larger cache size to try to improve this.

The following SQL statement can be used to measure cache-hit ratios for indexes:

```
mYdaTaBa53nAm3=> SELECT
mYdaTaBa53nAm3->    sum(idx_blks_read) as idx_read,
mYdaTaBa53nAm3->    sum(idx_blks_hit)  as idx_hit,
mYdaTaBa53nAm3->    (sum(idx_blks_hit) - sum(idx_blks_read)) /
sum(idx_blks_hit) as ratio
mYdaTaBa53nAm3-> FROM
mYdaTaBa53nAm3->    pg_statio_user_indexes;
 idx_read | idx_hit |          ratio
----------+---------+------------------------
       27 |      89 | 0.69662921348314606742
(1 row)
```

This indicates that you are hitting the cache only 69% of the time for your indexes. There is some room for improvement here with a larger database cache.

> **NOTE** *When experimenting with different Heroku Postgres plans, you can use fast database changeovers to move between plans while minimizing downtime. For more details about how to do this, see* https://devcenter.heroku.com/articles/fast-database-changeovers.

DELETING DATABASES

If you no longer need a database, you can destroy it completely or you can wipe the data and structure. Databases can be destroyed through either the web console or the command line. To destroy a database through the web console, go to the database's detail page, click the Destroy Database link at the bottom of the page (see Figure 8-7), type **destroy**, and click the Destroy button.

FIGURE 8-7

To destroy a database via the command line, use the following:

```
$ heroku addons:remove HEROKU_POSTGRESQL_VIOLET

!       WARNING: Destructive Action
!       This command will affect the app: test-db-app
!       To proceed, type "test-db-app" or re-run this command with --confirm test-db-app
> test-db-app
Removing HEROKU_POSTGRESQL_VIOLET from test-db-app... done, v5 ($200/mo)
```

If you want to simply reset the database to its initial empty form without destroying it completely, you can use the following command:

```
$ heroku pg:reset HEROKU_POSTGRESQL_YELLOW

!       WARNING: Destructive Action
!       This command will affect the app: test-db-app
!       To proceed, type "test-db-app" or re-run this command with --confirm test-db-app

> test-db-app
Resetting HEROKU_POSTGRESQL_YELLOW... done
```

This will delete all your data and remove any structure you have set up.

BACKING UP DATA

You can back up Heroku Postgres databases using the PG Backups add-on, which provides a robust backup manager.

To add PG Backups to your app, go to https://addons.heroku.com/pgbackups, click the Add button, and choose the app you want to add PG Backups to. You can also add the PG Backups free add-on by entering this command:

```
$ heroku addons:add pgbackups
Adding pgbackups to test-db-app... done, v7 (free)
You can now use "pgbackups" to backup your databases or import an external backup.
pgbackups documentation available at:
https://devcenter.heroku.com/articles/pgbackups
```

> **NOTE** *Several plans are available, depending on your automation needs, the number of exports you require, and how long they need to be retained. For a list of plans, see* `https://addons.heroku.com/pgbackups`. *Automated backup is performed on the database to which your* `DATABASE_URL` *config var points.*

To create a manual backup, use the following command:

```
$ heroku pgbackups:capture HEROKU_POSTGRESQL_YELLOW

HEROKU_POSTGRESQL_YELLOW  ----backup--->  b002

Capturing... done
Storing... done
```

Database backups are stored for later use, and you can view a list of backups with the following command:

```
$ heroku pgbackups
ID   | Backup Time         | Size  | Database
-----+---------------------+-------+-------------------------
b001 | 2012/07/01 20:15.57 | 1.4KB | HEROKU_POSTGRESQL_YELLOW
b002 | 2012/07/01 20:18.05 | 1.4KB | HEROKU_POSTGRESQL_YELLOW
```

The first column lists the ID of your backup, prefixed with either an "a" for automated backups or a "b" for manual backups. The time, size, and name of the database backed up is also available. If you need to access one of these databases, you can expose your backup file via a publicly available URL as follows:

```
$ heroku pgbackups:url b002
https://s3.amazonaws.com/hkpgbackups/app1234567@heroku.com/
b002.dump?AWSAccessKeyId=mYaCc355k3Y&Expires=1341199960&Signature=mYuN1qU351gNaTuR3
```

Visiting this publicly accessible URL in your browser enables you to download a `.dump` file that contains a standard Postgres dump of your database, suitable for importing into a Heroku or non-Heroku Postgres database. Be quick about making your download, though. This link expires after 10 minutes, after which you must run the command again to get a new link.

> **NOTE** *Very large backups are split up into multiple URLs. To join them back together into a single dump file, append the files with a command like the following:*
>
> ```
> cat b002.dump.aa b002.dump.ab b002.dump.ac > b002.dump
> ```

Only a limited number of backups are available, which varies according to the PG Backups add-on you choose. Therefore, you will occasionally have to delete your old backups, by running this command:

```
$ heroku pgbackups:destroy b001
Destroying b001... done

$ heroku pgbackups
ID    | Backup Time           | Size   | Database
------+-----------------------+--------+------------------------
b002  | 2012/07/01 20:18.05   | 1.4KB  | HEROKU_POSTGRESQL_YELLOW
```

Here you can see that the backup with ID b002 has been deleted. When creating new backups with the Heroku pgbackups:capture command, you can use the --expire command to rotate your backups by automatically deleting the old backup before creating the new one.

You can easily restore a backup from a previous version stored by PG Backups. The following restores from a backup with ID b002:

```
$ heroku pgbackups:restore HEROKU_POSTGRESQL_YELLOW b002

HEROKU_POSTGRESQL_YELLOW    <---restore---   b002
                                             HEROKU_POSTGRESQL_YELLOW
                                             2012/07/01 20:18.05
                                             1.4KB

!       WARNING: Destructive Action
!       This command will affect the app: test-db-app
!       To proceed, type "test-db-app" or re-run this command with --confirm test-db-app

> test-db-app

Retrieving... done
Restoring... done
```

> **WARNING** *Restoring a database backup overwrites the current database with the structure and contents of the previous backup. Therefore, it is recommended that you create a backup of the current database before overwriting it, just in case.*

IMPORTING DATA

When moving data from another database, you must first get your data into the Heroku Postgres database. Importing data into a Heroku Postgres database can be done with any Postgres dump, even a backup that you have downloaded onto your computer. If you are moving from an existing Postgres database, the first step is to create a dump of your database using the following command:

```
$ pg_dump -Fc --no-acl --no-owner old_postgres_db_name > old_database.dump
```

You will now have a file called old_database.dump that contains the contents and structure of your database. You can also use your favorite GUI to do a dump, by changing settings in your GUI tool to ensure that the dump file is compressed (custom format) and that no access privilege and ownership namespace information is saved with it.

> **NOTE** *Heroku provides an example dump file at* `https://heroku-data`
> `.s3.amazonaws.com/employees.dump` *that you can use to test the importing
> feature without having to create your own database from scratch and dump it.*

Next, create a new database using the instructions in the "Creating Databases" section (if you
don't create a new database, importing your data will overwrite the old data). You can import your
data either through the PG Backups restore function or using Postgres' command line `pg_restore`
tool. Importing your data with the PG Backups file requires that you have your database dump file
available via a public URL.

> **WARNING** *Having a dump of your database publicly available is a serious secu-
> rity risk if done improperly. It is recommended that you upload your database
> to Amazon S3 and create a temporary REST request authorization by setting an
> expiry date, as outlined in the example at* `http://docs.amazonwebservices`
> `.com/AmazonS3/2006-03-01/dev/RESTAuthentication`
> `.html#RESTAuthenticationQueryStringAuth.`

The following imports the database dump from a publicly available URL:

```
$ heroku pgbackups:restore HEROKU_POSTGRESQL_YELLOW
'https://heroku-data.s3.amazonaws.com/employees.dump'

HEROKU_POSTGRESQL_YELLOW   <---restore---   employees.dump

 !        WARNING: Destructive Action
 !        This command will affect the app: test-db-app
 !        To proceed, type "test-db-app" or re-run this command with --confirm test-db-app

 > test-db-app
Retrieving... done
Restoring... done

ckemp-ltr2:test-db-app ckemp$ heroku pg:psql HEROKU_POSTGRESQL_YELLOW
psql (9.1.4)
SSL connection (cipher: DHE-RSA-AES256-SHA, bits: 256)
Type "help" for help.

mYdaTaBa53nAm3=> select * from employees limit 2;
id    | birth_date | first_name     | last_name        | gender | hire_date
------+------------+----------------+------------------+--------+-------
10001 | 1953-09-02 | Georgi         | Facello          | M      | 1986-06-26
10002 | 1964-06-02 | Bezalel        | Simmel           | F      | 1985-11-21
```

This indicates that the database has been successfully imported. You can then run a query on the
Employees table to confirm that its data and structure were imported correctly. The following uses
the `pg_restore` command to import directly from a database dump on your local filesystem:

```
$ PGPASSWORD=mY53cr3tPa55pHrA53 pg_restore --verbose --clean --no-acl --no-owner
-h ec2-12-34-567-890.compute-1.amazonaws.com -U mYu53rNaM3 -d mYdaTaBa53nAm3
-p 5432 ~/Downloads/employees.dump
pg_restore: connecting to database for restore
[...]
```

> **NOTE** *If you are importing from another type of database, such as MySQL, you have to first convert it to work with Postgres. You can use an open source tool such as mysql2psql (https://github.com/maxlapshin/mysql2postgres) to convert the database. mysql2psql can load data directly from MySQL to your Heroku Postgres database and is very quick, transferring up to 100,000 records per minute. You can also copy and paste your ActiveRecord connection string from the Heroku Postgres web console's database detail page directly into the configuration file.*

USING ADVANCED FEATURES

Along with standard Postgres 9.1 functionality, Heroku Postgres contains a few features that are not available out-of-the-box, including data clips, hstore, and cancelable queries. Data clips provide a simple way to share data with others using a secure URL that shows the result of an SQL query. hstore enables you to use schema-free key-value storage with the Postgres database you know and love. Cancelable queries enable you to kill a long-running query that is taking your database to its knees.

Sharing Information with Data Clips

To create a new data clip, simply access your database's detail page in the Heroku Postgres web console. In the Data Clips section, click the plus (+) beside it. Then enter the SQL statement for which you want the data clip to expose results. For example, using the Employees test database you just imported, you can run the following query:

```
select * from employees limit 10;
```

> **NOTE** *Data clips will return results only for data sets with fewer than 10,000 records. If you are using real-time data clips, data is refreshed once every 60 seconds to minimize load on the database.*

When you click the Create Clip button, you are redirected to a screen with the results of the query, as shown in Figure 8-8.

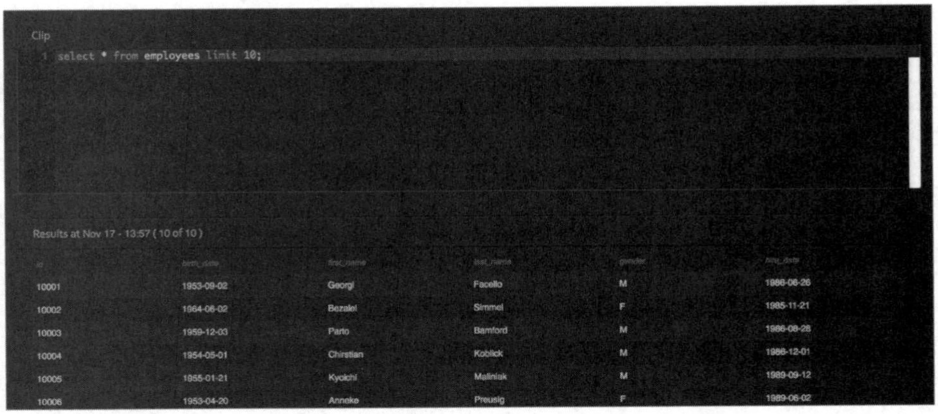

FIGURE 8-8

You can share the URL of this page with outsiders to expose this particular slice of data in your database. It is typically in the form `https://postgres.heroku.com/dataclips/mYuN1q3dAtAcL1pT0k3n`, where `mYuN1q3dAtAcL1pT0k3n` is replaced with the unique token for this particular data clip. By default, this clip is set to view the data at that particular point in time, but you can move the slider at the top of the page to Now for a real-time view of live data. Users can then use the download icon in the top-right corner to get a copy of the data in XLS, CSV, YAML, or JSON. This output can be used to create a lightweight integration with another system by pointing it to this URL.

> **WARNING** *Data clips should be used with caution, as you may potentially expose sensitive database information to outsiders. There is no guarantee that the person with whom you share the data clip URL will not share the URL with others.*

You can later delete a data clip by going back to the database's detail page and clicking the Delete button beside the data clip.

Using hstore for Schema-Free Data Storage

Heroku Postgres provides a schema-free data store using Postgres' `hstore` extension. This gives you the flexibility to store data without the constraint of a rigid structure, but still enjoy the reliability and durability of a Postgres database. Although this is a cutting-edge feature, some languages and frameworks, such as Django, Rails/ActiveRecord, Sequel, and Node.js, already have built-in or module-based support for `hstore`.

To use the `hstore` extension, you must first initialize it for use in your database:

```
mYdaTaBa53nAm3=> CREATE EXTENSION hstore;
WARNING:  => is deprecated as an operator name
DETAIL:  This name may be disallowed altogether in future versions of PostgreSQL.
CREATE EXTENSION
```

The following examples create a database of all the books in a personal library.

This command first creates a table, called `books`, that will hold the list of books:

```
mYdaTaBa53nAm3=> CREATE TABLE books (
       id SERIAL PRIMARY KEY,
       name VARCHAR,
       attributes HSTORE
);
NOTICE:  CREATE TABLE will create implicit sequence "products_id_seq" for
serial column "products.id"
NOTICE:  CREATE TABLE / PRIMARY KEY will create implicit index "products_pkey" for
table "products"
```

Notice that you are creating a regular field called `name` and a field for the key-value pairs, called `attributes`. You're going to store all the schema-free data in the `attributes` column.

The following inserts some data by adding a couple of books:

```
mYdaTaBa53nAm3=>INSERT INTO books (name, attributes) VALUES (
       'Atlas Shrugged',
       'author => "Ayn Rand",
       isbn   => "0-452-28636-0",
       type   => "paperback",
       pages  => 1168'
), (
       'Hindus (The Library of Religious Beliefs and Practices)',
       'author  => "Dr. Julius Lipner",
       isbn   => "0-415-05182-7",
       type   => "ebook",
       pages   => 332,
       formats => "ibook,kindle,pdf"'
);

INSERT 0 2
```

Now that two rows have been inserted successfully, you can do a query on the data. However, you're not going to do just any query; you're going to query from one of your key-value pairs, getting the name, author, and formats of all the books for which the value for the key `type` is `ebook`:

```
mYdaTaBa53nAm3=> SELECT name, attributes->'author' as author, attributes->'formats'
FROM books
WHERE attributes->'type'= 'ebook';
                         name                           |      author       |
?column?
-------------------------------------------------------+-------------------+
------------------
Hindus (The Library of Religious Beliefs and Practices) | Dr. Julius Lipner |
ibook,kindle,pdf
(1 row)
```

As you can see, you can do a query based on the key-value pairs; you can also do all sorts of other exciting stuff, such as index key-value pairs, do joins with key-value data, and parse XML data with XPath. You can even use PLV8, a PostgreSQL procedural language using Google's V8 JavaScript engine, to create advanced procedural functions. With `hstore`, you get maximum flexibility without any sacrifices.

Cancelling Queries

In the past, you had to cancel long-running queries by logging a ticket to the folks at Heroku support. Heroku Postgres now enables users to cancel their own requests. To test this out, open a terminal window and run a query that you know is going to take a while:

```
$ heroku pg:psql HEROKU_POSTGRESQL_YELLOW
psql (9.1.4)
SSL connection (cipher: DHE-RSA-AES256-SHA, bits: 256)
Type "help" for help.
mYdaTaBa53nAm3=> select * from employees;
```

Quickly open another terminal and use the following commands to cancel the running query:

```
$ heroku pg:psql HEROKU_POSTGRESQL_YELLOW
psql (9.1.4)
SSL connection (cipher: DHE-RSA-AES256-SHA, bits: 256)
Type "help" for help.
mYdaTaBa53nAm3=> SELECT pg_cancel_backend(procpid) FROM pg_stat_activity WHERE
current_query LIKE '%employees%';
ERROR:  canceling statement due to user request
```

When you go back to your original terminal, you can see the same message, indicating that your long-running query was cancelled, without requiring you to contact support.

CREATING A SAMPLE APP

In this section you are going to make a sample app that uses a Heroku Postgres back end to store data about your employees (code file: ch8-creating-a-sample-app.zip). You don't need to store much data — just their employee ID, name, and e-mail address. The quickest way to do this is to use Ruby on Rails and leverage its built-in scaffolding capabilities to create the code needed to list all the employees, as well as add, edit, and delete employees.

1. Create a new Rails app:

```
$ rails new heroku-postgres-ruby-example
      create
      create  README
      create  Rakefile
      create  config.ru
      [...]
Using turn (0.9.6)
Using uglifier (1.2.6)
Your bundle is complete! Use 'bundle show [gemname]' to see where a bundled
gem is installed.
```

> **NOTE** If you don't have the Rails gem installed already, use gem install rails to install it.

2. From the directory Rails just created, initialize a Git repository:

```
$ cd heroku-postgres-ruby-example/

$ git init
Initialized empty Git repository in
/Users/ckemp/Documents/Sites/heroku-postgres-ruby-example/.git/

$ heroku create heroku-postgres-ruby-example
Creating heroku-postgres-ruby-example... done, stack is cedar
http://heroku-postgres-ruby-example.herokuapp.com/ |
git@heroku.com:heroku-postgres-ruby-example.git
Git remote heroku added
```

3. You will use Rails to create the scaffolding for your Employees database table with the three fields you want to define:

```
$ rails generate scaffold employee id:integer name:string email:string
      invoke   active_record
      create   db/migrate/20120706193210_create_employees.rb
      create   app/models/employee.rb
      invoke   test_unit
      create   test/unit/employee_test.rb
  [...]
```

Now that you have the scaffolding set up for your app, you need to make some changes to the Gemfile to add dependencies for Postgres and Rake, a software task management tool for Ruby that is similar to the make command, which you will use to create your database migration script.

4. Open the auto-generated Gemfile in your text editor. Under the line that says gem 'rails', add the following:

```
gem 'rake'
```

5. On the line that says gem 'sqlite3', replace it with the following:

```
gem 'pg'
```

6. Update your dependencies with the changes to your Gemfile:

```
$ bundle update
Fetching source index for http://rubygems.org/
Using rake (0.9.2.2)
Using multi_json (1.3.6)
[...]
Your bundle is updated! Use 'bundle show [gemname]' to see where a bundled gem
is installed.
```

7. Create a Heroku app:

```
$ heroku create heroku-postgres-ruby-example
Creating heroku-postgres-ruby-example... done, stack is cedar
http://heroku-postgres-ruby-example.herokuapp.com/ |
git@heroku.com:heroku-postgres-ruby-example.git
Git remote heroku added
```

8. Add a Heroku Postgres production database to your app:

```
$ heroku addons:add heroku-postgresql:ronin
Adding heroku-postgresql:ronin to heroku-postgres-ruby-example... done, v2 ($200/mo)
Attached as HEROKU_POSTGRESQL_BRONZE
The database should be available in 3-5 minutes
Use 'heroku pg:wait' to track status
Use 'heroku addons:docs heroku-postgresql:ronin' to view documentation
```

> **WARNING** *The database we are using here is a production database, which you will be billed for by usage. Add-ons, like Heroku Postgres databases, are be billed by the second, so you should not get a large bill from running this example if you go through it at a reasonable pace and use* `heroku addons:remove <YOUR_DB_ NAME>` *once you have completed the example.*
>
> *If you prefer, you can use a development database that you will not be charged for, using* `heroku addons:add heroku-postgresql:dev` *instead. This will not affect the outcome of the example in any significant way, but some messages might differ slightly.*

9. When your database is ready, promote it to be the main database for your app:

```
$ heroku pg:promote HEROKU_POSTGRESQL_BRONZE
Promoting HEROKU_POSTGRESQL_BRONZE to DATABASE_URL... done
```

If you didn't do this, when you push your app to Heroku, it will automatically detect that you are using a Postgres database (remember the `gem 'pg'` line in step 5?) and add a shared database to your app's add-ons. Promoting your database will override the shared database for your DATABASE_URL config var, making your production database the default database for your app.

10. Now you can commit your app to your Git repository and push the code to Heroku:

```
$ git add .
$ git commit -am "intial commit"
[master (root-commit) 5128f46] intial commit
53 files changed, 1481 insertions(+), 0 deletions(-)\[...]
$ git push heroku master
[...]
-----> Launching... done, v6
       http://heroku-postgres-ruby-example.herokuapp.com deployed to Heroku

To git@heroku.com:heroku-postgres-ruby-example.git
* [new branch]      master -> master
```

11. Finally, use Rake to run your database migration script, adding the Employees table to your database. This will use the schema you defined when creating the scaffolding in step 3:

```
$ heroku run rake db:migrate
Running 'rake db:migrate' attached to terminal... up, run.1
Migrating to CreateEmployees (20120706193210)
==  CreateEmployees: migrating ================================================
```

```
-- create_table(:employees)
NOTICE:  CREATE TABLE will create implicit sequence "employees_id_seq" for serial
column "employees.id"
NOTICE:  CREATE TABLE / PRIMARY KEY will create implicit index "employees_pkey" for
table "employees"
-> 0.0552s
== CreateEmployees: migrated (0.0553s) =========================================
```

Now when you go to `http://<your-app-name>.herokuapp.com/employees`, you will see your Rails app, where you can view, add, delete, and edit employees in your employee database with this simple app. Behind the scenes, a Heroku Postgres production database is holding all your data, keeping it safe and secure, which means you don't incur any operational overhead to create and maintain this database.

SUMMARY

The Heroku Postgres offering provides a powerful and convenient DaaS that you can plug-and-play with your Heroku apps. Continuous protection makes Heroku Postgres databases highly durable, with built-in mechanisms for automated backups to ensure that your data is safe. Heroku uses automated health checks to monitor your databases around the clock. If something goes wrong, the engineers who built the Heroku Postgres service are the same folks who are alerted to investigate your issue.

Forking allows you to create a snapshot in time of your database's structure and contents — for example, for use as a staging or test database, without the additional setup work. Using followers, you can significantly increase the availability of your databases by keeping a forked database synchronized in near real-time with the database from which it was forked. Your databases can be monitored using the `psql` command or the Postgres GUI tool of your choice. Your database's performance is logged in the same logs as your app, providing easy access for monitoring and optimization.

Heroku Postgres' production database plans differ from one another by how much data is cached in memory and can be monitored to ensure that your database is using the optimal cache size. The PG Backups add-on can be leveraged to do both manual and automated backups of your database and export its contents. You can import data using a database dump, either from a backup or from an export from a non-Heroku Postgres database.

Advanced features like data clips can make information sharing and integration prototyping easy and painless, while `hstore` can be used to provide the flexibility of schema-less database systems with the durability of SQL-based database servers. Heroku Postgres provides a scalable, powerful database that can be leveraged, removing the headaches and business risk of managing database servers.

In the next chapter, we will look at Database.com, a DaaS that makes it easy to manage security and built-in, user-based authentication on top of a reliable and scalable data store.

Using Database.com as a Data Store for Your Heroku Applications

WHAT'S IN THIS CHAPTER?

➤ Getting started with Database.com

➤ Creating a database

➤ Importing and exporting data

➤ Managing your database

➤ Creating a sample application

➤ Managing users

➤ Using Database.com's advanced features

WROX.COM CODE DOWNLOADS FOR THIS CHAPTER

The wrox.com code downloads for this chapter are found at `www.wrox.com/remtitle`
`.cgi?isbn=1118508998` on the Download Code tab. The code is in the Chapter 9 download
and individually named according to the names throughout the chapter.

Most people mistakenly think that Database.com and Heroku are on the same infrastructure,
but they are not. Heroku is on the Amazon Elastic Compute Cloud (Amazon EC2)
infrastructure and Database.com is in Salesforce's data center. If you currently use Salesforce
for CRM, Service Cloud for customer service, or Force.com for creating custom apps, you
are already using Database.com to store that data. Database.com is also offered as a

standalone product that is an enterprise cloud-based data as a service (DaaS), ideal for mobile and social apps. This chapter will outline how to use Database.com's APIs, how to create and manage Database.com databases, and how to get data into Database.com.

GETTING STARTED WITH DATABASE.COM

To communicate between Heroku and Database.com, your app uses Database.com's open APIs. Database.com has a vast selection of APIs available:

- ➤ **Web Services:** The standard, general-use API that uses the SOAP protocol. This is a heavyweight API but has the most robust functionality.

- ➤ **REST:** A lightweight API ideal for interfacing with Database.com, and for use with mobile apps and web projects.

- ➤ **Bulk:** An API best suited for transferring large volumes of records, up to 10,000 per batch, asynchronously. This API is used to process data sets exceeding hundreds of thousands of records at a time and can process up to one million records per hour.

- ➤ **Streaming:** This API enables you to use a publish/subscribe model that provides asynchronous notifications about changes in data using the Bayeaux protocol instead of polling.

- ➤ **Chatter:** A REST-based API that enables you to leverage the built-in social functionality of Salesforce Chatter for such things such as feeds, comments, likes, users, and groups to make your custom app social.

- ➤ **Metadata:** An API for changing the customizations and data structure of your Database.com environment

Database.com has built-in user management, security, and authentication. You can add users either through the web interface or via the API. Users can have profile-based access controls to objects and fields or even fine-grained record-level security with sharing rules. This provides a database-level layer of security to ensure that users do not see information to which they are not authorized. Uses can be authenticated using OAuth or single sign-on with federated authentication (SAML) and delegated authentication.

> **NOTE** *An object in Database.com is the same thing as a* table *in traditional databases.*

Before choosing Database.com, you should be aware that the average time to make a request can take longer than traditional databases that reside in the same data center as the application server. Requests have to travel from your app on Heroku to Salesforce's servers and back. This is not very noticeable for mobile apps, as latency is typical on the carrier side anyway. However, you should test a simple proof of concept with any web app you make to ensure that this latency is acceptable for your use case.

Note that Database.com is not an SQL-based data store. It uses the Salesforce Object Query Language (SOQL) for querying, which is very easy to pick up if you know SQL because it is so familiar. However, readers who are used to advanced querying with SQL may find SOQL limited.

Database.com also has scheduled maintenance periods during which your database will not be available for short periods. For instance, three times a year, Salesforce releases a new version of its app, and all customers are automatically upgraded without having to do anything. Though the maintenance window allocates an hour of downtime while this happens, actual downtime in recent times has been less than five minutes. It is scheduled to occur overnight in North America, when apps mostly accessed by North American users experience less traffic.

> **NOTE** *Pricing for Database.com is based on number of users (and type), number of records stored in your database, and number of API calls made per month. The basic free account includes three Administration users, three Standard users, 100,000 records, and 50,000 transactions per month. To calculate pricing for additional services, see* `www.database.com/pricing`*.*

CREATING A DATABASE

The first step in creating a database on Database.com is to sign up for an account, if you do not already have one. To do so, go to `https://database.secure.force.com/signup/`. After filling out and submitting the sign-up form, you will receive an e-mail with a link to log in and set your password for the account. After setting your password, you are redirected to the System Overview page.

Alternatively, you can just create a Heroku app and use the Database.com add-on, as follows:

```
$ heroku addons:add database-com
```

> **NOTE** *At the time of writing, the Database.com add-on is in private beta.*

Database.com does not use the concept of separating multiple databases within a single account. Instead, you have a single database with a login, and you can create profiles to specify who has what permissions to which tables. Let's re-create the Employees table that you used in Chapter 8 as a Database.com object to show how it differs from using a traditional database server.

1. After you log in at `https://login.database.com`, you will be taken directly to the System Overview page. On the System Overview page, select App Setup ➪ Create ➪ Objects, and then click the New Custom Object button to create a new object.

2. For the label, enter **Employee**, which will automatically fill the Object Name field with "Employee" when you move the cursor to another field. Enter **Employees** in the Plural Label text box. Note that you use the singular form of the object name, and Database.com will automatically replace it with the plural form, when appropriate. The first three fields should look like those in Figure 9-1.

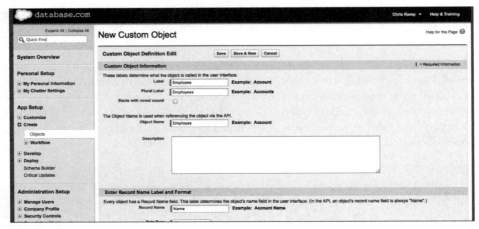

FIGURE 9-1

Basically, the label is the human-friendly name the user sees, and the object name is the unique, computer-readable name that you use to reference this object, post-fixed with "__c" (two underscores and a lowercase *c*) to indicate that it is a custom object, not a system object.

3. Optionally, enter a description to explain this object's purpose to other administrators.

4. Change the value of the Record Name text box to Name. You can make this an automatically assigned ID or a text field in which you have to enter your own auto-incrementing, unique value by choosing Auto Number in the Data Type drop-down list. For this example, select Text in the drop-down list.

5. You can track the field's history, keeping a record of when the value changed and what it was previously, by checking off the Track Field History checkbox. Setting the Deployment Status to In Deployment enables you to make objects invisible to non-administrators while you test them. Make this object Deployed by selecting the corresponding radio button so that you can start using it right away.

> **NOTE** *If you are tracking field history for a custom object, a new object is created to store records with the old and new values each time changes are made to field values. To access this field history, the convention* ObjectName__history *is used as the object name in your query, where* ObjectName *is the name of your object. (Note that this does not include the* __c *postfix you typically use when accessing custom objects.) In this example, the new object created to track changes is called* Employee__history.
>
> *See* www.salesforce.com/us/developer/docs/api/Content/sforce_api_calls_soql_relationships.htm#i1422454 *for an example of a SOQL query on field history records.*

6. The remaining fields should look like those in Figure 9-2. Save your new object by clicking the Save button.

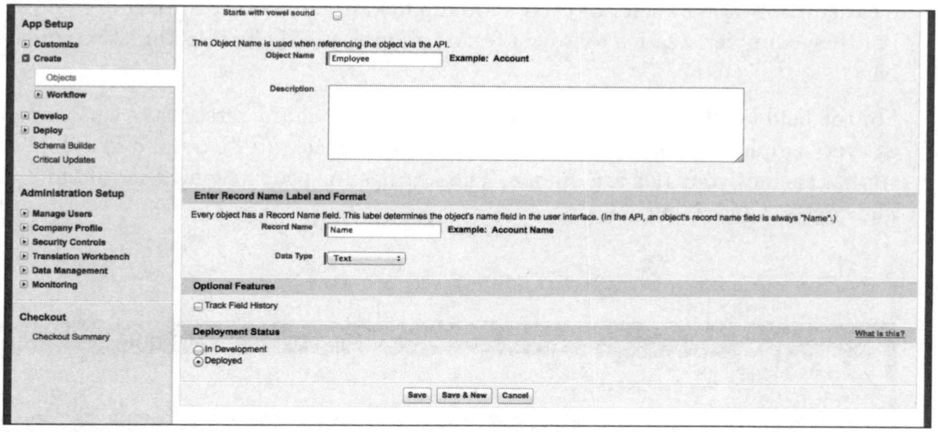

FIGURE 9-2

After saving your object, you are brought to the Custom Object Definition Detail screen, as shown in Figure 9-3. Here you can create new fields and relationships with other objects, make validation rules to enforce standards for values entered in records, and create sharing rules that are defined programmatically.

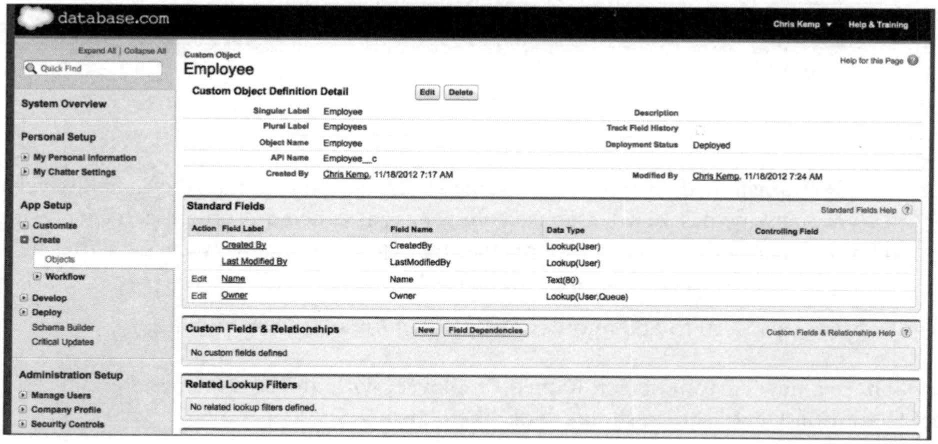

FIGURE 9-3

7. Add a field by clicking the New button beside the Custom Fields & Relationships heading. The "Choose the field type" screen appears.

8. Choose a type for your new field. You can make your field a date field, a number field, a picklist (drop-down) field, or even a lookup field (to create a relationship to other objects). For this example, create a text field for your employee ID by selecting Text and clicking Next.

9. For the field label, enter **ID**, and make the length 10 characters. Make this value required, as every employee will need an employee ID, and check off "Do not allow duplicate values" so that each of your IDs are unique. The settings for your new field should look like Figure 9-4. Click Next.

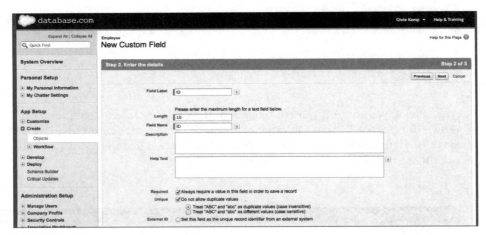

FIGURE 9-4

10. The "Establish field level security" screen enables you to establish the field-level security for your new field. Every Database.com user is assigned a profile. Each time you create a field, you can set which of those profiles can view and change values for that field. For this example, use the default settings and click Save.

11. Repeat steps 7–10 to add another field, called **Email**, of type Email.

You now have a new custom object, named Employee, with an ID, name, and e-mail. Your Custom Object Definition Detail screen should look like Figure 9-5.

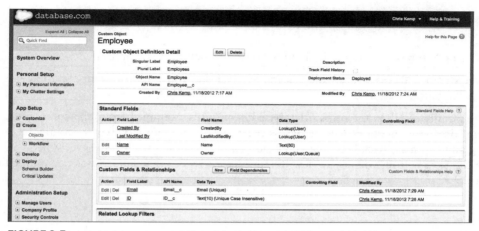

FIGURE 9-5

You could have used the Schema Builder as a more GUI-based way to create custom objects and fields.

To access Schema Builder, go to App Setup ⇨ Schema Builder. Here you can see a schema of your objects — in this case, just your Employee object, as shown in Figure 9-6. You can also see other objects here, with lines between the objects showing their different relationships. Click the User checkbox to see the User object and its relationships to the Employee table. You can click the Elements tab to see a list of field and relationship types that you can drag and drop onto an object to create a new field.

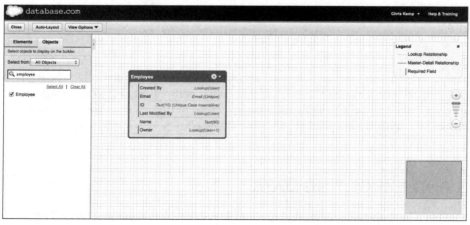

FIGURE 9-6

To access Database.com via the REST API, you need to generate OAuth credentials by creating a Remote Access record.

1. If you are still in the Schema Builder, click the Close button to return to the System Overview.

2. Select App Setup ➪ Develop ➪ Remote Access, and click the New button.

3. On the Remote Access screen, call this app **My Heroku App** and fill in your e-mail address in the Contact E-mail field.

4. For the Callback URL, use **https://databasedotcom-rails-example.herokuapp.com/_auth**, where "databasedotcom-rails-example" is the name of your app. You won't actually be doing an OAuth callback here, but you need to add a URL in this field to save. When you click the Save button, you have a new Remote Access record that should look something like Figure 9-7.

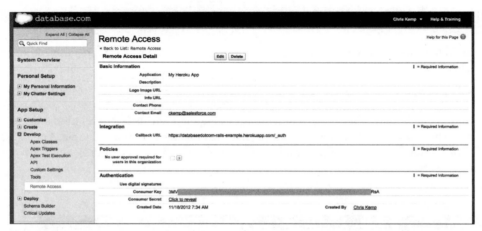

FIGURE 9-7

You also have to generate an API key (also known as a security token) in order to use the REST API to communicate with your database. To do so, select Personal Setup ➪ My Personal Information ➪ Reset My Security Token and click the Reset Security Token button. Within the next couple of minutes you will be e-mailed a security token. Keep this on hand, because you will be using it shortly.

IMPORTING AND EXPORTING DATA

You can use a number of tools to get data in and out of Database.com, including the following:

➤ **Data Loader:** If you are a Windows user, you can use Salesforce's official data-loading program to import data into Salesforce, export data, and even transfer very large volumes of data with the Bulk API. To download the Data Loader and find more information about how to use it, see `http://wiki.developerforce.com/page/Data_Loader`.

➤ **LexiLoader:** This is an unofficial OS X build of the Data Loader. To download it, go to `www.pocketsoap.com/osx/lexiloader/`.

➤ **Workbench:** Salesforce employee Ryan Brainard created this handy online utility that interfaces with Salesforce's various APIs using authentication with OAuth. To use Workbench, visit `https://workbench.developerforce.com`.

➤ **Jitterbit Data Loader:** This is a more robust version of Salesforce's Data Loader. It includes features such as importing from an ODBC or JDBC database, even in the free edition. With the paid edition you can do more advanced things, such as integrate directly with other web services, integrate data between Salesforce organizations, and more advanced synchronizations. Jitterbit Data Loader is available for both Mac and Windows at `http://info.jitterbit.com/SFDCDataLoaderDownload.html`.

The following steps describe how to use Workbench to import test data. Workbench was chosen for this example because it does not require installing anything else and is operating system agnostic.

1. Create a comma-separated value (CSV) spreadsheet. Use three columns, called `ID__c`, `Name`, and `Email__c`, and fill in the spreadsheet with a few rows of test data, as shown in Figure 9-8. Be sure to save the spreadsheet as a CSV spreadsheet, not an Excel spreadsheet or other format.

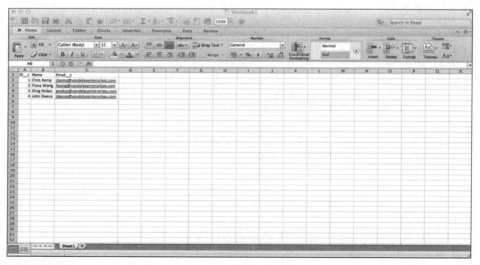

FIGURE 9-8

2. Go to the Workbench site, select the default API, and click the checkbox to accept the terms and conditions for use. You may also select which Database.com environment to use here: Production, Pre-Release, and Sandbox. Database.com makes new versions available before they are released for testing, called *Pre-Release environments*. Sandboxes can be used for testing changes in a staging environment. Leave the environment setting on Production, since you only have one environment in your Database.com setup.

3. Workbench's OAuth login will redirect you to a Database.com login screen. Enter your Database.com credentials and then select Data ➪ Insert. You will be redirected back to Workbench and the Insert dialog, shown in Figure 9-9, will appear.

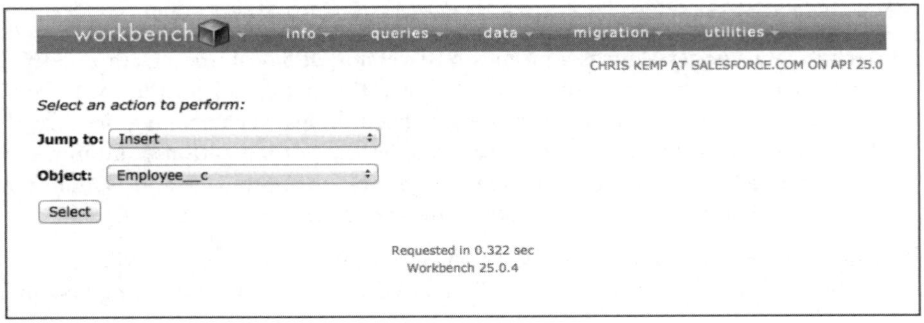

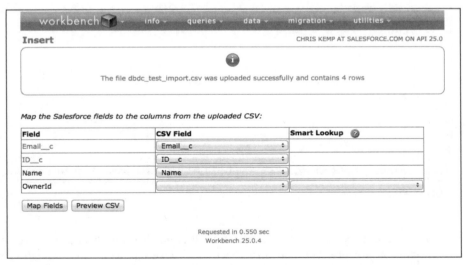

FIGURE 9-9

4. Choose Employee__c as your object and select the CSV file from which the data should be imported, and then click Next. The Insert screen appears.

5. The CSV fields from the spreadsheet you imported should have auto-matched the Salesforce fields if they were named the same, and your screen should look like Figure 9-10. If not, match up your fields now. Click Map Fields and, on the subsequent screen, confirm your mappings by clicking Confirm Insert.

FIGURE 9-10

The results screen should show that you have imported the data from your spreadsheet to Database.com successfully (see Figure 9-11).

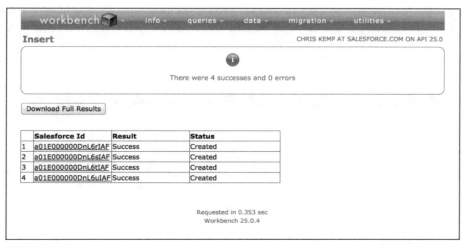

FIGURE 9-11

MANAGING YOUR DATABASE

Database.com includes several built-in options for monitoring a database. The first and most obvious option is the System Overview page (see Figure 9-12). This is the page you see when you first log in to Database.com. It contains key information, such as how many API requests you have made against your daily limit, how many data records you have created, how many objects you have created, and how many user licenses you have. This page provides a quick status check of your database at a glance.

FIGURE 9-12

You can also take a closer look at how many records you have in your database by either clicking on the number underneath the Data Records heading or going to Administration Setup ⇨ Data Management ⇨ Storage Usage. The Storage Usage page shows how much of the two types of storage you are currently using (see Figure 9-13). *Data storage* is just regular records of data, whereas *file storage* is any documents you are storing (see the "Storing Files" section). You can use the Data Loader or other similar tools mentioned in the "Importing and Exporting Data" section to delete multiple records when needed.

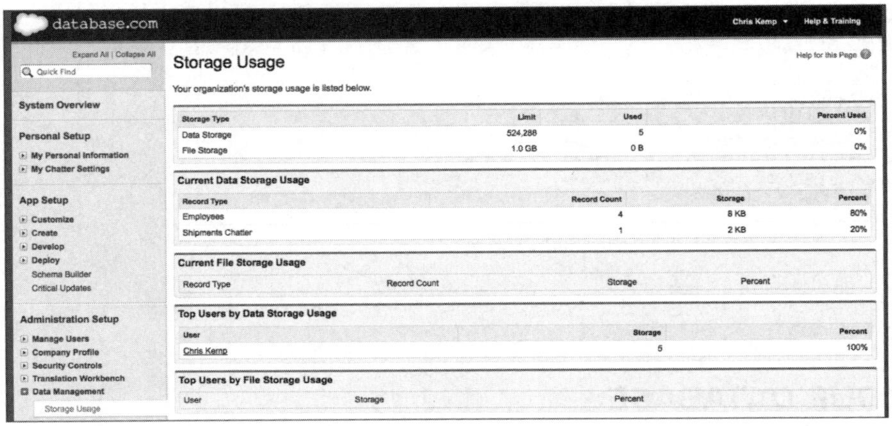

FIGURE 9-13

After you have used all your available API requests in a rolling 24-hour period, your Database.com organization's API is immediately shut off. Therefore, it is important that you monitor usage. To set up API usage notifications, select Administration Setup ➪ Monitoring ➪ API Usage Notifications. On the API Usage Notifications page, shown in Figure 9-14, you can click the New button and set a Notification Recipient (which user should receive the notifications), threshold (what percentage of usage should trigger notifications), and a threshold notification interval (just leave this at 24). These notifications ensure that you are aware of nearing your limits; and, if set properly, they should give you enough time to purchase more API calls. To purchase additional transactions, select Checkout ➪ Checkout Summary and follow the instructions.

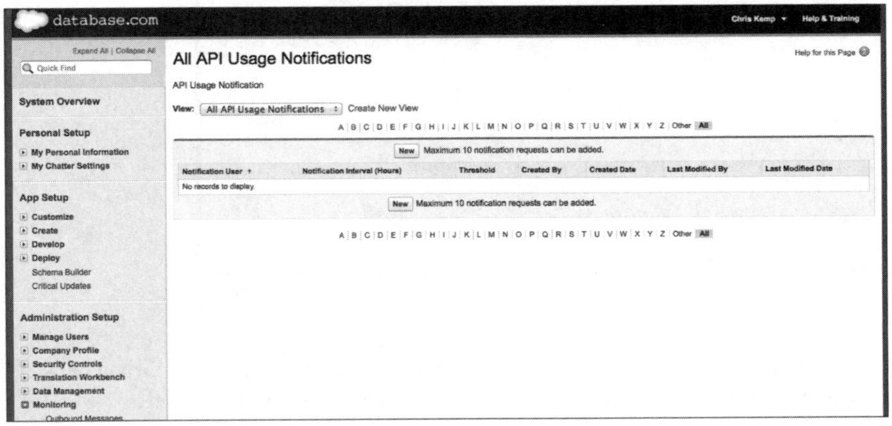

FIGURE 9-14

CREATING A SAMPLE APPLICATION

This section describes how to create a sample Ruby on Rails app to interface with the Employee object you created in Database.com and imported data into in the previous sections (code file: `ch9-creating-a-sample-application.zip`).

1. Create a Rails app, which will create a new directory with the same name, and change to the new directory:

    ```
    $ rails new dbdc-rails-example
            create
            create  README.rdoc
            create  Rakefile
            create  config.ru
            [...]
            run  bundle install
    Fetching gem metadata from https://rubygems.org/........
    Using rake (0.9.2.2)
    Using i18n (0.6.0)
    [...]
    Your bundle is complete! Use `bundle show [gemname]` to see where a bundled gem
    is installed.

    $ cd  dbdc-rails-example/
    ```

    Now you have the basic framework for your Rails app.

2. Create the routings for the app by adding the following lines anywhere between the first and last lines in your automatically generated `config/routes.rb` Ruby script:

    ```
    root :to => "employees#index"
    resources :employees
    ```

    The first line will route requests from the root of your app to your index page. The second line defines your resource for Employee objects in your model.

3. Now you need to make a controller for your app. To do this, create an `app/controllers/employees_controller.rb` file and add the following code:

    ```
    class EmployeesController < ApplicationController
        include Databasedotcom::Rails::Controller

        # GET /employee__cs
        def index
            @employees = Employee__c.all
        end

        # GET /employee__cs/1
        def show
            @employee = Employee__c.find(params[:id])
        end

        # GET /employee__cs/new
        def new
            @employee = Employee__c.new
    ```

```
        end

        # POST /employee__cs
        def create
            @employee = Employee__c.new(params[:employee__c])
            @employee['OwnerId'] = User.first.Id

            if @employee.save
                redirect_to employees_url, notice:
                    'Employee was successfully created.'
            else
                render action: "new"
            end
        end

        # DELETE /employee__cs/1
        def destroy
            @employee = Employee__c.find(params[:id])
            @employee.delete

            redirect_to employees_url
        end
    end
```

On the line after the class definition, you extend the `databasedotcom` gem's controller, inheriting useful methods to retrieve records from Database.com. The block of code under `GET /employee__cs/1` gets a list of all Employee records to pass into the view. The code under `GET /employee__cs/1` retrieves a single record for your view.

The code under `GET /employee__cs/new` creates a new Employee object in Ruby. This is used with the form that the user fills out to create a new record. The code under `POST /employee__cs` fills in the record with the values from the form used to add new Employee records.

Every Database.com record needs an owner, so the line where you define `@employee['OwnerId']` gets the first user in the system and assigns the record to him/her. `@employee.save` does the actual saving. The code under `DELETE /employee__cs/1` deletes the Employee record retrieved on the previous line.

4. Create a directory called `app/views/employees` in the application directory. Create a view for your index page, where all your Employee records are listed. Call this file `app/views/employees/index.html.erb`:

```
<h1>Listing Employees</h1>

<table>
  <tr>
      <th>ID</th>
      <th>Name</th>
      <th>E-mail</th>
      <th></th>
      <th></th>
  </tr>

<% @employees.each do |employee| %>
```

```
<tr>
    <td><%= employee.ID__c %></td>
    <td><%= employee.Name %></td>
    <td><%= employee.Email__c %></td>
    <td><%= link_to 'Show', 'employees/' + employee.Id %></td>
    <td><%= link_to 'Destroy', 'employees/' + employee.Id, method: :delete, data:
        { confirm: 'Are you sure?' } %></td>
  </tr>
<% end %>
</table>

<br />

<%= link_to 'New Employee', new_employee_path %>
```

The bold code iterates through each of the Employee records in the `@employees` array
passed in from the controller, creating a row in the table and filling in the information from
the record.

5. To create the view to show a single record, create a new file called `app/views/employees/`
`show.html.erb`:

```
<p id="notice"><%= notice %></p>
<p>
    <b>Id :</b>
    <%= @employee.ID__c %>
</p>

<p>
    <b>Name:</b>
    <%= @employee.Name %>
</p>

<p>
    <b>Email:</b>
    <%= @employee.Email__c %>
</p>
<%= link_to 'Back', employees_path %>
```

This view simply takes the `@employee` variable from the controller and displays its values.

6. Create a view to create a new Employee record in `app/views/employees/new.html.erb`:

```
<h1>New Employee</h1>
<%= render 'form' %>
<%= link_to 'Back', employees_path %>
```

This is self-explanatory; you simply call your form with `render 'form'`.

7. Define your form in `app/views/employees/_form.html.erb`:

```
<%= form_for @employee, :url => employees_url do |f| %>
  <div class="field">
      ID: <br />
      <%= f.text_field :ID__c %>
  </div>
  <div class="field">
```

```
    Name: <br />
    <%= f.text_field :Name %>
</div>
<div class="field">
    E-mail: <br />
    <%= f.text_field :Email__c %>
</div>
<div class="actions">
    <%= f.submit "Create Employee" %>
</div>
<% end %>
```

This view will simply render an HTML form with three text fields: - ID, name, and e-mail. These form elements will bind with the fields you created on the Employee object.

8. Edit the auto-generated `config/databasedotcom.yml` file, which defines your Database. com credentials:

```
client_id: mYc0N5uM3rK3y
client_secret: 01234567890123456789
username: herokubook@database.com

password: pA55w0Rd53CuR1tYT0k3N
host: login.salesforce.com
debugging: true
```

> **NOTE** *Typically, you would want to put your Database.com credentials in configuration variables (config vars) as a best practice, but you'll add them directly to a configuration file to save time and keep the example simple.*

The first two values are from when you set up your remote access in Database.com (refer to Figure 9-7), with `client_id` representing the value of the Consumer Key and `client_secret` representing the Consumer Secret. The `username` is your Database.com username and the `password` is your Database.com password with the API key (aka security token) appended. For example, if your password were `pA55w0Rd` and your security token were `53CuR1tYT0k3N`, then this value would be `pA55w0Rd53CuR1tYT0k3N`. The `host` is typically `login.salesforce.com`, unless you are accessing a sandbox, in which case you should use `test.salesforcecom` instead. You can set the `debugging` value to provide more pedantic output for debugging purposes.

9. Edit your `Gemfile`, which contains your application's dependencies, by adding the lines:

```
gem 'databasedotcom'
gem 'databasedotcom-rails'
gem 'pg'
```

and removing the following line:

```
gem 'sqlite3'
```

This will add your libraries for Database.com apps and replace the default SQLite database with a Postgres database. Even though you are not storing your data in the Postgres database, you still need to use it to store Rails' session information. A free Heroku

Postgres development database will automatically be provisioned when you first push your application.

10. Add these dependencies to your bundle by running the following:

```
$ bundle update
Fetching gem metadata from https://rubygems.org/........
Using rake (0.9.2.2)
Using i18n (0.6.0)
[...]
Your bundle is updated! Use 'bundle show [gemname]' to see where a bundled
gem is installed.
```

11. Finally, create your app and push it to Heroku:

```
$ git init
Initialized empty Git repository in /Users/ckemp/Documents/Sites/
dbdc-rails-example/.git/

$ heroku create dbdc-rails-example
Creating dbdc-rails-example... done, stack is cedar
http://dbdc-rails-example.herokuapp.com/ | git@heroku.com:dbdc-rails-example.git
Git remote heroku added

$ git add .

$ git commit -am "Initial commit"
[master (root-commit) c922111] Initial commit
43 files changed, 1098 insertions(+), 0 deletions(-)
create mode 100644 .gitignore
[...]

$ git push heroku master
Counting objects: 70, done.
Delta compression using up to 4 threads.
Compressing objects: 100% (57/57), done.
Writing objects: 100% (70/70), 25.93 KiB, done.
Total 70 (delta 2), reused 0 (delta 0)

-----> Heroku receiving push
-----> Ruby/Rails app detected
-----> Installing dependencies using Bundler version 1.2.0.pre
[...]
-----> Compiled slug size is 9.6MB
-----> Launching... done, v4
       http://dbdc-rails-example.herokuapp.com deployed to Heroku

To git@heroku.com:dbdc-rails-example.git
 * [new branch      master -> master

$ heroku open
```

Now, when you visit your sample app's URL in your browser, you can see your list of Employee records, add new Employee records, and delete Employee records from your data store on Database.com.

> **NOTE** *You created an application in Ruby in this example, but you may want to connect to Database.com with other languages and frameworks. Developerforce's integration page (*http://wiki.developerforce.com/page/Integration*) has a number of toolkits and code samples for making integration to Database.com easier with a variety of languages and frameworks.*

MANAGING USERS

You can create and manage users using either the Database.com web console or the SOAP or REST APIs. Each user has a unique username, a password, a profile, and a license type. There are three license types for Database.com users:

➤ **Admin users:** These users can access the web-based console and perform administrative tasks to which they have permissions, such as adding other users, changing the data model, etc.

➤ **Standard users:** These users are similar to Admin users but are allowed more fine-grained access control with record-level access restrictions like roles, sharing rules (rules defined using point and click), and Apex sharing rules (rules defined using code).

➤ **Light users:** These users access data via the API by using profiles and object- and field-level access restrictions.

> **NOTE** *The basic, free Database.com account includes three Admin users and three Standard users. You can purchase additional users of each license type by selecting Checkout ➪ Checkout Summary and following the instructions there.*

Authenticating Users

You can authenticate users to any of Database.com's APIs using one of the following four options:

➤ A combination of username, password, and security token

➤ OAuth

➤ Federated authentication with SAML

➤ Delegated authentication

Authenticating users with a username/password/security token combination is appropriate if you want to access the database as a single user. Use this option only if you do not want to use Keep "Database.com's" unbroken authentication and you simply want to access the database with your app without utilizing Database.com's data layer permissions and sharing model.

Authenticating users with OAuth enables you to write an app that grants access to Database.com using an access token. This token is generated by redirecting to a Database.com login indicating that the app wants access. The login passes back an access token to the app upon successful login, so the app never has any knowledge of the credentials themselves. The token acts as a "valet key" for that Database.com user's access, in that it can be revoked at any time for that specific app. This permits your app to access that user's data via the API and uses the permissions and sharing model for that particular user to determine the objects, records, and fields to which the logged in user has access.

Federated and delegated authentication allow you to use other systems to authenticate users with single sign-on. With both methods, users log in with their username and password, which are passed to a third-party identity provider to verify on Database.com's behalf. With federated authentication, the Security Assertion Markup Language (SAML) standard is used. With delegated authentication, when a user tries to log in to Database.com, a web service request is made with the credential entered to a third-party system that returns true or false, either allowing access to Database.com or denying it, respectively. Both methods allow single-sign on with other systems, without requiring users to manage a second set of credentials.

> **NOTE** *You can use just-in-time (JIT) provisioning with SAML to create accounts on-the-fly as users log in. When a user logs in to Database.com with federated authentication set up, the credentials are verified with the identity provider. If this login is valid but does not match up with an existing Database .com user, one is automatically created at that time. For more information, see* http://docs.database.com/dbcom/en-us/db_help/sso_jit_about.htm.

USING DATABASE.COM'S ADVANCED FEATURES

Many advanced features are available with Database.com to make database administration, user access, and automation behind the scenes easier. The following sections highlight a few of the most important ones, but you should take the time to explore the others in order to get the most from your account.

Understanding Profiles and Sharing

When you log in to any of the Database.com APIs as a specific user, Database.com uses your permissions to determine which records and fields you can and cannot access. Database.com uses three primary methods for determining access:

- ➤ Profiles
- ➤ Record ownership
- ➤ Sharing

Each user created in Salesforce is assigned one profile only. The user's assigned profile determines system-level access, including time and IP restrictions; object-level access, to determine create, read, update, and delete (CRUD) permissions on each object; and field-level access, to determine which fields the user can see.

Each record created on Database.com must be assigned a user as an owner for that particular record. Record owners are afforded full access to any records they own, including permissions to read, update, and delete those records. Each object is assigned a sharing model called *organization-wide defaults*, which can be private, public read only, or public read/write. Private sharing allows only the owner to see and alter the record. Public read allows all users to read the record but only the owner to edit or delete the record. Public read/write allows all users full access to records. You should set organization-wide defaults as strictly as possible for each object as a baseline, and extend them as necessary with other methods.

You can enable sharing using a number of methods, including role hierarchies, groups, and sharing rules. Role hierarchies enable you to define a tree that represents the organizational hierarchy of users. This allows users above the record owner to access records by checking off Grant Access Using Hierarchies in the organization-wide defaults for an object. Public groups enable you to define a set of users who can be granted the required level of access. Sharing rules enable you to define a group's access to an object or to set custom criteria based on the values for each record. Finally, if none of the preceding options are appropriate, you can write code using Apex sharing rules to define highly customized record-based sharing.

> **NOTE** *Record visibility for standard Database.com users uses all sharing rules, while Light Database.com users do not allow record-based sharing with public groups, sharing rules, or Apex sharing rules.*

Enforcing Data Integrity with Validation Rules

Database.com lets you define rules that are validated on the database level to ensure data integrity. Using syntax similar to that used in Excel, you can create a condition formula that will return an error message if the expression evaluates as true. In the following example, you will create a validation rule to ensure that e-mail addresses entered for new Employee records include an at (@) symbol.

1. On the System Overview page of Database.com, choose App Setup ⇨ Create ⇨ Objects.

2. On the object page, select the Employee object.

3. On the Employee object page, click the New button beside the Validation heading.

4. On the validation rule creation page, create a rule called "At_Symbol_in_Email_Address" and click Insert Field.

5. In the dialog, select the Email field on the Employee object (as shown in Figure 9-15) and click Insert. This adds `Email__c`, the name of your e-mail field.

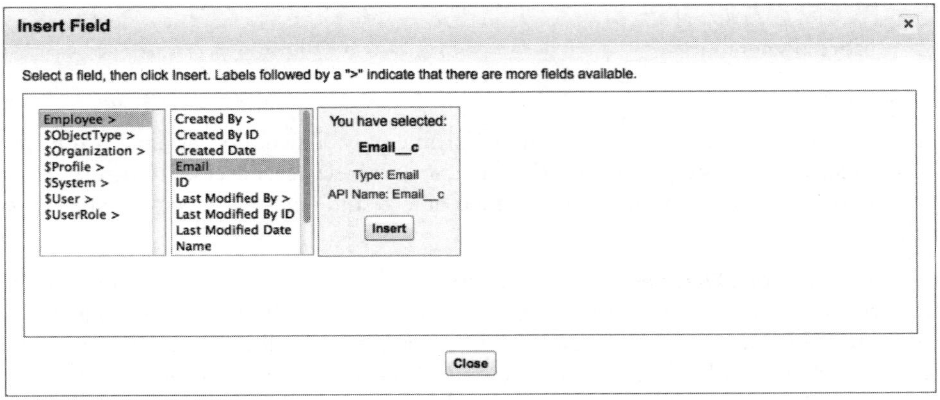

FIGURE 9-15

6. Use the Functions section on the right to find "CONTAINS." Double-clicking this adds it to the formula. Replace all the text in your textbox to read **NOT(CONTAINS(Email__c, '@'))**. Your screen should look like Figure 9-16.

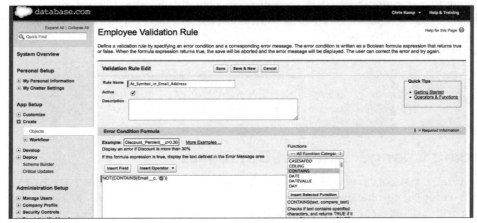

FIGURE 9-16

7. Enter a human-readable error message in the Error Message field (e.g., **The e-mail address must contain an at symbol**) and click Save.

This validation rule you created now ensures that if text entered in the e-mail field contains an at symbol, the formula evaluates to false and you can save the record. If it fails, the record cannot be saved and the error message in step 7 is shown.

Automating with Workflow Rules

You can use workflow rules in Database.com to automatically trigger actions when a record is created and/or updated. The two types of workflow in Database.com are field updates and outbound messages. As you would expect, a *field update* simply updates a field automatically when a record is created or changed. For example, in a project-management app, the project might move to the next stage if all the checkboxes on the record that define substeps are checked off. An *outbound message* sends an XML message via web services to a pre-defined outside system. This can be used to trigger actions in other third-party systems when records meet specific criteria, providing a mechanism for light, one-way data synchronization.

For each rule defined on an object, you must define when the rule is triggered, what criteria must be met for the workflow to run, and what actions should be taken if the workflow is triggered and meets the criteria. Rules can be triggered as follows:

➤ When a record is created or when a record is edited and did not previously meet the rule criteria

➤ Only when a record is created

➤ Every time a record is created or edited

The criteria can either set what the field values must be in order for the rule to be triggered or set a formula that must evaluate to a true value to trigger the workflow.

Workflow actions can be either immediate or time-dependent, and can trigger field updates or outbound messages. Immediate workflow actions are self-explanatory; time-dependent actions can be set to occur after a specified amount of time has elapsed after the record is created, or they can be triggered based on a date or time set in a field value. For instance, you may want to trigger a notification to another system using an outbound message when a record in your database representing a project is three days to the due date.

> **NOTE** *If you are using a full Salesforce account (not Database.com), you can also trigger actions to create a task or send an e-mail using workflows.*

Managing Change with Test Databases

When using Database.com to develop your app, you will need a development database to act as a sandbox for change management. Test databases serve as a staging environment for use when developers need a place to point Heroku apps before going live. You can create a test database by choosing Administration Setup ➪ Data Management ➪ Test Database.

There are two different types of test databases: quality assurance (QA) databases and staging databases. A *QA database* gives you a copy of your production database without the data but with all configuration changes included and enough room for 10MB of test data. This type of database is suitable for development testing by a single developer. A *staging database* is a replica of your production database, including all configuration changes and data pre-loaded. This database is more suitable as a testing environment for pushing team changes to production by a member of the QA team. Figure 9-17 shows the Test Database screen after a QA database has been set up.

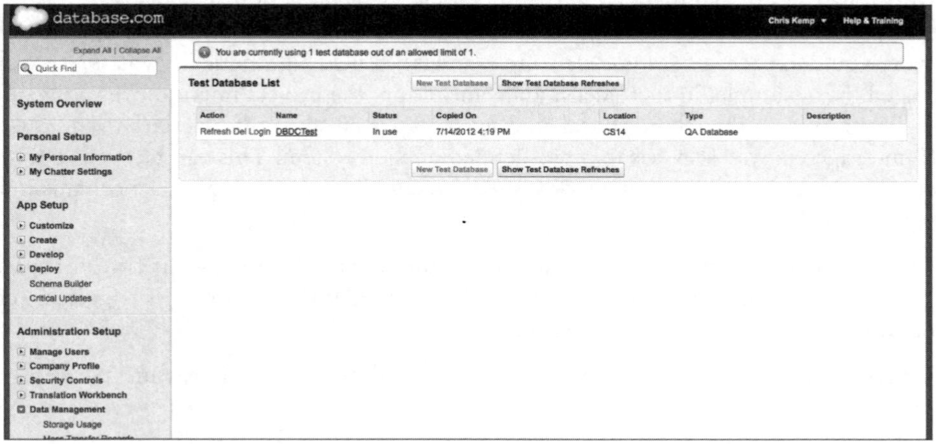

FIGURE 9-17

> **NOTE** *Free Database.com accounts include one QA database. You can add more databases by contacting a Salesforce.com support representative.*

Changes made in test databases can be migrated to the production database using *change sets*, which package together new objects created, fields added, and other customizations made, but not records. Deployment connections are used to define which test databases can migrate changes to other databases. For instance, you might allow staging databases to only deploy change sets to the QA database, not directly to the production database, providing a mechanism for change management by defining who on the development team can deploy changes to production with deployment connections.

Databases can be refreshed, enabling you to create a fresh new copy containing all the changes made to the database since the last refresh. QA databases can be refreshed daily, whereas staging databases can be refreshed only once every 30 days. To do a refresh, go to Administration Setup ⇨ Data Management ⇨ Test Database, select the database you want to refresh in your Test Database list, and then click the Refresh button. You can copy from 0 to 180 days of data for staging databases. By choosing a smaller window, you can restrict how much data is imported, speeding up the time it takes to create the test database.

> **WARNING** *Refreshing a database will overwrite all the previous data and customizations, so. you should refresh a database only if you are sure you want to overwrite the contents of the current database as well as any changes that have been made since its creation or last refresh.*

Storing Files

In addition to storing data, Database.com allows you to store files. You can use the SOAP or REST APIs to manage files. Using the `ContentVersion` object, you can not only store a file, but also different versions of the same file. You can upload binary files up to 38MB of base 64-encoded data using these APIs. The MIME multipart content-type standard is used to upload new files without having to use further encoding.

> **NOTE** *For an example of how* `ContentVersion` *can be used to store files using REST, see* `www.salesforce.com/us/developer/docs/api_rest/Content/dome_sobject_insert_update_blob.htm#inserting_a_contentversion`.

Automating with Apex Triggers

Workflows enable you to define simple automation with point and click. If more complex behaviour is required, Apex triggers enable you to perform highly customized actions using code in a similar way to traditional database triggers. For example, if you had an Order object in your database and wanted to create an associated Delivery object automatically every time you create a new record, you can do this with a few lines of code in an Apex trigger. Triggers are run after each creation of, or change to, a record.

Apex is a Java-like language that Salesforce uses for creating custom logic in your apps. Triggers cannot be created in a production database, only in a test database and then deployed to a production database with a change set deployed over a deployment connection.

> **NOTE** *For more information on the command syntax used for writing Apex code, see the "Force.com Apex Code Developer's Guide" at* `www.salesforce.com/us/developer/docs/apexcode/index.htm`.
>
> *For an example of an Apex trigger, see* `www.salesforce.com/us/developer/docs/apexcode/Content/apex_qs_trigger.htm`.

Leveraging Social Graphs

Social graphs in Database.com enable you to access functionality from Salesforce Chatter to make your Heroku app social. The Chatter REST API enables users to access their Chatter feeds, comments, likes, groups, and private messages in their external apps. This can be leveraged to make any app that you are developing social.

For instance, suppose you have been tasked with developing an app for a travel agency selling tours. They want the app to support discussions among the tour guides about tours they have led. If you create a Heroku app to manage this, you can have a Chatter feed on your tour records so tour guides who are conducting the same tours can ask questions, share best practices, and discuss upcoming tours. The Chatter API restricts access to Chatter feeds on tour records using Database .com's sharing engine, so anyone not allowed to view a record cannot see Chatter feeds or add comments.

> **NOTE** *For an example of a social app built with the Chatter API, see Chapter 16, "Building Social Applications with Heroku."*

SUMMARY

Database.com can be used as a powerful DaaS that saves you the time and effort needed to add authentication and data-layer security to your application. Configuration and management is done using a point-and-click interface, minimizing the amount of code you need to write and maintain. Database maintenance and monitoring is done without the hassle of running commands on your database server.

Several APIs are available, each fitting a different use case based on how data is being used in your application. You can define your database structures using point-and-click, making it quick and simple to create and change databases. There are a number of tools available, both as downloads and accessed online, that can be used to import and export data from Database.com.

Your database is monitored with Database.com's web interface. User management is also done in the same web interface, and there are different levels of access for different user types. You are given a number of standards-based options for authenticating with Database.com, including OAuth and SAML. Profiles and sharing are used to restrict what objects, records, and fields that users can access. Access can be controlled with a point-and-click interface or through code for very complex criteria.

Validation rules help to ensure data integrity by creating rule-based criteria that must pass for a record to be saved. Workflow can be used to create automation that happens behind the scenes to update fields on a record or send XML messages to other systems when certain criteria are met. Apex triggers can also be used to automate more complex behavior with code, similar to database triggers. Test databases can be created for QA and testing purposes. Files can also be stored in Database.com through the SOAP or REST APIs. The Chatter API uses social graphs to make applications social.

In the next chapter, you will learn about alternative data stores, such as NoSQL stores, and explore the options available in the Heroku ecosystem.

10

Using Third-Party Data Stores for Your Heroku Applications

WHAT'S IN THIS CHAPTER?

➤ SQL-based options

➤ NoSQL-based options

➤ Attaching existing data stores

You've already explored a few data store options in this part of the book — specifically, the Heroku Postgres and Salesforce Database.com services — but what if these don't satisfy your requirements? Not to worry, as the Heroku platform is extensible, supporting a wide assortment of third-party data stores, many of which are available directly through the Heroku add-on ecosystem. Even if you require external data store services not provided via the Heroku add-ons library, you can attach them to your apps using configuration variables (config vars). This chapter explores several SQL and NoSQL options from the Heroku add-ons library and describes how to attach stores already in use to your Heroku apps.

SQL-BASED OPTIONS

Traditional or relational databases, commonly referred to *SQL DBs*, are one of the primary options available to your apps on Heroku. Relational SQL databases are defined by a schema consisting of various tables, each table consisting of unique columns or field names with keys that tie each table together to "relate" the data. To create, read, update, or delete any data within the database, you define statements (queries) using SQL to act on the data as desired.

There are two primary options for SQL-based databases: Postgres (explored in Chapter 8 via the Heroku Postgres service) and MySQL. This section describes how to leverage MySQL, and then discusses JustOneDB, an alternative method to Heroku Postgres.

MySQL

Projects often require the use of MySQL for various reasons: organizational requirements and standards, developer expertise and preference, or language/framework compatibility. Fortunately, several options are available within the Heroku ecosystem. This section explores two MySQL service provider options: the ClearDB MySQL Database (ClearDB) add-on and the Amazon Relational Database Service (RDS), which can be connected to your Heroku app using an integration add-on.

ClearDB

ClearDB is a MySQL database service provider available to all Heroku users via the add-ons library. If MySQL is your database of choice but you don't want to be saddled with any of the operational headaches associated with running a MySQL instance, ClearDB offers a complete MySQL data as a service (DaaS).

ClearDB provides some unique and useful features, such as in-place upgrades/migrations, as well as "multi-master" setups across separate Amazon regions, providing higher availability for apps that require it. Because ClearDB is provided via the add-ons library, it's available to all apps running on the Heroku platform. Here are the steps to add a ClearDB database to your app.

You can add your database to the app either via the command line or via the Heroku Dashboard (see Figure 10-1).

From the command line:

```
$ heroku addons:add cleardb:punch
Adding cleardb:punch on brads-www... done, v42 ($9.99/mo)
Use 'heroku addons:docs cleardb:punch' to view documentation.
```

From the Dashboard:

1. Visit the app detail page within Heroku Dashboard.

2. Click the Get Addons button.

3. Navigate to, then select, the ClearDB service.

4. Select the appropriate plan based on your sizing requirements. (This example uses the "Punch" option.)

5. Verify, and the installation will commence.

FIGURE 10-1

Now pull the ClearDB instance URL from your Heroku config:

```
$ heroku config
=== brads-octopress Config Vars
BLITZ_API_KEY: 60ca103f-c751f473-dda605ae-a1384991
BLITZ_API_USER: brad@heroku.com
CLEARDB_DATABASE_URL: mysql://bb3a16878e727a:4b1ec86f@us-cdbr-east-02.cleardb.com/
heroku_9441295e3c77c83?reconnect=true
GEM_PATH:vendor/bundle/ruby/1.9.1
```

At this point, you can either configure your app to use this config var or set your app to use `DATABASE_URL` alone:

```
$ heroku config:add DATABASE_URL=mysql://bb3a16878e727a:4b1ec86f@us-cdbr-
east-02.cleardb.com/
heroku_9441295e3c77c83?reconnect=true
Setting config vars and restarting brads-www... done, v45
DATABASE_URL: mysql://bb3a16878e727a:4b1ec86f@us-cdbr-east-02.cleardb.com/
heroku_9441295e3c77c83?reconnect=true
```

When the database is up and running, you can view the instance via the Heroku Dashboard, as shown in Figure 10-2.

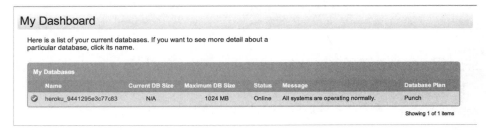

FIGURE 10-2

Within the Dashboard, clicking on your database instance name will provide you with a few administrative options:

➤ **Performance:** This highlights your Query Performance both in quantity and speed (in seconds), as well as your Database Growth (in megabytes).

➤ **Backups & Jobs:** This enables you to define any recurring jobs, such as backups, restores, migrations, and view the available backups for restore or local export.

➤ **Endpoint Information:** This shows your database username and password. This information is also available by running `heroku config` and finding the `CLEARDB_DATABASE_URL`.

➤ **Support Cases:** This lets you create a new support ticket and view any open ones.

All other administration or development work is done via the command line in the same fashion as a typical MySQL database.

Amazon Relational Database Service

Amazon Relational Database Service (Amazon RDS) is an enterprise-ready, fault-tolerant database service that can be run across multiple regions and availability zones within the Amazon Web Services (AWS) infrastructure. It enables customers to choose from several database platforms and runs in a distributed fashion.

Heroku enables you to leverage Amazon RDS for your data store in a similar fashion to Amazon S3 for storage, via an available integration add-on. The following steps describe how to create a new RDS instance of MySQL:

1. Log into the AWS Management Console, as shown in Figure 10-3. The Console is available via any browser, at `https://console.aws.amazon.com/`.

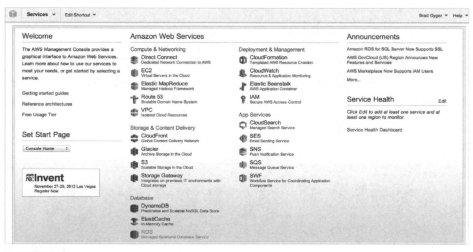

FIGURE 10-3

> **NOTE** *You should already have an AWS account set up from earlier in this book, when you created Amazon S3 buckets to store your app's static assets.*

2. To create a new RDS instance of MySQL, begin by navigating to "RDS" under the Database section and clicking the Launch a DB Instance button (see Figure 10-4). The Launch DB Instance Wizard appears (see Figure 10-5).

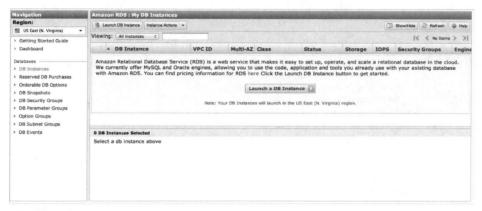

FIGURE 10-4

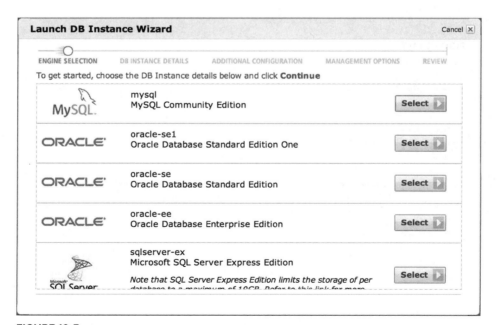

FIGURE 10-5

3. Step through the Launch DB Instance Wizard, specifying all the options that you require:

    a. Select MySQL.

    b. Configure the options for your database (see Figure 10-6).

    c. Add any additional configuration settings you require (see Figure 10-7).

    d. Tune your management options for backup and maintenance windows (see Figure 10-8).

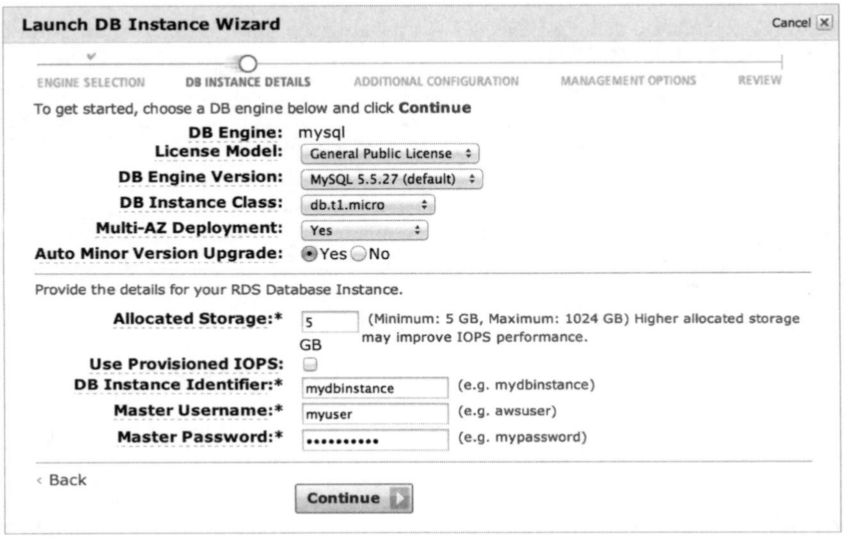

FIGURE 10-6

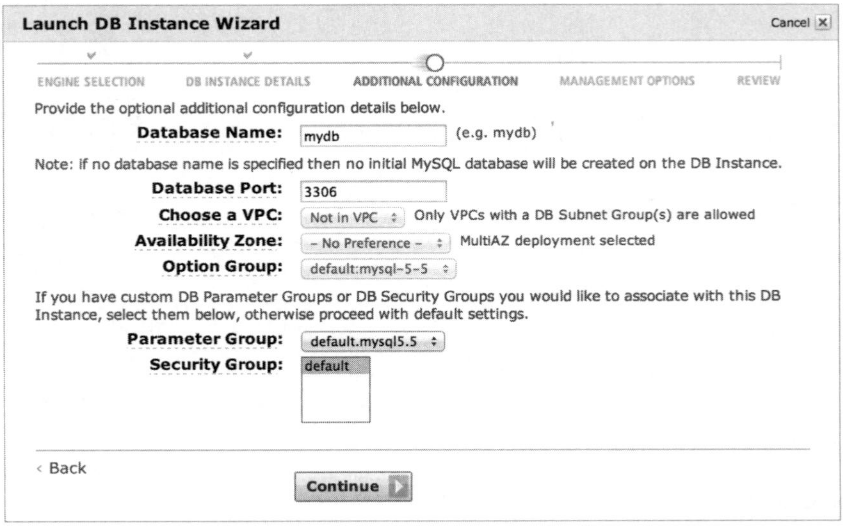

FIGURE 10-7

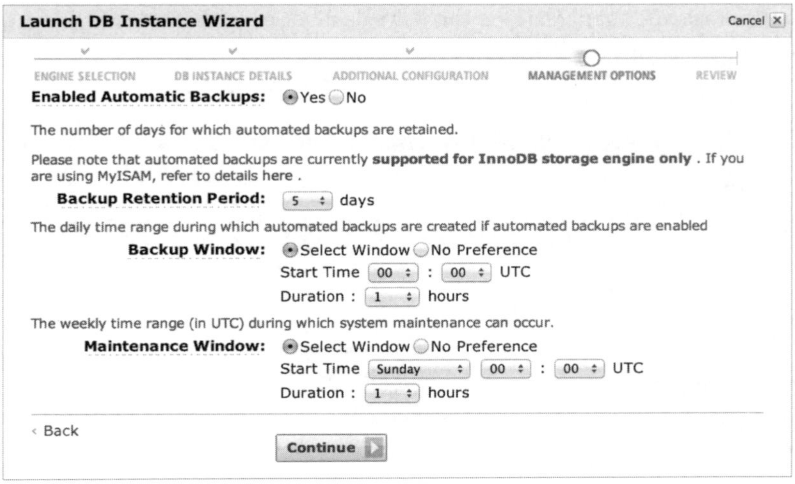

FIGURE 10-8

Once completed, confirm your settings and click the Launch DB Instance button, as shown in Figure 10-9. If you want to change anything, click the Back button and make your modifications before proceeding.

FIGURE 10-9

4. Access the database and manage it via the RDS dashboard within the AWS Management Console, as shown in Figure 10-10.

FIGURE 10-10

Now that your Amazon RDS instance is set up, you need to set up your local machine and Heroku environment.

5. Download and install the RDS command-line tools from `http://aws.amazon.com/developertools/2928`.

   a. Download the zip and unpack it:

```
$ curl -O http://s3.amazonaws.com/rds-downloads/RDSCli.zip
$ unzip RDSCli.zip
$ cd RDSCli-1.10.003/
```

   b. Set your `AWS_RDS` and `JAVA_HOME` environment variables in your active command-line session or within your `.profile` or shell config file:

```
export AWS_RDS_HOME=/your/rds-install/path
export JAVA_HOME=/your/java/path
```

   c. Configure your AWS credentials via the credential file or using certificates. In this case, use the template credential file called `credential-file-path.template` located within your RDS command-line tools directory (It should be named something like `RDSCli-<version>` on your local machine.) Your credentials then can be found within the AWS Management Console.

   i. From the drop-down (Your name) in the upper right, select Security Credentials.

ii. Once dropped into the Security Credentials page, scroll down to the Access Keys.

iii. Cut/paste your Access Key ID into the credential file:

```
AWSAccessKeyId=<YourAWSAccessKeyID>
```

iv. Hit "Show" for the Secret Access Key, and then cut/paste that value into the credential file:

```
AWSSecretKey=<YourAWSSecretAccessKey>
```

v. Save the file, and then set your AWS_CREDENTIAL_FILE environment variable to the file you just edited (again, this can be in the active session or saved to your shell config file):

```
export AWS_CREDENTIAL_FILE=/Users/Brad/Projects/personal/
    RDSCli-1.10.003/credential-file-path.template
```

If all is set accordingly, running RDS commands from the toolkit should return data from services:

```
$ rds rds-describe-db-instances
DBINSTANCE  my-db  2012-10-10T05:08:25.230Z  db.t1.micro  mysql  100  bradgyger
available  my-db.cig7fzazeizk.us-east-1.rds.amazonaws.com  3306  us-east-1b  1  n
5.5.27  general-public-license
    SECGROUP  default  active
    PARAMGRP  default.mysql5.5  in-sync
    OPTIONGROUP  default:mysql-5-5  in-sync
```

6. Finally, you must authorize Heroku to access your RDS instance and add the add-on:

```
$ rds-authorize-db-security-group-ingress -db-security-group-name default
  --ec2-security-group-name default
  --ec2-security-group-owner-id 098166147350
  --aws-credential-file ../credential-file-path.template

$ heroku addons:add amazon_rds url=mysql2://bradgyger:mysecretpassword@
  my-db.cig7fzazeizk.us-east-1.rds.amazonaws.com/my-db
```

Congratulations! You now have an Amazon RDS instance of MySQL running and connected to your app on Heroku. Remember that the AWS Management Console is your home for managing RDS as well as Amazon S3 (for asset storage) as well as any other services you run within Amazon that will connect to your apps on Heroku. However, you can now directly connect to your database at the API and SQL level with the tools you've installed, and your Heroku app will be able to leverage RDS as a data store — the same as any other database or service you'd want to read or write data to and from.

Alternative Postgres — JustOneDB

If you find that Heroku Postgres is not optimal for your app but want to run a flavor of Postgres, check out JustOneDB. Based on the open-source PostgreSQL project and designed for large volumes of data, JustOneDB is a customized version of the project with the primary focus of delivering a fast database.

Here's how you can add a JustOneDB instance to your Heroku app:

1. Select Get Add-ons from your app's resource detail page within your Heroku Dashboard. Once within the add-ons library, navigate to JustOneDB and select the plan you want.

   Alternatively, you can enable the service from the command line:

   ```
   $ heroku addons:add justonedb
   Adding justonedb on brad-gyger-www... done, v53 (free)
   Use 'heroku addons:docs justonedb' to view documentation.
   ```

2. Visit your Heroku Dashboard and verify JustOneDB successfully installed.

3. View your database page via the Heroku Dashboard, as shown in Figure 10-11.

FIGURE 10-11

And quickly display your settings using `heroku config`. These will be important, depending on how you decide to interact with the database.

```
$ heroku config | grep JUSTONEDB

JUSTONEDB_DBI_URL:

postgres://tq0mejlo7eb6v0ixshx:ipqbu1qn9yte840fmo32p16jhlwt6shq@
   lambda-1.justonedb.com:10301/mf0mejlo7ebb50ixsiu

JUSTONEDB_REST_BASE:

https://tq0mejlo7eb6v0ixshx:ipqbu1qn9yte840fmo32p16jhlwt6shq@
   lambda-1.justonedb.com:31418/justonedb/

JUSTONEDB_REST_DB: database/mf0mejlo7ebb50ixsiu

JUSTONEDB_SUPPORT_ID: 0eef9a19
```

4. Now that your JustOneDB instance is available, you can access it via three mechanisms:

➤ **REST API:** JustOneDB has created its own REST interface over HTTPS, eliminating the need to make direct SQL calls. If you decide to leverage this option, note the REST config vars that are available for connecting to the service. The full reference for the API can be found at `www.justonedb.com/wp-content/uploads/2011/07/JustOneDB-REST-Reference-Jul-2011.pdf`.

➤ **DBI:** DBI (*Database Interface*) is a more standard access mechanism. The DBI URL from your Heroku config provides the data required to leverage this. You can either point your Heroku app's `DATABASE_URL` to this value or update your app's database config file, typically a `Database.yml` file, with the database credentials you've gotten above:

```
production:
  adapter: postgresql
  database: mf0mejlo7ebb50ixsiu
  username: tq0mejlo7eb6v0ixshx
  password: ipqbu1qn9yte840fmo32p16jhlwt6shq
  host: lambda-1.justonedb.com
  port: 10301
```

➤ **ActiveRecord:** ActiveRecord is an object-relational mapping (ORM) interface for Ruby (Rails) that allows you to write queries using application code rather than SQL. You can use the same DBI URL as above and let ActiveRecord provide an abstraction layer on top of the database itself so that you don't have to write SQL code as well as app code. Add the following to your application initialization file(s):

```
ActiveRecord::Base.establish_connection(ENV['JUSTONEDB_DBI_URL'])
```

> **NOTE** *We'll explore ActiveRecord more in Chapter 11, "Developing with Ruby."*

Now you have an alternative Postgres service available to your app! Remember that Heroku Postgres and JustOneDB may appear to be similar services, but they are quite different under the hood. Make sure you evaluate which will best serve your app's needs. If all else fails, try them both to see which fits your requirements and performs the best based on your architecture.

NOSQL-BASED OPTIONS

In many modern web application architectures, leveraging a relational, SQL-based database is overkill. Creating a complex schema to represent a relatively simple data model is often not a worthwhile endeavor for most developers. Enter the NoSQL data store. NoSQL stores empower developers to still write their application data to a "store," much like a traditional database but without the complexity. The NoSQL community is full of options, optimized for various types of apps. While we won't dive into each option, we provide a few common options. If you have a preferred option that isn't listed in this section, take a walk around the Heroku add-ons library and see if it's available. If not, e-mail the folks at Heroku to see if any plans to offer it are pending. The list of data store providers in the cloud will continue to grow.

MongoDB

MongoDB (commonly referred to as simply *Mongo*), a play on the term "humongous," is a general-purpose NoSQL database that provides many large-scale features, such as indexing, sharing, and map/reduce (distributed computing) for big data processing. It is well suited for scenarios in which data is stored in flat files, can leverage JavaScript Object Notation (JSON), or where a schema-free or dynamic-schema approach is required for the data model. Mongo typically is not as effective when an app may have been previously backed by a SQL/RDBMS system and the goal of moving to Mongo is a performance gain. That's typically because the impetus of such a move is often large and very complex data-transaction processing apps whose data model may already be suited to an RDBMS.

The Heroku add-on ecosystem offers two Mongo options: MongoLab and MongoHQ. While both provide similar features and functionality, this example uses MongoLab.

1. Add your Mongo instance to the app, via either the command line (as follows) or the Heroku Dashboard (see Figure 10-12):

```
$ heroku addons:add mongolab:small
Adding mongolab:small on brad-gyger-www... done, v56 ($10/mo)
Welcome to MongoLab.
Use 'heroku addons:docs mongolab:small' to view documentation.
```

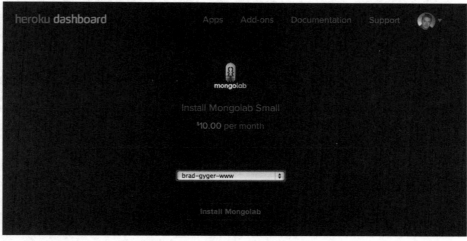

FIGURE 10-12

2. Now that your MongoDB instance is ready to go, you can configure your app to use it. Pull your MongoLab config var from the app, as you'll need it to complete the configuration:

```
$ heroku config | grep MONGOLAB
MONGOLAB_URI: mongodb://heroku_app2094323:
bs6fjtnhmdfqvta1msu2uebbt6@ds033867.mongolab.com:33867/heroku_app2094323
```

Before proceeding any further, ensure that your app requires/includes the appropriate libraries, packages, and/or dependencies to leverage MongoDB. In the case of a Ruby app, make sure that you include rubygems, uri, and mongo within your Gemfile and any other config files (config.ru). This will ensure that you include the Ruby driver to connect your app to the MongoDB instance.

Then you can leverage the following sample snippet to connect in your app:

```
uri  = URI.parse(ENV['MONGOLAB_URI'])
conn = Mongo::Connection.from_uri(ENV['MONGOLAB_URI'])
db   = conn.db(uri.path.gsub(/^\//, ''))
db.collection_names.each { |name| puts name }
```

3. Now you can start using your MongoLab instance. If you need to do any administration, Figure 10-13 shows the main console. There are a few tabs to navigate through, based on what you need to do:

➤ **Collections:** This represents all your existing databases within MongoLab. Note that, by default, system collections for indexes, namespaces, and users are created automatically. To create a new collection, click the Add button, provide a Collection Name, and click Create. The following options are available:

➤ **Search or create new documents:** This is where your objects can be created from the GUI.

➤ **Add new indexes:** Any additional indexes you require for an app can be added here.

➤ **View collection level stats:** Provides detailed usage metrics on the collection statistics.

➤ **Leverage usability tools:** Runs interactive query sessions on the collection data or import/export data sets.

➤ **Users:** If you require additional users to have access to your MongoLab DBs, you can add them here. Enter a username and password, select whether they will be read-only, and then click Create. This becomes helpful if you have other apps or services that may need to connect to the same MongoLab instance.

➤ **Stats:** This provides the usage metrics for your instance as both a chart and raw key-value output for exported use (if required).

➤ **Tools:** This gives you an interactive mechanism to run API requests against your instance with responses in key-value format. It can be useful for quick calls to the system.

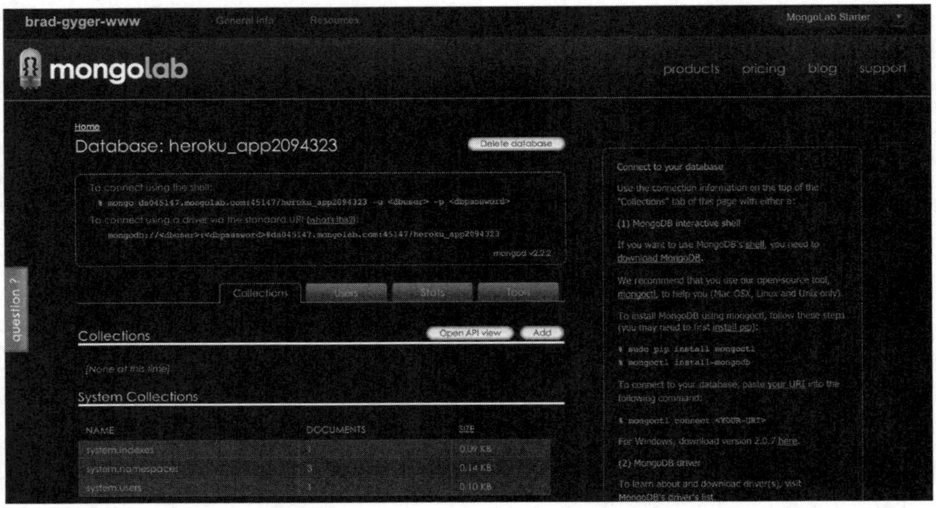

FIGURE 10-13

With Mongo ready to go, it's important to remember that although it can be a very performant option for apps that require big data with distributed, compute-type requirements, existing apps with SQL-based DBs behind them may not be the best migration candidates if you want to leverage Mongo for the first time. Instead, examine your data model and data set to see if there's a fit before betting on MongoDB.

> **NOTE** *For additional documentation on using MongoDB, visit the project's site at* www.mongodb.org.

Redis

Redis is a very lightweight yet highly performant key-value store. It is not meant to be a true NoSQL alternative to SQL-based or RDBMS options; however, if you have a relatively small data set that can fit in memory (cache, session, small data row count), Redis is a great option to keep your app blazingly fast.

Within the Heroku add-ons library are several great options for Redis: RedisGreen, RedisCloud, OpenRedis, and RedisToGo. All are solid options, but this example highlights RedisGreen as the provider.

Here's how to add and configure a RedisGreen instance to your app. As with previous data stores, this can be done either via the Heroku Dashboard or from the command line.

1. Add RedisGreen to your app:

```
$ heroku addons:add redisgreen:basic
Adding redisgreen:basic on brad-gyger-www... done, v84 ($169/mo)
Use 'heroku addons:docs redisgreen:basic' to view documentation.
```

2. When the add-on is installed, you can quickly configure the app to leverage Redis. In the case of Ruby/Rails apps, there are a few quick steps.

   a. Add the gems `redis` and `hiredis` to your `Gemfile`, and then run `bundle install` from the command line:

   ```
   gem 'redis'
   gem 'hiredis'

   $ bundle install
   ```

   b. Pull the RedisGreen instance's config var:

   ```
   $ heroku config | grep REDISGREEN
   REDISGREEN_URL:
       redis://rg:04911a61dfbd49e4bc809a83961157de@
       clever-ponderosa-503.redisgreen.net:11040/
   ```

   c. You will now create a new initializer file that will connect to your Redis instance (on RedisGreen) every time your app loads. It will simply contain the `$redis` setting, pointing to your `REDISGREEN_URL` using the `hiredis` gem.

      i. Create/edit the new initializer file:

      ```
      $ vi config/initializers/redis.rb
      ```

      ii. Add the connection string and then save the file:

      ```
      $redis = Redis.new(url: ENV["REDISGREEN_URL"], driver: hiredis)
      ```

3. Now that your application configuration is complete, you can manage your instance from the RedisGreen Dashboard (available within the Heroku Dashboard). As shown in Figure 10-14, the following tabs are available:

   ➤ **Graphs:** This displays usage statistics around your RedisGreen instance, such as Memory, CPU, Keys, and Clients.

   ➤ **Slow Queries:** This is a graphical representation of the SLOWLOG command. SLOWLOG is a Redis standard command that will display any commands that are taking longer than a specified time. Rather than having to do this on your own, RedisGreen provides this data as part of this service.

   ➤ **Info:** This provides all the instance-level details that could also be provided running the INFO command. INFO is another standard Redis command that users can run within an instance. RedisGreen takes care of this for you.

   ➤ **Backups:** All your RedisGreen backups are available here for migration, export or failover.

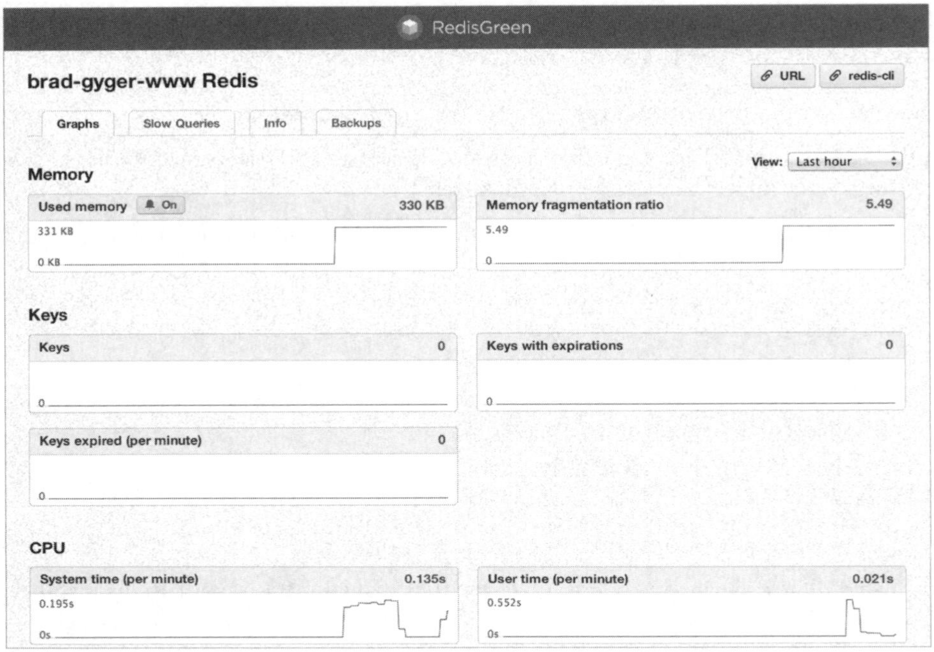

FIGURE 10-14

Now your Heroku RedisGreen add-on is ready to be populated with application data. Remember that you can also view your RedisToGo instance at any time via the Heroku Dashboard or by running `heroku addons:open redisgreen` from your command line.

> **NOTE** *For additional documentation on using Redis, visit the project's site at* `http://redis.io/`.

Apache Cassandra

Apache Cassandra is another option in the NoSQL family. Originally written by members of the Facebook Data team, Cassandra's aim is to handle big data sets across a distributed infrastructure. Now Cassandra is run as an open-source project under the Apache Software Foundation.

> **NOTE** *As of this book's publication, CassandraIO is offered as a Beta service.*

Cassandra is provided within the Heroku add-on ecosystem from CassandraIO. Like the other add-ons described previously, you can add it to your app via the Dashboard or via the command line, as you will explore here.

1. Add CassandraIO to your app:

```
$ heroku addons:add cassandraio
Adding cassandraio on brad-gyger-www... done, v87 (free)
Use 'heroku addons:docs cassandraio' to view documentation.
```

2. Now that you have the Cassandra instance provisioned, you can visit its administration console, shown in Figure 10-15, at any time via the Heroku Dashboard. Notice that it identifies only credentials and plan details; everything else must be done via the command line.

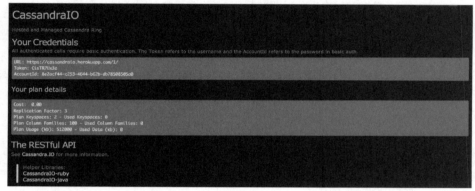

FIGURE 10-15

3. Grab the Heroku config var for your CassandraIO instance. As you've already discovered with the other stores, you'll need this soon:

```
$ heroku config | grep cassandra
CASSANDRAIO_URL: https://CisTR7Ux3z:8e2acf44-c253-4644-b62b-
  db78508505a0@api.cassandra.io/1/welcome
```

4. You will need the client helper libraries to properly interact with your CassandraIO instance via Java, Ruby, or PHP on Heroku.

   a. Visit the Cassandra site (http://cassandra.io/#heroku-platforms) to locate the appropriate Client Toolkit libraries. This will redirect to the appropriate git repositories.

   b. git clone the repositories to your local machine:

```
$ git clone https://github.com/m2mIO/cassandraio-client-libraries.git
Cloning into 'cassandraio-client-libraries'...
remote: Counting objects: 227, done.
remote: Compressing objects: 100% (173/173), done.
remote: Total 227 (delta 82), reused 168 (delta 23)
Receiving objects: 100% (227/227), 3.19 MiB | 488 KiB/s, done.
Resolving deltas: 100% (82/82), done.
```

5. Now that you have the service installed on your app and the appropriate libraries, update your app accordingly.

    a. Include everything in the app for Cassandra to function, adding `require '.cassandraio'` to the Ruby app.

    b. Include the connection details:

```
cIO = CassandraIO.new(
    :heroku => 'api.cassandra.io/1/welcome',
    :port => 443,
    :ssl => 'true',
    :token => 'CisTR7Ux3z',
    :accountID => '8e2acf44-c253-4644-b62b-db78508505a0')
```

        You can also simplify this by passing just your token and account ID credentials within the connection settings.

CassandraIO is now configured and ready to accept data from your app. Remember that the offering is still in beta within the Heroku ecosystem, so you'll likely need to leverage the community resources if this is your first foray into Cassandra as a data store.

> **NOTE** *For additional documentation on using Cassandra, visit the Apache Project page at* `http://cassandra.apache.org/.`

Apache CouchDB

Apache CouchDB (commonly referred to as *Couch*) is another NoSQL option to consider. One of the main advantages it offers compared with something like Mongo is that its primary communication protocol is REST-based — making interaction a bit more familiar. It best serves (very quickly) data sets that don't often change or environments where pre-defined searches/queries are frequently run. Similar to Cassandra, CouchDB is also maintained as an Apache project.

In the Heroku add-on ecosystem, Cloudant is the only vendor that provides a CouchDB-compatible service for apps to consume. As described in the preceding examples, you can add the service via the Heroku Dashboard or via the command line, as you'll explore here.

1. Add Cloudant to your app:

```
$ heroku addons:add cloudant
Adding cloudant on brad-gyger-www... done, v89 (free)
Use 'heroku addons:docs cloudant' to view documentation.
```

By default running `addons:add cloudant` will provision an "Oxygen" instance of the Cloudant service. Cloudant provides several different instance sizes, with increasing amounts of storage. Be sure to size appropriately to start, and then scale up as needed.

2. Visit the Cloudant administration console by selecting it from the app detail page within Heroku Dashboard. Note that it provides a bit more interactivity than the previous providers described.

You can also open the Cloudant console from the command line.

```
$ heroku addons:open cloudant
Opening cloudant:oxygen for brad-gyger-www... done
```

3. Create a new database. As shown in Figure 10-16, the Cloudant admininistration console allows you to create a database from with the UI. Enter a name and click Create.

FIGURE 10-16

4. With your Cloudant instance running a new database, you can now create documents that are searchable for that database. The idea of a document is that it's basically the key-value pair you will want to store in the database. Figure 10-17 shows a few example key-value pairs. Note that you can even upload attachments as part of the data set. Remember to click Save Document if you add any data (documents) to your database.

FIGURE 10-17

5. Now configure your Heroku app with the Cloudant service. As always, the first thing to do is to pull the appropriate config var:

```
$ heroku config | grep cloudant
CLOUDANT_URL:           https://app2094323.heroku:dVVARImFdLtMq80jHKlL2jmo@
app2094323.heroku.cloudant.com
```

6. Interact with your Cloudant instance on Heroku using the REST client, which can be downloaded/cloned from GitHub (https://github.com/archiloque/rest-client):

```
$ git clone https://github.com/archiloque/rest-client.git
Cloning into 'rest-client'...
remote: Counting objects: 2393, done.
remote: Compressing objects: 100% (783/783), done.
remote: Total 2393 (delta 1679), reused 2212 (delta 1539)
Receiving objects: 100% (2393/2393), 406.66 KiB | 274 KiB/s, done.
Resolving deltas: 100% (1679/1679), done.
```

7. Modify your app to pull a document from your database. The following example adds a route to a Sinatra (Ruby) app that retrieves the specific document you need:

```
DB = "#{ENV['CLOUDANT_URL']}/test"

get "/doc/:doc" do
  doc = RestClient.get("#{DB}/#{params[:doc]}")
  @result = JSON.parse(doc)
  haml :doc_id
end
```

8. Update your app's view to display the document:

```
%h1 Brads Cloudant Doc
  - @result.each do |k,v|
    %b=k
    %em=v
    %br
```

9. To test your app, enter http://brad-gyger-www.herokuapp.com/test/<doc>' in a web browser. The document in question should render.

Congratulations! You have successfully configured your Cloudant instance running CouchDB on Heroku.

ATTACHING EXISTING DATA STORES

The preceding sections have covered several types of data stores available within the Heroku add-on ecosystem, but remember that existing stores can also be leveraged for your Heroku app. If you already run cloud-based data services (either private or public) elsewhere, Heroku config vars provide the means to do so. By specifying any connection data required in a custom config var, you can attach your existing store(s) much like any other service (e-mail, CDN, etc.) to your app.

If you are running services on AWS, specifically Amazon Elastic Compute Cloud (Amazon EC2) in the US-East Region, you'll see extremely low latency because you're running in the same region as Heroku itself. Here's how you can connect an external data store (in this case, running on Amazon EC2):

1. To allow Heroku access to your separate Amazon EC2 instances, run the following command:

```
$ ec2-authorize <groupname>  -P tcp -p 3306 -u 098166147350 -o default
```

> **NOTE** *You can find out more about the AWS EC2 API tools and associated documentation at* http://aws.amazon.com/developertools/351.

2. If you have a remote MySQL database to which you'd like to connect, first get your CA certificate, and then add it to your local working app directory:

```
$ mkdir -p config/ca
$ cp <ca_path>/cert-name.pem config/ca
```

3. Ensure that your Gemfile includes the appropriate mysql gem, and then create a Git repository and add and commit the changes:

```
$ git add .
$ git commit -v -m "adding CA and Gemfile update"
```

4. Add your config vars and git push:

```
$ heroku config:add EXTERNAL_DATABASE_URL=
'mysql://<username>:<password>@<server>/<dbname>'
$ heroku config:add EXTERNAL_DATABASE_CA= ',cert-name>.pm'
$ git push heroku master
```

Now your app is set up to connect to the remote MySQL database, but you're not done yet. You still need to allow incoming connections to your remote data service (in this case, MySQL) and update any whitelist requirements if they are enforced. Heroku provides an add-on called Proximo (see Figure 10-18) that enables you to do this elegantly, as apps on Heroku do not receive a single, dedicated IP address. You can add Proximo using either the Heroku Dashboard or the command line.

FIGURE 10-18

5. Add the Proximo service to your app:

```
$ heroku addons:add proximo:development
Adding proximo:development on brad-gyger-www... done, v69 ($5/mo)
Your static IP address is 23.21.235.22
Use 'heroku addons:docs proximo:development' to view documentation.
```

6. Pull the Heroku config var for Proximo:

```
$ heroku config | grep proximo
PROXIMO_URL: http://proxy:65f90a50dd03-4196-89f2-5098b8db058f@
  proxy-23-21-235-22.proximo.io
```

The @proxy segment of the string is your IP, which you can add to any IP whitelisting, firewall, or general security/operational requirements you need to fulfill to allow inbound traffic from your Heroku app to an outside service or system.

7. Now add your Proximo proxy to the app itself. Proximo requires that a small piece of software be installed directly to your app. The binary wraps your processes and automatically forwards outbound TCP connections to your proxy, essentially a process wrapper to send all requests through Proximo. To install the code:

    a. Move into your top-level app directory:

```
$ cd /brads-app
```

    b. Download the file and uncompress it from the command line:

```
$ curl -O http://downloads.proximo.io/proximo-stacklet.tgz
$ tar xz http://downloads.proximo.io/proximo-stacklet.tgz
```

    c. Add and commit your changes into your app's git repository:

```
$ git add bin/proximo vendor/dante
$ git commit -m " adding proximo"
```

8. Modify your Heroku Procfile to have all processes run within the Proximo wrapper:

```
web: bin/proximo [your standard app process]
```

9. You can also modify the way that Proximo routes traffic:

➤ PROXIMO_MASK: This provides the ability to mask traffic to a subset of destinations. The following snippet would send any traffic destined for the given IP ranges through your Proximo proxy:

```
$ heroku config:add PROXIMO_MASK="75.101.128.0/17"
```

➤ PROXIMO_URL: This is your standard Proximo config var with Heroku. It also enables you to use Proximo as a standard HTTP proxy over port 80. For example, if you wanted to implement this feature within your Ruby app, you would add the following to your app:

```
require "rest-client"

RestClient.proxy = ENV["PROXIMO_URL"] if ENV["PROXIMO_URL"]

res = RestClient.get("http://get.yourwebservice.com/endpoint")
puts "status code: ", res.code
puts "headers: ", res.headers
```

10.   Explicitly grant privileges for the data service or system itself. Here's the MySQL way from within the SQL prompt:

```
GRANT ALL PRIVILEDGES ON <db-name>.* TO
  <user-name>@<heroku-proximo-ip-address>
  IDENTIFIED BY '<password>';
```

Now your external data store is attached to your Heroku app. Although the exact steps and commands may vary according to the technology or organizational requirements, the general flow is the same:

1.   Include authentication from your Heroku app.

2.   Modify your app and config vars to connect to the service.

3.   Update/redeploy your Heroku app with changes.

4.   Enable your Heroku source IP via Proximo (if required).

5.   Allow inbound connections to your data store.

SUMMARY

This chapter discussed alternative data stores that you can use to back your apps. SQL, NoSQL and existing external stores are all viable options when deploying on Heroku. It's important to take into consideration your use case (which data service will fit best with your app or service), latency and response times (which will provide the best user experience), as well as the overall effectiveness of the technology (how savvy are you, your team, and supporting resources/infrastructure). The beauty of Heroku and the various stores available to you is that you can find an option that's best for the project at hand.

PART IV
Programming on Heroku's Polyglot Platform

11

Developing with Ruby

WHAT'S IN THIS CHAPTER?

➤ Understanding Ruby

➤ Installing Ruby on your local workstation

➤ Managing dependencies

➤ Creating an application with the Rails framework

➤ Creating an application with the Sinatra framework

➤ Using Delayed Job for background jobs

➤ Caching with Ruby

➤ Porting Ruby applications to Heroku

WROX.COM CODE DOWNLOADS FOR THIS CHAPTER

The wrox.com code downloads for this chapter are found at www.wrox.com/remtitle
.cgi?isbn=1118508998 on the Download Code tab. The code is in the Chapter 11 download
and individually named according to the names throughout the chapter.

This chapter explores how to run Ruby apps on Heroku. To create Ruby apps on Heroku,
you first must install Ruby locally. Dependencies in Ruby are managed using Bundle. You
can create Ruby apps using a number of frameworks, including the popular Rails and Sinatra
frameworks.

Background jobs are used for long-running tasks and Delayed Job can be used in Ruby to
run these jobs. Caching is important to ensure that Ruby apps run quickly, and a number of

different strategies can be employed in Ruby. There are also a number of important considerations to keep in mind when porting apps on Ruby to ensure it runs properly.

UNDERSTANDING RUBY

When Heroku launched in 2007, Ruby was the only supported language. It has since evolved into a polyglot platform, but Ruby still remains Heroku's most popular language because of its roots in the Ruby development community. Heroku's commitment to Ruby is so strong that on July 12, 2011, Yukihiro "Matz" Matsumoto, Ruby's creator, was hired as Chief Architect of Ruby. This appointment gives Matz and the core Ruby development team the stability they need to focus on continuing to develop and improve Ruby.

Ruby is well known for being a language that enables programmers to develop web apps quickly, which complements the core principles of agile methodologies. Ruby had already been around for almost 10 years before the Rails framework was introduced by David Heinemeier Hansson, but the Rails framework is often credited with putting Ruby on the map, with its focus on using convention over configuration to reduce the amount of code needed. Rails also subscribes to the "don't repeat yourself" principle, facilitating rapid development through eliminating the tedious duplication of work inherent in traditional programming languages. Rails is a mature framework that is an excellent fit for large, enterprise web apps.

Sinatra is a popular, Rack-based alternative framework for Ruby. Unlike Rails, Sinatra does not adhere strictly to the traditional model-view-controller (MVC) pattern typically seen in modern frameworks, though MVC can be used easily enough. Like Rails, Sinatra's focus is on minimizing the effort needed to build web apps quickly, but it takes this to a whole new level of simplicity. It is best suited for small, utility apps, quick prototyping, and writing web services in a single file. Its small footprint also makes it a very lightweight framework to use with minimal overhead, and it has inspired numerous similar frameworks in many other languages.

Though you can write code using virtually any framework on Heroku, including Rack-based frameworks such as Ramaze and Camping, this chapter focuses on the popular Rails and Sinatra frameworks.

INSTALLING RUBY ON YOUR LOCAL WORKSTATION

You will need to install a number of programs on your workstation to run Ruby apps locally using popular frameworks. To install the programs needed, use the following instructions.

1. Mac OS X comes pre-installed with Ruby. Mac OS X Tiger comes with version 1.8.2; Leopard with version 1.8.6; and Lion and Mountain Lion with version 1.8.7. If your workstation does not have Ruby installed, you can install it by first installing Homebrew, an easy to use package manager for Mac OS X, with the following command:

   ```
   ruby -e "$(curl -fsSkL raw.github.com/mxcl/homebrew/go)"
   ```

   Once Homebrew is installed, you can install Ruby with the following command:

```
$ brew install ruby
```

If you are using Windows, download and install RubyInstaller (`http://rubyinstaller.org/`) to use Ruby.

2. Heroku supports many different versions of Ruby. You can run multiple different versions of Ruby on the same workstation using the Ruby Version Manager (RVM). To install RVM, go to `https://rvm.io/rvm/install/#explained` and follow the instructions. You can then install a specific version using the following command:

```
$ rvm install <version number>
```

You will need to replace `<version number>` with the version of Ruby you want to install (e.g. 1.9.2).

3. Install Rails, a popular framework for Ruby, using the following command:

```
$ gem install rails
```

4. Another popular framework for Ruby is Sinatra. You can install Sinatra with the following command:

```
$ gem install sinatra
```

MANAGING DEPENDENCIES

Dependency management with Ruby apps is done with RubyGems using the Bundler application dependency manager — specifically, version 1.2.0. RubyGems is a package management facility that supplies a standard format for libraries (called *gems*) and supporting apps that makes it easy to distribute and install them, similar to yum or apt for Linux. To get started with dependency management with Ruby, you must first install the Bundler gem:

```
$ gem install bundler
Fetching: bundler-1.1.5.gem (100%)
Successfully installed bundler-1.1.5
1 gem installed
Installing ri documentation for bundler-1.1.5...
Installing RDoc documentation for bundler-1.1.5...
```

Now that you have Bundler installed, you can create a file called `Gemfile` in the root directory of your applications. This file contains a list of the dependencies that your Heroku Ruby app requires to run. Use the following to create a simple `Gemfile`:

```
source "http://rubygems.org"
gem "sinatra", "1.2.6"
gem "pg"
```

The first line tells Bundler from which RubyGem server the dependencies should be obtained. In this case, you are using RubyGems.org, the community RubyGems host. The second line is an example that defines which specific version of a gem you want to use — in this case, version 1.2.6 of the Sinatra framework. Version numbers can also contain basic logic, such as `>=1.0` to get any version later than 1.0. The last line simply indicates the latest version you have of the Postgres gem by omitting the specific version number.

Now that you have your dependencies defined, ensure that your gems are installed:

```
$ bundle install
Fetching gem metadata from http://rubygems.org/....
Using pg (0.14.0)
Using rack (1.4.1)
Using tilt (1.3.3)
Using sinatra (1.2.6)
Using bundler (1.1.5)
Your bundle is complete! Use 'bundle show [gemname]' to see where a bundled gem is
installed.
```

As you can see, the dependencies have been downloaded, along with any dependencies of dependencies. They are all now available locally for your app to use in your system's default location for gems. A Gemfile.lock file has also been created, which will be committed with your source code as a snapshot that other developers will use to ensure they are using the exact same version of gems that you are.

> **NOTE** *Even if you do not have any dependencies in your app, you still must include an empty file named* Gemfile *in the root directory. This is the file that identifies to Heroku that you are deploying a Ruby app.*

Upgrading to the latest, greatest version of a gem is simple. For example, you can edit the Gemfile so the Sinatra line looks like this:

```
gem "sinatra", "1.3.2"
```

Now you can update Gemfile.lock to include your latest version and the correct dependencies for the new version:

```
$ bundle install
Using pg (0.14.0)
Using rack (1.4.1)
Using rack-protection (1.2.0)
Using tilt (1.3.3)
Using sinatra (1.3.2)
Using bundler (1.1.5)
Your bundle is complete! Use 'bundle show [gemname]' to see where a bundled gem is
installed.
```

You can also specify different libraries to be used for different environments. For instance, if you do not have Postgres installed locally but want to use the Postgres database, you can swap in SQLite locally instead, using dependency groups:

```
group :development do
    gem 'sqlite3'
end

group :production do
    gem 'pg'
end
```

> **NOTE** *Using two different databases for development and production generally isn't recommended, as you ideally want to keep development environments as similar as possible to production. However, if you can't get a specific gem working locally but need it for your production app, you can use this as a workaround. An acceptable use would be having a group called* test *that includes gems such as RSpec that are only needed locally for testing and will reduce your slug size.*

The following command creates a `Gemfile.lock` for use with local testing:

```
$ bundle install --without production
Using rack (1.4.1)
Using rack-protection (1.2.0)
Using tilt (1.3.3)
Using sinatra (1.3.2)
Using sqlite3 (1.3.6)
Using bundler (1.1.5)
Your bundle is complete! Use 'bundle show [gemname]' to see where a bundled gem is
installed.
```

Heroku will now use SQLite locally. When you push your app to production, you can see some interesting behavior:

```
$ git push heroku master
Counting objects: 6, done.
Delta compression using up to 4 threads.
Compressing objects: 100% (4/4), done.
Writing objects: 100% (6/6), 659 bytes, done.
Total 6 (delta 0), reused 0 (delta 0)

-----> Heroku receiving push
-----> Ruby app detected
-----> Installing dependencies using Bundler version 1.2.0.pre
       Running: bundle install --without development:test --path vendor/bundle
       --binstubs bin/ --deployment
       Fetching gem metadata from http://rubygems.org/....
       Installing pg (0.14.0) with native extensions
       Installing rack (1.4.1)
       Installing rack-protection (1.2.0)
       Installing tilt (1.3.3)
       Installing sinatra (1.3.2)
       Using bundler (1.2.0.pre)
       Your bundle is complete! It was installed into ./vendor/bundle
       Cleaning up the bundler cache.
-----> Discovering process types
[...]
```

When Heroku pushes apps, the gems are downloaded and installed for your app to use, and the development and test groups are specifically excluded. In this case, your Postgres gem was included and SQLite was not. By getting a fresh copy, you are ensuring that dependencies are isolated and that no developer has leaked in manual changes to the gem that may later break your code when you upgrade to the latest version.

You can even specify the version of Ruby you would like to run by declaring it as a dependency. The current default version of Ruby is 1.9.2p290; alternate versions of Ruby available are 1.8.7 and 1.9.3. To include a version of Ruby other than the default, simply add something like `ruby '1.9.3'` to your `Gemfile`. When you push your app, this is automatically detected and you will see the version of Ruby explicitly specified in the output (shown bolded) during the push:

```
$ git push heroku master
Counting objects: 16, done.
Delta compression using up to 4 threads.
Compressing objects: 100% (10/10), done.
Writing objects: 100% (10/10), 808 bytes, done.
Total 10 (delta 7), reused 0 (delta 0)

-----> Heroku receiving push
-----> Ruby/Rails app detected
-----> Using Ruby version: ruby-1.9.3
[...]
```

> **NOTE** *For the latest list of supported Ruby versions on Heroku, go to* https://devcenter.heroku.com/articles/ruby-support#ruby_versions.

CREATING AN APPLICATION WITH THE RAILS FRAMEWORK

You have already seen a basic app used to test out the Postgres Heroku database. The following example of a Rails app takes this one step further by demonstrating how you can use the Rails framework to create a handy app for use as a phone-based employee directory (code file: `ch11-ruby-rails-example.zip`). This example uses the Twilio REST API to create an interactive voice response (IVR) system whereby users can hear a list of employees and their extensions and then enter an extension number on their phone's keypad to be connected to a specific employee.

Writing the Application

You will create a Rails app that users access to manage employee records in the directory. The Twilio API will also access the same app when people call your Twilio phone number, handling the logic in your IVR system. For instance, when the caller inputs an extension belonging to an employee, the app will find the employee in the Heroku Postgres database and use Twilio to connect the caller to the corresponding employee's phone number.

1. To begin, create a new app with Rails 3:

```
$ rails new employee-directory
      create
      create  README.rdoc
      create  Rakefile
      create  config.ru
      create  .gitignore
      create  Gemfile
```

```
        create  app
        create  app/assets/images/rails.png
  [...]
        run  bundle install
Fetching gem metadata from https://rubygems.org/........
Using rake (0.9.2.2)
Using i18n (0.6.0)
Using multi_json (1.3.6)
  [...]
```

2. After creating the Rails app, access the directory and initialize a Git repository:

```
$ cd employee-directory/

$ git init
Initialized empty Git repository in /Users/ckemp/Documents/Sites/employee-directory/
.git/
```

3. Create a Rails scaffolding:

```
$ rails generate scaffold employee name:string extension:integer phone:string
        invoke active_record
        create db/migrate/20120719213432_create_employees.rb
        create app/models/employee.rb
        invoke test_unit
  [...]
```

This scaffolding automatically creates the model, views, and controller for the list of employees, extensions, and phone numbers to connect to.

4. Add your dependencies to your Rails app's `Gemfile`:

```
gem 'rake'
gem 'pg'
gem 'twilio-ruby'
```

Here you are adding the Rake gem to migrate your database, the Postgres gem to interface with the database server, and the Twilio Ruby gem to access the Twilio API for telephony-related actions, such as answering calls, sending text messages, and dialing numbers.

> **WARNING** *This example uses the built-in development Postgres database to save time. If you are writing a production app, it is suggested that you use the Dev database for testing, and one of the Production database plans for your production app's database. See Chapter 8, "Using Heroku Postgres as a Data Store for Your Heroku Applications," for more information on adding Dev and Production databases to your app.*

5. Use Bundler to install your gems:

```
$ bundle install
Using rake (0.9.2.2)
Using i18n (0.6.0)
Using multi_json (1.3.6)
```

```
[...]
Using twilio-ruby (3.7.0)
Using uglifier (1.2.6)
Your bundle is complete! Use 'bundle show [gemname]' to see where a bundled gem is
installed.
```

6. The following command creates your app on Heroku:

```
$ heroku create twilio-phone-directory-rails
Creating twilio-phone-directory-rails... done, stack is cedar
http://twilio-phone-directory-rails.herokuapp.com/ |
git@heroku.com:twilio-phone-directory-rails.git
Git remote heroku added
```

7. Now that your app has been added to Heroku, you must write the code for it. First, open
app/controllers/employees_controller.rb, which was automatically generated when
we created the scaffolding, and add the following lines of code before your final end tag,
replacing [your-app-name] in the value of BASE_URL with your Heroku app's base URL:

```
# base URL of this application
BASE_URL = "http://[your-app-name].herokuapp.com/employees"

# GET /employees/directory
def directory
    @post_to = BASE_URL + '/menu'
    render :action => "directory.xml.builder", :layout => false
    return
end

# POST /employees/menu
def menu
    @post_to = BASE_URL + '/extension'

    # If 1 is entered, do extension entry
    if params['Digits'] == '1'
        render :action => "extension.xml.builder", :layout => false
        return
    end

    # If 2 is entered, list all employees
    if params['Digits'] == '2'
        @employees = Employee.all
        render :action => "list.xml.builder", :layout => false
        return
    end
end

# POST /employees/extension
def extension
    # Get employee with extension entered from database
    @employees = Employee.where("extension = ?", params['Digits']).limit(1)

    if @employees.count == 1
        # Connect to phone number entered
        @employee = @employees[0]
```

```
            render :action => "call.xml.builder", :layout => false
        else
            # No entry found for extension entered
            @entry = params['Digits']
            @post_to = BASE_URL + '/menu'
            render :action => "notfound.xml.builder", :layout => false
        end
        return
    end
```

The first method, `directory`, is the method that will be called when the user first calls your Twilio phone number. When this number is called, you want to fire off a script that welcomes the caller and lists the initial options. You will use Builder to generate the XML needed to define the scripts that Twilio will follow during the call.

Twilio uses an XML markup language called *TwiML* for this. In this method, you also use the `@post_to` variable. When passed and used in your generated XML, this variable tells Twilio where to send an HTTP POST when input is entered on the phone's keypad. In this case, you will send the POST to your `menu` method, which handles the caller's input.

The `menu` method is passed the POST with the `Digits` parameter, filled with the digit(s) entered by the user. In your app, two options should be available to callers: entering an extension if "1" is first selected (if the caller already knows the employee's extension) or pressing "2" to get a list of all employees and their extensions. This method will route to the appropriate XML file, based on what was entered.

The `extension` method receives a POST with four digits in the `Digits` parameter indicating the extension the caller wishes to reach. A database lookup is done, and the caller is connected to the correct phone number based on the extension entered. An error message is generated if the extension is invalid.

8. Phone numbers saved in the database must be cleaned of any non-numeric characters, such as dashes and parentheses, that users may enter. To do this, add the following lines to `app/models/employee.rb`, which was automatically generated when you created the scaffolding, before the last line:

```
before_save :clean_phone

def clean_phone
    self.phone = self.phone.gsub(/[^0-9]/i, '')
end
```

This block of code will automatically be run each time you add a new employee to your database or edit an employee record, eliminating any non-numeric characters from the phone number.

9. Add your XML builders to define the call scripts that will be generated. To do this, add a file called `app/views/employees/directory.xml.builder` with the following code:

```
xml.instruct!
xml.Response do
    xml.Gather(:action => @post_to, :numDigits => 1) do
        xml.Say("Welcome to the Employee Directory.", :voice => "woman")
        xml.Say("If you know the extension of the person ", :voice => "woman")
```

```
            xml.Say("you wish to speak to, press 1. Please ", :voice => "woman")
            xml.Say("press 2 to hear a list of employees and ", :voice => "woman")
            xml.Say("their extensions.", :voice => "woman")
        end
end
```

When run, the preceding will generate an XML file that looks like this:

```
<?xml version="1.0" encoding="UTF-8"?>
<Response>
    <Gather action="http://employee-directory.herokuapp.com/employees/menu"
            numDigits="1">
        <Say voice="woman">Welcome to the Employee Directory.</Say>
        <Say voice="woman">If you know the extension of the person you wish to speak to,
press 1.</Say>
        <Say voice="woman">Please press 2 to hear a list of employees and their
            extensions.</Say>
    </Gather>
</Response>
```

The `<Gather>` tag instructs Twilio that you want to gather numeric input from the caller, with the `numDigits` attribute indicating that only a single digit should be gathered. The `action` attribute points to the URL to which you want to POST the response. The `<Say>` tag tells Twilio that you want the voice to read the text inside the tags using an American woman's voice, as specified using the `voice` attribute. (You can use a male or female British, Spanish, French, or German voice.)

> **NOTE** *For complete documentation on TwiML usage, see* `www.twilio.com/docs/api/twiml`.

10. Add a file in the same directory called `list.xml.builder`, so if "2" is pressed in the main menu, all employees will be listed:

```
xml.instruct!
xml.Response do
    xml.Gather(:action => @post_to, :numDigits => 4) do
        @employees.each do |employee|
            xml.Say(employee.name + " at extension " +
                employee.extension.to_s(), :voice => "woman")
        end
        xml.Say("Please enter the 4 digit extension now.", :voice => "woman")
    end
end
```

This XML builder will loop through the list of all employees in the database, passed in with the `@employees` variable, reading the name and extension of each employee aloud. Finally, you prompt for the four-digit extension the caller wishes to reach.

11. If users press "1" in the same menu, they are prompted to enter the extension of the employee they want to reach. Use the following code to add `extension.xml.builder` to the same directory:

```
xml.instruct!
xml.Response do
    xml.Gather(:action => @post_to, :numDigits => 4) do
        xml.Say("Enter the 4 digit extension now.", :voice => "woman")
    end
end
```

12. Add `call.xml.builder` to make the call to the employee users want to reach:

```
xml.instruct!
xml.Response do
    xml.Say("Connecting to ", :voice => "woman")
    xml.Say(@employee.name, :voice => "woman")
    xml.Dial @employee.phone
end
```

The `<Dial>` tag instructs Twilio to connect the caller to the number inside that tag — in this case, the phone number belonging to the employee whose extension was entered by the caller.

13. Add `notfound.xml.builder` to deal with situations in which an invalid extension is entered:

```
xml.instruct!
xml.Response do
    xml.Gather(:action => @post_to, :numDigits => 1) do
        xml.Say("The extention you entered, " + @entry, :voice => "woman")
        xml.Say(" was not found. To try another extension, press 1.  For a ",
            :voice => "woman")
        xml.Say("list of extensions, press 2.", :voice => "woman")
    end
end
```

14. Add the following lines before the `resources :employees` line in your `config/routes.rb` file, which was automatically generated when you created the scaffolding:

```
match 'employees/directory', :to => 'employees#directory'
match 'employees/menu', :to => 'employees#menu'
match 'employees/extension', :to => 'employees#extension'
match 'employees/call', :to => 'employees#call'
```

This will route your web app URLs to the appropriate actions in the controller.

15. Let's pretty up the phone numbers a bit. Because the model saves the phone number as a series of numbers only, you should make them a bit more human-readable. Therefore, in `app/views/employees/show.html.erb`, which was automatically generated when you created scaffolding, replace the following line:

```
<%= @employee.phone %>
```

with the following line:

```
<%= number_to_phone(@employee.phone, :area_code => true) %>
```

16. Likewise, in `app/views/employees/index.html.erb`, which was automatically generated when you created scaffolding, replace the following line:

```
<td><%= employee.phone %></td>
```

with this:

```
<td><%= number_to_phone(employee.phone, :area_code => true) %></td>
```

That will change your purely numeric phone number (e.g., "5555555555") into a phone number formatted for the U.S. or Canada (e.g., "(555) 555-5555").

Signing Up for a Twilio Account

You have to sign up for a Twilio trial account to use the Twilio API.

1. Go to Twilio's trial account registration page at `www.twilio.com/try-twilio`. Enter your name, e-mail address, and password, and click the Get Started button.

2. Verify a phone number where you can receive calls with your trial account (you can only text and call numbers that have been verified with a trial account). On the next screen, you will be presented with a Twilio number that you can use to take incoming calls. If possible, choose a local number here so you don't rack up long-distance bills while testing your app. If you're satisfied with the number provided, click Get Started and you will be taken to your account dashboard.

3. You are redirected to the Twilio account dashboard page, which includes debugging information when something goes wrong, as well as metrics detailing when calls and text messages are made with your Twilio account. This page also contains your credentials, which consists of an Account SID and Auth Token needed to access the Twilio API. You will need to add those to your application's config vars in a later step. You can display the value of the Auth Token by clicking the key icon beside the Auth Token label.

4. Before leaving the Twilio account dashboard, let's add a Voice Request URL. This is the URL that Twilio will visit when someone calls your Twilio number. The TwiML returned from visiting this URL will define the flow of your interactive phone responses. To set your Voice Request URL, click Numbers, and then click the phone number that you set up during registration. Replace the value of "Voice Request URL" with `http://[your-app-name]` `.herokuapp.com/employees/directory` and click Save Changes.

5. Add your Twilio credentials to your app's configuration variables (config vars) in Heroku:

```
$ heroku config:add TWILIO_ACCOUNT_SID="mYtW1l10aCc0UnT51D"
TWILIO_AUTH_TOKEN="mYtW1l10aUtHt0K3n"
Setting config vars and restarting twilio-phone-directory-rails... done, v2
TWILIO_ACCOUNT_SID: mYtW1l10aCc0UnT51D
TWILIO_AUTH_TOKEN:  mYtW1l10aUtHt0K3n
```

Deploying the Application to Heroku

Now that you have written the code for your app, signed up for Twilio, and added your credentials to your app's config vars, you must deploy your app to Heroku.

1. Commit your code and push your app to Heroku:

```
$ git add .

$ git commit -am "init"
[master (root-commit) 71e391f] init
```

```
58 files changed, 1618 insertions(+), 0 deletions(-)
create mode 100644 .gitignore
create mode 100644 Gemfile
[...]

$ git push heroku master
Counting objects: 95, done.
Delta compression using up to 4 threads.
Compressing objects: 100% (85/85), done.
Writing objects: 100% (95/95), 31.72 KiB, done.
Total 95 (delta 6), reused 0 (delta 0)

-----> Heroku receiving push
-----> Ruby/Rails app detected
-----> Installing dependencies using Bundler version 1.2.0.rc
       Running: bundle install --without development:test --path vendor/bundle
       --binstubs bin/ --deployment
       Fetching gem metadata from https://rubygems.org/.......
       Installing rake (0.9.2.2)
       Installing i18n (0.6.0)
[...]
-----> Discovering process types
       Procfile declares types   -> (none)
       Default types for Ruby/Rails -> console, rake, web, worker
-----> Compiled slug size is 9.7MB
-----> Launching... done, v5
       http://twilio-phone-directory-rails.herokuapp.com deployed to Heroku

To git@heroku.com:twilio-phone-directory-rails.git
 * [new branch]     master -> master
```

When deploying a Ruby on Rails app, Heroku will automatically detect that a Rails app
is being deployed. You can see this on the line in the output that says, "Ruby/Rails app
detected"; also detected is the version of Rails needed for the app. If a `config/environment.rb`
file is present in your app, a Rails 2 app is created on Heroku. If a `config/application.rb` file
is present in your app and contains the string `Rails::Application`, this signals to Heroku
that it is dealing with a Rails 3 app.

The following four default process types are created when you deploy an app

➤   `console`: This process type defines your interactive Ruby shell (IRB) used to test
    code against your database or run one-off Ruby commands

➤   `rake`: This process type enables you to run database migrations to initialize or alter
    the database for your app. You will see an example of this shortly.

➤   `web`: This process type is your default process type, the one to which HTTP traffic
    is routed by default. It uses the `rails server` command (Webrick) as a web server.
    You can use a different server, such as Thin, by adding it to your `Gemfile` and
    `Procfile`.

➤   `worker`: This process type defines background workers, as outlined in the section
    "Using Delayed Job for Background Jobs" later in this chapter.

2. Check your config vars:

```
$ heroku config
=== Config Vars for twilio-phone-directory-rails
DATABASE_URL:           postgres://mYu53RnAm3:MyPa55W0rD@ec2-123-45-678-901.
                        compute-1.amazonaws.com/sHaR3dDbNaM3
GEM_PATH:               vendor/bundle/ruby/1.9.1
LANG:                   en_US.UTF-8
PATH:                   bin:vendor/bundle/ruby/1.9.1/bin:/usr/local/bin:/usr/bin:/bin
RACK_ENV:               production
RAILS_ENV:              production
HEROKU_POSTGRESQL_ONYX_URL: postgres://mYu53RnAm3:MyPa55W0rD@ec2-123-45-678-901.
                        compute-1.amazonaws.com/sHaR3dDbNaM3
TWILIO_ACCOUNT_SID:     mYtW1l10aCc0UnT51D
TWILIO_AUTH_TOKEN:      mYtW1l10aUtHt0K3n
```

As you would expect, your `DATABASE_URL` and `HEROKU_POSTGRESQL_ONYX_URL` config vars are the same, because you are using a Dev database as your app's main database. You previously set your `TWILIO_ACCOUNT_SID` and `TWILIO_AUTH_TOKEN` values manually. A number of config vars are automatically set. `GEM_PATH`, `LANG`, and `PATH` are added for any Ruby app deployed to Heroku. `RACK_ENV` and `RAILS_ENV` are set on deployment when a Rails app is detected.

When you deploy a Rails app, the `config/database.yml` file in your code base is overwritten with one provided by Heroku that injects your `DATABASE_URL` value that points to your app's database. If it does not exist, one is created for you. The following shows what that looks like:

```
$ heroku run bash
Running 'bash' attached to terminal... up, run.1

~ $ cat config/database.yml
<%

require 'cgi'
require 'uri'

begin
  uri = URI.parse(ENV["DATABASE_URL"])
rescue URI::InvalidURIError
  raise "Invalid DATABASE_URL"
end

raise "No RACK_ENV or RAILS_ENV found" unless ENV["RAILS_ENV"] || ENV["RACK_ENV"]

def attribute(name, value, force_string = false)
  if value
      value_string =
      if force_string
      '"' + value + '"'
      else
      value
      end
      "#{name}: #{value_string}"
```

```
      else
          ""
      end
  end

  adapter = uri.scheme
  adapter = "postgresql" if adapter == "postgres"

  database = (uri.path || "").split("/")[1]

  username = uri.user
  password = uri.password

  host = uri.host
  port = uri.port

  params = CGI.parse(uri.query || "")

%>

<%= ENV["RAILS_ENV"] || ENV["RACK_ENV"] %>:
  <%= attribute "adapter",  adapter %>
  <%= attribute "database", database %>
  <%= attribute "username", username %>
  <%= attribute "password", password, true %>
  <%= attribute "host",     host %>
  <%= attribute "port",     port %>

<% params.each do |key, value| %>
  <%= key %>: <%= value.first %>
<% end %>
```

3. Run the migration script, which uses the default `rake` process type:

```
$ heroku run rake db:migrate
Running 'rake db:migrate' attached to terminal... up, run.1
Connecting to database specified by DATABASE_URL
Migrating to CreateEmployees (20120726014820)
==  CreateEmployees: migrating ==================================================
-- create_table(:employees)
   -> 0.0584s
==  CreateEmployees: migrated (0.0585s)=========================================
```

Your app is now deployed to Heroku and ready to test.

Testing the Application

Your phone-based employee directory app is running on Heroku, so the final step is to test your app. When you visit http://[your-app-name].herokuapp.com/employees, you can manage the employee database used for your directory, as shown in Figure 11-1. After your app loads, click New Employee and add a name, a four-digit extension, and a valid phone number.

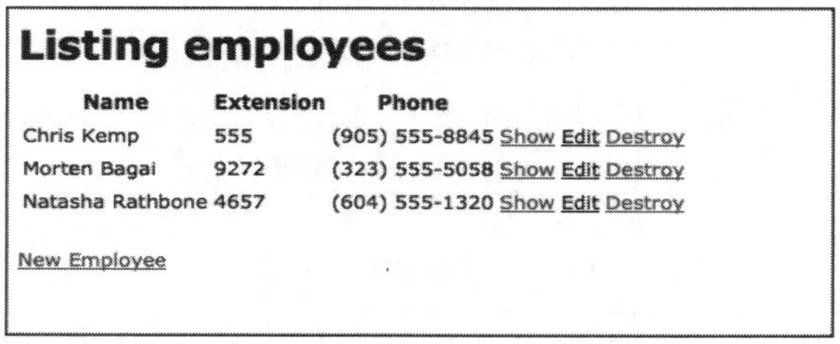

Listing employees

Name	Extension	Phone			
Chris Kemp	555	(905) 555-8845	Show	Edit	Destroy
Morten Bagai	9272	(323) 555-5058	Show	Edit	Destroy
Natasha Rathbone	4657	(604) 555-1320	Show	Edit	Destroy

New Employee

FIGURE 11-1

When you call the Twilio phone number you set up initially, you should reach your phone directory, be able to list the employees and their extensions (in this case, the single entry made thus far), and connect to that phone number when you enter the correct extension. You now have a working phone-based employee directory built with Rails and the Twilio API.

CREATING AN APPLICATION WITH THE SINATRA FRAMEWORK

While Rails typically is the framework of choice for large, complex Ruby apps, Sinatra's strength lies in its ability to facilitate very quick development with a very small footprint. In this section you will build an app using the Sinatra framework, again leveraging the Twilio API (code file: ch11-ruby-sinatra-example.zip). The app will verify that users are human by sending them a PIN in a text message via SMS using the Twilio API. Sinatra is a Rack-based framework, so similar principles can be extended to use the Ramaze and Camping frameworks with Heroku.

> **NOTE** *To see examples of apps using the Ramaze and Camping frameworks on Heroku, visit* https://devcenter.heroku.com/articles/rack. *The example app in this section does not use a backing database, but you will also find examples demonstrating how to access a database with Rack-based apps in the same article.*

Writing the Application

You will create a Sinatra app on Heroku that uses the Twilio API to send an SMS message to the user's phone with a random PIN. After sending the text message, the next screen shown to the user prompts him or her to enter the PIN that was just sent. The PIN the user has entered is then verified against the PIN that was texted to the user's phone.

1. Sinatra apps typically start with a `config.ru` file in the root directory of the code base:

```
# config.ru
require './app'
run Sinatra::Application
```

The existence of a `config.ru` file signals to Heroku that the app uses the Sinatra framework. This is also the file that the Rack web server will run if no `Procfile` is included. If Thin is included in the app's `Gemfile`, Heroku will automatically use the Thin web server instead, also executing the `config.ru` file by default. If you choose to not include a `config.ru` file, you can run whatever file you want by indicating this in a `Procfile` pushed with your app.

2. Create an `app.rb` file in the root directory. This file contains the core code for your app, which `config.ru` will run:

```
# app.rb
require "twilio-ruby"
require 'sinatra'
require 'builder'
```

```ruby
require 'digest/md5'

# Your Twilio authentication credentials
ACCOUNT_SID = ENV['TWILIO_ACCOUNT_SID']
ACCOUNT_TOKEN = ENV['TWILIO_AUTH_TOKEN']

# Your verified Twilio number
CALLER_ID = ENV['TWILIO_VERIFIED_PHONE_NO']

# Salt for making the hash used for passing the PIN unguessable.  You should
# change this to something different, like a random phrase.
SALT = 'mY5@Lt'

get '/' do
    erb :index
end

post '/pin_entry' do
    # Generate random number and translate to four digit PIN and hash it
    random_number = Random.rand(10000)
    pin = "%04d" % random_number
    @pin_md5 = Digest::MD5.hexdigest(pin + SALT)

    if params['number'].empty?
        redirect "/?msg=Invalid%20phone%20number"
        return
    end

    # parameters sent to Twilio REST API
    data = {
        :from => CALLER_ID,
        :to => params['number'],
        :body => 'This is an automated message from the SMS Phone ' +
            'Verification system.  Your PIN is ' + pin + '.'
    }

    begin
        # Use Twilio's REST API to send SMS message
        client = Twilio::REST::Client.new(ACCOUNT_SID, ACCOUNT_TOKEN)
        client.account.sms.messages.create data
    rescue StandardError => bang
        redirect "/?msg=" + URI.escape('Error ' + bang.to_s())
        return
    end

    erb :pin_entry
end

post '/verify' do
    # Check PIN entered against hash of PIN generated
    if params['pin'] != Digest::MD5.hexdigest(params['entry'] + SALT)
        redirect "/?msg=" + URI.escape('Incorrect PIN entered.  Try again.')
    end

    erb :verify
end
```

After including the required libraries, you define placeholders for your Twilio credentials, which you will add as config vars shortly. You also add the Twilio verified phone number to be used as the Caller ID for the text messages you send. Directly following is a salt, a random string used to minimize the risk of an attacker using lookup tables to determine hash values. The salt is used for the one-way hash function that you are going to use for passing the secret PIN number between web requests. As a security best practice, change the salt to a random value.

The first block of code is executed when the user visits the root URL of the app. It simply shows the view, which collects the phone number of the user to whom you are going to send the text message. The second block of code is passed the phone number from the previous form. It creates the four-digit PIN, hashes it along with your salt, and sends a text message with the four-digit PIN to the number the user entered. The hash of the PIN is inserted in a hidden field on the form on which the user enters the PIN from the text message he or she just received. The final block of code hashes the PIN the user entered and confirms that it matches the hash of the PIN generated by the app.

> **NOTE** *When using a Twilio trial account, you can send text messages only to numbers that have been verified through your account dashboard.*

3. Add your first view by creating a directory named "views" and a file named `views/index.erb`, adding the following code:

```
<h1>SMS Phone Number Verification: Step 1</h1>
<h2 style="color: #ff0000"><%= params['msg'] %></h2>
<h3>Enter your phone number to receive an SMS message with a PIN number you
will need to enter on the next screen</h3>
<form action="/pin_entry" method="post">
    <input type="text" name="number" />
    <input type="submit" value="Text me!">
</form>
```

This view has a straightforward purpose: to enable users to enter the phone number to which they want to be texted and to redirect to /pin_entry.

4. Create a file called `views/pin_entry.erb`: and add the following code:

```
<h1>SMS Phone Number Verification: Step 2</h1>
<h2 style="color: #ff0000"><%= params['msg'] %></h2>
<h3>A text message has been sent to <%= params['number'] %> with a four digit
PIN.  When you receive the text message, please enter the PIN below.</h3>
<form action="/verify" method="post">
    <input type="text" name="entry" />
    <input type="hidden" name="pin" value="<%= @pin_md5 %>" />
    <input type="submit" value="Submit">
</form>
```

Here you can see that after the text message is sent, you show the user a form on which they can enter the PIN they received, which contains a hidden field with an MD5 hash representation of the PIN with the salt appended.

5. Create a file called `views/verify.erb`, adding the following code:

```
<h1>SMS Phone Number Verification Complete</h1>
<h3>You have entered the correct PIN and have been successfully verified.</h3>
```

This view is simply static HTML that is displayed to the user if the PIN entered matches the one generated by the app and sent via SMS.

6. Add your `Gemfile`, to include dependencies that the app needs to run:

```
source :rubygems
gem 'sinatra'
gem 'thin'
gem 'twilio-ruby'
```

7. Add your dependencies to your Gem bundle:

```
$ bundle install
Using builder (3.0.0)
Using daemons (1.1.8)
Using eventmachine (0.12.10)
Using multi_json (1.3.6)
Using jwt (0.1.5)
Using rack (1.4.1)
Using rack-protection (1.2.0)
Using tilt (1.3.3)
Using sinatra (1.3.2)
Using thin (1.4.1)
Using twilio-ruby (3.7.0)
Using bundler (1.1.5)
Your bundle is complete! Use 'bundle show [gemname]' to see where a bundled gem is
installed.
```

Your Sinatra app's code is now complete and you are ready to deploy it to Heroku.

Deploying the Application to Heroku

Now that you have written the code for your app, you must add your Twilio API credentials to your config vars and deploy your app to Heroku.

1. Create your Git repository and Heroku app and commit your code:

```
$ git init
Initialized empty Git repository in /Users/ckemp/Documents/Sites/test-sinatra/.git/

$ $ heroku create twilio-verify-sms-sinatra
Creating twilio-verify-sms-sinatra... done, stack is cedar
http://twilio-verify-sms-sinatra.herokuapp.com/ |
git@heroku.com:twilio-verify-sms-sinatra.git
Git remote heroku added

$ git add .

$ git commit -am "Initial commit"
[master (root-commit) e4dc08c] Initial commit
 7 files changed, 119 insertions(+), 0 deletions(-)
 create mode 100644 Gemfile
```

```
create mode 100644 Gemfile.lock
create mode 100644 app.rb
create mode 100644 config.ru
create mode 100644 views/index.erb
create mode 100644 views/pin_entry.erb
create mode 100644 views/verify.erb
```

2. Push your Sinatra app to Heroku:

```
$ git push heroku master
Counting objects: 10, done.
Delta compression using up to 4 threads.
Compressing objects: 100% (10/10), done.
Writing objects: 100% (10/10), 2.28 KiB, done.
Total 10 (delta 0), reused 0 (delta 0)

-----> Heroku receiving push
-----> Ruby/Rack app detected
-----> Installing dependencies using Bundler version 1.2.0.rc
       Running: bundle install --without development:test --path vendor/bundle
       --binstubs bin/ --deployment
       Fetching gem metadata from http://rubygems.org/.....
       Installing builder (3.0.0)
[...]
       Installing twilio-ruby (3.7.0)
       Using bundler (1.2.0.rc)
       Your bundle is complete! It was installed into ./vendor/bundle
       Cleaning up the bundler cache.
-----> Discovering process types
       Procfile declares types   -> (none)
       Default types for Ruby/Rack -> console, rake, web
-----> Compiled slug size is 2.7MB
-----> Launching... done, v3
       http://twilio-verify-sms-sinatra.herokuapp.com deployed to Heroku

To git@heroku.com:twilio-verify-sms-sinatra.git
 * [new branch]      master -> master
```

At the beginning of your deployment, you can see that Heroku indicates "Ruby/Rack app detected" because of the presence of the config.ru file. You can also see that only three processes are automatically defined for Rack-based apps: web, console, and rake. A worker process is not defined automatically, as it is with Rails apps. One other thing to note is that the slug size is smaller than the Rails app; as a result, the deployment is likely to be noticeably faster. This lightweight approach is one of the key reasons why Sinatra advocates prefer this framework for simple apps.

3. Add the config vars with your Twilio credentials and Twilio verified number:

```
$ heroku config:add TWILIO_ACCOUNT_SID="mYtW1l10aCc0UnT51D"
TWILIO_AUTH_TOKEN="mYtW1l10aUtHt0K3n" TWILIO_VERIFIED_PHONE_NO="5555555555"
Setting config vars and restarting twilio-verify-sms-sinatra... done, v4
TWILIO_ACCOUNT_SID:       mYtW1l10aCc0UnT51D
TWILIO_AUTH_TOKEN:        mYtW1l10aUtHt0K3n
TWILIO_VERIFIED_PHONE_NO: 5555555555
```

4. Note the config vars set in your app:

```
$ heroku config
=== Config Vars for twilio-verify-sms-sinatra
GEM_PATH:                  vendor/bundle/ruby/1.9.1
LANG:                      en_US.UTF-8
PATH:                      bin:vendor/bundle/ruby/1.9.1/bin:/usr/local/bin:/usr/bin:/bin
RACK_ENV:                  production
TWILIO_ACCOUNT_SID:        AC188b2ecc01c20a436bd3c557d19cdf73
TWILIO_AUTH_TOKEN:         d3011b5120344d3a8c3a0512f5b2dfa7
TWILIO_VERIFIED_PHONE_NO:  6479311574
```

Similar to your Rails app, a number of environment variables have been set for you automatically. In comparison, only two are missing: RAILS_ENV, which is not needed because this is not a Rails app, and DATABASE_URL, because this app does not use a backing database.

Testing the Application

Now you can test the app by typing the following at the command line:

```
$ heroku open
```

You will be asked to enter a phone number to which the text message can be sent, as shown in Figure 11-2, which must be verified on Twilio beforehand (only if using a trial account). You will then be sent a text message containing the four-digit pin to input in the form on the next page. If the correct PIN is entered, you are successfully verified by the app. That completes your simple, lightweight app built on the Sinatra framework, using the Twilio API.

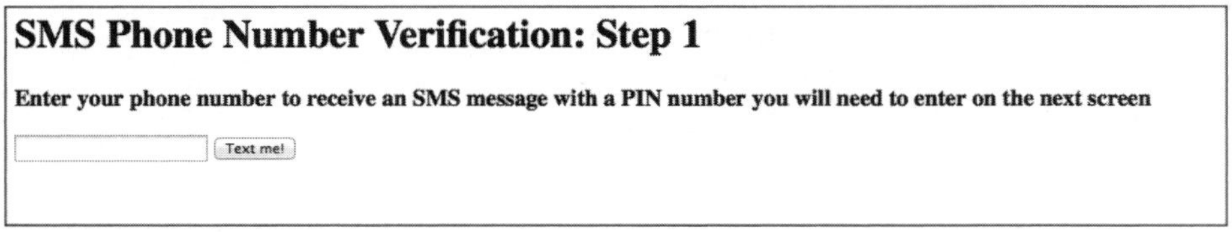

SMS Phone Number Verification: Step 1

Enter your phone number to receive an SMS message with a PIN number you will need to enter on the next screen

[   ] [Text me!]

FIGURE 11-2

USING DELAYED JOB FOR BACKGROUND JOBS

Delayed Job (DJ) enables you to use worker dynos running in the background to asynchronously do work for your app. As a best practice for creating apps with a scalable architecture, you should use background jobs for units of work that don't require an immediate response, that may take a long time, or that rely on a backing service.

This is especially important when writing Heroku apps because your dyno will not respond to new HTTP web requests while waiting to get a response from the backing service or while executing long-running code. This results in long queue times for new HTTP requests from users while the dyno is blocked, or waiting, which negatively affects the user's experience of your app. Poorly architected apps can cause you to use more dyno hours than necessary, as you will have to scale up your app in order to minimize queuing time.

For instance, if your app supports sending e-mail, you do not need to make the user wait while your mail server sends the message. If sending a message takes longer than expected for some reason, it could even timeout your app, as Heroku has a maximum response time before closing connections. For example, for maximum scalability, you could re-architect the previous app you created, to verify users with text messages, by changing the call to the Twilio API (to send the text message) to run as a background job, rather than using synchronous execution. (We leave that as an exercise for the reader.)

As shown in Figure 11-3, three HTTP requests are made. In the example architecture without background jobs (on the left-hand side), the second and third requests are queued while the dyno is tied up waiting for an API response from a backing service, which may be running slower than normal. Conversely, in the architecture with background jobs (on the right-hand side), all three responses are returned quickly; and the second and third jobs are queued, where they are processed after the first delayed job completes. In this scenario, your users making the second and third requests are happy because the app appears to be snappy. The backing service will eventually complete its work, reaching the end of the request queue, and it is unlikely that the user will realize or care if it does not happen immediately.

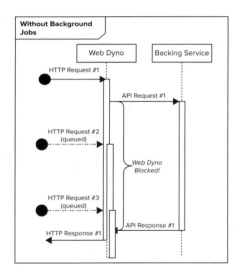
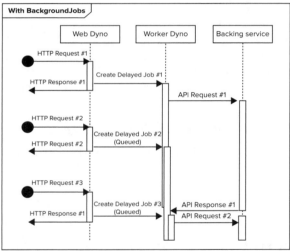

FIGURE 11-3

Keep in mind that in Heroku's process model, web and worker dynos can be scaled independently of one another. This means that if you notice that your delayed job queue is getting backed up, you can add more worker dynos to complete the work in parallel without having to scale web workers as well. This is especially useful for work that you can break down into small chunks. For instance, suppose you need to do a complex calculation on each row of your 100,000-row database. If each 1,000 rows takes one hour to compute, you can either do all the rows with one worker process running for 100 hours, or you can run 100 dynos for a single hour. Either way, you are using 100 dyno hours, costing you the same. However, in the latter scenario, the calculations are performed two orders of magnitude faster.

To demonstrate how you can create background jobs in Ruby, you will create a Rails app architected to use Delayed Job to complete some work asynchronously (code file: `ch11-ruby-delayed-job.zip`).

Setting Up Delayed Job

You will write a Rails app with two classes: `DjController`, representing a web process receiving requests, and `WorkUnit`, representing a background worker processing jobs asynchronously. The web process will simulate placing ten jobs on a Delayed Job queue. This process uses the `ruby-delayed-job` gem to place a new job on the queue every 1½ seconds. The background worker uses Delayed Job to pull jobs off the queue and simulates taking 4 seconds to process them. This app uses a Heroku Postgres database to store the job queue.

1. Create your Rails app:

    ```
    $ rails new ruby-delayed-job
          create
          create    README.rdoc
          create    Rakefile
          create    config.ru
          create    .gitignore
          create    Gemfile
          create    app
          create    app/assets/images/rails.png
    [...]
          Using uglifier (1.2.6)
    Your bundle is complete! Use 'bundle show [gemname]' to see where a bundled gem is
    installed.
    ```

2. Add Delayed Job to your `Gemfile` by adding the following line:

    ```
    gem 'delayed_job_active_record'
    ```

3. Use Bundler to update your dependencies:

    ```
    $ bundle install
    Fetching gem metadata from https://rubygems.org/.........
    Using rake (0.9.2.2)
    Using i18n (0.6.0)
    [...]
    Using uglifier (1.2.6)
    Your bundle is complete! Use 'bundle show [gemname]' to see where a bundled gem is
    installed.
    ```

4. Add a jobs table to your database migration script to store queued background jobs, like this:

    ```
    $ rails generate delayed_job:active_record
          create    script/delayed_job
          chmod     script/delayed_job
          create    db/migrate/20120728210000_create_delayed_jobs.rb
    ```

5. Delayed Job can use any Active Record–supported database. To use the default development database, replace in your `Gemfile`:

    ```
    gem 'sqlite3'
    ```

with this line:

```
gem 'pg'
```

6. Run `bundle install` again:

```
$ bundle install
Using rake (0.9.2.2)
[...]
Using uglifier (1.2.6)
Your bundle is complete! Use 'bundle show [gemname]' to see where a bundled gem is
installed.
```

7. Now create your app's controller by adding a `app/controllers/dj_controller.rb` file with this code:

```
class DjController < ApplicationController

    # GET /dj
    def index
        $i = 0;
        $num = 10;

        while $i < $num  do
            $i += 1;
            puts("Adding to queue job #$i");
            work_unit = WorkUnit.new($i)
            work_unit.delay.do_work

            # simulate time between requests
            sleep(1.5)
        end
    end
end
```

The loop is iterated 10 times, each time creating a new work unit object, which will represent some work that needs to be completed. Note that on the bolded line of code you use Delayed Job's `delay` method, chained before the `do_work` method. The `delay` method adds a job to the queue to execute the method that follows it — in this case, `do_work`. The worker dyno simply picks jobs off the queue that were added in this way and executes the method indicated. Finally, you call the `sleep` method to add a second-and-a-half interval between requests.

8. Create the model for your unit of work by creating the file `app/models/work_unit.rb` and adding the following code:

```
class WorkUnit
    def initialize(i)
        @id = i
    end

    def do_work
        # simulate doing some work that takes a while
        sleep(4)
        puts("Completed work unit #{@id}");
    end
end
```

Here, the constructor adds the ID passed in to the object. The `do_work` method mimics the app performing some sort of long-running work by pausing for four seconds. In real-life usage, this is where the app would complete complex calculations, send e-mails, or call some external API.

Alternatively, instead of using the `delay` method when calling the `do_work` method, you can declare a method to always be run asynchronously using the `handle_asynchronously` declaration, like this:

```
class WorkUnit
    def do_work
        # do something
    end
    handle_asynchronously :do_work
end
```

The `handle_asynchronously` declaration should be made after the method declaration, and it can include optional parameters, such as to set priority with `priority` or set a delay interval before the job is run with `run_at`.

9. You also use a very simple view to indicate to the web visitor that the jobs have been queued. This is done by creating the file `app/views/dj/index.html.erb` and adding the following code:

```
<p>Jobs added to queue.</p>
```

10. Add a line after the first line of the automatically generated `config/routes.rb` file to reroute requests to the root URL to our controller's `index` action:

```
root :to => "dj#index"
```

11. Remove the default generated HTML index:

```
$ rm public/index.html
```

Deploying the Application to Heroku

Now that you have written the code for your two processes, you must deploy your app to Heroku. Deploying the app to Heroku will start your web dyno automatically, but you must start a worker process manually to pick jobs off the queue in the background.

1. Commit and push your app to Heroku:

```
$ git add .

$ git commit -am "init"
[master (root-commit) 951d573] init
 43 files changed, 1282 insertions(+), 1 deletions(-)
 create mode 100644 .gitignore
 create mode 100644 .project
 create mode 100644 Gemfile
 [...]

$ git push heroku master
Counting objects: 76, done.
Delta compression using up to 4 threads.
```

```
Compressing objects: 100% (63/63), done.
Writing objects: 100% (76/76), 28.04 KiB, done.
Total 76 (delta 5), reused 0 (delta 0)

-----> Heroku receiving push
-----> Ruby/Rails app detected
[...]
-----> Launching... done, v4
       http://ruby-delayed-job.herokuapp.com deployed to Heroku

To git@heroku.com:ruby-delayed-job.git
 * [new branch]      master -> master
```

2. Run your migration script to create the job table needed for Delayed Job to operate correctly:

```
$ heroku run rake db:migrate
Running 'rake db:migrate' attached to terminal... up, run.1
==  CreateDelayedJobs: migrating ==============================================
-- create_table(:delayed_jobs, {:force=>true})
   -> 0.0262s
-- add_index(:delayed_jobs, [:priority, :run_at], {:name=>"delayed_jobs_priority"})
   -> 0.0101s
==  CreateDelayedJobs: migrated (0.0366s) =====================================
```

3. You also need to add a worker dyno because only a web dyno is added automatically. This worker dyno will pick jobs off of the queue and complete them:

```
$ heroku ps:scale worker=1
Scaling worker processes... done, now running 1
```

Testing Delayed Job

Now watch your logs in real time with the following command, and visit your web app with your browser to start queuing jobs:

```
$ heroku logs --tail
2012-07-29T12:54:04+00:00 app[web.1]: Started GET "/" for 99.230.250.230 at 2012-07-29
12:54:04 +0000
2012-07-29T12:54:04+00:00 app[web.1]: Processing by DjController#index as HTML
2012-07-29T12:54:04+00:00 app[web.1]: Adding to queue job 1
2012-07-29T12:54:06+00:00 app[web.1]: Adding to queue job 2
2012-07-29T12:54:07+00:00 app[web.1]: Adding to queue job 3
2012-07-29T12:54:09+00:00 app[web.1]: Adding to queue job 4
2012-07-29T12:54:09+00:00 app[worker.1]: Completed work unit 1
2012-07-29T12:54:09+00:00 app[worker.1]: [Worker(host:a34b8004-9eec-4b8d-9211-
a024690f7c39 pid:2)] WorkUnit#do_work completed after 4.0083
2012-07-29T12:54:10+00:00 app[web.1]: Adding to queue job 5
2012-07-29T12:54:12+00:00 app[web.1]: Adding to queue job 6
2012-07-29T12:54:13+00:00 app[worker.1]: Completed work unit 2
2012-07-29T12:54:13+00:00 app[worker.1]: [Worker(host:a34b8004-9eec-4b8d-9211-
a024690f7c39 pid:2)] WorkUnit#do_work completed after 4.0068
2012-07-29T12:54:13+00:00 app[web.1]: Adding to queue job 7
2012-07-29T12:54:15+00:00 app[web.1]: Adding to queue job 8
2012-07-29T12:54:16+00:00 app[web.1]: Adding to queue job 9
2012-07-29T12:54:17+00:00 app[worker.1]: Completed work unit 3
2012-07-29T12:54:17+00:00 app[worker.1]: [Worker(host:a34b8004-9eec-4b8d-9211-
```

```
a024690f7c39 pid:2)] WorkUnit#do_work completed after 4.0080
2012-07-29T12:54:18+00:00 app[web.1]: Adding to queue job 10
2012-07-29T12:54:19+00:00 app[web.1]:   Rendered dj/index.html.erb within
layouts/application (0.0ms)
2012-07-29T12:54:19+00:00 app[web.1]: Completed 200 OK in 15177ms (Views: 4.5ms |
ActiveRecord: 91.0ms)
2012-07-29T12:54:19+00:00 heroku[router]: GET ruby-delayed-job.herokuapp.com/
dyno=web.1 queue=0 wait=0ms service=15185ms status=304 bytes=0
[...]
2012-07-29T12:54:21+00:00 app[worker.1]: Completed work unit 4
2012-07-29T12:54:21+00:00 app[worker.1]: [Worker(host:a34b8004-9eec-4b8d-9211-
a024690f7c39 pid:2)] WorkUnit#do_work completed after 4.0055
2012-07-29T12:54:25+00:00 app[worker.1]: Completed work unit 5
2012-07-29T12:54:25+00:00 app[worker.1]: [Worker(host:a34b8004-9eec-4b8d-9211-
a024690f7c39 pid:2)] WorkUnit#do_work completed after 4.0075
2012-07-29T12:54:29+00:00 app[worker.1]: Completed work unit 6
2012-07-29T12:54:29+00:00 app[worker.1]: [Worker(host:a34b8004-9eec-4b8d-9211-
a024690f7c39 pid:2)] WorkUnit#do_work completed after 4.0449
2012-07-29T12:54:33+00:00 app[worker.1]: Completed work unit 7
2012-07-29T12:54:33+00:00 app[worker.1]: [Worker(host:a34b8004-9eec-4b8d-9211-
a024690f7c39 pid:2)] WorkUnit#do_work completed after 4.0151
2012-07-29T12:54:37+00:00 app[worker.1]: Completed work unit 8
2012-07-29T12:54:37+00:00 app[worker.1]: [Worker(host:a34b8004-9eec-4b8d-9211-
a024690f7c39 pid:2)] WorkUnit#do_work completed after 4.0104
2012-07-29T12:54:41+00:00 app[worker.1]: Completed work unit 9
2012-07-29T12:54:41+00:00 app[worker.1]: [Worker(host:a34b8004-9eec-4b8d-9211-
a024690f7c39 pid:2)] WorkUnit#do_work completed after 4.1067
2012-07-29T12:54:45+00:00 app[worker.1]: Completed work unit 10
2012-07-29T12:54:45+00:00 app[worker.1]: [Worker(host:a34b8004-9eec-4b8d-9211-
a024690f7c39 pid:2)] WorkUnit#do_work completed after 4.0657
2012-07-29T12:54:45+00:00 app[worker.1]: [Worker(host:a34b8004-9eec-4b8d-9211-
a024690f7c39 pid:2)] 10 jobs processed at 0.2478 j/s, 0 failed ...
```

This output indicates that the web dyno is putting jobs on the queue and the worker dyno is asynchronously completing the job. Because the time spent completing the work is much longer than the time between jobs being added to the queue, the work takes a very long time to complete — approximately about 41 seconds.

The following scales up your workers to get this work done faster:

```
$ heroku ps:scale worker=3
Scaling worker processes... done, now running 3

$ heroku logs --tail
2012-07-29T12:55:08+00:00 heroku[api]: Scale to web=1, worker=3 by ckemp@salesforce.com
2012-07-29T12:55:11+00:00 heroku[worker.2]: Starting process with command 'bundle exec
rake jobs:work'
2012-07-29T12:55:12+00:00 heroku[worker.2]: State changed from starting to up
2012-07-29T12:55:12+00:00 heroku[worker.3]: Starting process with command 'bundle exec
rake jobs:work'
2012-07-29T12:55:13+00:00 heroku[worker.3]: State changed from starting to up
2012-07-29T12:55:17+00:00 app[worker.3]: [Worker(host:14b3f5a7-792e-4362-980c-
4bb2dcc26178 pid:2)] Starting job worker
2012-07-29T12:55:17+00:00 app[worker.2]: [Worker(host:089bd029-bf34-44d4-ac9e-
e21bc9c36449 pid:2)] Starting job worker
2012-07-29T12:55:43+00:00 app[web.1]:
```

```
2012-07-29T12:55:43+00:00 app[web.1]:
2012-07-29T12:55:43+00:00 app[web.1]: Started GET "/" for 99.230.250.230 at 2012-07-29
12:55:43 +0000
2012-07-29T12:55:43+00:00 app[web.1]: Processing by DjController#index as HTML
2012-07-29T12:55:43+00:00 app[web.1]: Adding to queue job 1
2012-07-29T12:55:45+00:00 app[web.1]: Adding to queue job 2
2012-07-29T12:55:46+00:00 app[web.1]: Adding to queue job 3
2012-07-29T12:55:48+00:00 app[web.1]: Adding to queue job 4
2012-07-29T12:55:49+00:00 app[web.1]: Adding to queue job 5
2012-07-29T12:55:50+00:00 app[worker.1]: Completed work unit 1
2012-07-29T12:55:50+00:00 app[worker.1]: [Worker(host:a34b8004-9eec-4b8d-9211-
a024690f7c39 pid:2)] WorkUnit#do_work completed after 4.0100
2012-07-29T12:55:51+00:00 app[web.1]: Adding to queue job 6
2012-07-29T12:55:51+00:00 app[worker.3]: Completed work unit 2
2012-07-29T12:55:51+00:00 app[worker.3]: [Worker(host:14b3f5a7-792e-4362-980c-
4bb2dcc26178 pid:2)] WorkUnit#do_work completed after 4.0941
2012-07-29T12:55:52+00:00 app[worker.2]: Completed work unit 3
2012-07-29T12:55:52+00:00 app[worker.2]: [Worker(host:089bd029-bf34-44d4-ac9e-
e21bc9c36449 pid:2)] WorkUnit#do_work completed after 4.0560
2012-07-29T12:55:52+00:00 app[web.1]: Adding to queue job 7
2012-07-29T12:55:54+00:00 app[web.1]: Adding to queue job 8
2012-07-29T12:55:54+00:00 app[worker.1]: Completed work unit 4
2012-07-29T12:55:54+00:00 app[worker.1]: [Worker(host:a34b8004-9eec-4b8d-9211-
a024690f7c39 pid:2)] WorkUnit#do_work completed after 4.0054
2012-07-29T12:55:55+00:00 app[worker.3]: Completed work unit 5
2012-07-29T12:55:56+00:00 app[web.1]: Adding to queue job 9
2012-07-29T12:55:56+00:00 app[worker.3]: [Worker(host:14b3f5a7-792e-4362-980c-
4bb2dcc26178 pid:2)] WorkUnit#do_work completed after 4.1914
2012-07-29T12:55:56+00:00 app[worker.2]: Completed work unit 6
2012-07-29T12:55:56+00:00 app[worker.2]: [Worker(host:089bd029-bf34-44d4-ac9e-
e21bc9c36449 pid:2)] WorkUnit#do_work completed after 4.0775
2012-07-29T12:55:57+00:00 app[web.1]: Adding to queue job 10
2012-07-29T12:55:58+00:00 app[worker.1]: Completed work unit 7
2012-07-29T12:55:58+00:00 app[worker.1]: [Worker(host:a34b8004-9eec-4b8d-9211-
a024690f7c39 pid:2)] WorkUnit#do_work completed after 4.0081
2012-07-29T12:55:59+00:00 app[web.1]:    Rendered dj/index.html.erb within
layouts/application (0.0ms)
2012-07-29T12:55:59+00:00 app[web.1]: Completed 200 OK in 15315ms (Views: 10.4ms |
s: 235.7ms)
2012-07-29T12:55:59+00:00 heroku[router]: GET ruby-delayed-job.herokuapp.com/
dyno=web.1 queue=0 wait=0ms service=15328ms status=304 bytes=0
2012-07-29T12:56:00+00:00 app[worker.3]: Completed work unit 8
2012-07-29T12:56:00+00:00 app[worker.3]: [Worker(host:14b3f5a7-792e-4362-980c-
4bb2dcc26178 pid:2)] WorkUnit#do_work completed after 4.0189
2012-07-29T12:56:00+00:00 app[worker.3]: [Worker(host:14b3f5a7-792e-4362-980c-
4bb2dcc26178 pid:2)] 3 jobs processed at 0.2417 j/s, 0 failed ...
2012-07-29T12:56:00+00:00 app[worker.2]: Completed work unit 9
2012-07-29T12:56:00+00:00 app[worker.2]: [Worker(host:089bd029-bf34-44d4-ac9e-
e21bc9c36449 pid:2)] WorkUnit#do_work completed after 4.0349
2012-07-29T12:56:00+00:00 app[worker.2]: [Worker(host:089bd029-bf34-44d4-ac9e-
e21bc9c36449 pid:2)] 3 jobs processed at 0.2371 j/s, 0 failed ...
2012-07-29T12:56:02+00:00 app[worker.1]: Completed work unit 10
2012-07-29T12:56:02+00:00 app[worker.1]: [Worker(host:a34b8004-9eec-4b8d-9211-
a024690f7c39 pid:2)] WorkUnit#do_work completed after 4.0057
2012-07-29T12:56:02+00:00 app[worker.1]: [Worker(host:a34b8004-9eec-4b8d-9211-
a024690f7c39 pid:2)] 4 jobs processed at 0.2493 j/s, 0 failed ...
```

As shown in the output, the three workers get all the jobs done in less than half the time, about 19 seconds. Clearly, executing background jobs in parallel results in less collective average time queuing for jobs, providing better overall performance.

> **WARNING** *When scaling up workers to get through a backed-up queue, remember to scale down later once the queue is back in a manageable state to avoid needlessly consuming dyno hours. Even if your worker dyno is not actively processing jobs, you will still be charged for dyno hours while the worker dynos are waiting for new jobs.*

Delayed Job enables you to write hooks that can be called at specific checkpoints in a job's life cycle, such as when it is enqueued, before it starts, and after it either completes successfully or fails (see `https://github.com/collectiveidea/delayed_job#hooks` for examples). If errors occur during execution of Delayed Job, the source of the errors is captured in the `job` table in the database. The error message will appear in the `last_error` column of the record. If you want to empty out the job queue, use the following command to flush all jobs:

```
heroku run rake jobs:clear
```

CACHING WITH RUBY

Caching is an important part of application architecture, to reduce the load on the app and increase efficiency. Several different strategies can be used to cache Ruby apps, but many of them were not designed for a highly scalable platform like Heroku. The Varnish reverse proxy was once provided as a built-in part of the stack when running Ruby apps on the now-deprecated Aspen and Bamboo stacks. However, with Cedar's added support for advanced HTTP features such as long polling, Varnish is no longer automatically available. This makes caching a more challenging exercise, as it necessitates either moving caching functionality to the application layer or implementing external services.

Three primary types of caching can be done:

➤ **Page caching:** This involves caching either entire web pages requested or parts of them (single actions or partial pages).

➤ **Data caching:** This saves data, typically in-memory, when it would normally have to be retrieved by accessing a database or third-party service.

➤ **HTTP caching:** This describes approaches that can be used to cache content using distributed methods (such as with CloudFront); to cache content locally in the user's browser; or to cache content with a proxy (as described earlier with Varnish).

Rails has a convenient, built-in caching mechanism used by the web server to do page caching by storing cached copies of a page in the local filesystem. Given the distributed nature of dynos and the ephemeral nature of the filesystem, this does not work optimally with Heroku apps. However, Rails' internal caching functionality can still be used for action and fragment caching, and Memcached can used for caching presentation layer assembly (see `https://devcenter.heroku.com/articles/caching-strategies` for more information on those). You have a choice of Memcached add-ons to use, including Memcachier (`https://addons.heroku.com/memcachier`).

The bulk of an app's delays is oftentimes at the data layer, either accessing information from the database or through a third-party API, making data layer caching important. The Memcachier add-on is well suited for caching information and can be used with a Simple Authentication and Security Layer (SASL) enabled client. The Dalli Memcached client is recommended for maximum compatibility with Heroku apps. The `memcached-northscale` gem is also available, but it's only recommended in cases for which it is needed for backward compatibility.

Rails uses the `Rails.cache` object to store and retrieve cache information with Memcachier or whatever alternative caching system or data store you use. This object has four main methods:

- ➤ `read`: To get a cached value with the key
- ➤ `write`: To write a new key-value pair
- ➤ `delete`: To delete a key-value pair
- ➤ `fetch`: To attempt to get a cached value with a key or store a new value on a cache miss

A `stats` method provides important statistical information from Dalli for things such as cache hits and misses.

For Sinatra apps, you can enable Memcached caching with Dalli by adding the following to the beginning of your Sinatra app:

```
set :cache, Dalli::Client.new
```

The `settings.cache.set` method sets a key-value pair. The `settings.cache.get` method will return either the value for a given key for a cache hit or `nil` for a cache miss.

> **NOTE** *For detailed information on configuring and using Memcachier with Ruby, see* `https://devcenter.heroku.com/articles/memcachier#ruby`.

HTTP caching can be done on the application layer as an alternative to more complex and costly methods like using content delivery networks (CDNs) or external proxy servers, though it will not perform as well as these methods in most cases. `Rack::Cache` is lightweight middleware that can be used to cache static assets in a caching system or data store of your choice, responding to requests without having them go through your Ruby app. It is recommended that `Rack::Cache` be used on Heroku using a Memcached storage engine, with the Dalli client for metadata (e.g., HTTP request and response headers) and the file storage engine for EntityStore, the content payload.

> **NOTE** *Detailed information and instructions for* `Rack::Cache` *is available at* `https://devcenter.heroku.com/articles/rack-cache-memcached-static-assets-rails31`.

PORTING RUBY APPLICATIONS TO HEROKU

This section discusses some considerations to keep in mind when porting Ruby apps to Heroku. The principles outlined in Chapter 3, "Porting Your Applications to Heroku," apply to any apps written in any language. Here we recap the key points for Ruby architects:

➤ **Filesystem differences:** Make sure your Ruby app does not rely on any file being used after the current request has been completed, because of the ephemeral nature of a dyno's filesystem.

➤ **Data stores:** This chapter provided an example that uses Heroku Postgres as a data store, but any data store of your choice should work; and you can check the add-ons to find a cloud-based provider for your Heroku app.

➤ **Session management:** Rails sessions are stored client-side in an encrypted cookie by default. However, this also means that you may eventually run out of room in the cookie if more than 4,096 bytes are stored. In this case, some information may have to be transferred to a backing data store instead of being stored in the session, or you can configure your app to use Memcached or ActiveRecord as the backing storage for cookie information.

Sinatra apps also use encrypted cookies, but some configuration is necessary to get them to work properly. Sinatra apps will not have the same key, `session_secret`, across dynos, meaning dynos other than the one that created the session cannot read the session information because it was encrypted by a different key. To fix this, add a config var to share the session key across dynos with some arbitrary (and ideally, long) value:

```
$ heroku config:add SESSION_KEY=50m3V3rY10nG53Cr3tPhR@53
```

Then, in your Sinatra app, add the following lines to set the session key:

```
enable :sessions
set :session_secret, ENV['SESSION_KEY']
```

➤ **Caching:** See the "Caching with Ruby" section earlier in this chapter.

➤ **Static assets:** Because of the 200MB maximum slug size, apps with a lot of static assets should store them outside of the app, in Amazon S3 or using Amazon CloudFront for distributed asset storage.

➤ **Config vars:** You saw many examples of using config vars in this chapter to manage environment variables such as DATABASE_URL. Use similar techniques for credential storage for backing third-party apps upon which your app relies.

➤ **Web servers and containers:** You saw an example earlier that used Webrick to run your Rails app. You can use whatever web server you choose with your app by bundling it into your dependencies and adding it to your Gemfile and Procfile.

➤ **Managing dependencies:** As shown in the "Managing Dependencies" section earlier in this chapter, Bundle is used by Heroku to manage dependencies for Ruby apps.

➤ **E-mailing from your apps:** Third-party add-ons such as SendGrid (https://devcenter .heroku.com/articles/sendgrid#ruby-rails) or your own SMTP server can be used for sending e-mail with Ruby apps on Heroku, and configured appropriately in your app according to the provider's Ruby setup instructions.

➤ **Logging:** Logs can be sent out to a sink server or third-party log manager, such as Loggly (http://wiki.loggly.com/rubylogging) or Logentries (https://blog.logentries.com/2011/07/logging-its-a-gem).

➤ **Relying on external programs:** An app should not rely on programs external to itself, such as using %x notation, backticks, exec(), or system() to run cURL. As a best practice to simplify delivery, all libraries needed to run should be a dependency of the app.

➤ **Scaling up vs. scaling out:** App memory should be managed efficiently, as failing to do so can cause memory to page if the 512MB limit is reached. You can use a simple memory logger like Memorylogic (https://github.com/binarylogic/memorylogic) or Bleakhouse (http://railsguides.heroku.com/2.3.5/debugging_rails_applications.html#debugging-memory-leaks) to profile memory. See http://railslab.newrelic.com/2009/10/23/episode-20-on-the-edge-part-2 for some common causes of memory bloat, including using too many ActiveRecord objects in your app.

Your app's code base should also be kept as lean as possible to ensure that scaling can be done quickly. As mentioned earlier, storing assets externally can reduce slug size. It is recommended that you use GitHub's general Ruby .gitignore file or the one appropriate for your Ruby framework (see https://github.com/github/gitignore for some pre-built files) in all your projects as a best practice, to ensure that only necessary artifacts are included in the slug.

➤ **Binding to ports:** Port binding in the default web servers is done using the automatically created Procfile. You should configure other web servers in a similar way or bind manually in the code base using the port passed in through the config var.

➤ **Long-running processes:** Long-running processes should be run with a worker dyno in the background to avoid automatic connection closing upon timeout. As a best practice for scalability, you should re-architect your apps to use background processes for any third-party backing service used. You saw an example that demonstrated how much faster it is in the section "Using Delayed Job for Background Jobs" earlier in this chapter.

➤ **Shutting down gracefully:** Your app can be signaled at any time to shutdown or restart. Therefore, you need to write logic into your app to register a shutdown hook for SIGTERM and gracefully deal with the impending shutdown. As a best practice, you should try to complete any work that was not completed and respond to the web request, or any work that is not complete should be put back on a queue for a worker to pick up later.

On Rails, you can achieve this using something like the following:

```
Signal.trap("TERM") do
    // do actions for graceful shutdown here
end
```

Trapping a SIGTERM on a Sinatra app is done in a similar way:

```
trap("SIGTERM") {
    // do actions for graceful shutdown here
}
```

➤ **Moving your domain:** Using DNS settings, you can point domains in Ruby apps in the same way that you would in any other apps.

Following these important points ensures that your Ruby apps will be well prepared for a move to the Heroku platform.

SUMMARY

In this chapter, you saw how Ruby apps are architected and deployed to Heroku. Ruby, RVM, Rails, and Sinatra should be installed in order to write Ruby apps on Heroku. Bundler is used as a dependency manager on Ruby and will package RubyGems that your application relies on to run on Heroku. Rails is a very mature and popular framework for writing enterprise apps on Ruby. Sinatra is a lightweight framework, best suited for quickly turning around useful apps with a small footprint.

Caching should be used when possible to speed up application delivery and minimize server load and response time. Delayed Job is used to asynchronously run processes in the background, adhering to the web-worker model, which will minimize queuing time for your app's users. Heroku works differently from traditional platforms, which requires you to follow best practices in order to make Ruby apps ported to Heroku work as expected.

In the next chapter, you will see how Java apps can be run on Heroku in the same way.

12

Developing with Java

WHAT'S IN THIS CHAPTER?

➤ Understanding Java

➤ Writing enterprise applications on Heroku

➤ Installing the Java Development Kit

➤ Managing dependencies

➤ Writing a containerless application with embedded Jetty

➤ Writing an application with the Spring Framework and Hibernate on Apache Tomcat

➤ Writing an application with the Play framework

➤ Deploying a Web application ARchive (WAR) file directly to Heroku

➤ Additional considerations

WROX.COM CODE DOWNLOADS FOR THIS CHAPTER

The wrox.com code downloads for this chapter are found at www.wrox.com/remtitle .cgi?isbn=1118508998 on the Download Code tab. The code is in the Chapter 12 download and individually named according to the names throughout the chapter.

This chapter explores how Java apps can be written and deployed on Heroku. Java has evolved from a simple, portable language to a powerful development platform that has spawned other languages that run on this common platform. In recent times, development on Java has also evolved from built-for-distribution, where developer operations (DevOps) teams are required to deploy apps infrequently, to built-for-deployment, where rapid and continuous deployment of incremental improvements is favoured.

To test apps before deploying them to Heroku, you must first install the Java Development Kit (JDK) on your workstation. Java uses Apache Maven for managing dependencies and building your Heroku apps. The embedded Jetty web server is a popular tool used for running containerless Java apps. You can leverage the mature trio of the Spring Framework, Hibernate object-relational mapping, and an Apache Tomcat web server for writing enterprise-class apps.

Play is an up-and-coming framework that equips developers with the ability to develop apps rapidly while leveraging widely used Java-based standards to provide a stable and reliable core. Web application ARchive files (WAR files) can be deployed directly on Heroku. Existing Java apps can be ported to Heroku, but such an undertaking must be done with care for them to continue to run properly.

UNDERSTANDING JAVA

In modern programming, Java is often thought of as the de facto open-source, enterprise programming language. Designed by Dr. James A. Gosling at Sun Systems, the Java programming language started with more humble beginnings as a simpler, portable alternative to C/C++. Over the years, it grew in popularity to the point where today most computer science students across the world either have had to learn it as part of their studies or have had some exposure to the platform during their tutelage. Now, with those developers in the workforce, it is one of the most popular languages for professional development.

One of the primary goals of Java is to provide a "write once, run anywhere" platform that enables developers to write code that is not platform-specific, as was the practice with traditional, compiled languages. This is made possible through the Java virtual machine (JVM), which uses a platform-specific compiler to produce bytecode. This code can be run as is on any platform on which the JVM can run. This capability has made Java a preferred development choice for platform-independent apps.

In recent times, the portable nature of the JVM has made it a popular platform to write languages on top of. Brand-new languages such as Scala have been developed on top of the JVM, as well as dialects of existing languages, such as Clojure as a Lisp dialect. Ports of other languages, like JRuby (Ruby) and Jython (Python), enable developers to leverage familiar languages while using tight integration with the Java stack to write multilingual programs, whereby code written in different languages can access Java classes and be compiled to bytecode.

> **NOTE** *Writing apps in JVM languages on Heroku with Clojure and Scala is covered in Chapter 13, "Developing with Other Supported Languages."*

WRITING ENTERPRISE APPLICATIONS ON HEROKU

Heroku represents a paradigm shift from traditional Java Platform, Enterprise Edition (Java EE) development practices. Traditional Java EE development began for server-side application development when the Internet was still in its infancy and provides a standard API for developing apps. As development needs matured, this resulted in the emergence of a number of middleware vendors, such as Websphere and Weblogic, that built on this API to provide feature-rich solutions for making apps reliable, scalable, and easier to deploy. However, this resulted in a number of tradeoffs for this perceived convenience.

Though in some cases the benefits provided by middleware for building Java apps makes sense, this luxury comes with certain costs. As vendors matured, they began to deliver more and more features that affected an app's portability, locking in developers to a particular middleware vendor. This provided a steady income stream for vendors, but it strayed from the write once, run anywhere philosophy on which Java was based. Swapping out individual components soon became a nightmare of compatibility issues; and it also meant that many organizations had to rely on middleware-specific knowledge for configuration, tuning, and deployment, affecting the company's ability to easily staff its development teams. Creating apps that are loosely coupled with the application server quickly became a struggle.

Speed to deployment also suffered as the features began to introduce increasing complexity to apps. Most containers employ an "everything including the bathroom sink" feature set whereby a small subset is needed for any given project. This often meant that a complex deployment process was needed to configure and deploy apps — in many cases requiring development operations teams with specialized roles for each part of the process. This also slowed down the development group's ability to pick and choose the best components for an app; and slowed innovation, making the process of turning around a quick form-based app take hours or days instead of minutes. Developer productivity shifted from writing code to heavy configuration.

One of the most fundamental issues with traditional Java EE development is that it relies on a built-for-distribution model, rather than built-for-deployment. Built-for-distribution apps involve packaging, distributing, and installing apps. This makes sense when you want to build an app that may be used by other teams and organizations, but it adds unnecessary complexity for web apps that simply need to be deployed and run. This runs contrary to continuous deployment practices when rapid feature delivery is slowed by this antiquated and extraneous process. Built-for-deployment apps can be coded and deployed by the same team and organization, enabling greater development agility.

Over time, factions of the Java community shifted to lightweight tools for developing Java apps. The Spring Framework emerged, reducing the reliance on using a container with EJB compliance. Enterprises started building apps on Apache Tomcat to reduce the complexity of deployments; and the emergence of rapid application development tools, like Spring Roo, enabled Java developers to spend less time configuring and more time coding by adopting principles of convention over configuration. Then along came platform-as-a-service (PaaS) providers like Heroku, eliminating the need for heavyweight application containers to provide mechanisms for deployment, scaling, load balancing, failover, logging, and service binding.

Java developers are no longer handicapped by the need for application containers to run their apps. Java EE APIs can still be used when packaged with an app as needed, and apps are deployed with an embedded web stack declared as a dependency of the app. For instance, Tomcat and Jetty can be used to write and run servlets and JavaServer Pages (JSP). Packaging these as dependencies results in simpler, more lightweight apps and provides environmental parity, as the application environment used to develop locally will be identical to the environment to which the app is deployed, resulting in less debugging to determine environment-specific bugs that surface as a result of environment differences.

With Heroku, deployment mechanisms are built in and do not rely on WAR files, Enterprise Archive (EAR) files, or other means of packaging to deploy your app. Nor do you need to create complex deployment scripts to deploy your Java app; and upload tools to deploy WAR files are no longer required. Heroku's provides a built-in deployment mechanism with Git that will push your source assets. Apache Maven takes care of dependency management and builds your app's artifacts. Scripts to push code and minimize downtime during pushes are also unnecessary, as Heroku's dyno manifold swaps the running instance of your app with the newly deployed one without added legwork; and starting, stopping, and restarting your server is taken care of by Heroku's built-in deployment mechanisms. Script maintenance headaches simply go away.

> **NOTE** *For more information on Maven, see the "Managing Dependencies" section later in this chapter.*

Traditional Java application containers often require complex configuration to manage scaling mechanisms and processes. Often, this is done with stateful sessions or state replication across a cluster of servers, adding complexity to configure and deploy these apps. Heroku apps must be stateless, with state moved into layers that are better suited for it, like a data store or client-side. Key-value stores like Redis and Memcached are ideal for this. This stateless, share-nothing architecture allows for rapid scaling, with a simple command or a few clicks of a mouse in Heroku's Dashboard.

Including load balancing and failover in an app adds more complexity to the app's architecture. It typically requires configuration or adding a load-balancing solution to the system and monitoring the health of nodes to detect failure and reroute traffic to healthy nodes. Heroku's dyno manifold takes care of this behind the scenes, transparently to the developer. Each running dyno is continuously monitored, and misbehaving dynos (e.g., crashed apps, apps with memory leaks that runaway with resources) are automatically restarted, providing erosion resistance and high availability. Load balancing is done by the dyno routing layer, and configuration and script writing are not needed to scale your app up and down.

Logging is also something that Java developers commonly had to manage with strategies for routing and rotating logs. This requires effort to configure and bind them to the application layer. Heroku provides built-in logging functionality with Logplex, which bridges from common frameworks such as Simple Logging Facade for Java (SLF4J) or Log4j. Application output is streamed and can be sent to other servers or your choice of third-party services for archival and advanced reporting. The Loggly add-on provides an excellent service that aggregates logs, provides monitoring and alerts, and empowers users with log-analysis tools.

Deployment descriptors describe how your app should be deployed and bound to services. Service configuration is done with deployment descriptors, server console, and Java Naming and Directory Interface (JDNI) services, usually relying on a combination of these to define bindings. Heroku does this in its most simple form by configuring services explicitly on the application layer. For more complex bindings, configuration files can be used in conjunction with configuration variables (config vars) for environment-specific differences. Config vars take care of context-specific binding information, such as defining port binding.

This lightweight approach that Heroku takes to Java application development frees the developer from reliance on middleware vendors and enables a more agile approach to developing web apps. The need for containers to take care of mechanisms that happen behind the scenes to ensure scalability and reliability are abstracted, simplifying the development process. This approach can provide transformational change for Java developers, who can focus their efforts on delivering code instead of wasting time on configuring and managing complexity.

INSTALLING THE JAVA DEVELOPMENT KIT

The first thing you need to do to develop Java apps locally is to install the Java Development Kit (JDK). This collection of tools varies according to the platform you are using and you can find instructions for each one here. If you want to skip this part and simply develop and test your apps directly on Heroku instead of locally, you can do so without the JDK.

Installing on Windows

Heroku runs apps that use the Open Java Development Kit (OpenJDK) 6. Writing Java apps for Heroku with Windows can be either very easy or very hard. The easy way is to simply install Oracle's Java SE 6 JDK (`www.oracle.com/technetwork/java/javase/downloads/index.html`) even though it is not the same as OpenJDK. Though they are different, if you go to OpenJDK's home page (`http://openjdk.java.net/`), they suggest installing Oracle's JDK because it is so similar to OpenJDK (in theory, the JVMs on both should work the same). However, some purists might shun using slightly different JDKs for development and production, as it could cause issues whereby something may work in development but not in production as a result of minute differences. For most purposes, however, you will be fine with Oracle's JDK.

If you want to get a working copy of OpenJDK 6 working on your Windows machine or you are simply a masochist, you can build it from the source on your computer using the instructions at `https://blogs.oracle.com/poonam/entry/building_openjdk_on_windows`. This process involves getting the source code, installing Microsoft Visual Studio (to compile the code), installing numerous other supporting tools (Cygwin, Apache Ant, Direct X 9, and NetBeans, amongst many others), and running a complex set of configurations. It can take hours, but you will have a copy of OpenJDK 6 running on Windows that was compiled for that machine.

> **NOTE** *OpenCSG maintains an OpenJDK 6 binary (`www.openscg.com/se/openjdk/`) that can be used on 32-bit Windows machines. This might suit a purist's purposes for having OpenJDK 6 installed and may be worth trying before going through the preceding process.*

Maven 3 is needed for dependency management. You can download it from `http://maven.apache.org/download.html` and follow the instructions to install it.

Installing on Mac OS X

The easiest way to install Java on Mac OS X is by going to Applications ➪ Utilities ➪ Java Preferences. If you do not have any versions of Java installed, you will be prompted to download and install it. This should also install Maven, which is needed for dependency management. If you cannot install it in this manner or have an older version, you can install OpenJDK instead.

To install OpenJDK 6 on Mac OS X, you can use MacPorts, a handy package management system. Before you install MacPorts, you need to download Apple's Xcode Developer Tools, a package needed by MacPorts to run. To do this, go to `http://developer.apple.com/`, download the latest copy of Xcode, and follow the instructions in the package to install it.

> **NOTE** *Xcode is a very large app — nearly 2GB. It takes a long time to download and install, but luckily you have to do this only once.*

To install MacPorts, go to `www.macports.org/install.php` and follow the instructions there on installing it from a package. To get OpenJDK 6 running on your Mac, open the Terminal and type the following commands to use MacPorts to install OpenJDK 6:

```
$ port search openjdk6
$ sudo port install openjdk6
```

> **NOTE** *Ideally, you should have the exact same version of the JVM that you are going to run apps on, even though OpenJDK 7 is already out. For those who are more cutting-edge, OpenJDK 7 and 8 can be used by adding* `java.runtime.version=1.7` *or* `java.runtime.version=1.8` *to your* `system.properties` *file.*

Installing on Linux

With Linux, you can install OpenJDK 6 in a couple of different ways, depending on what package manager you use. If you use the Advanced Package Tool (APT), primarily found on Debian and Ubuntu flavours of Linux, then you can use the following command to install OpenJDK 6:

```
$ sudo apt-get install openjdk-6-jdk
```

If you use Yum as a package manager — found on Red Hat Enterprise and Fedora distributions, amongst others — you can use the following command:

```
$ su -c "yum install java-1.6.0-openjdk-devel"
```

MANAGING DEPENDENCIES

Dependency management for Heroku apps is done with Apache Maven. Maven uses a Project Object Model (POM), which encapsulates information about the project (e.g., name, version, etc.) and the process to build it. Maven 3.0.3 is used for build automation on Heroku, using a `pom.xml` file located in the root directory to determine which libraries are needed to build the project. Maven can either download dependencies from a public repository or package local libraries. However, in the interest of dependency isolation, using libraries from a public repository is recommended whenever possible. When pushing your app, Maven will package your app with its dependencies, producing a slug that will run on your Heroku dynos.

Maven is very easy to use. When you want to run a Java app locally, simply run the following:

```
mvn package
```

Maven will do its magic, downloading and installing the required packages to a local repository specified in the pom.xml file. Maven uses cached copies of local libraries when possible to speed up the build process by preventing a download of all your dependencies on each build.

When you push your code to Heroku and a pom.xml file is detected, Maven is run as part of Heroku's build process with this command:

```
mvn -B -DskipTests=true clean install
```

The basic structure of a pom.xml file looks something like this:

```
<?xml version="1.0" encoding="UTF-8"?>
<project xmlns="http://maven.apache.org/POM/4.0.0"
    xmlns:xsi="http://www.w3.org/2001/XMLSchema-instance"
    xsi:schemaLocation="http://maven.apache.org/POM/4.0.0
        http://maven.apache.org/maven-v4_0_0.xsd">

    <modelVersion>4.0.0</modelVersion>
    <groupId>com.organizationname.appname</groupId>
    <version>1.0</version>
    <artifactId>myappname</artifactId>
    <name>My Application Name</name>

    <dependencies>
        <dependency>
            <groupId>org.provider.projectname</groupId>
            <artifactId>library-name</artifactId>
            <version>1.2.3</version>
        </dependency>
    </dependencies>
</project>
```

The elements in this file are as follows:

➤ modelVersion: Defines which POM version Maven should use to read the file. It should always be 4.0.0 for your Heroku projects.

➤ groupId: Specifies a unique identifier for your organization or project. It doesn't have to use dot notation or correspond with the package structure of the project, but it is still used this way for most libraries.

➤ artifactId: Denotes the name of your project.

➤ version: Indicates the version number of the app you are building.

➤ name: Defines the name of your app.

The dependencies block defines each dependency by using its unique groupId, artifactId, and version. The combination of these three identifiers points to a particular version of the library on which your app depends, using the same identification structure described in the previous paragraph for the app you are creating. In your example `pom.xml` file, you are getting the library `library-name` that is part of the project `org.provider.projectname`. You specifically want version 1.2.3 of this library to be used. By default, Maven will attempt to download the specified version of this library from the central repository found at `http://repo.maven.apache.org/maven2/`.

> **NOTE** *You can search Maven's central repository for libraries you need at* `http://search.maven.org/#browse`.

Sometimes you will want to include libraries in your project that aren't in Maven's central repository. For instance, if you want to include a Java ARchive (JAR) file as a dependency for your project, you can create a `repo` directory in the root of the project with a folder hierarchy underneath matching the group name, library name, and version of the dependency. In the previous example, if your group name were `org.provider.projectname`, then your library would live at `repo/org/provider/projectname/library-name/1.2.3/library-name-1.2.3.jar`.

You would then have to define your local repository in your `pom.xml` file, by adding a `repositories` tag under the `project` element that points to your local repository, as follows:

```
<repositories>
    <repository>
        <id>project.local</id>
        <name>project</name>
        <url>file:${project.basedir}/repo</url>
    </repository>
</repositories>
```

Now your dependency can be declared in the same way as before:

```
<dependency>
    <groupId>org.provider.projectname</groupId>
    <artifactId>library-name</artifactId>
    <version>1.2.3</version>
</dependency>
```

Your local repository must be checked in with the rest of your code, and Maven will resolve your unmanaged dependency to this local repository.

If you prefer to use another build manager, such as Apache Ant, you can do so. However, because Heroku's build mechanism relies upon a `pom.xml` file being present for Java apps, the script used to manage dependencies would have to be initiated by a Maven script. Here is an example of a `pom.xml` file in which Maven initiates an Ant task:

```
<?xml version="1.0" encoding="UTF-8"?>
<project xmlns="http://maven.apache.org/POM/4.0.0"
    xmlns:xsi="http://www.w3.org/2001/XMLSchema-instance"
    xsi:schemaLocation="http://maven.apache.org/POM/4.0.0
        http://maven.apache.org/maven-v4_0_0.xsd">

    <modelVersion>4.0.0</modelVersion>
    <groupId>com.organizationname.appname</groupId>
    <version>1.0</version>
    <artifactId>myappname</artifactId>
```

```
<name>My Application Name</name>

    <build>
    <plugins>
        <plugin>
        <artifactId>maven-antrun-plugin</artifactId>
        <version>1.1</version>
        <executions>
            <execution>
                <phase>generate-sources</phase>
                <configuration>
                <tasks>
                    <exec dir="${project.basedir}"
                    executable="${project.basedir}/scripts/some-script.sh"
                    failonerror="true">
                    <arg line="firstArgument secondArgument" />
                    </exec>
                </tasks>
                </configuration>
                <goals>
                <goal>run</goal>
                </goals>
            </execution>
        </executions>
        </plugin>
    </plugins>
    </build>
</project>
```

Here, the `some-script.sh` script located in the `scripts` directory is run by Ant with the arguments `"firstArgument secondArgument"`. This is done in Maven's generate-sources phase where code used for compilation is generated.

> **NOTE** *For a list of Maven's build phases, see* `http://maven.apache` `.org/guides/introduction/introduction-to-the-lifecycle` `.html#Lifecycle_Reference.`

Maven must be installed locally to get the dependencies needed for local testing. To build and install Maven, go to `http://maven.apache.org/download.html` and follow the instructions in the section "Unix-based Operating Systems (Linux, Solaris and Mac OS X)."

WRITING A CONTAINERLESS APPLICATION WITH EMBEDDED JETTY

In order to run your Java apps, you need a web server on which to run it. As discussed earlier in the chapter, apps running on Heroku must embed everything needed to run as a dependency. Heroku supports either using an embedded Jetty web server, the Jetty Runner, to run your app's JAR or using an embedded Tomcat server. Embedded Jetty enables you to run a servlet using Java's Servlet API, and provides support for using JSPs.

The following example creates a very simple app to demonstrate how you can write containerless apps on Heroku with an embedded Jetty web server (code file: `ch12-java-embedded-jetty-example.zip`).

1. Create your `pom.xml` file, which includes your dependencies, as described in the previous section:

```xml
<?xml version="1.0" encoding="UTF-8"?>
<project xmlns="http://maven.apache.org/POM/4.0.0"
        xmlns:xsi="http://www.w3.org/2001/XMLSchema-instance"
        xsi:schemaLocation="http://maven.apache.org/POM/4.0.0
            http://maven.apache.org/maven-v4_0_0.xsd">
    <modelVersion>4.0.0</modelVersion>
    <groupId>com.professional-heroku-programming.java-embedded-jetty-example</groupId>
    <version>1.0</version>
    <artifactId>java-embedded-jetty-example</artifactId>
    <name>Embedded Jetty Example with Java</name>
    <dependencies>
        <dependency>
            <groupId>org.eclipse.jetty</groupId>
            <artifactId>jetty-servlet</artifactId>
            <version>7.6.4.v20120524</version>
        </dependency>
        <dependency>
            <groupId>javax.servlet</groupId>
            <artifactId>servlet-api</artifactId>
            <version>2.5</version>
        </dependency>
    </dependencies>
    <build>
        <plugins>
            <plugin>
                <groupId>org.apache.maven.plugins</groupId>
                <artifactId>maven-dependency-plugin</artifactId>
                <version>2.4</version>
                <executions>
                    <execution>
                        <id>copy-dependencies</id>
                        <phase>package</phase>
                        <goals>
                            <goal>copy-dependencies</goal>
                        </goals>
                    </execution>
                </executions>
            </plugin>
        </plugins>
    </build>
</project>
```

Here, in the `dependencies` section, the first dependency defined, `jetty-servlet`, is the lightweight Jetty servlet container that will run the servlet you are creating. Your `javax .servlet` dependency defines the standard API for Java servlets that Jetty will use; and the `maven-dependency-plugin` tells Maven to package your web app by copying the dependencies to the default directory.

2. Define the Java servlet that you want to run. To do this, add the file `src/main/java/JavaEmbeddedJettyExample.java`:

```
import java.io.IOException;
import javax.servlet.ServletException;
import javax.servlet.http.*;
import org.eclipse.jetty.server.Server;
import org.eclipse.jetty.servlet.*;

public class JavaEmbeddedJettyExample extends HttpServlet {

    public static void main(String[] args) throws Exception {
        Server server = new Server(Integer.valueOf(System.getenv("PORT")));
        ServletContextHandler context =
            new ServletContextHandler(ServletContextHandler.SESSIONS);
        context.setContextPath("/");
        server.setHandler(context);
        context.addServlet(new ServletHolder(new JavaEmbeddedJettyExample()),"/*");
        server.start();
        server.join();
    }

    @Override
    protected void doGet(HttpServletRequest req, HttpServletResponse resp)
            throws ServletException, IOException {
        resp.getWriter().print("<h1>This is my first Java app running on
            Heroku!</h1>\n");
    }
}
```

Here, when the main class is entered, in the first line in this code block, you tell the Jetty server to which port it should bind. This is defined as an environment variable in Heroku because it varies on every dyno on which your app is run. The `context` object instance is used to set the handling of web requests that arrive at the root directory with `setContextPath()`. The `addServlet()` method will run the servlet you defined within this context. The `start()` and `join()` methods start your app server. In the `doGet()` method, you simply write out a response to web browsers with your message.

3. Add a `Procfile` to tell Heroku how to start the embedded Jetty server to run your app:

```
web: java -cp target/classes:target/dependency/* JavaEmbeddedJettyExample
```

Because there is no standard process as there is with other languages supported by Heroku (like Ruby), you must explicitly define your processes here. The following defines the targets for your classes and dependencies (which Maven copied here as instructed in the `pom.xml` file) and tells Jetty which class the `main` method is in.

4. Package up your dependencies using Maven:

```
$ mvn package
[INFO] Scanning for projects...
[INFO]
[INFO] ------------------------------------------------------------------------
[INFO] Building Embedded Jetty Example with Java 1.0
[INFO] ------------------------------------------------------------------------
Downloading: http://repo1.maven.org/maven2/org/apache/maven/plugins/maven-resources-
```

```
plugin/2.4.3/maven-resources-plugin-2.4.3.pom
Downloaded: http://repo1.maven.org/maven2/org/apache/maven/plugins/maven-resources-
plugin/2.4.3/maven-resources-plugin-2.4.3.pom (6 KB at 34.4 KB/sec)
Downloading: http://repo1.maven.org/maven2/org/apache/maven/plugins/maven-plugins/18/
maven-plugins-18.pom
Downloaded: http://repo1.maven.org/maven2/org/apache/maven/plugins/maven-plugins/18/
maven-plugins-18.pom (13 KB at 96.9 KB/sec)
...
[INFO] Copying jetty-server-7.6.4.v20120524.jar to /Users/ckemp/Documents/Sites/java-
embedded-jetty-example/target/dependency/jetty-server-7.6.4.v20120524.jar
[INFO] Copying jetty-continuation-7.6.4.v20120524.jar to /Users/ckemp/Documents/Sites/
java-embedded-jetty-example/target/dependency/jetty-continuation-7.6.4.v20120524.jar
[INFO] ------------------------------------------------------------------------
[INFO] BUILD SUCCESS
[INFO] ------------------------------------------------------------------------
[INFO] Total time: 31.386s
[INFO] Finished at: Mon Aug 20 19:09:24 EDT 2012
[INFO] Final Memory: 12M/81M
[INFO] ------------------------------------------------------------------------
```

Now, all your dependencies are packaged up in the target directory.

5. Run your app locally by setting the environment variable for the port on which it will run:

```
$ export PORT=5000
$ java -cp target/classes:"target/dependency/*" JavaEmbeddedJettyExample
2012-08-20 19:10:02.558:INFO:oejs.Server:jetty-7.6.4.v20120524
2012-08-20 19:10:02.625:INFO:oejsh.ContextHandler:started
o.e.j.s.ServletContextHandler
{/,null}
2012-08-20 19:10:02.658:INFO:oejs.AbstractConnector:Started SelectChannelConnector@
0.0.0.0:5000
```

Your app is now available when you visit `http://localhost:5000` in your browser. Now that you know your apps works, the next step is to deploy it to Heroku.

6. To deploy to Heroku, first initialize your Git repository, create your Heroku app, and commit your code:

```
$ git init
Initialized empty Git repository in /Users/ckemp/Documents/Sites/java-embedded-jetty-
example/.git/

$ heroku create java-embedded-jetty-example
Creating java-embedded-jetty-example... done, stack is cedar
http://java-embedded-jetty-example.herokuapp.com/ | git@heroku.com:java-embedded-jetty-
example.git
Git remote heroku added

$ git add .

$ git commit -am "Initial commit"
[master (root-commit) 0f052e1] Initial commit
 3 files changed, 65 insertions(+), 0 deletions(-)
 create mode 100644 Procfile
 create mode 100644 pom.xml
 create mode 100644 src/main/java/JavaEmbeddedJettyExample.java
```

7. Push the app to Heroku:

```
$ git push heroku master
Counting objects: 8, done.
Delta compression using up to 4 threads.
Compressing objects: 100% (6/6), done.
Writing objects: 100% (8/8), 1.41 KiB, done.
Total 8 (delta 0), reused 0 (delta 0)

-----> Heroku receiving push
-----> Java app detected
-----> Installing Maven 3.0.3..... done
-----> Installing settings.xml..... done
-----> executing /app/tmp/repo.git/.cache/.maven/bin/mvn -B -Duser.home=/tmp/build_
       1u7nmdhqbznst -Dmaven.repo.local=/app/tmp/repo.git/.cache/.m2/repository -s
       /app/tmp/repo.git/.cache/.m2/settings.xml -DskipTests=true clean install
       [INFO] Scanning for projects...
       [INFO]
       [INFO] ------------------------------------------------------------------------
       [INFO] Building Embedded Jetty Example with Java 1.0
       [INFO] ------------------------------------------------------------------------
       Downloading: http://s3pository.heroku.com/jvm/org/apache/maven/plugins/maven-
       dependency-plugin/2.4/maven-dependency-plugin-2.4.pom
       Downloaded: http://s3pository.heroku.com/jvm/org/apache/maven/plugins/maven-
       dependency-plugin/2.4/maven-dependency-plugin-2.4.pom (11 KB at 50.4 KB/sec)
       Downloading: http://s3pository.heroku.com/jvm/org/apache/maven/plugins/maven-
       dependency-plugin/2.4/maven-dependency-plugin-2.4.jar
       Downloaded: http://s3pository.heroku.com/jvm/org/apache/maven/plugins/maven-
       dependency-plugin/2.4/maven-dependency-plugin-2.4.jar (132 KB at 744.1 KB/sec)
...
       [INFO] --- maven-compiler-plugin:2.3.2:compile (default-compile) @ java-
       embedded-jetty-example ---
       [INFO] Compiling 1 source file to /tmp/build_1u7nmdhqbznst/target/classes
...
       [INFO] --- maven-jar-plugin:2.3.1:jar (default-jar) @ java-embedded-jetty-
       example ---
       [INFO] Building jar: /tmp/build_1u7nmdhqbznst/target/java-embedded-jetty-
       example-1.0.jar
       [INFO]
...
       [INFO] --- maven-install-plugin:2.3.1:install (default-install) @ java-embedded-
       jetty-example ---
       [INFO] Installing /tmp/build_1u7nmdhqbznst/target/java-embedded-jetty-example-
       1.0.jar to /app/tmp/repo.git/.cache/.m2/repository/com/professional-heroku-
       programming/java-embedded-jetty-example/java-embedded-jetty-example/1.0/
       java-embedded-jetty-example-1.0.jar
       [INFO] Installing /tmp/build_1u7nmdhqbznst/pom.xml to /app/tmp/repo.git/.cache/
       .m2/repository/com/professional-heroku-programming/java-embedded-jetty-example/
       java-embedded-jetty-example/1.0/java-embedded-jetty-example-1.0.pom
       [INFO] ------------------------------------------------------------------------
       [INFO] BUILD SUCCESS
       [INFO] ------------------------------------------------------------------------
       [INFO] Total time: 8.913s
       [INFO] Finished at: Sat Aug 18 17:42:05 UTC 2012
       [INFO] Final Memory: 12M/490M
```

```
        [INFO] ------------------------------------------------------------
-----> Discovering process types
       Procfile declares types -> web
-----> Compiled slug size is 1.0MB
-----> Launching... done, v5
       http://java-embedded-jetty-example.herokuapp.com deployed to Heroku

To git@heroku.com:java-embedded-jetty-example.git
 * [new branch]      master -> master
```

As shown in the preceding output, a Java app is detected through the existence of a `pom.xml` file. Next, Maven is installed and the build script is run. Maven begins the build process by downloading all the dependencies defined, as well as their subdependencies. Your app and its dependencies are then compiled, JAR'd, and installed. Finally, the `web` process defined in the `Procfile` is detected and your app server is launched by Heroku.

8.   Test your app with the following command:

```
$ heroku open
```

You should see your successfully running, containerless Java app with embedded Jetty, as shown in Figure 12-1.

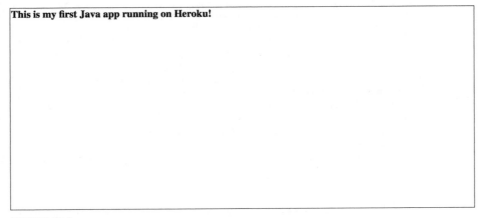

This is my first Java app running on Heroku!

FIGURE 12-1

9.   Finally, take a look at your config vars:

```
$ heroku config
=== java-embedded-jetty-example Config Vars
DATABASE_URL:                      postgres://mYu53Rn@M3:mYp@55W0rD@ec2-123-45-678-909.
                                   compute-1.amazonaws.com:5432/mYd@T@b@53n@M3
HEROKU_POSTGRESQL_VIOLET_URL: postgres://mYu53Rn@M3:mYp@55W0rD@ec2-123-45-678-909.
                                   compute-1.amazonaws.com:5432/mYd@T@b@53n@M3
JAVA_OPTS:                         -Xmx384m -Xss512k -XX:+UseCompressedOops
MAVEN_OPTS:                        -Xmx384m -Xss512k -XX:+UseCompressedOops
PATH:                              /app/.jdk/bin:/usr/local/bin:/usr/bin:/bin
```

You have seen DATABASE_URL before, and the HEROKU_POSTGRES_VIOLET_URL simply refers to the connection string for the same database. Heroku automatically adds a Heroku Dev database to every app. JAVA_OPTS and MAVEN_OPTS are flags that define options for the JVM when running your app. You can use this to tweak memory settings, but the standard settings should work for most apps; and changes should be carefully considered, as you may start consuming more than the 512MB limit and begin to page to disk, adversely affecting performance. PATH sets the location of directories containing programs needed to run your app.

WRITING AN APPLICATION WITH THE SPRING FRAMEWORK AND HIBERNATE ON TOMCAT

One of the most common frameworks on which modern enterprise Java apps are written is the Spring Framework. The Spring Framework provides an Inversion of Control (IoC) application framework on top of the Java EE platform. The IoC container enables you to configure and manage Java objects called Beans using dependency injection, where components are included in the app at run time rather than during the build. The Spring Framework's aspect-oriented programming (AOP) also enables developers to reuse a single routine across selected objects, using a flexible engine to do so. Java Database Connectivity (JDBC) and object-relational mapping (ORM) tools such as Hibernate can be used to connect to databases. Enterprise application development with the Spring Framework is made easy with its robust built-in feature set, ease of use, and quick learning curve.

Apps using the Spring Framework can be run with your choice of web containers. In this example, you will use the popular Apache Tomcat 7 web server. The Catalina servlet container enables you to run JSPs, and the Coyote web server will run your Java apps. Tomcat can be used for any Java app, not just apps using the Spring Framework. In the example app, you will run an app using the Spring Framework with an embedded Tomcat web server that uses Hibernate to access the data store in a Heroku Postgres database.

Creating Spring Framework apps from scratch can be a complex and time-consuming task. You would have to create your model, view, and controller; configure your Beans to connect all the pieces together; and do all your dependency declarations for the various components of the framework. Luckily, there is an open-source tool that makes this a quick and painless process, enabling quick creation of the basic scaffolding needed to rapidly make a Spring Framework app.

Spring Roo is a rapid application development tool used to create Java applications on the Spring Framework, leveraging convention over coding. It is similar to the Rails scaffolding tool, which can be used to quickly create Ruby on Rails applications, enabling Java developers to quickly create the basics of a Spring Framework application and build on that. It uses the Java Persistence API (JPA), JSP, and AspectJ for AOP to create Spring Framework-based applications that use Maven for dependency management, which makes deployment to Heroku a snap. Spring Roo can be used to create scaffolding that is defined either interactively using the Spring Roo command-line interface (CLI) or by loading scripts that Spring Roo will parse to create standalone apps using the Spring Framework that don't rely on any Spring Roo–specific runtime components, enabling maximum portability.

In the next example, you are going to create a Spring Framework Java app that will run on a Tomcat server (code file: ch12-spring-tomcat-roo-example.zip). To quickly create this app, you will use Spring Roo to build the scaffolding. Similar to previous examples, you will create an app for maintaining a database of employees, each of which has an employee ID, name, and e-mail address. You will set up a Spring Roo script to create your code, add the database credentials for your Heroku Postgres database, and then deploy your app directly to Heroku.

> **NOTE** *To install Spring Roo, you can either download it from* `www.springsource` `.org/spring-roo#try` *or, if you have a Mac with Homebrew installed, use* `brew install spring-roo.`

1. Create an `employees.roo` file, which will define a Spring Roo script to set up your database model and the scaffolding, almost effortlessly:

```
project --topLevelPackage com.professionalherokuprogramming.javaspringexample

persistence setup --provider HIBERNATE --database POSTGRES

entity jpa --class ~.domain.Employee  --testAutomatically

field number --fieldName id --type java.lang.Integer --min 0 --class ~.domain.Employee
field string --fieldName name --notNull --sizeMin 3 --sizeMax 100
field string --fieldName email --notNull --sizeMin 3 --sizeMax 100

web mvc setup
web mvc all --package ~.web

selenium test --controller ~.web.EmployeeController

logging setup --level DEBUG
```

The `project` command sets up the namespace for your project. The `persistence setup` command tells Spring Roo that you want to use a Postgres database as the backing data store for the app. The line beginning with `entity jpa` defines the table that you want to set up for the `Employee` object. The three lines that use the `field` command define the properties for the `Employee` object — in this example, ID, name, and e-mail address.

The lines beginning with `web mvc` tell Spring Roo to set up the scaffolding with the model, view, and controller for your object. The `selenium test` command automatically sets up a test script that you can run to test your app's scaffolding, using the popular web-testing framework, Selenium. The line beginning with `logging setup` configures logging for Log4j, which is included in Spring Roo.

2. Now use Spring Roo's interactive CLI to run your script:

```
$ roo
```

```
                       1.2.2.RELEASE [rev 7d75659]


Welcome to Spring Roo. For assistance press TAB or type "hint" then hit ENTER.

roo> script employees.roo
```

```
project --topLevelPackage com.professionalherokuprogramming.javaspringexample
Created ROOT/pom.xml
Created SRC_MAIN_RESOURCES
Created SRC_MAIN_RESOURCES/log4j.properties
Created SPRING_CONFIG_ROOT
Created SPRING_CONFIG_ROOT/applicationContext.xml

persistence setup --provider HIBERNATE --database POSTGRES
Created SPRING_CONFIG_ROOT/database.properties
Please update your database details in src/main/resources/META-INF/spring/database.
properties.
Updated SPRING_CONFIG_ROOT/applicationContext.xml
Created SRC_MAIN_RESOURCES/META-INF/persistence.xml
Updated ROOT/pom.xml [added dependencies postgresql:postgresql:9.1-901.jdbc3,
org.hibernate:hibernate-core:3.6.9.Final, org.hibernate:hibernate-entitymanager:3.6.9.
Final, org.hibernate.javax.persistence:hibernate-jpa-2.0-api:1.0.1.Final, commons-
collections:commons-collections:3.2.1, org.hibernate:hibernate-validator:4.2.0.Final,
javax.validation:validation-api:1.0.0.GA, cglib:cglib-nodep:2.2.2, javax.transaction:
jta:1.1, org.springframework:spring-jdbc:${spring.version}, org.
springframework:spring-
orm:${spring.version}, commons-pool:commons-pool:1.5.6, commons-dbcp:commons-dbcp:1.3]

entity jpa --class ~.domain.Employee  --testAutomatically
Created SRC_MAIN_JAVA/com/professionalherokuprogramming/javaspringexample/domain
...

web mvc setup
Created ROOT/src/main/webapp/WEB-INF/spring
Created ROOT/src/main/webapp/WEB-INF/spring/webmvc-config.xml
...

logging setup --level DEBUG
Updated ROOT/src/main/resources/log4j.properties
Script required 4.942 seconds to execute
~.web roo> quit
```

In this case you ran a script, but you could also enter each command line by line, in the CLI. The first section sets up the basics for any Spring Roo app. The second section sets up the Maven dependencies and Hibernate object-relational mapping (ORM) configuration that is needed to use Postgres as your data store. The third section sets up the model for your app, including the database migration scripts needed. The fourth and fifth sections set up the model-view-controller and logging, as per the script. You now have the scaffolding for a running Spring Framework app set up. Spring Roo has not yet set up the database or installed your embedded Tomcat server, so you'll do that next.

3. Modify the database properties to pull in your Heroku Postgres credentials from the DATABASE_URL config var. Set your Bean to point to these by modifying src/main/resources/META-INF/spring/applicationContext.xml inside the bean tag:

```
<bean class="java.net.URI" id="dbUrl">
    <constructor-arg value="${DATABASE_URL}"/>
</bean>
```

4. Find the following section in the same file:

```
<bean class="org.apache.commons.dbcp.BasicDataSource" destroy-method="close"
    id="dataSource">
<property name="driverClassName" value="${database.driverClassName}"/>
<property name="url" value="${database.url}"/>
<property name="username" value="${database.username}"/>
<property name="password" value="${database.password}"/>
...
```

And replace the preceding four property values with your database credentials from the parsed config var:

```
<property name="driverClassName" value="${database.driverClassName}"/>
<property name="url" value="#{ 'jdbc:postgresql://' + @dbUrl.getHost() +
    @dbUrl.getPath() }"/>
<property name="username" value="#{ @dbUrl.getUserInfo().split(':')[0] }"/>
<property name="password" value="#{ @dbUrl.getUserInfo().split(':')[1] }"/>
```

Your Heroku Postgres database is set up and ready to roll.

5. Add the Webapp Runner, an embedded version of a Tomcat container, to run the app. To do that, edit the pom.xml file by adding the following lines to the plugins section:

```
<plugin>
    <groupId>org.apache.maven.plugins</groupId>
    <artifactId>maven-dependency-plugin</artifactId>
    <version>2.3</version>
    <executions>
        <execution>
            <phase>package</phase>
            <goals>
                <goal>copy</goal>
            </goals>
            <configuration>
                <artifactItems>
                    <artifactItem>
                        <groupId>com.github.jsimone</groupId>
                        <artifactId>webapp-runner</artifactId>
                        <version>7.0.22.3</version>
                        <destFileName>webapp-runner.jar</destFileName>
                    </artifactItem>
                </artifactItems>
            </configuration>
        </execution>
    </executions>
</plugin>
```

> **NOTE** *This example uses the Webapp Runner created by Heroku's John Simone (https://github.com/jsimone/webapp-runner). Apache's official Tomcat Maven plugin was a work-in-progress when Heroku first started supporting Java and did not work without some tweaking. You can use the official Apache plugin instead by following the instructions at https://devcenter.heroku.com/articles/java-tomcat7-maven-plugin.*

6. Set up your `Procfile` to use Webapp Runner to run your app:

```
web:  java $JAVA_OPTS -jar target/dependency/webapp-runner.jar --port $PORT target/*.war
```

> **NOTE** *To run the same app with Jetty Runner, use the snippet for* `pom.xml` *at* `https://devcenter.heroku.com/articles/spring-mvc-hibernate#add-jetty-runner`, *along with the* `Procfile` *command in the "Declare process types with Procfile" section in the same Dev Center article instead.*

7. Follow the regular Heroku methodology for committing, pushing, and testing the app:

```
$ git init
Initialized empty Git repository in /Users/ckemp/Documents/Sites/java-spring-tomcat-
roo-example/.git/

$ heroku create java-spring-tomcat-roo-example
Creating java-spring-tomcat-roo-example... done, stack is cedar
http://java-spring-tomcat-roo-example.herokuapp.com/ | git@heroku.com:java-spring-
tomcat-roo-example.git
Git remote heroku added

$ git add .

$ git commit -am "Initial commit"
[master (root-commit) 7e78453] Initial commit
 91 files changed, 4193 insertions(+)
 create mode 100644 Procfile
 create mode 100644 employees.roo
 create mode 100644 log.roo
 create mode 100644 pom.xml
...

$ git push heroku master
Counting objects: 125, done.
Delta compression using up to 4 threads.
Compressing objects: 100% (116/116), done.
Writing objects: 100% (125/125), 72.78 KiB, done.
Total 125 (delta 29), reused 0 (delta 0)

-----> Heroku receiving push
-----> Java app detected
...
-----> Launching... done, v5
       http://java-spring-tomcat-roo-example.herokuapp.com deployed to Heroku

To git@heroku.com:java-spring-tomcat-roo-example.git
 * [new b ranch]      master -> master

$ heroku open
```

When the Spring Roo-generated app is up and running successfully on Heroku, you should see a screen like the one shown in Figure 12-2.

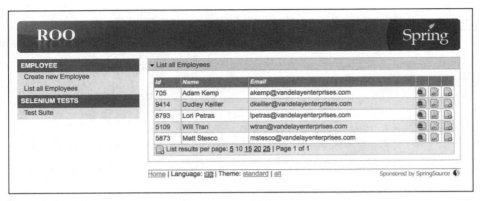

FIGURE 12-2

In your app, Spring Roo has set up three links on the sidebar. Create a new Employee will insert a new employee record into the database. List all Employees displays the contents of your database table, and you can use the links there to view individual records, edit them, and delete them. The last menu option, Test Suite, can be used to test your app with a Selenium test script auto-generated with Spring Roo. Spring Roo also sets up JUnit tests for testing your code.

Now take a look at the headers returned by the server for your app:

```
$ curl -i http://java-spring-tomcat-roo-example.herokuapp.com
HTTP/1.1 200 OK
Content-Language: en-US
Content-Type: text/html;charset=UTF-8
Date: Fri, 24 Aug 2012 20:55:41 GMT
Server: Apache-Coyote/1.1
...
```

Here you can see that Tomcat's Coyote HTTP 1.1 web server is responding to your web requests. The Spring Framework app is running successfully on the embedded Tomcat server. You can now take this scaffolding code and modify it to meet your app's requirements.

WRITING AN APPLICATION WITH THE PLAY FRAMEWORK

The Play framework is a model-view-controller (MVC) platform that can be used for writing both Java and Scala programs. Like Spring Roo or Ruby on Rails, you can use Play to rapidly create apps, prioritizing convention over configuration for maximum developer productivity. A JBoss Netty web server is embedded in Play apps to serve requests. Apache Ivy is used for dependency management for Play apps, and Simple Build Tool (commonly known as sbt) is used as the build tool.

The Play framework is very well suited for writing apps that are run on the Heroku platform because of its stateless nature and capability to perform asynchronous I/O for long-running processes. A share-nothing model is used for sessions, making scaling with Heroku effortless. The nonblocking approach for I/O means that if you want to do something such as generate a PDF, you can do so in the background while continuing to service new requests. This means that the dyno will not be blocked while this processing happens, making it an efficient approach for Heroku apps.

To get started with the Play framework, download the Play 2 framework from `www.playframework .org/download` and follow the installation instructions at `www.playframework.org/ documentation/2.0/Installing`. If you are using a Mac, you can install Play with Homebrew, using the following command:

```
$ brew install play
```

When Play is installed, you can create the example app. As in previous sections, it will be used to display an employee list from a Heroku Postgres database (code file: `ch12-java-play-example.zip`).

1. Run the `play new` command to create a new Play app:

```
$ play new java-play-example

       _            __ _ __  _|_|
      | '_ \| |/ _' | || |_|
      |  __/|_|\___|\__ (_)
      |_|              |_/

play! 2.0.3, http://www.playframework.org

The new application will be created in /Users/ckemp/Documents/Sites/java-play-example

What is the application name?
> java-play-example

Which template do you want to use for this new application?

  1 - Create a simple Scala application
  2 - Create a simple Java application
  3 - Create an empty project

> 2

OK, application java-play-example is created.

Have fun!

$ cd java-play-example/

$ ls -a | cat
.
..
.gitignore
README
app
conf
project
public
```

Play has created a simple Java app. Examining the directory structure automatically generated for you, you see the following:

➤ `app`: This directory contains subdirectories with the controllers and views. In the next step, you will put the model here as well.

➤ `conf`: This directory is where configuration lives. The `application.conf` file is the main configuration for your app, and `routes` defines the routing for requests. Heroku will detect a Play app with the presence of `conf/application.conf` in any directory except for the `modules` directory.

➤ `project`: This directory contains the build information needed by sbt in order to build the app.

➤ `public`: This directory is the home for an app's public assets, such as images, JavaScript scripts, and CSS files. Notice that in the `javascript` subdirectory, the popular JQuery JavaScript library is already installed for convenience.

2. Set up the model for the `Employee` object in `app/models/Employee.java`:

```java
package models;

import play.db.ebean.*;

import javax.persistence.*;

import java.util.*;

@Entity
public class Employee extends Model {

    @Id
    public Long id;

    public String name;

    public String email;

    public static Finder<Long,Employee> find = new Finder(
        Long.class, Employee.class
    );

    public Employee(Long id, String name, String email) {
        this.id = id;
        this.name = name;
        this.email = email;
    }

    public static List<Employee> all() {
        return Employee.find.all();
    }

    public static Integer count() {
        return Employee.find.all().size();
    }

}
```

This represents and defines the Employee object you will be using to represent employees in the app. As in previous examples, you include an ID, name, and e-mail address for each employee. You also create an Ebean Finder that is used to query your database, as shown in the code block where the find variable is declared. The all() method uses the Finder to get all Employee records. The count() method simply gets a count of all Employee records.

3. Create your controller by editing the app/controllers/Application.java file:

```
package controllers;

import play.*;
import play.mvc.*;

import models.Employee;

import views.html.*;

public class Application extends Controller {

    public static Result index() {
        return ok(
            views.html.index.render(Employee.all())
        );
    }
}
```

In the Employee class, you get all of your employee records, using the Employee.all() model method defined in the previous class. The HTML is rendered using the views.html helpers for HTML templates and passes in the list of employees.

4. Create a view by editing the sample view that Play provides at app/views/index.scala .html:

```
@(employeeList: List[Employee])

@import helper._

@main("Employee List") {

        <h1>Employee List</h1>
        <table>
        <tr>
                <th>Id</th>
                <th>Name</th>
                <th>E-mail Address</th>
        </tr>

        @for(employee <- employeeList) {
                <tr>
                <td>@employee.id</td>
                <td>@employee.name</td>
                <td>@employee.email</td>
                </tr>
        }
        </table>
}
```

5. Modify the route configuration to your controller in the `conf/routes` file so it looks like this:

```
# Routes
# This file defines all application routes (Higher priority routes first)
# ~~~~

# Employee list method
GET     /                           controllers.Application.index()

# Map static resources from the /public folder to the /assets URL path
GET     /assets/*file               controllers.Assets.at(path="/public", file)
```

6. Configure your app to point to your Heroku Postgres database by adding the following lines to the `conf/application.conf` file:

```
ebean.default="models.*"
db.default.driver=org.postgresql.Driver
db.default.url=${?DATABASE_URL}
```

The first line sets up Ebean ORM as your default model engine for accessing data from the default data store. The next line adds support for the Postgres driver needed to access your Heroku Postgres database. The last line pushes in the DATABASE_URL config var with the location and credentials for your backing data store.

7. Add the Postgres driver to your build script at `project/Build.scala` by replacing the line:

```
val appDependencies = Seq(
    // Add your project dependencies here,
)
```

with the following line, which adds the Postgres driver as a dependency:

```
val appDependencies = Seq(
    "postgresql" % "postgresql" % "8.4-702.jdbc4"
)
```

8. Add some test data to initially populate the app by creating a `conf/initial-data.yml` file with a handful of records:

```
employees:

        - !!models.Employee
        id: 1034
        name: Alice Tien
        email: atien@vandelayenterprises.com

        - !!models.Employee
        id: 2319
        name: Dina Lafoyiannis
        email: dlafoyiannis@vandelayenterprises.com

        - !!models.Employee
        id: 7721
        name: Jeff Dickie
```

```
        email: jdickie@vandelayenterprises.com

        - !!models.Employee
        id: 9393
        name: Lucia Orsini
        email: lorsini@vandelayenterprises.com
```

9. Write a bootstrap method to load the test data into your database by creating a file called app/Global.java:

```java
import play.*;
import play.libs.*;

import java.util.*;

import play.db.ebean.*;
import com.avaje.ebean.*;

import models.Employee;

public class Global extends GlobalSettings {

    @Override
    public void onStart(Application app) {
        InitialData.insert(app);
    }

    static class InitialData {

        public static void insert(Application app) {

            if (Ebean.find(Employee.class).findRowCount() == 0) {

                Map<String,List<Object>> all =
                    (Map<String,List<Object>>)Yaml.load("initial-data.yml");

                // Insert employees
                Ebean.save(all.get("employees"));
            }
        }
    }
}
```

This class extends the GlobalSettings annotation, telling Play to execute this class at run time. In GlobalSettings classes, the onStart() and onStop() methods are executed at the appropriate time in the life cycle of your app. Other methods can also be defined in this class to handle missing action methods and define an app error page. The onStart() method simply calls your nested class to insert the test data.

The findRowCount() method in the bootstrapping class first determines whether you have an empty database because you don't want to add duplicates each time the app is started. If no records are found, the test data is loaded from the initial-data.yml file you created into the variable named all. The save() method does the database insert for these new test records with the Ebeans ORM.

10. Deploy the app to Heroku, just as you would for any other app:

```
$ git init
Initialized empty Git repository in /Users/ckemp/Documents/Sites/java-play-example/.git/

$ heroku create java-play-example
Creating java-play-example... done, stack is cedar
http://java-play-example.herokuapp.com/ | git@heroku.com:java-play-example.git
Git remote heroku added

$ git add .

$ git commit -am "Initial commit"
[master (root-commit) 4308ea2] Initial commit
 15 files changed, 205 insertions(+)
 create mode 100644 .gitignore
 create mode 100644 README
 create mode 100644 app/Bootstrap.java
 ...


$ git commit -am "Initial commit"
[master 88c4d5a] Initial commit
 1 file changed, 5 insertions(+), 5 deletions(-)
cK-MacBook-Air:java-play-example ckemp$ git push heroku master
Counting objects: 7, done.
Delta compression using up to 4 threads.
Compressing objects: 100% (4/4), done.
Writing objects: 100% (4/4), 457 bytes, done.
Total 4 (delta 2), reused 0 (delta 0)

-----> Heroku receiving push
-----> Removing .DS_Store files
-----> Play 2.0 - Java app detected
-----> Running: sbt clean compile stage
       Getting net.java.dev.jna jna 3.2.3 ...
       :: retrieving :: org.scala-sbt#boot-jna
             confs: [default]
             1 artifacts copied, 0 already retrieved (838kB/18ms)
 ...
       [info] Compiling 4 Scala sources and 4 Java sources to
       /tmp/build_3eymsr0v0n2sy/
       target/scala-2.9.1/classes...

 ...
       [success] Total time: 17 s, completed Aug 27, 2012 4:42:49 AM
       [info] Packaging /tmp/build_3eymsr0v0n2sy/target/scala-2.9.1/java-play-example_
       2.9.1-1.0-SNAPSHOT.jar ...
       [info] Done packaging.
       [info]
       [info] Your application is ready to be run in place: target/start
       [info]
       [success] Total time: 1 s, completed Aug 27, 2012 4:42:50 AM
-----> Dropping ivy cache from the slug
-----> Discovering process types
```

```
        Procfile declares types        -> (none)
        Default types for Play 2.0 - Java -> web
-----> Compiled slug size is 47.7MB
-----> Launching... done, v7
        http://java-play-example.herokuapp.com deployed to Heroku

To git@heroku.com:java-play-example.git
   c8a3b90..88c4d5a  master -> master
```

Notice that Heroku detects specifically that you are pushing a Play 2.0 Java app. It will also detect Play 1.2.x Java apps, as well as Play 2.0 Scala apps.

11. Use sbt to build the app by running the following command for Play 2.0 apps:

```
sbt clean compile stage
```

12. You do not have to supply a `Procfile` telling Heroku how to run your app because Heroku automatically adds one with a web process. The following command starts the default web process for Play 2.0 apps:

```
web: target/start -Dhttp.port=$PORT $JAVA_OPTS
```

13. Initialize the structure for your Heroku Postgres database:

```
$ heroku pg:psql
psql (9.1.4, server 9.1.5)
SSL connection (cipher: DHE-RSA-AES256-SHA, bits: 256)
Type "help" for help.

mYdAtAbA5eNaM3=> CREATE TABLE employee (
mYdAtAbA5eNaM3(>    id     integer NOT NULL CONSTRAINT firstkey PRIMARY KEY,
mYdAtAbA5eNaM3(>    name   varchar(100) NOT NULL,
mYdAtAbA5eNaM3(>    email  varchar(255) NOT NULL
mYdAtAbA5eNaM3(> );
NOTICE:  CREATE TABLE / PRIMARY KEY will create implicit index "firstkey" for table
"employee"
CREATE TABLE
mYdAtAbA5eNaM3=> \q
```

14. Now that the Play app is deployed to Heroku, take a look at the config vars before testing it out:

```
$ heroku config
=== java-play-example Config Vars
DATABASE_URL:               postgres://dBu53RnAm3:dBpA55w0Rd@ec2-123-45-678-901.
                            compute-1.amazonaws.com:5432/dBnAm3
HEROKU_POSTGRESQL_TEAL_URL: postgres://dBu53RnAm3:dBpA55w0Rd@ec2-123-45-678-901.
                            compute-1.amazonaws.com:5432/dBnAm3
JAVA_OPTS:                  -Xmx384m -Xss512k -XX:+UseCompressedOops
PATH:                       .sbt_home/bin:/usr/local/bin:/usr/bin:/bin
REPO:                       /app/.sbt_home/.ivy2/cache
SBT_OPTS:                   -Xmx384m -Xss512k -XX:+UseCompressedOops
```

The first two config vars represent the connection string for your Heroku Postgres database. JAVA_OPTS defines the JVM parameters you are going to use to run the app. Like all Heroku apps you have seen thus far, the PATH is the standard Unix-style path variable.

REPO points Apache Ivy, the dependency manager for Play apps, to the correct directory with the dependency cache. SBT_OPS defines the default parameters for sbt to use when building your app.

Employee List

Id	Name	E-mail Address
1034	Alice Tien	atien@vandelayenterprises.com
2319	Dina Lafoyiannis	dlafoyiannis@vandelayenterprises.com
7721	Jeff Dickie	jdickie@vandelayenterprises.com
9393	Lucia Orsini	lorsini@vandelayenterprises.com

FIGURE 12-3

15. Test the app:

```
$ heroku open
```

You should now see the employee list with the test data pre-loaded, as shown in Figure 12-3.

> **NOTE** *You can use the* heroku run sbt play *command to experiment with Play's interactive CLI, running on a Heroku instance.*

DEPLOYING A WAR FILE DIRECTLY TO HEROKU

Typically when writing apps on Heroku, you compile your app as part of the standard build process. Sometimes Java developers want to deploy only compiled versions of their apps. For instance, if you use your own continuous integration system and you will only be pushing stable versions of your app that have already passed unit, integration, and acceptance tests, you probably don't want to recompile when deploying to Heroku.

A WAR file is a standard used to package components that make up a Java web app into a single file. WAR files must adhere to a specific directory structure, including a WEB-INF directory with a web .xml file that contains the deployment descriptor (DD) files, tag library descriptor (TLD) files, server-side classes in a classes directory, and a lib directory with the JAR libraries on which your app depends. The JAR tool distributed with the JDK can be used to create these WAR files, or you can write your own scripts to create the archive using the build tool of your choice (e.g., Ant, Maven, or your IDE).

Recall from earlier chapters that Heroku plugins are used to add functionality to the standard Heroku CLI. In order to deploy WAR files directly on Heroku, you must first install the heroku-deploy plugin for the Heroku CLI:

```
$ heroku plugins:install https://github.com/heroku/heroku-deploy
Installing heroku-deploy... done
```

Next, you need a WAR to deploy. For this example, you will use the Build File for the Sample Ant Build page from DZone at www.dzone.com/tutorials/java/ant/ant-sample-build-file-war-1.html and use the built-in Ant script to create a WAR file:

```
$ ant war
Buildfile: /Users/ckemp/Documents/Sites/java-war-deploy-example/build.xml

init:
        [mkdir] Created dir: /Users/ckemp/Documents/Sites/java-war-deploy-example/build/
```

```
        classes
        [mkdir] Created dir: /Users/ckemp/Documents/Sites/java-war-deploy-example/dist

compile:
        [javac] /Users/ckemp/Documents/Sites/java-war-deploy-example/build.xml:16:
        warning: 'includeantruntime' was not set, defaulting to
        build.sysclasspath=last; set to false for repeatable builds
        [javac] Compiling 4 source files to /Users/ckemp/Documents/Sites/java-war-
        deploy-example/build/classes
        [javac] Note: /Users/ckemp/Documents/Sites/java-war-deploy-example/src/com/
        vaannila/web/UserController.java uses or overrides a deprecated API.
        [javac] Note: Recompile with -Xlint:deprecation for details.

war:
        [war] Building war: /Users/ckemp/Documents/Sites/java-war-deploy-example/dist/
        AntExample.war

BUILD SUCCESSFUL
Total time: 1 second
```

Next, create your Heroku app and point the `heroku-deploy` plugin to your WAR file (using the full pathname here) and the app:

```
$ heroku create java-war-deploy-example
Creating java-war-deploy-example... done, stack is cedar
http://java-war-deploy-example.herokuapp.com/ |
git@heroku.com:java-war-deploy-example.git

$ heroku deploy:war --war ~/Documents/Sites/java-war-deploy-example/dist/AntExample.war
--app java-war-deploy-example
Uploading /Users/ckemp/Documents/Sites/java-war-deploy-example/dist/AntExample.war.....
.........................................
Uploading /Users/ckemp/Documents/Sites/java-war-deploy-example/dist/AntExample.war.....
.........................................................done
Deploying to java-war-deploy-example....done
```

Now when you access your app's URL (in this case, `http://java-war-deploy-example.herokuapp.com/userRegistration.htm`), you can see that the WAR file has deployed successfully (see Figure 12-4).

FIGURE 12-4

ADDITIONAL CONSIDERATIONS

This section covers some additional topics related to porting Java apps to Heroku, including session management and caching, memory management, and continuous integration. Special considerations must be taken into account when porting apps to Heroku because of the scalable nature of the platform. Session management and caching on Heroku is important because of the share-nothing nature of the platform. Managing the JVM's memory footprint is critical because of the limited memory on dynos.

Porting Java Applications to Heroku

Chapter 3, "Porting Your Applications to Heroku," outlined the general principles governing the architecture of all Heroku apps, and these principles apply to any apps you run on Heroku. The following list summarizes the key points relevant to *Java* architects:

➤ **Filesystem differences:** Make sure your Java app does not rely on any file being used after the current request has been completed, because of the ephemeral nature of a dyno's filesystem.

➤ **Data stores:** This chapter demonstrated how to use Heroku Postgres as a data store. Any data store of your choice should work, however, and you can search the add-ons to find a cloud-based provider that can easily be added to your Heroku app.

➤ **Session management and caching:** See the "Session Management and Caching" section that follows.

➤ **Static assets:** Because of the 200MB maximum slug size, apps with numerous static assets should store them outside of the app, in Amazon S3 or using Amazon CloudFront, for distributed asset storage.

➤ **Config vars:** You saw many examples of using config vars in this chapter to manage environment variables, such as DATABASE_URL. Use similar techniques for credential storage for backing third-party apps on which your app relies.

➤ **Web servers and containers:** This chapter's examples used a number of embedded web servers, such as Jetty, Tomcat, and Jetty Runner. Heroku's built-in functionality for scaling, deploying, and load balancing eliminates developers' dependency on containers for these functions. Containerless application development results in faster releases and apps with smaller footprints. Modern frameworks, such as Play, offer rapid development tools that provide more agility. Be sure to keep the considerations in this section in mind when configuring your framework to run on a scalable platform (e.g., keeping sessions out of memory or the local file system).

➤ **Managing dependencies:** Maven is the required tool for dependency and build management for all non-Play Java apps. Play uses Apache Ivy and sbt for dependency and build management, respectively. Other tools, such as Ant, can be initiated with a Maven script.

➤ **E-mailing from your apps:** Third-party add-ons, such as SendGrid (http://docs .sendgrid.com/documentation/get-started/integrate/examples/ java-email-example-using-smtp/), or your own SMTP server can be used to send e-mail with Java apps on Heroku when configured appropriately in your Java app according to the provider's Java setup instructions.

➤ **Logging:** Logs can be sent out to a sink server, or a third-party log manager such as Loggly can be used for more robust log management (instructions for integrating with Log4J can be found at http://wiki.loggly.com/log4j).

➤ **Relying on external programs:** An app should not rely on programs external to itself — for instance, using Runtime.getRuntime().exec() to run cURL. As a best practice for simplifying delivery, all libraries needed to run your app should be declared as dependencies.

➤ **Scaling up vs. scaling out:** Java apps can consume a lot of memory if they are not architected properly. Memory management should be tuned to stay within the 512MB limit for Heroku apps; otherwise, memory will be swapped to disk and performance will greatly suffer. For more details, see the section "Memory Management."

Your app's code base should also be kept as lean as possible to ensure that scaling can be done quickly. It is recommended that you use GitHub's general Java.gitignore file or the one appropriate for your Java framework (see https://github.com/github/gitignore for some pre-built files) in all your projects as a best practice, to ensure that only necessary artifacts are included in the slug.

➤ **Binding to ports:** You have seen how to bind your web server to the port exposed by Heroku using the PORT config var. Apps requiring more than one incoming port will need to be re-architected, as Heroku provides only a single port to bind to per each running process.

➤ **Long-running processes:** Long-running processes should be run with a worker dyno in the background to avoid automatic connection closing upon timeout. As a best practice for scalability, you should rearchitect your apps to use background processes for any third-party backing service used. For an example of using RabbitMQ for a web-worker model on Java, see https://devcenter.heroku.com/articles/run-non-web-java-processes-on-heroku.

➤ **Shutting down gracefully:** Your app can be signaled at any time to shutdown or restart. Therefore, it is important that you write logic into your app to register a shutdown hook for SIGTERM and gracefully deal with the impending shutdown with Runtime.addShutdownHook(). As a best practice, try to complete any outstanding work and respond to the web request. Any work that is not complete should be put back on a queue for a worker to pick up later.

➤ **Moving your domain:** Domains for Java apps can be pointed in the same way as any other apps using DNS settings. Heroku's SSL endpoint proxy will replace the "https" in the URL and add an X-Forwarded-Proto HTTP header indicating the protocol used to send the request from the user's browser (e.g., "https"). Some older versions of Spring Security force pages to be accessed over SSL by looking for "https" in the URL. This results in an infinite redirect loop. To fix this, either upgrade your version of Spring Security or use subclasses to override decide(), as outlined at http://stackoverflow.com/questions/6732453/spring-security-requires-channel-https-behind-ssl-accelerator.

Session Management and Caching

All apps running on Heroku must be completely stateless and share nothing because of their ephemeral nature. For this reason, distributed sessions with techniques like memory sharing are not well suited for a highly scalable platform. Any stateful data must live in a data store external to each dyno. Databases and distributed data stores like Memcache are well suited for session management with Heroku apps.

Some Java apps rely on javax.servlet.http.HttpSession for state storage. To run these apps, you should instead use a session manager that uses a central data store, such as Memcachier. (See https://devcenter.heroku.com/articles/memcachier#java for setup instructions.) This add-on or other similar data stores designed for fast key-value retrieval are used for caching and storing session data as a best practice.

Memory Management

Typically, when an app is architected such that each node does not use excessive amounts of memory, it will run just fine on Heroku with no tuning necessary. As mentioned elsewhere in this chapter, each dyno on Heroku is allocated 512MB of memory, and exceeding this results in disk swapping, adversely affecting your app's performance. The default Java memory settings in Heroku's buildpacks are as follows:

```
-Xmx384m -Xss512k -XX:+UseCompressedOops
```

This allocates your app's threads only 512KB of memory each, rather than the standard 1MB.

If you are seeing R14 errors in your logs, you may need to take action. The New Relic Java agent (`https://devcenter.heroku.com/articles/newrelic#java`) can be used to monitor your app. Heroku also has an article (`https://devcenter.heroku.com/articles/java-memory-issues`) outlining other methods for monitoring memory and understanding its usage to reduce your app's memory footprint to one within Heroku's ideal boundaries.

Continuous Integration

Java apps often use a continuous integration server as part of their software development life cycle. Heroku supports a number of popular continuous integration solutions, including open-source Jenkins and Atlassian Bamboo (not to be confused with the Bamboo stack on Heroku). The Heroku team maintains a Jenkins plugin that can be used with Jenkins app (see `https://github.com/heroku/heroku-jenkins-plugin/blob/master/README.md`). You can find instructions on using Atlassian Bamboo at `https://devcenter.heroku.com/articles/heroku-bamboo-plugin`. Both deploy a WAR file generated by your app's build file.

> **NOTE** *Atlassian Bamboo integration is currently offered only with Heroku Enterprise for Java packages.*

SUMMARY

Heroku empowers Java developers to shift from large and infrequent deployments, made by a dedicated operations team, to continuous deployment by individual developers. To test apps that are being deployed to Heroku, the JDK must be installed locally. You can develop containerless apps using embedded web servers, such as Jetty Runner, because Heroku takes care of many of the typical features that containers provide, including rapid deployment, scaling, and load balancing.

Mature, enterprise frameworks like the Spring Framework can be used to write Java apps on Heroku. The Spring Framework is often used in conjunction with ORMs, like Hibernate, and embedded web servers, like Tomcat. Configuring the Spring Framework with Hibernate and Tomcat requires heavy configuration. Spring Roo can significantly boost productivity by automatically configuring these components to work together for you. Play is an alternative framework that uses convention over configuration for rapid application development. WAR files can also be deployed directly on Heroku dynos.

Porting existing Java apps should be done with care because Heroku differs greatly from traditional platforms on which Java apps typically are developed. Development on Heroku makes session management and caching in a centralized location imperative. You must also make sure that memory usage in your app is minimized to avoid performance degradation when memory limits are reached.

In the next chapter, we will look at how to do the same things on Heroku's other supported languages, including a number of JVM-based languages.

13

Developing with Other Supported Languages

WHAT'S IN THIS CHAPTER?

➤ Developing with Python

➤ Developing with Node.js

➤ Developing with Clojure

➤ Developing with Scala

➤ Developing with Groovy using the Grails framework

➤ Developing non-Facebook applications on PHP

WROX.COM CODE DOWNLOADS FOR THIS CHAPTER

The wrox.com code downloads for this chapter are found at `www.wrox.com/remtitle .cgi?isbn=1118508998` on the Download Code tab. The code is in the Chapter 13 download and individually named according to the names throughout the chapter.

In the last two chapters, we took an in-depth look at how to run Ruby and Java apps on Heroku. Although those are the most common languages with which apps are written, Heroku's polyglot capabilities enable you to select the best tool for the job at hand. Heroku also officially supports Python, Clojure, Scala, Node.js, and Groovy. You will explore how to develop applications with each of these languages in this chapter.

At the time of writing, PHP is supported for writing Facebook apps only. However, you can use Heroku to run non-Facebook PHP apps. Even though full support is not quite available yet, this chapter takes a look at writing PHP apps on Heroku as well.

DEVELOPING WITH PYTHON

Python is a versatile, interpreted language that is easy to understand and read, using strict indentation for determining code blocks. Since its release in the 1980s, it has grown in popularity steadily and has built on its feature set, moving from its roots in simple script building to enterprise application development. Along with its development, many powerful and easy to use frameworks have emerged, including Django, Flask, and Zope, amongst many others.

Heroku supports any Web Server Gateway Interface (WSGI)-compliant web server for running Python web apps, and runs CPython 2.7.2 (64-bit), contained within a distribute-flavored `virtualenv`. The example demonstrated in this section revisits the employee list apps, creating a Heroku Postgres database-backed app in Python using the Django framework. Django is a lightweight web framework that uses model-view-controller (MVC) patterns and contains an easy to use object-relational mapping (ORM) that makes Python-based web application development easy and fast.

> **NOTE** *For instructions on running web apps on alternative Python web servers, such as Gunicorn and gevent, see* `https://devcenter.heroku.com/articles/django#using-a-different-wsgi-server`.

You are going to create an example app written in Python and using the popular Django framework (code file: `ch13-python-django-example.zip`). You will revisit an example that should be familiar now, an employee directory. Your employee directory will use a Heroku Postgres database to store your data.

1. Install Python, `virtualenv` 1.7.2, and pip 1.1. The Python documentation outlines platform-specific install instructions under "Properly Installing Python" at `http://docs` `.python-guide.org/en/latest/index.html`.

   To get Python working on a Mac, run the following:

```
$ brew install python --framework
$ sudo easy_install pip
$ sudo pip install virtualenv
```

2. The following command creates the `virtualenv` virtual environment for your app, to be used with `pip`, the dependency manager for Python apps, and activates it:

```
$ mkdir python-django-example

$ cd python-django-example

$ virtualenv venv --distribute
New python executable in venv/bin/python
Installing distribute...........................................................
...............................................................................
............................................done.

Installing pip..............done.

$ source venv/bin/activate
```

Your prompt, which should now indicate that you are inside your virtual environment, may look something like this:

```
(venv)My-Computer-Name:python-django-example ckemp$
```

> **NOTE** *You can use only one virtual environment per open terminal, and the following commands will not run properly unless you are in the virtual environment.*

3. Use `pip` to download and install the dependencies needed to run your app:

```
$ pip install Django psycopg2 dj-database-url
Downloading/unpacking Django
   Downloading Django-1.4.1.tar.gz (7.7Mb): 7.7Mb downloaded
   Running setup.py egg_info for package Django

Downloading/unpacking psycopg2
   Downloading psycopg2-2.4.5.tar.gz (719Kb): 719Kb downloaded
   Running setup.py egg_info for package psycopg2
...
```

4. Instantiate the app, here called `python_django_example`, with Django:

```
$ django-admin.py startproject python_django_example .
```

5. If everything has worked properly thus far, you can now run a Django test app to verify your setup:

```
$ python manage.py runserver
Validating models...

0 errors found
Django version 1.4.1, using settings 'python_django_example.settings'
Development server is running at http://127.0.0.1:8000/
Quit the server with CONTROL-C.
```

Django has now created the basic scaffolding for your app. If you visit `http://127.0.0.1:8000/`, you can see a test page that looks like what is shown in Figure 13-1.

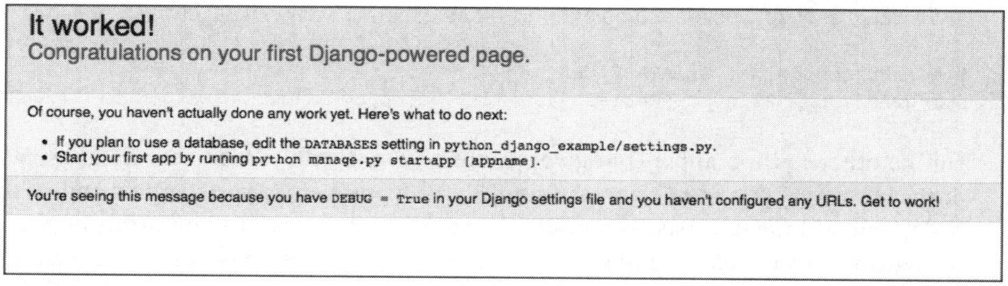

FIGURE 13-1

6. Use the following command to take a snapshot of your app's requirements:

```
$ pip freeze > requirements.txt
```

7. Look in the `requirements.txt` file. Here, you can see the dependencies for your Python app:

```
Django==1.4.1
distribute==0.6.27
dj-database-url==0.2.1
psycopg2==2.4.5
wsgiref==0.1.2
```

This `requirements.txt` file is needed in order for Heroku to detect that you are trying to deploy a Python-based app. If Heroku also finds `Django` listed here as a dependency, as well as a `settings.py` file in your app (you will create this shortly), then Heroku detects a Python Django app push, specifically. You can also add modules with C extensions here, as long as they install properly with `pip`.

> **NOTE** *You can find an in-depth article on dependency management with* `pip` *at* `https://devcenter.heroku.com/articles/python-pip`.

8. Initialize your repository and create a backing database for your app:

```
$ git init
Initialized empty Git repository in /Users/ckemp/Documents/Sites/python-django-
example/.git/

$ heroku create python-django-example
Creating python-django-example... done, stack is cedar
http://python-django-example.herokuapp.com/ | git@heroku.com:python-django-example.git
Git remote heroku added

$ heroku addons:add heroku-postgresql:dev
Adding heroku-postgresql:dev on python-django-example... done, v2 (free)
Attached as HEROKU_POSTGRESQL_TEAL
Database has been created and is available
Use 'heroku addons:docs heroku-postgresql:dev' to view documentation.

$ heroku pg:promote HEROKU_POSTGRESQL_TEAL_URL
Promoting HEROKU_POSTGRESQL_TEAL (DATABASE_URL) to DATABASE_URL... done

$ heroku config:get DATABASE_URL
postgres://dBu53r:dBp@55@ec1-23-45-678-90.compute-1.amazonaws.com:5432/dBnAm3
```

Unlike other Python apps, Django apps are automatically allocated a database when you push. However, you need to create your Heroku app before you commit and push your code, and add the database manually to get the URL for your configuration files with the configuration variables (config vars). You need to note the `DATABASE_URL` for the next step.

9. Open the `settings.py` file in the directory with the same name as your app (in this example, `python_django_example/settings.py`) and locate the following lines:

```
DATABASES = {
        'default': {
        'ENGINE': 'django.db.backends.',  # Add 'postgresql_psycopg2', 'mysql', 'sqlite3'
                                           # or 'oracle'.
        'NAME': '',                        # Or path to database file if using sqlite3.
        'USER': '',                        # Not used with sqlite3.
        'PASSWORD': '',                    # Not used with sqlite3.
        'HOST': '',                        # Set to empty string for localhost. Not used
                                           # with sqlite3.
        'PORT': '',                        # Set to empty string for default. Not used with
                                           # sqlite3.
        }
}
```

Replace the entire preceding block of code with the following code, which will point to your Heroku Postgres database with the proper config vars found, by replacing the example Postgres URL with your `DATABASE_URL` noted earlier:

```
import dj_database_url
DATABASES = {
    'default': dj_database_url.config(
        default='postgres://dBu53r:dBp@55@ec1-23-45-678-90.compute-1.amazonaws.com:
            5432/dBnAm3'
    )
}
```

10. Normally, it is a best practice to use the `DATABASE_URL` string directly, rather than cut and paste the Heroku Postgres URL, but environment variables are unavailable in this configuration file, so you must directly use the connection string. Activate the model for use by finding the section in the same file that looks like this:

```
INSTALLED_APPS = (
        'django.contrib.auth',
        'django.contrib.contenttypes',
        'django.contrib.sessions',
        'django.contrib.sites',
        'django.contrib.messages',
        'django.contrib.staticfiles',
        # Uncomment the next line to enable the admin:
        # 'django.contrib.admin',
        # Uncomment the next line to enable admin documentation:
        # 'django.contrib.admindocs',
)
```

Before the closing bracket, add the following line:

```
        'python_django_example',
        'django.contrib.admin',
```

This also enables Django's built-in administration console, enabling you to quickly create your database-backed app.

11. Locate the following lines in `urls.py`:

```
# Uncomment the next two lines to enable the admin:
# from django.contrib import admin
# admin.autodiscover()
...
    # url(r'^admin/', include(admin.site.urls)),
```

Uncomment the second and third lines to get the following:

```
# Uncomment the next two lines to enable the admin:
from django.contrib import admin
admin.autodiscover()
...
    url(r'^admin/', include(admin.site.urls)),
```

12. Create your model by creating a file, `models.py`, in whatever your application directory is called:

```
from django.db import models

class Employee(models.Model):
    employeeId = models.IntegerField()
    name = models.CharField(max_length=200)
    email = models.CharField(max_length=200)
```

This defines your three fields — employee ID, name, and e-mail — similar to the model you have used with other example apps.

13. Register this model with Django's administration console by adding an `admin.py` script to your application directory that looks like this:

```
from django.contrib import admin
from python_django_example.models import Employee
admin.site.register(Employee)
```

14. You don't want your `virtualenv` files creating slug bloat when you push your app, so create a `.gitignore` file to exclude extraneous artifacts:

```
venv
*.pyc
```

> **NOTE** *You can also use Github's gitignore repository (*`https://github.com/github/gitignore`*) to provide more extensive, automatic removal, and even install it system-wide for added convenience.*

15. Deploy your app to Heroku as follows:

```
$ git commit -am "Initial commit"
[master (root-commit) a76f77d] Initial commit
 8 files changed, 220 insertions(+)
 create mode 100644 .gitignore
 create mode 100644 manage.py
 create mode 100644 python_django_example/__init__.py
...


$ git push heroku master
Counting objects: 7, done.
Delta compression using up to 4 threads.
Compressing objects: 100% (4/4), done.
Writing objects: 100% (4/4), 503 bytes, done.
Total 4 (delta 3), reused 0 (delta 0)

-----> Heroku receiving push
-----> Python/Django app detected
-----> Preparing Python interpreter (2.7.2)
-----> Creating Virtualenv version 1.7.2
       New python executable in .heroku/venv/bin/python2.7
...
-----> Activating virtualenv
-----> Installing dependencies using pip version 1.1
...
       Cleaning up...
-----> Collecting static files
       72 static files copied.

-----> Discovering process types
       Procfile declares types          -> (none)
       Default types for Python/Django -> web
-----> Compiled slug size is 9.3MB
-----> Launching... done, v15
       http://python-django-example.herokuapp.com deployed to Heroku

To git@heroku.com:python-django-example.git
   7ae5826..a236e80  master -> master
```

Here you can see that Heroku automatically detects a Python/Django app, as described earlier. It then defines a virtual environment and automatically creates a `Procfile` with a web process that looks like this:

```
web: python python_django_example/manage.py runserver 0.0.0.0:$PORT --noreload
```

Normally, non-Django Python apps require a `Procfile` and will bind to the `PORT` config var in the app code (see `https://devcenter.heroku.com/articles/django` for an example), with your resulting `Procfile` looking something like this:

```
web: python app.py
```

16. Sync the database, which will create the Employees table and the tables needed for Django's administration console to work:

```
$ heroku run python manage.py syncdb
Running 'python manage.py syncdb' attached to terminal... up, run.1
Creating tables ...
Creating table auth_permission
Creating table auth_group_permissions
Creating table auth_group
Creating table auth_user_user_permissions
Creating table auth_user_groups
Creating table auth_user
Creating table django_content_type
Creating table django_session
Creating table django_site
Creating table django_admin_log
Creating table python_django_example_employee

You just installed Django's auth system, which means you don't have any superusers
defined.
Would you like to create one now? (yes/no): yes
Username (leave blank to use 'u23585'): myAdminName
E-mail address: ckemp@salesforce.com
Password:
Password (again):
Superuser created successfully.
Installing custom SQL ...
Installing indexes ...
Installed 0 object(s) from 0 fixture(s)
```

Note that the preceding output also prompts you to create a superuser in order to log in to the Django administration console for the first time. Follow the prompts to create one, using whatever username and password with which you want to log in.

17. Inspect your config vars before testing your app on Heroku:

```
$ heroku config
=== python-django-example Config Vars
DATABASE_URL:              postgres://dBu53r:dBp@55@ec1-23-45-678-90.compute-1.
                           amazonaws.com:5432/dBnAm3
HEROKU_POSTGRESQL_TEAL_URL: postgres://dBu53r:dBp@55@ec1-23-45-678-90.compute-1.
                           amazonaws.com:5432/dBnAm3
LANG:                      en_US.UTF-8
LD_LIBRARY_PATH:           /app/.heroku/vendor/lib
LIBRARY_PATH:              /app/.heroku/vendor/lib
PATH:                      /app/.heroku/venv/bin:/bin:/usr/local/bin:/usr/bin
PYTHONHASHSEED:            random
PYTHONHOME:                /app/.heroku/venv/
PYTHONPATH:                /app/
PYTHONUNBUFFERED:          true
```

The standard DATBASE_URL and PATH are set here, along with a number of environment variables on which Python relies.

Now that the app is ready, simply visit `http://python-django-example.herokuapp.com/admin/`, logging in with the username and password you just created. Figure 13-2 shows the "Add employee" dialog of the new app, where you can add new employees to your Python app.

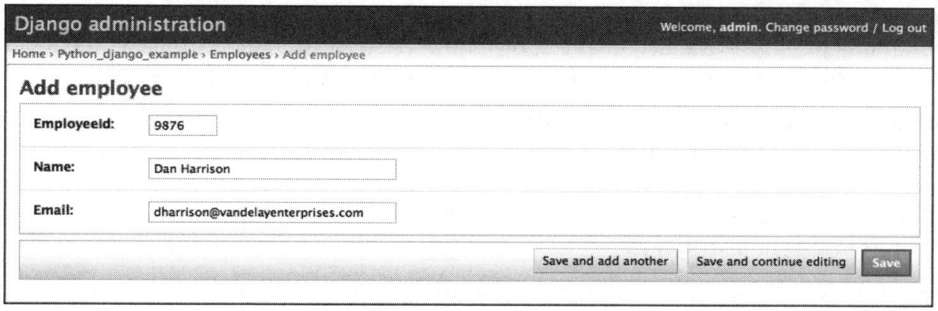

FIGURE 13-2

Additional Considerations

When developing new Python apps or porting them from other platforms, keep the following things in mind

> **Filesystem differences:** Make sure your Python app does not rely on any file being used after the current request has been completed, because of the ephemeral nature of a dyno's filesystem.

> **Data stores:** Although this chapter uses Heroku Postgres as a data store, any data store of your choice should work; and you can search the add-ons to find a cloud-based provider that can easily be added to your Heroku app.

> **Session management:** By default, Django and many other popular frameworks store session data in the backing database. Ensure that any framework you are using is configured to store session information in a central location, as requests for the same session could be stored on different dynos if your framework is configured to store session information locally.

> **Caching:** Information can be cached using a solution such as the Memcachier add-on. For an example of how to add this to a Django-based app, see `https://devcenter .heroku.com/articles/django-memcache`.

> **Static assets:** Because of the 200MB maximum slug size, apps with a lot of static assets should store them outside of the app, in Amazon Simple Storage Service (Amazon S3) or using Amazon CloudFront for distributed asset storage. As part of the Django app deployment process, Heroku runs *collectstatic*, which you can configure to centralize static assets somewhere such as Amazon S3. For more information, see `https://devcenter .heroku.com/articles/django-assets`.

> **Config vars:** This chapter contains examples that use config vars to manage environment variables, like DATABASE_URL. Use similar techniques for credential storage for backing third-party apps on which your app relies.

➤ **Web servers and containers:** Mature Python HTTP servers such as Gunicorn, gevent, and Eventlet are recommended for production apps, though any WSGI-compatible HTTP server that runs on Linux can be used. Nginx reverse proxying is not needed, as Heroku takes care of functionality that reverse proxies normally deliver.

➤ **Managing dependencies:** All Python apps use `pip` for dependency management. For a deeper understanding of `pip`'s advanced features, including Git-backed, remote-backed, and local file-backed distributions, see `https://devcenter.heroku.com/articles/python-pip`.

➤ **E-mailing from your apps:** To send e-mail with Python apps on Heroku, you can use third-party add-ons such as SendGrid (`http://docs.sendgrid.com/documentation/get-started/integrate/examples/python-email-example-using-smtp/`) or your own SMTP server, configured appropriately in your app's codebase according to the provider's Python-specific setup instructions.

➤ **Logging:** Logs can be sent to a sink server or third-party log manager, such as Loggly, using the `Hoover` library (see `http://wiki.loggly.com/hooverguide`).

➤ **Relying on external programs:** An app should not rely on programs external to itself, like cURL. As a best practice for simplifying delivery, all libraries needed to run your application should be declared as dependencies.

➤ **Scaling up vs. scaling out:** App memory should be managed efficiently, as failing to do so can cause memory to page if the 512MB limit is exceeded. Tools like New Relic (`https://newrelic.com/docs/python/python-agent-and-heroku`) and Heapy (`http://guppy-pe.sourceforge.net/#Heapy`) can be used to profile memory if R14 errors are encountered.

Your app's code base should also be kept as lean as possible to ensure that scaling can be done quickly. See the previous "Static assets" bullet for tips on how storing assets externally can reduce slug size. As a best practice, it is recommended that you use a `.gitignore` file appropriate for the Python framework that you use in all of your projects (see `https://github.com/github/gitignore` for some pre-built files), to ensure that only necessary artifacts are included in the slug.

➤ **Binding to ports:** Port binding in Django apps is done automatically. For non-Django apps, port binding must be done in your app's code. For an example, see `https://devcenter.heroku.com/articles/python`.

➤ **Long-running processes:** You should use a worker dyno in the background for long-running processes in order to avoid automatic connection closing upon timeout. Ported apps should be re-architected to use background processes for any third-party backing service used as a best practice for scalability. For an example of using Redis Queue (RQ) for a web-worker model on Python, see `https://devcenter.heroku.com/articles/python-rq`.

➤ **Shutting down gracefully:** Your app can be signaled at any time to shut down or restart. Therefore, it is important for you to write logic into your app to set handlers for SIGTERM events and to gracefully deal with the impending shutdown. As a best practice, try to complete any work that was not completed and respond to the web request, or any work that is not complete should be put back on a queue for a worker to pick up later. For more information on setting signal handlers in Python apps, including an example, see `http://docs.python.org/library/signal.html`.

➤ **Moving your domain:** Domains for Python apps can be pointed in the same way as with any other apps, using DNS settings.

DEVELOPING WITH NODE.JS

Node.js and Heroku seem to have been made for each other, given their shared focus on scalability. Node.js uses Google's V8 JavaScript engine, a highly performant server-side JavaScript engine, optimal for apps that need to run extremely quickly. Moreover, because the JavaScript language is used to write programs, this makes Node.js very accessible to even adventurous web designers who know JavaScript. It is well suited for highly concurrent apps, because of its event-based and asynchronous/nonblocking nature. For example, Node.js works well as a backing service for a video game server or mobile phone app that will be broadly distributed, just as it can be used to serve plain old HTTP.

Node.js has also proven itself ready for the enterprise, with many prominent tech giants using it for their apps. LinkedIn uses Node.js for its mobile client's back end, reducing its server footprint from 15 physical servers with 15 virtual machines on each, to just four with twice the capacity of their original infrastructure. Similarly, Walmart uses Node.js for its mobile app back end. eBay uses Node.js for API access to its infrastructure, with a single machine able to handle more than 120,000 concurrent connections per process, each only consuming 2KB of memory each. Node.js has proven itself to be a strong up-and-coming language.

In this section you are going to create a Node.js program that displays a list of employees, similar to many of the other examples in this book, using the Express framework and a Heroku Postgres data store (code file: `ch13-nodejs-express-example.zip`).

1. Install Node.js and `npm`, its dependency manager. First, download the installer from `http://nodejs.org/download/`. This installer will also conveniently install `npm` for you.

2. Add a `web.js` file, which defines the core JavaScript source code for your app:

```
// web.js

var express = require('express');

var app = express.createServer(express.logger());

app.get(
    '/', function(request, response) {

    var pg = require('pg');

    // Connect to the DB
    pg.connect(
```

```
        process.env.DATABASE_URL, function(err, client) {

            if (err) {
                // Output error to console if can't connect
                console.log(err);

            } else {

                // Get all employees
                client.query(
                    'SELECT id, name, email FROM employees', function(err, result) {

                        response.writeHead(200, {'Content-Type': 'text/html'});
                        response.write('<h1>Employee List</h1>');

                        response.write('<table>' +
                            '<tr>' +
                            '    <th>Id</th>' +
                            '    <th>Name</th>' +
                            '    <th>E-mail</th>' +
                            '</tr>'
                        );

                        // Output each row of result
                        for (var i = 0; i < result.rows.length; i++) {

                            response.write('<tr>' +
                                '    <td>' + result.rows[i].id + '</td>' +
                                '    <td>' + result.rows[i].name + '</td>' +
                                '    <td>' + result.rows[i].email + '</td>' +
                                '</tr>');
                        }

                        response.write('</table>');
                        response.end();
                    }
                );
            }
        }
    )
    }
);

var port = process.env.PORT || 5000;
app.listen(
    port, function() {
        console.log("Node.js server listening on " + port);
    }
);
```

Setting the express and app variables, you instantiate the Express framework and define a route for GET HTTP methods for your app. pg.connect will create the connection to your Postgres database, using the DATABASE_URL config var to point to the correct database. If an error occurs while connecting to the database, the err variable is set and the exception is handled.

client.query will define your database SQL query to get all the employees. The for loop inside client.query will iterate through the results, printing one employee per row in your HTML table. Finally, app.listen will bind to the defined port, listening for incoming requests — in this case, the PORT config var set by the dyno.

3. Declare dependencies for the dependency manager, npm, to resolve. To do that, create a package.json file:

```
{
    "name": "nodedotjs-sample",
    "version": "1.0.0",
    "dependencies": {
        "express": "2.5.x",
        "pg": "0.8.2"
    },
    "engines": {
        "node": "0.8.x",
        "npm": "1.1.x"
    }
}
```

The existence of a package.json file in the root directory indicates to Heroku that a Node .js app is being pushed to Heroku. Here, you use name and version to define the name and version of the program you are writing. You then declare your dependencies for this program. In this case, you are using Express 2.5 and the Postgres driver version 0.8.

> **NOTE** *You can use semantic versioning to define specific versions of dependencies to use with* npm, *similar to dependency declaration in Gemfiles with Ruby.*

The engines section defines the run-time and dependency manager versions you will use with your app. The default versions used by Heroku are Node.js 0.4.7 and 1.0.106, respectively, but you can add whatever versions suit your needs here. See the manifests for each at https://devcenter.heroku.com/articles/nodejs-versions/ for available versions.

4. No default web process is defined for Node.js, so you must create a Procfile to point to your web app:

```
web: node web.js
```

5. Install the dependencies for your app, using npm:

```
$ npm install
npm WARN package.json nodedotjs-sample@1.0.0 No README.md file found!
npm http GET https://registry.npmjs.org/express
npm http GET https://registry.npmjs.org/pg/0.8.2
npm http 200 https://registry.npmjs.org/pg/0.8.2
...
```

```
npm http GET https://registry.npmjs.org/formidable

> pg@0.8.2 install /Users/ckemp/Documents/Sites/nodedotjs-postgres-sample/node_modules/
  pg
> node-gyp rebuild || (exit 0)

npm http 200 https://registry.npmjs.org/formidable
  CXX(target) Release/obj.target/binding/src/binding.o
  SOLINK_MODULE(target) Release/binding.node
  SOLINK_MODULE(target) Release/binding.node: Finished
express@2.5.11 node_modules/express
├── qs@0.4.2
├── mime@1.2.4
├── mkdirp@0.3.0
└── connect@1.9.2 (formidable@1.0.11)

pg@0.8.2 node_modules/pg
└── generic-pool@1.0.12
```

npm has successfully retrieved and installed the dependencies in the appropriate subdirectories of the `node_modules` directory of your code base.

6. Create your Heroku app:

```
$ git init
Initialized empty Git repository in /Users/ckemp/Documents/Sites/nodedotjs-postgres-
sample/.git/

$ heroku create nodedotjs-postgres-sample
Creating nodedotjs-postgres-sample... done, stack is cedar
http://nodedotjs-postgres-sample.herokuapp.com/ | git@heroku.com:nodedotjs-postgres-
sample.git
Git remote heroku added

$ git add .

$ git commit -am "Initial commit"
[master (root-commit) c46f4e7] Initial commit
 338 files changed, 25825 insertions(+)
 create mode 100644 .DS_Store
 create mode 100644 Procfile
 create mode 120000 node_modules/.bin/express
...
```

7. Attach a Heroku Postgres database to your app. The following creates a Dev database that you can use to test your app:

```
$ heroku addons:add heroku-postgresql:dev
Adding heroku-postgresql:dev on nodedotjs-postgres-sample... done, v2 (free)
Attached as HEROKU_POSTGRESQL_WHITE
Database has been created and is available
Use 'heroku addons:docs heroku-postgresql:dev' to view documentation.
```

8. Set up your table structure and add some initial test data to the app:

```
$ heroku pg:psql HEROKU_POSTGRESQL_WHITE
psql (9.1.4, server 9.1.5)
SSL connection (cipher: DHE-RSA-AES256-SHA, bits: 256)
Type "help" for help.

dBnAm3=> CREATE TABLE employees (
dBnAm3(>    id      integer NOT NULL CONSTRAINT firstkey PRIMARY KEY,
dBnAm3(>    name    varchar(100) NOT NULL,
dBnAm3(>    email   varchar(255) NOT NULL
dBnAm3(> );
NOTICE:  CREATE TABLE / PRIMARY KEY will create implicit index "firstkey" for table
"employees"
CREATE TABLE
dBnAm3=>
dBnAm3=> INSERT INTO employees (id, name, email) VALUES
dBnAm3->    ('1', 'Ren Ramkhelawan', 'ren@vandelayenterprises.com'),
dBnAm3->    ('2', 'Adrien Selim', 'aselim@vandelayenterprises.com'),
dBnAm3->    ('3', 'Adam Latour', 'alatour@vandelayenterprises.com');
INSERT 0 3
dBnAm3=> \q
```

9. Set your NODE_ENV config var in Heroku. Node.js uses this to determine important behaviors behind the scenes, such as caching view templates only when the NODE_ENV variable indicates that the app is running in production. Or, if you want to specify that a particular behavior should occur in development, you can use code like the following to do so:

```
app.configure('development', function() {
    // Do some development-specific action
});

app.configure('production', function() {
    // Do production-specific action
});
```

This is especially useful for doing things like setting different databases for production and development environments. You can use whatever names you want, but note that "production" is a special parameter for use only with production apps.

10. Set the NODE_ENV config var, as follows:

```
$ heroku config:add NODE_ENV=production
Setting config vars and restarting nodedotjs-postgres-sample... done, v3
NODE_ENV: production
```

11. Push to Heroku:

```
$ git push heroku master
Counting objects: 416, done.
Delta compression using up to 4 threads.
```

```
Compressing objects: 100% (374/374), done.
Writing objects: 100% (416/416), 357.66 KiB | 46 KiB/s, done.
Total 416 (delta 14), reused 0 (delta 0)

-----> Heroku receiving push
-----> Removing .DS_Store files
-----> Node.js app detected
-----> Resolving engine versions
        Using Node.js version: 0.8.7
        Using npm version: 1.1.49
-----> Fetching Node.js binaries
-----> Vendoring node into slug
-----> Installing dependencies with npm
...
        Dependencies installed
-----> Building runtime environment
-----> Discovering process types
        Procfile declares types -> web
-----> Compiled slug size is 5.8MB
-----> Launching... done, v6
        http://nodedotjs-postgres-sample.herokuapp.com deployed to Heroku

To git@heroku.com:nodedotjs-postgres-sample.git
 * [new branch]      master -> master
```

The existence of the `package.json` file alerts Heroku that a Node.js app is being pushed, enabling retrieval of the engines indicated in this file. Dependencies are then resolved and installed, and the slug is created and launched on Heroku's dynos.

12. Check out your app running on Heroku:

```
$ heroku open
Opening http://nodedotjs-sample.herokuapp.com/
```

Now your Node.js apps is launched and you should be able to see the list of employees, as shown in Figure 13-3.

Take a closer look at your config vars:

Employee List

Id	Name	E-mail
1	Ren Ramkhelawan	ren@vandelayenterprises.com
2	Adrien Selim	aselim@vandelayenterprises.com
3	Adam Latour	alatour@vandelayenterprises.com

FIGURE 13-3

```
$ heroku config
=== nodedotjs-postgres-sample Config Vars
DATABASE_URL:                postgres://dBu53r:dBp@55@ec1-23-45-678-90.compute-1.
                             amazonaws.com:5432/dBnAm3dBnAm3
HEROKU_POSTGRESQL_WHITE_URL: postgres://dBu53r:dBp@55@ec1-23-45-678-90.compute-1.
                             amazonaws.com:5432/dBnAm3dBnAm3
NODE_ENV:                    production
PATH:                        bin:node_modules/.bin:/usr/local/bin:/usr/bin:/bin
```

Here you can see the DATABASE_URL and Postgres database you have added, along with the NODE_ENV variable discussed earlier. The only other variable added was the standard PATH variable.

Additional Considerations

Node.js development typically takes a stateless approach, making designing apps for Heroku and porting apps to Heroku fairly simple. However, some considerations should be kept in mind:

➤ **Filesystem differences:** Make sure your Node.js app does not rely on any file being used after the current request has been completed, because of the ephemeral nature of a dyno's file system.

➤ **Data stores:** This chapter demonstrated using Heroku Postgres as a data store, but any data store of your choice should work, and you can search the add-ons to find a cloud-based provider that can easily be associated with your Heroku app.

➤ **Session management:** The bundled session manager in Express uses a local memory store, which does not work across dynos. You must switch to a strategy that uses a backing data store of your choice instead. See `http://soenkerohde.com/2012/04/using-redis-as-node-js-express-session-storage-on-heroku/` for an example of using a Redis data store for session information, using the Redis To Go add-on (`https://addons.heroku.com/redistogo`).

➤ **Caching:** Information can be cached using a solution such as the Memcachier add-on or Redis To Go, as previously discussed. Memcache can be used with Node.js using the Node .js Memcache client at `https://github.com/elbart/node-memcache`.

➤ **Static assets:** Because of the 200MB maximum slug size, apps with a lot of static assets should store them outside of the app, in Amazon S3 or using Amazon CloudFront, for distributed asset storage. It is generally recommended not to use Node.js to serve static assets unless necessary, to keep load minimal, or use node-static-asset (`https://github.com/bminer/node-static-asset`) for caching.

➤ **Config vars:** This chapter contains many examples that use config vars to manage environment variables, such as `DATABASE_URL`. Use similar techniques for credential storage for backing third-party apps on which your app relies.

➤ **Web servers and containers:** Node.js provides the container needed to run your app, so you only need to worry about frameworks. The example used Express as the framework, but other frameworks, such as Geddy (`http://geddyjs.org/`), can also be used.

➤ **Managing dependencies:** As shown in the example app, you manage your dependencies using npm, and you can define versions of both Node.js and npm itself in the `engines` section of the dependencies.

➤ **E-mailing from your apps:** To send e-mail with Node.js apps on Heroku, you can use third-party add-ons such as SendGrid (`https://github.com/sendgrid/sendgrid-nodejs`) or your own SMTP server, configured appropriately in your app's codebase according to the provider's Node.js-specific setup instructions.

➤ **Logging:** Logs can be sent to a sink server or third-party log manager, such as Loggly, using the Node.js library (see `www.loggly.com/blog/2011/03/using-the-loggly-node-js-library/`).

➤ **Relying on external programs:** An app should not rely on programs external to itself, such as cURL. As a best practice for simplifying delivery, all libraries needed to run your application should be declared as dependencies.

➤ **Scaling up vs. scaling out:** Node.js apps are generally very lean on memory, but app memory should be managed efficiently, as failing to do so can cause memory to page if the 512MB limit is exceeded. You can use tools such as Nodetime (`http://nodetime.com/`) to profile memory if R14 errors are encountered.

Keep your app's code base as lean as possible to ensure that scaling can be done quickly. Refer to the discussion on static assets for tips on how storing assets externally can reduce slug size. As a best practice to ensure that only necessary artifacts are included in the slug, use GitHub's general Node.js `.gitignore` file or the one appropriate for your Node.js framework (see `https://github.com/github/gitignore` for some pre-built files) in all your projects.

➤ **Binding to ports:** Port binding in Express apps is achieved by binding to the `PORT` config var. In Geddy apps, you must specify the port in the `Procfile` and configuration of your app, as outlined at `http://stackoverflow.com/questions/10145960/starting-geddy-on-heroku-fails-with-error-r11-bad-bind-what-is-wrong-with-the`.

➤ **Long-running processes:** To avoid automatic connection closing upon timeout, long-running processes should use a worker dyno in the background. Ported apps should be re-architected to use background processes for any third-party backing service used as a best practice for scalability. The node-webworkers module (`https://github.com/pgriess/node-webworker`) can be used to facilitate such an architecture. CloudAMPQ can also be used as a queuing mechanism for work, as described at `https://devcenter.heroku.com/articles/cloudamqp#use-with-nodejs`.

Note that Socket.IO, often used for real-time browser- or mobile-based applications, can be used with Heroku; but it must be configured properly to use long polling and not use Websockets, as outlined at `https://devcenter.heroku.com/articles/using-socket-io-with-node-js-on-heroku`.

➤ **Shutting down gracefully:** Your app can be signaled at any time to shut down or restart. Therefore, it is important to write logic into your app to set handlers for `SIGTERM` events and gracefully deal with the impending shutdown. As a best practice, try to complete any work that was not completed and respond to the web request, or any work that is not complete should be put back on a queue for a worker to pick up later. To capture a `SIGTERM` in Node.js, you would use something like the following:

```
process.on('SIGTERM',
    function() {
        // do stuff to shut down gracefully here
        process.exit(1);
    }
);
```

➤ **Moving your domain:** Domains for Node.js apps can be pointed in the same way as with any other apps, using DNS settings.

DEVELOPING WITH CLOJURE

Clojure is a Lisp-based functional programming language that runs on the Java Virtual Machine (JVM). Rich Hickey created Clojure to provide a modern implementation of Lisp that enables the easy use of multithreading and concurrency to create robust, parallelizable apps. Immutable states and data structures further facilitate the scalable nature of apps built using Clojure, making it a powerful development language. The JVM provides a strong platform beneath the covers and helps with interoperability with other JVM-based applications.

The following example creates a Clojure app on Heroku using a Heroku Postgres database to store an employee list (code file: ch13-clojure-example.zip).

1. Install the Java 6 JDK (as outlined in the previous chapter), Clojure, and Leiningen. To do so, follow the instructions at http://clojure.org/getting_started and https://github.com/technomancy/leiningen#installation, or use the following commands using Homebrew on a Mac:

```
$ brew install clojure
$ brew install leiningen
```

2. Leiningen will serve as the build automation tool and dependency manager. It enables you to quickly set up a scaffold for your project. To create your app with Leiningen, use the following command:

```
$ lein new clojure-postgres-example
Created new project in: /Users/ckemp/Documents/Sites/clojure-postgres-example
Look over project.clj and start coding in clojure_postgres_example/core.clj
```

3. Modify the project.clj file Leiningen has created for you in the root directory, replacing the code with this:

```
(defproject clojure-postgres-example "1.0.0"
    :description "Clojure Postgres Example"
    :dependencies [
        [org.clojure/clojure "1.3.0"]
        [postgresql/postgresql "8.4-702.jdbc4"]
        [org.clojure/java.jdbc "0.1.1"]
        [ring/ring-jetty-adapter "0.3.10"]
        [compojure "0.6.4"]
        [hiccup "0.3.6"]
        ]
)
```

This defines the parameters of your app (including the name, version, and description), and declares the dependencies needed to run it. Here you added Clojure, Postgres, and Java's JDBC driver to access your Heroku Postgres database. You also included the Ring web application library, which is similar to Python's WSGL and Ruby's Rack. This includes binding to the Jetty web server from the Ring project to run your app. Compojure is used as the routing library, and Hiccup is used to template and render HTML.

4. Replace the pre-built `core.clj` file in your application's directory (in this case, `clojure_postgres_example/core.clj`) with the following code:

```
(ns clojure-postgres-example.core
    (:use [compojure.core :only [defroutes]])
    (:require [compojure.route :as route]
        [compojure.handler :as handler]
        [ring.adapter.jetty :as ring]
        [clojure-postgres-example.controllers.employees]
        [clojure-postgres-example.views.layout :as layout]
    )
)

(defroutes routes
    clojure-postgres-example.controllers.employees/routes
    (route/resources "/")
    (route/not-found (layout/four-oh-four))
)

(def application (handler/site routes))

(defn start [port]
    (ring/run-jetty #'application {:port (or port 8080) :join? false})
)

(defn -main []
    (let [port (Integer. (System/getenv "PORT"))]
        (start port)
    )
)
```

The code block inside `ns clojure-postgres-example.core` defines the core of your app, setting up Compojure routing and adding Jetty as the embedded web server. You also add a controller and layout to your app in the same code block. The code block inside `defroutes routes` defines the routes taken when a web visitor accesses the root directory, generating a 404 error when a page doesn't exist. The code block inside `defn start [port]` binds the web server to the port Heroku will define in your config vars (set with `System/getenv "PORT"`) and starts the web server.

5. Add the controller for your app in the application directory as `controllers/employees.clj`:

```
(ns clojure-postgres-example.controllers.employees
    (:use [compojure.core :only [defroutes GET POST]])
    (:require [clojure.string :as str]
        [ring.util.response :as ring]
        [clojure-postgres-example.views.employees :as view]
        [clojure-postgres-example.models.employee :as model]
    )
)

(defn index []
    (view/index (model/all))
```

```
)

(defroutes routes
    (GET "/" [] (index))
)
```

The code in the ns `clojure-postgres-example.controllers.employees` block sets up Compojure in the controller and initializes the view and model. The `index` function sets up the view by injecting the result of the `all` function defined in the model to add the list of all employees from the database. The `defroutes routes` code block sets up the routing that defines a user's visit to the website's root.

6. Your app's model defines an `Employee` object that you will store in the database. Create this file in your application's directory under `models/employee.clj`:

```
(ns clojure-postgres-example.models.employee
    (:require [clojure.java.jdbc :as sql])
)

(defn all []
    (sql/with-connection (System/getenv "DATABASE_URL")
        (sql/with-query-results results
            ["select * from employees"]
            (into [] results)
        )
    )
)
```

The model uses the JDBC connector to connect to your Heroku Postgres database using the DATABASE_URL config var as a connection string. It then queries all employees using the SQL statement `select * from employees` and returns the result.

7. In the application directory, add `views/layout.clj` and define the base layout for your views:

```
(ns clojure-postgres-example.views.layout
    (:use [hiccup.core :only [html]]
        [hiccup.page-helpers :only [doctype include-css]])
)

(defn common [title & body]
    (html
        (doctype :html5)
        [:head [:meta {:charset "utf-8"}]]
        [:body
            [:div {:id "header"}
                [:h1 {:class "container"} "Employee List"]
            ]
            [:div {:id "content" :class "container"} body]
        ]
    )
```

```
    )

(defn four-oh-four []
    (common "Page Not Found"
        [:div {:id "four-oh-four"} "The page you requested could not be found"]
    )
)
```

The code block inside `ns clojure-postgres-example.views.layout` tells Clojure to use Hiccup as the templating engine. The `common` function defines the HTML structure of your layout. Clojure's functional structure builds XML for the layout according to the nested structure you define here, inserting closing tags when blocks of code are closed. The `four-oh-four` function will be called if a web visitor tries to access a page that doesn't exist.

8. Define a view for displaying the employee records. To do this, add `views/employees.clj` to the application's directory:

```
(ns clojure-postgres-example.views.employees
    (:use [hiccup.core :only [html h]]
        [hiccup.page-helpers :only [doctype]]
    )
    (:require [clojure-postgres-example.views.layout :as layout])
)

(defn list-employees [employees]
    [:table
        [:tr
            [:th "Employee ID"] [:th "Name"] [:th "E-mail Address"]
        ]
        (map
            (fn [employee]
                [:tr
                    [:td (h (:id employee))]
                    [:td (h (:name employee))]
                    [:td (h (:email employee))]
                ]
            )
        employees)
    ]
)

(defn index [employees]
    (layout/common "clojure-postgres-example"
        (list-employees employees)
    )
)
```

The `ns clojure-postgres-example.views.employees` code block uses Hiccup to specify your layout and embed your view. The `list-employees` function creates the table structure for your HTML and fills it with the controller's employee list. Inside this function, the code block inside of `fn [employee]` actually loops through the list. The `index` function binds the employee list from the controller to the index page.

9. Set up your database and add some initial test data by creating `models/migration.clj` in your application's directory:

```clojure
(ns clojure-postgres-example.models.migration
    (:require [clojure.java.jdbc :as sql])
)

(defn create-employees []
    (sql/with-connection (System/getenv "DATABASE_URL")
        (sql/create-table :employees
            [:id :integer "NOT NULL" "CONSTRAINT firstkey" "PRIMARY KEY"]
            [:name "varchar(100)"]
            [:email "varchar(255)"]
        )
    )
)

(defn add-employee-test-data []
    (sql/with-connection (System/getenv "DATABASE_URL")
        (sql/insert-values :employees [:id :name :email]
            [6440 "Chip Arnaldo" "farnaldo@vandelayenterprises.com"]
            [9567 "Ed Cassola" "ecassola@vandelayenterprises.com"]
            [6603 "Angela Gil" "agil@vandelayenterprises.com"]
        )
    )
)

(defn -main []
    (print "Migrating Employee database...") (flush)
    (create-employees)
    (add-employee-test-data)
    (println " done")
)
```

This file will be run as a migration script, similar to how a Rake database migration script would be run in the Ruby world. The code inside the `ns clojure-postgres-example` `.models.migration` block sets up the JDBC connection. Your database is created in the `create-employees` function, including an employee ID, name, and e-mail address. The `add-employee-test-data` function adds your test data, and the `main` function executes the migration.

10. Add your `Procfile`, as there are no pre-defined process types:

```
web: lein trampoline run -m clojure-postgres-example.core
```

11. Initialize your Git repository and create your Heroku app:

```
$ git init
Initialized empty Git repository in /Users/ckemp/Documents/Sites/clojure-postgres-example/.git/

$ heroku create clojure-postgres-example
Creating clojure-postgres-example... done, stack is cedar
```

```
http://clojure-postgres-example.herokuapp.com/ | git@heroku.com:clojure-postgres-
example.git
Git remote heroku added
```

12. No database is added by default to Clojure apps pushed to Heroku, so add one with the following command:

```
$ heroku addons:add heroku-postgresql:dev
Adding heroku-postgresql:dev on clojure-postgres-example... done, v4 (free)
Attached as HEROKU_POSTGRESQL_NAVY
Database has been created and is available
Use `heroku addons:docs heroku-postgresql:dev` to view documentation.

$ heroku pg:promote HEROKU_POSTGRESQL_NAVY_URL
Promoting HEROKU_POSTGRESQL_NAVY to DATABASE_URL... done
```

13. Do the push:

```
$ git add .

$ git commit -am "Initial commit"
[master (root-commit) 3bae273] Initial commit
 11 files changed, 177 insertions(+)
 create mode 100644 .gitignore
 create mode 100644 Procfile
 create mode 100644 README
 create mode 100644 project.clj
 create mode 100644 src/clojure_postgres_example/controllers/employees.clj
 create mode 100644 src/clojure_postgres_example/core.clj
...

$ git push heroku master
Counting objects: 21, done.
Delta compression using up to 4 threads.
Compressing objects: 100% (18/18), done.
Writing objects: 100% (21/21), 3.24 KiB, done.
Total 21 (delta 0), reused 0 (delta 0)

-----> Heroku receiving push
-----> Clojure app detected
-----> Installing Leiningen
       Downloading: leiningen-1.7.1-standalone.jar
       To use Leiningen 2.x, add this to project.clj: :min-lein-version "2.0.0"
       Downloading: rlwrap-0.3.7
       Writing: lein script
-----> Building with Leiningen
       Running: lein deps
       Downloading: org/clojure/clojure/1.3.0/clojure-1.3.0.pom from repository central
       at http://repo1.maven.org/maven2
       Transferring 5K from central
...
       Copying 18 files to /tmp/build_2xg6ho4ustm52/lib
-----> Discovering process types
       Procfile declares types -> web
```

```
-----> Compiled slug size is 13.0MB
-----> Launching... done, v3
       http://clojure-postgres-example.herokuapp.com deployed to Heroku

To git@heroku.com:clojure-postgres-example.git
 * [new branch]      master -> master
```

Your app is correctly identified as a Clojure app by Heroku because of the presence of `project.clj` in the root directory. Leiningen 1.7.1, the default version used for Clojure apps (unless otherwise specified as directed in the output shown), is used; and dependencies are retrieved and installed. The web process from the `Procfile` is used to define the process formation, and your app is launched.

14. Do your database migration:

```
$ heroku run lein run -m clojure-postgres-example.models.migration
Running 'lein run -m clojure-postgres-example.models.migration' attached to
   terminal... up, run.1
Migrating Employee database... done
```

15. Test your Clojure app:

```
$ heroku open
```

You should now see the Employee list, as shown in Figure 13-4.

Employee List

Employee ID	Name	E-mail Address
6440	Chip Arnaldo	farnaldo@vandelayenterprises.com
9567	Ed Cassola	ecassola@vandelayenterprises.com
6603	Angela Gil	agil@vandelayenterprises.com

FIGURE 13-4

16. Inspect the config vars to ensure they are set up properly:

```
$ heroku config
=== clojure-postgres-example Config Vars
DATABASE_URL:              postgres://dBu53r:dBp@55@ec1-23-45-678-90.compute-1.
                           amazonaws.com:5432/dBnAm3
HEROKU_POSTGRESQL_NAVY_URL: postgres://dBu53r:dBp@55@ec1-23-45-678-90.compute-1.
                           amazonaws.com:5432/dBnAm3
JVM_OPTS:                  -Xmx400m
LEIN_NO_DEV:               true
PATH:                      .lein/bin:/usr/local/bin:/usr/bin:/bin
```

You can see your `DATABASE_URL` and Heroku Postgres database string. `JVM_OPTS` can be used to adjust JVM settings, such as memory size — here set to 400MB. The `LEIN_NO_DEV` config var is used to tell Leiningen that you are running your app in production. The standard `PATH` variable is set automatically.

Additional Considerations

Clojure apps can be written or ported to Heroku in a straightforward manner with a few considerations kept in mind

➤ **Filesystem differences:** Make sure your app does not rely on any file being used after the current request has been completed — for instance, using `Java.io`'s file access functions — because of the ephemeral nature of a dyno's filesystem.

➤ **Data stores:** This chapter uses Heroku Postgres as a data store, but you can choose any data store you prefer; and you can search the add-ons to find a cloud-based provider that can easily be added to your Heroku app.

➤ **Session management:** Ring does not define a scalable way to store session information by default, preferring to store it either to memory or disk. This does not work with an inherently distributed system like Heroku. Use a library such as `mongodb-session` for Ring (`https://github.com/hozumi/mongodb-session`) to store shared session data in a centrally accessible location.

➤ **Caching:** Information can be cached in Clojure using the `clojure.core.cache` library (`https://github.com/clojure/core.cache`), Memcached (`https://github.com/shughes/clojure-memcached`), or a similar mechanism.

➤ **Static assets:** Because of the 200MB maximum slug size, an app with a lot of static assets should store them outside of itself, in Amazon S3 or using Amazon CloudFront, for distributed asset storage. If needed, you can serve some static assets with Clojure using the Dieter ring middleware (`https://github.com/edgecase/dieter`).

➤ **Config vars:** This chapter contains many examples using config vars to manage environment variables, such as `DATABASE_URL`. Use similar techniques for credential storage for backing third-party apps on which your app relies.

➤ **Web servers and containers:** You saw an example in this section that used an embedded Jetty web server to run your app. You can use use frameworks such as Noir to run apps on Heroku. See `http://thecomputersarewinning.com/post/clojure-heroku-noir-mongo/` for an example app.

➤ **Managing dependencies:** You have seen how to manage dependencies using Leiningen and how to define the version used by specifying `:min-lein-version` in `project.clj` — for instance, to run Leiningen 2.0 apps on Heroku.

➤ **E-mailing from your apps:** To send e-mail, use your own SMTP server with Clojure apps on Heroku, using a library such as `mail` (`http://nakkaya.com/2009/11/10/using-java-mail-api-from-clojure/`), which uses Java's `javax.mail` API. Alternatively, you can plug in to other APIs for third-party services to send e-mail, such as the SendGrid add-on

(http://blog.flurdy.com/2012/05/send-email-via-sendgrid-on-heroku-using
.html), but you might have to write your own interface, as few are readily available.

➤ **Logging:** Logs can be sent to a sink server or third-party log manager, such as Loggly, using the `clj-loggly` library (see https://github.com/markgunnels/clj-loggly).

➤ **Relying on external programs:** An app should not rely on programs external to itself, such as using `exec` to run cURL. As a best practice for simplifying delivery, all libraries needed to run your application should be declared as dependencies.

➤ **Scaling up vs. scaling out:** With the JVM's memory footprint on top of your app, it is important to manage memory efficiently, as failing to do so can cause memory to page if the 512MB limit is exceeded. JVisualVM can be used to monitor the JVM's memory usage (as described at www.fatvat.co.uk/2009/05/jvisualvm-and-clojure.html) if R14 errors are encountered.

Keep your app's code base as lean as possible to ensure that scaling can be done quickly. See the "Static assets" bullet earlier for tips on how storing assets externally can reduce slug size. As a best practice to ensure that only necessary artifacts are included in the slug, it is recommended that you use GitHub's general Clojure `.gitignore` file or the one appropriate for your Clojure framework (see https://github.com/github/gitignore for some pre-built files) in all your projects.

➤ **Binding to ports:** Port binding in your apps is done in your app's code by binding Jetty to the `PORT` config var. You can bind to the correct port in Noir apps as follows:

```
(server/start (Integer/parseInt (or (System/getenv "PORT") "8080")))
```

➤ **Long-running processes:** To avoid automatic connection closing upon timeout, long-running processes should be run with a worker dyno in the background. Ported apps should be re-architected to use background processes for any third-party backing service used as a best practice for scalability. You can use the CloudAMPQ (https://devcenter.heroku
.com/articles/cloudamqp#use-with-clojure) or IronMQ (https://github.com/
iron-io/iron_mq_clojure) for message queuing for background tasks.

Running processes on Heroku can be debugged in real time using Drawbridge, as outlined at https://devcenter.heroku.com/articles/debugging-clojure.

➤ **Shutting down gracefully:** Your app can be signaled at any time to shut down or restart. Therefore, it is important that you write logic into your app to set handlers for `SIGTERM` events and gracefully deal with the impending shutdown. As a best practice, try to complete any work that was not completed and respond to the web request, or any work that is not complete should be put back on a queue for a worker to pick up later. To capture a `SIGTERM` in Clojure with a JVM hook, you would use something like the following:

```
(defn -main []
    (.addShutdownHook (Runtime/getRuntime) (Thread. #(println "shutdown gracefully")))
    ...
)
```

➤ **Moving your domain:** Domains for Clojure apps can be pointed in the same way as with any other apps, using DNS settings.

DEVELOPING WITH SCALA

Much like Clojure, Scala apps are also run on the JVM. Scala is considered a multi-paradigm language because it intermingles aspects of both functional and object-oriented programming. Unlike Clojure, it is statically typed and strongly object oriented. It is typically considered a more clean and concise way to write Java-like code, making Scala a beneficial alternative. Access to the JVM also provides access to the Java APIs, making Scala apps very powerful and extensible.

In this section, you will again revisit the employee list example to write a sample Scala app (code file: `ch13-scala-play-example.zip`), but adding a twist. Instead of displaying a typical HTML page, you will simply output the JSON containing the employees' names and IDs. You will write the app using the Play framework, similar to the Java Play app you wrote in the previous chapter. Anorm (which stands for Anorm is Not an Object Relational Mapper) is the default Scala Play database mapper. However, we want to do automatic mapping with an ORM, so you will instead use a Hibernate-like ORM for Scala called *Squeryl*, with a few additional steps.

1. Create your Scala app with Play:

```
$ play new scala-play-example
       _            _
 _ __ | | __ _ _  _| |
| '_ \| |/ _' | || |_|
|  __/|_|\__,_|\__ (_)
|_|            |_/

play! 2.0.3, http://www.playframework.org

The new application will be created in /Users/ckemp/Documents/Sites/scala-play-example

What is the application name?
> scala-play-example

Which template do you want to use for this new application?

  1 - Create a simple Scala application
  2 - Create a simple Java application
  3 - Create an empty project

> 1

OK, application scala-play-example is created.

Have fun!
```

This is very similar to the process you used to create your Java Play app, except you specify a Scala app instead. Similarly, Play creates the skeleton of your app for you automatically.

2. Create a file in the root directory called `Global.scala`:

```
import org.squeryl.adapters.PostgreSqlAdapter
import org.squeryl.internals.DatabaseAdapter
import org.squeryl.{Session, SessionFactory}
```

```scala
import play.api.db.DB
import play.api.GlobalSettings

import play.api.Application

object Global extends GlobalSettings {

    override def onStart(app: Application) {
        SessionFactory.concreteFactory =
                app.configuration.getString("db.default.driver") match {
            case Some("org.postgresql.Driver") => Some(() =>
                getSession(new PostgreSqlAdapter, app))
            case _ => sys.error("Failed loading org.postgresql.Driver")
        }
    }

    def getSession(adapter:DatabaseAdapter, app: Application) =
        Session.create(DB.getConnection()(app), adapter)
}
```

This file defines the Postgres database driver and initializes it for your app's use.

3. Add the dependencies to `project/Build.scala`, inserting them where the comment "Add your project dependencies here" appears, in order for `sbt` (the Simple Build Tool) to retrieve and install the appropriate libraries:

```scala
val appDependencies = Seq(
    "org.scalatest" %% "scalatest" % "1.8" % "test",
    "org.squeryl" %% "squeryl" % "0.9.5-2",
    "postgresql" % "postgresql" % "9.1-901-1.jdbc4"
)
```

4. Create the project framework using IntelliJ:

```
$ play idea
[info] Loading project definition from /Users/ckemp/Documents/Sites/test-scala/project
[info] Set current project to scala-play-example (in build file:/Users/ckemp/Documents/
       Sites/test-scala/)
[info] Trying to create an Idea module scala-play-example
[info] Updating {file:/Users/ckemp/Documents/Sites/test-scala/}scala-play-example...
...
[info] Created /Users/ckemp/Documents/Sites/test-scala/.idea_modules/scala-play-example-
       build.iml
```

5. Edit your `app/controllers/Application.scala` controller, replacing the generated code with this:

```scala
package controllers

import play.api.mvc._

import com.codahale.jerkson.Json
import play.api.data.Form
```

```scala
import play.api.data.Forms.{mapping, text, optional}

import org.squeryl.PrimitiveTypeMode._
import models.{AppDB, Employee}

object Application extends Controller {

    def getEmployees = Action {
        val json = inTransaction {
            val employees = from(AppDB.employeeTable) (
                employeeTable => select(employeeTable)
            )
            Json.generate(employees)
        }
        Ok(json).as(JSON)
    }
}
```

Here you are defining the getEmployees action, which generates JSON from the employee list retrieved by your model, which you will write next.

6. Create a file called app/models/Employee.scala with the following code:

```scala
package models

import org.squeryl.{Schema, KeyedEntity}

case class Employee(name: Option[String]) extends KeyedEntity[Long] {
    val id: Long = 0
}

object AppDB extends Schema {
    val employeeTable = table[Employee]("employee")
}
```

The class Employee function creates an object for your employee records, extending Squeryl's KeyedEntity, which enables you to look up and delete records by id, also defined here. The AppDB function maps your model to the correct database table.

7. Replace your automatically generated view in app/views/index.scala.html with a view to display the employees:

```html
@main("Employee List") {

    <script src="@routes.Assets.at("javascripts/index.min.js")"
        type="text/javascript">
    </script>
    <ul id="employees"></ul>

}
```

This doesn't really do much except include a JavaScript script and add a placeholder for employees to be added. Notice that you are pointing to `javascripts/index.min.js`, which doesn't exist. This points to the CoffeeScript script that you will create in the next step to retrieve and display the JSON.

8. Create your CoffeeScript script in `app/assets/javascripts/index.coffee` to retrieve and display the data:

```
$ ->
    $.get "/", (data) ->
        $.each data, (index, item) ->
            $("#employees").append $("<li>").text item.name
```

This will take your JSON data and display each item in your employee list by injecting it into the view.

9. In `conf/routes`, change the line

```
# Home page
GET     /                           controllers.Application.index
```

to point your routing to the correct action in your controller, `getEmployees`:

```
# Home page
GET     /                           controllers.Application.getEmployees
```

10. Create a database migration script at `conf/evolutions/default/1.sql`:

```
# --- First database schema

# --- !Ups

create sequence s_employee_id;

create table employee (
    id      bigint,
    name    varchar(100),
    email   varchar(255)
);

INSERT INTO employee (id, name, email) VALUES
    ('9664', 'Janice Wong', 'jwong@vandelayenterprises.com'),
    ('5634', 'Justin Sit', 'jsit@vandelayenterprises.com'),
    ('0580', 'Kyle Shantz', 'southern@vandelayenterprises.com');

# --- !Downs

drop table employee;
drop sequence s_employee_id;
```

Evolutions provides Play developers with a sophisticated tool for managing database migrations. Typically, when you use JPA, Hibernate takes care of migrations, making Evolutions a valuable tool for replacing this functionality. The `!Ups` section defines the scripts that need to be run to build the database, including your test data. The `!Downs` section defines the opposite, SQL commands that can be run to undo these changes. If you wanted to define another migration, you would call it 2.sql and define it in the same way. In production, Evolution checks whether these scripts have been run, and runs any required in sequence.

11. Declare your `Procfile` to override the default for your Play app:

```
web: target/start -Dhttp.port=${PORT} -DapplyEvolutions.default=true
-Ddb.default.driver=org.postgresql.Driver -Ddb.default.url=${DATABASE_URL} ${JAVA_OPTS}
```

Notice that you are also injecting the driver type and DATABASE_URL in your startup command for Play. This means you do not have to include this config var in the code at all.

12. Deploy your app to Heroku:

```
$ git init
Initialized empty Git repository in /Users/ckemp/Documents/Sites/scala-play-example/
.git/

$ heroku create scala-play-example
Creating scala-play-example... done, stack is cedar
http://scala-play-example.herokuapp.com/ | git@heroku.com:scala-play-example.git
Git remote heroku added

$ git commit -am "Initial commit"
[master (root-commit) 9257813] Initial commit
 118 files changed, 1383 insertions(+)
 create mode 100644 .gitignore
 create mode 100644 .idea/IdeaProject.iml
 create mode 100644 .idea/encodings.xml
 create mode 100644 .idea/libraries/cglib_cglib_nodep_2_1_3_test.xml
 create mode 100644 .idea/libraries/cglib_cglib_nodep_2_2.xml
...


$ git push heroku master
Counting objects: 4, done.
Delta compression using up to 4 threads.
Compressing objects: 100% (3/3), done.
Writing objects: 100% (3/3), 396 bytes, done.
Total 3 (delta 1), reused 0 (delta 0)

-----> Heroku receiving push
-----> Removing .DS_Store files
-----> Play 2.0 - Scala app detected
-----> Running: sbt clean compile stage
       Getting net.java.dev.jna jna 3.2.3 ...
       :: retrieving :: org.scala-sbt#boot-jna
             confs: [default]
             1 artifacts copied, 0 already retrieved (838kB/14ms)
...
       [info] Compiling 7 Scala sources and 1 Java source to /tmp/build_2q02jvu44hd51/
       target/scala-2.9.1/classes...
       [success] Total time: 9 s, completed Sep 2, 2012 2:54:20 PM
       [info] Packaging /tmp/build_2q02jvu44hd51/target/scala-2.9.1/
       scala-play-example_2.9.1-1.0-SNAPSHOT.jar ...
```

```
[info] Done packaging.
[info]
[info] Your application is ready to be run in place: target/start
[info] [info]
[success] Total time: 3 s, completed Sep 2, 2012 2:54:23 PM
-----> Dropping ivy cache from the slug
-----> Discovering process types
       Procfile declares types -> web
-----> Compiled slug size is 50.2MB
-----> Launching... done, v6
       http://scala-play-example.herokuapp.com deployed to Heroku

To git@heroku.com:scala-play-example.git
   9257813..8383351  master -> master
```

Here, you can see that Heroku detects that you are pushing a Play 2 app written with Scala, because you have included a /conf/application.conf file. For non-Play Scala apps, a Scala app is detected during the push if any of the following patterns match:

```
/*.sbt
/project/*.scala
/project/build.properties
/.sbt/*.scala
```

The sbt version specified in project/build.properties is used to resolve your dependencies with Apache Ivy, a dependency manager for JVM-based languages, and build the app. You must use sbt v0.11.0 or later with a proper release because release candidates are not allowed. sbt then compiles and JARs your app for deployment. The web process, as defined in your Procfile, is launched. If you did not include a Procfile, the default for Scala apps is as follows:

```
web: target/start -Dhttp.port=$PORT $JAVA_OPTS
```

A development database is provisioned automatically with Scala apps, so you do not need to create one. When you run heroku open, the JSON output from your app is returned, listing the employees and their associated IDs:

```
[{"name":"Janice Wong","id":9664},{"name":"Justin Sit","id":5634},{"name":"Kyle
Shantz","id":580}]
```

13. Inspect its config vars to ensure they are set up properly:

```
$ heroku config
=== scala-play-example Config Vars
DATABASE_URL:                  postgres://dBu53r:dBp@55@ec1-23-45-678-90.compute-1.
                               amazonaws.com:5432/dBnAm3
HEROKU_POSTGRESQL_VIOLET_URL: postgres://dBu53r:dBp@55@ec1-23-45-678-90.compute-1.
                               amazonaws.com:5432/dBnAm3
JAVA_OPTS:                     -Xmx384m -Xss512k -XX:+UseCompressedOops
PATH:                          .sbt_home/bin:/usr/local/bin:/usr/bin:/bin
REPO:                          /app/.sbt_home/.ivy2/cache
SBT_OPTS:                      -Xmx384m -Xss512k -XX:+UseCompressedOops
```

The first two variables identify your Heroku Postgres database. JAVA_OPTS defines the parameters used for the JVM — in this case, the default of 384MB maximum heap size and 512KB stack size. SBT_OPS defines the same thing for when sbt is run. PATH is your standard OS path, and REPO points to your Apache Ivy dependency repository.

Additional Considerations

Keep the following points in mind for Scala apps written or architected for deployment to Heroku:

➤ **Filesystem differences:** Make sure your app does not rely on any file being used after the current request has been completed — for instance, using Java.io's file access functions — because of the ephemeral nature of a dyno's filesystem.

➤ **Data stores:** This chapter uses Heroku Postgres as a data store but you can use any data store of your choice, and you can search the add-ons to find a cloud-based provider that can easily be added to your Heroku app.

➤ **Session management:** Play stores session and flash information in cookies on the client side. However, it uses a secret key that is automatically generated for each instance if none is defined in conf/application.conf using application.secret. You should use config vars to share this across dynos; otherwise, a request to a dyno that did not set this session will not be able to read the session and create a new one. Other frameworks that do not do this by default, such as Scalatra, should be configured to use a similar approach or store session information in a backing data store instead.

➤ **Caching:** Information can be cached in Scala using a backing data store such as Memcached using the scala-memcached (https://github.com/argan/scala-memcached) or SMemcached libraries (https://github.com/victori/smemcached).

➤ **Static assets:** Because of the 200MB maximum slug size, any app with a lot of static assets should store them outside of itself, in Amazon S3 or using Amazon CloudFront, for distributed asset storage. Play enables you to define routes to static assets, and other frameworks should be configured accordingly if needed.

➤ **Config vars:** Many examples use config vars in this chapter to manage environment variables, like DATABASE_URL. Use similar techniques for credential storage for backing third-party apps on which your app relies.

➤ **Web servers and containers:** You used the Play 2 framework in the example app, but you can also use other frameworks such as Scalatra (see an example Heroku app at https://gist.github.com/1209277) or Lifty (example app at https://github.com/ghostm/lift_blank_heroku) using an embedded Jetty server.

➤ **Managing dependencies:** The example app managed your dependencies using Apache Ivy, built by sbt. If you are porting an app that uses a version of sbt prior to 0.11, you must upgrade to a more recent version to deploy to Heroku. You can also use Apache Maven to build your apps, but this forces your app to be treated as a Java app when pushed to Heroku.

➤ **E-mailing from your apps:** You should use your own SMTP server to send e-mail with Scala apps on Heroku, using a library such as `http://langref.org/scala/networking/smtp/send-an-email`, which uses Java's `javax.mail` API. Alternatively, you can plug in to other APIs for add-on services to send e-mail, such as SendGrid with the Play framework (as outlined in `http://blog.flurdy.com/2012/05/send-email-via-sendgrid-on-heroku-using.html`).

➤ **Logging:** Logs can be sent to a sink server or third-party log manager. Wrappers for Java's popular logging frameworks are often used for logging with Scala (see `http://stackoverflow.com/questions/978252/logging-in-scala`).

➤ **Relying on external programs:** An app should not rely on programs external to itself, such as using `Runtime.exec()` to run cURL. As a best practice for simplifying delivery, all libraries needed to run your application should be declared as dependencies.

➤ **Scaling up vs. scaling out:** With the JVM's memory footprint on top of your app, it is important to manage memory efficiently, as failing to do so can cause memory to page if the 512MB limit is exceeded. Performance management techniques can be used to profile JVM's memory usage (as described at `http://docs.scala-lang.org/overviews/parallel-collections/performance.html`) if R14 errors are encountered.

Keep your app's code base as lean as possible to ensure that scaling can be done quickly. See the discussion of static assets earlier for tips such as storing assets externally to reduce slug size. It is recommended that you use GitHub's general Scala `.gitignore` file or one appropriate for the Scala framework you use (see `https://github.com/github/gitignore` for some pre-built files) in all your projects as a best practice, to ensure that only necessary artifacts are included in the slug.

➤ **Binding to ports:** Port binding for Scala Play apps is done by passing the `PORT` config var in with the `Procfile's` process definitions. Other frameworks should be configured in a similar way, or bind manually in the code base using the port passed in through the config var.

➤ **Long-running processes:** To avoid automatic connection closing upon timeout, long-running processes should be run with a worker dyno in the background. Ported apps should be re-architected to use background processes for any third-party backing service used as a best practice for scalability. The Akka middleware (`https://devcenter.heroku.com/articles/scaling-out-with-scala-and-akka`) provides a web-worker pattern that can be used for message queuing of background tasks, and it provides strong concurrency using actor patterns.

➤ **Shutting down gracefully:** Your app can be signaled at any time to shut down or restart. Therefore, it is important to write logic into your app to set handlers for `SIGTERM` events and gracefully deal with the impending shutdown. As a best practice, try to complete any work that was not completed and respond to the web request, or any work that is not complete should be put back on a queue for a worker to pick up later. To capture a `SIGTERM` in Scala with a JVM hook, use something like the following:

```
Runtime.getRuntime.addShutdownHook(
    // do graceful shutdown here
)
```

➤ **Moving your domain:** Domains for Scala apps can be pointed in the same way as with any other apps, using DNS settings.

DEVELOPING WITH GROOVY USING THE GRAILS FRAMEWORK

Much like Clojure and Scala, Grails builds on top of the power and reliability provided by the JVM. Programming on Grails is done using the Groovy programming language, which will be very familiar to users of Java, but borrowing aspects of Ruby and Perl as well. Groovy bolts on features such as static and dynamic typing, closures, operator overloading, and native support for data structures and regular expressions, which are not available in Java.

The Grails framework leverages Hibernate and Spring, enabling developers using these technologies to learn it quickly and easily. Convention over coding or configuration is embraced by the framework, making it similar to Rails for Ruby in its capacity to facilitate rapid app development. It uses MVC principles to decouple the models, views, and controllers, similar to most modern frameworks.

> **NOTE** *Support for Grails on Heroku is currently in beta.*

In the following Grails example, you will implement the now familiar employee list app with the Grails framework (code file: `ch13-groovy-grails-example.zip`). You will use Grails 2.1, though Heroku also supports Grails 1.3.7 apps. The Grails app will use Apache Maven to manage your dependencies and build the app.

1. Install the Grails framework by following the instructions at `http://grails.org/doc/latest/guide/gettingStarted.html#requirements`. Grails can be installed on a Mac with Homebrew using the following command:

```
$ brew install grails
```

You must also have the Java JDK and Apache Maven installed to create Grails apps.

2. Create your application skeleton:

```
$ grails CreateApp_ groovy-grails-example
| Created Grails Application at /Users/ckemp/Documents/Sites/groovy-grails-example
```

3. Create the scaffolding for the `Employee` object:

```
$ cd groovy-grails-example

$ grails create-domain-class org.example.Employee
| Created file grails-app/domain/org/example/Employee.groovy
| Created file test/unit/org/example/EmployeeTests.groovy
```

4. The previous step has created a skeleton model in `grails-app/domain/org/example/Employee.groovy`, which you replace with the following:

```
package org.example

class Employee {
    Integer id
    String name
    String email

    static constraints = {
        id(blank: false)
    }
}
```

Here, the first three lines in the `Employee` class define the employee's properties, including ID, name, and e-mail address. The `constraints` block provides built-in validation rules for your properties.

5. Create a controller for your app. To do so, again use Grails to build the skeleton controller:

```
$ grails create-controller org.example.Employee
| Created file grails-app/controllers/org/example/EmployeeController.groovy
| Created file grails-app/views/employee
| Created file test/unit/org/example/EmployeeControllerTests.groovy
```

6. Replace the generated `grails-app/controllers/org/example/EmployeeController.groovy` file with the following:

```
package org.example

class EmployeeController {
    def scaffold = Employee
}
```

Here, you simply tell the controller to use Grails' built-in scaffolding, instead of having to create this functionality by hand. This clearly demonstrates Grails' convention over coding principle.

7. Replace the code in `grails-app/conf/BootStrap.groovy` to load some test data into your database when the app starts:

```
import org.example.Employee

class BootStrap {
    def init = { servletContext ->

        // Only add data if the DB is empty
        if (!Employee.count()) {
            new Employee(
                id:   1320,
                name: "Natasha Rathbone",
```

```
                   email: "nrathbone@vandelayenterprises"
            ).save(failOnError: true)

            new Employee(
                id:     1510,
                name:   "Peter Reeve",
                email: "preeve@vandelayenterprises"
            ).save(failOnError: true)

            new Employee(
                id:     6456,
                name:   "Mike Plonka",
                email: "mplonka@vandelayenterprises"
            ).save(failOnError: true)
        }
    }

    def destroy = { }
}
```

The code in the `init` block is run each time the app is started, and the `destroy` block is run upon termination.

8. Grails uses an in-memory Hyper Structured Query Language Database (HSQLDB) database by default, but this won't work with a share-nothing architecture like Heroku. You have to change this to point to your Heroku Postgres database. To do that, open `grails-app/conf/DataSource.groovy`, where your backing data stores are configured, and keeping the rest intact, replace the `production` block with this code:

```
production {
    dataSource {
        dbCreate = "update"
        driverClassName = "org.postgresql.Driver"
        dialect = org.hibernate.dialect.PostgreSQLDialect

        uri = new URI(System.env.DATABASE_URL)

        url = "jdbc:postgresql://"+uri.host+uri.path
        username = uri.userInfo.split(":")[0]
        password = uri.userInfo.split(":")[1]
    }
}
```

This will get your DATABASE_URL Heroku Postgres connection string and parse it to get the username and password.

9. Add the Postgres driver to your dependencies, by editing the `grails-app/conf/BuildConfig.groovy` file used to declare them, adding the following line to the dependencies section:

```
dependencies {
...
    runtime 'postgresql:postgresql:8.4-702.jdbc3'
}
```

This tells Apache Ivy to include the Postgres driver in your app build.

10. A Heroku database is auto-provisioned for you, but you need the DATABASE_URL to be available at build time; otherwise, your build will fail. Therefore, use the following to create a Heroku Postgres database, using the user-env-compile Heroku Labs tool to make config vars accessible at build time:

```
$ git init
Initialized empty Git repository in /Users/ckemp/Documents/Sites/groovy-grails-
example/.git/

$ heroku create groovy-grails-example
Creating groovy-grails-example... done, stack is cedar
http://groovy-grails-example.herokuapp.com/ | git@heroku.com:groovy-grails-example.git
Git remote heroku added

$ git add .

$ git commit -am "Initial commit"
[master (root-commit) 227e9e9] Initial commit
 63 files changed, 2964 insertions(+)
 create mode 100644 .classpath
 create mode 100644 .project
 create mode 100644 .settings/org.codehaus.groovy.eclipse.preferences.prefs
 create mode 100644 application.properties
 create mode 100644 grails-app/conf/ApplicationResources.groovy
 create mode 100644 grails-app/conf/BootStrap.groovy
...

$ heroku addons:add heroku-postgresql:dev
Adding heroku-postgresql:dev on groovy-grails-example... done, v2 (free)
Attached as HEROKU_POSTGRESQL_COBALT
Database has been created and is available
Use 'heroku addons:docs heroku-postgresql:dev' to view documentation.

$ heroku pg:promote HEROKU_POSTGRESQL_COBALT_URL
Promoting HEROKU_POSTGRESQL_COBALT to DATABASE_URL... done

$ heroku config
...

$ export DATABASE_URL="postgres://dBu53Rn4m3:dBp455W0rD@ec2-123-45-678-901.compute-1.
amazonaws.com:5432/dBn4M3"

$ heroku labs:enable user-env-compile
Enabling user-env-compile for groovy-grails-example... done
WARNING: This feature is experimental and may change or be removed without notice.
For more information see: http://devcenter.heroku.com/articles/labs-user-env-compile
```

Here, you copy the output from heroku config's DATABASE_URL to a local environment variable with the same name. The user-env-compile tool will use your local environment variables for the config vars used to build your app, so you must manually add variables such as JAVA_OPTS to compile properly. Alternatively, you can simply hardcode the value of the DATABASE_URL in the appropriate section for the environment in Datasource.groovy instead.

> **NOTE** *The* user-env-compile *tool is experimental and will cause your app to not be redeployed if you change config vars. You must do a new code push to use the updated config vars. You can disable* user-env-compile *at any time using the following command:*
>
> ```
> $ heroku labs:disable user-env-compile
> ```

11. Push the app to Heroku:

```
$ git push heroku master
Counting objects: 89, done.
Delta compression using up to 4 threads.
Compressing objects: 100% (77/77), done.
Writing objects: 100% (89/89), 100.86 KiB, done.
Total 89 (delta 3), reused 0 (delta 0)

-----> Heroku receiving push
-----> Grails app detected
-----> Grails 2.1.0 app detected
       WARNING: The Grails buildpack is currently in Beta.
-----> Installing Grails 2.1.0.....
-----> Done
-----> Executing grails -Divy.default.ivy.user.dir=/app/tmp/repo.git/.cache compile
       --non-interactive

          | Loading Grails 2.1.0
          | Configuring classpath
          | Downloading: ivy-1.0.1.RELEASE.xml
          | Downloading: ivy-2.4.1.xml
...

          |Compiling 10 source files
          ...........
          |Compiling 3 GSP files for package [testGrails]
          ..
          |Compiling 4 GSP files for package [databaseMigration]
          ..
          |Building WAR file
          .......................................
          |Done creating WAR target/test-grails-0.1.war
-----> No server directory found. Adding jetty-runner 7.5.4.v20111024 automatically.
-----> Discovering process types
          Procfile declares types  -> (none)
          Default types for Grails -> web
-----> Compiled slug size is 32.5MB
-----> Launching... done, v5
          http://groovy-grails-example.herokuapp.com deployed to Heroku

To git@heroku.com:groovy-grails-example.git
 * [new branch]      master -> master
```

You can see that Heroku has detected a Grails app and is indicating that the Grails 2.1.0 buildpack is in beta. You then use Apache Ivy to install your dependencies and package the Grails app as a WAR file. You have not added a web server, so Heroku automatically adds Jetty Runner, for convenience. Nor did you add a `Procfile`, so Heroku creates a default web process type with the following parameters:

```
web: java $JAVA_OPTS -jar server/jetty-runner.jar --port $PORT target/*.war
```

12. Test out your application:

```
$ heroku open
```

If all goes well, after the app loads you should see the "Welcome to Grails" screen. The scaffolding you used has also created facilities for listing, viewing, creating, updating, and deleting employee records. For example, click the "org.example.EmployeeController" link and you should be taken to a page where you can see the test records you added in your migration script, as shown in Figure 13-5.

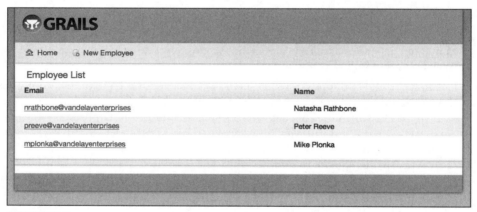

FIGURE 13-5

You have successfully created your first Groovy app with the Grails framework on Heroku. Now you can alter the scaffolding to make the app look and behave however you want.

Additional Considerations

Keep the following points in mind for Scala apps written or architected to be deployed to Heroku:

➤ **Filesystem differences:** Make sure your app does not rely on any file being used after the current request has been completed — for instance, using Java.io's file-access functions — because of the ephemeral nature of a dyno's filesystem.

➤ **Data stores:** This chapter uses Heroku Postgres as a data store, but any data store of your choice should work, and you can search the add-ons to find a cloud-based provider that can easily bolt on to your Heroku app.

➤ **Session management:** Grails stores session information in memory by default, meaning configuration is required to move to a share-nothing architecture like Heroku's. This can be done with Burt Beckwith's Database Session Plugin (`http://grails.org/plugin/database-session`) or Robert Fisher's Grails Database Session Plugin (`https://github.com/RobertFischer/grails-database-session`).

➤ **Caching:** Hibernate's second-level cache can be used for caching in Grails (see `http://grails.org/doc/2.1.0/guide/single.html#caching`).

➤ **Static assets:** Because of the 200MB maximum slug size, any app with a lot of static assets should store them outside of itself, in Amazon S3 or using Amazon CloudFront, for distributed asset storage. The Amazon S3 Plugin (`http://grails.org/plugin/amazon-s3`) can help facilitate this. Static assets can also be placed in the `web-app` directory and served from there, if necessary.

➤ **Config vars:** Many of the chapter's examples use config vars to manage environment variables, like `DATABASE_URL`. Use similar techniques for credential storage for backing third-party apps on which your app relies.

➤ **Web servers and containers:** Heroku automatically adds Jetty Runner to serve up your app. As shown previously with the Java examples, you can include whatever web server you want for Grails apps in a similar fashion.

➤ **Managing dependencies:** Your app demonstrates how you manage dependencies using Apache Ivy and build the app with Apache Maven.

➤ **E-mailing from your apps:** To send e-mail in Grails apps on Heroku, use your own SMTP server using Grails Plugins such as the standard Mail Plugin (`http://grails.org/plugin/mail`), which uses Spring's MailSender, or Mail from Grails (`http://grails.org/Mail+from+Grails`), which uses Spring's JavaMailSender. Alternatively, you can use a Heroku add-on, such as SendGrid (with the Grails SendGrid Plugin at `http://grails.org/plugin/sendgrid`), or another third-party service.

➤ **Logging:** Grails uses Log4J for logging, and the output can be sent to a sink server or third-party log manager. You can plug the popular Heroku log manager add-on Loggly into Log4j to use for logging (see `http://wiki.loggly.com/log4j` for instructions).

➤ **Relying on external programs:** An app should not rely on programs external to itself, such as using `Runtime.exec()` to run cURL. As a best practice for simplifying delivery, all libraries needed to run your application should be declared as dependencies.

➤ **Scaling up vs. scaling out:** Your Grails app can consume a lot of memory with Groovy, Grails, and the JVM's memory footprint on top of it. It is therefore important to manage memory efficiently, as failing to do so can cause memory to page if the 512 MB limit is exceeded. The JavaMelody monitoring tool (`http://code.google.com/p/javamelody/`) can be integrated with Grails via the JavaMelody Grails Plugin (`http://grails.org/plugin/grails-melody`) to profile memory.

Keep your app's code base as lean as possible to ensure that scaling can be done quickly. See the earlier discussion about static assets for tips such as storing assets externally to reduce slug size. In addition, as a best practice to ensure that only necessary artifacts are included in the slug, use Github's Grails `.gitignore` file at `https://github.com/github/gitignore/blob/master/Grails.gitignore` in all your projects.

➤ **Binding to ports:** Port binding for Grails apps is done by passing the PORT config var in with the Procfile's process definitions. Other web servers should be configured in a similar way or bind manually in the code base using the port passed in through the config var.

➤ **Long-running processes:** Long-running processes should be run with a worker dyno in the background to avoid automatic connection closing upon timeout. Ported apps should be re-architected to use background processes for any third-party backing service used as a best practice for scalability. The BackgroundThread plugin (http://grails.org/plugin/background-thread) provides a framework for asynchronous processing, or you can create your own with the Java Message Service (JMS) plugin (http://grails.org/plugin/jms) using a JMS provider like OpenMQ or ActiveMQ for messaging.

➤ **Shutting down gracefully:** Your app can be signaled at any time to shut down or restart. Therefore, it is important that you write logic into your app to set handlers for SIGTERM events and gracefully deal with the impending shutdown. As a best practice, try to complete any work that was not completed and respond to the web request, or any work that is not complete should be put back on a queue for a worker to pick up later. To capture a SIGTERM in Scala with a JVM hook, you would use something like the following:

```
Runtime.runtime.addShutdownHook {
    // do graceful shutdown here
}
```

➤ **Moving your domain:** Domains for Groovy apps can be pointed in the same way as with any other apps, using DNS settings.

DEVELOPING NON-FACEBOOK APPLICATIONS ON PHP

In the heyday of the dot-com boom, PHP quickly gained massive popularity for web development. PHP's original creator, Danish-Canadian developer Rasmus Lerdorf, designed the language to be easy to use for scripting dynamic web apps. As PHP matured, it introduced built-in features such as object-oriented programming and security, which helped build credibility with the established development community. This increased popularity made the LAMP (Linux, Apache, MySQL, PHP) stack one of the most popular, with 75% of all websites in 2007 being built in PHP.

Though Heroku fully supports PHP development for Facebook apps (see Chapter 16 for an example Facebook app written with PHP), PHP for non-Facebook apps is not yet officially supported. However, Heroku users are free to push and run apps through PHP, and they will run just fine. However, if you experience problems with your PHP app, an answer from Heroku's support team is not guaranteed.

In this section, you will create a basic PHP app to (you guessed it) display a list of employees from a Heroku Postgres database (code file: php-non-facebook-example.zip). You will run your app on Heroku, using the default Apache 2.2.22 web server and PHP version 5.3.10.

1. Install PHP for local testing. Modern Linux and OS X operating systems typically come with PHP pre-installed, but you may have to upgrade to a more recent version to ensure compatibility. MAMP (www.mamp.info/en/index.html) is an excellent package that can be installed to work with very little configuration. This project is based on the popular Windows WampServer (www.wampserver.com/en/), which provides the same ease of use for Windows users.

2. Create an `index.php` file in your root directory. Even if you are not going to use this file (for instance, with an `.htaccess Redirect`), it must be included for Heroku to detect that a PHP app is being pushed. Add the following code:

```php
<?php

    // Creates the connection string for our Postgres DB using DATABASE_URL
    extract(parse_url($_ENV["DATABASE_URL"]));
    $pg_conn = "user=$user password=$pass host=$host dbname=" . substr($path, 1) .
        " sslmode=require";
    $db = pg_connect($pg_conn);

    // Get all employee records
    $result = pg_query($db, "SELECT * FROM employees");

?>
<html>
    <head>
        <title>Employee List</title>
    </head>
    <body>

        <h1>Employee List</h1>

        <table>
            <tr>
                <th>Employee Id</th>
                <th>Name</th>
                <th>E-mail Address</th>
            </tr>
<?php

    // Go through each record returned
    while ($row = pg_fetch_row($result)) {
        print "<tr>\n";
        print "<td>" . $row[0] . "</td>\n";
        print "<td>" . $row[1] . "</td>\n";
        print "<td>" . $row[2] . "</td>\n";
        print "</tr>\n";
    }

?>
    </table>
    </body>
</html>
```

3. Push your PHP app to Heroku in the usual fashion:

```
$ git init
Initialized empty Git repository in /Users/ckemp/Documents/Sites/php-non-facebook-
example/.git/

$ heroku create php-non-facebook-example
```

```
Creating php-non-facebook-example... done, stack is cedar
http://php-non-facebook-example.herokuapp.com/ | git@heroku.com:php-non-facebook-
example.git
Git remote heroku added

$ git add .

$ git commit -am "Initial commit"
[master (root-commit) d72555e] Initial commit
 3 files changed, 52 insertions(+)
 create mode 100644 .DS_Store
 create mode 100644 index.php
 create mode 100644 insert.sql

$ git push heroku master
Counting objects: 5, done.
Delta compression using up to 4 threads.
Compressing objects: 100% (5/5), done.
Writing objects: 100% (5/5), 1.11 KiB, done.
Total 5 (delta 0), reused 0 (delta 0)

-----> Heroku receiving push
-----> Removing .DS_Store files
-----> PHP app detected
-----> Bundling Apache version 2.2.22
-----> Bundling PHP version 5.3.10
-----> Discovering process types
       Procfile declares types -> (none)
       Default types for PHP  -> web
-----> Compiled slug size is 9.5MB
-----> Launching... done, v3
       http://php-non-facebook-example.herokuapp.com deployed to Heroku

To git@heroku.com:php-non-facebook-example.git
 * [new branch]      master -> master
```

Note that no `Procfile` is needed. The Heroku PHP buildpack will automatically configure and start Apache for you.

4. Create the Heroku Postgres database you will use as a data store and populate it with some initial data:

```
$ heroku addons:add heroku-postgresql:dev
Adding heroku-postgresql:dev on php-non-facebook-example... done, v4 (free)
Attached as HEROKU_POSTGRESQL_RED
Database has been created and is available
Use 'heroku addons:docs heroku-postgresql:dev' to view documentation.

$ heroku pg:promote HEROKU_POSTGRESQL_RED_URL
Promoting HEROKU_POSTGRESQL_RED to DATABASE_URL... done

$ heroku pg:psql
psql (9.1.4, server 9.1.5)
SSL connection (cipher: DHE-RSA-AES256-SHA, bits: 256)
```

```
Type "help" for help.

mYdBn4M3=> create table employees (
mYdBn4M3(>   id     bigint,
mYdBn4M3(>   name  varchar(100),
mYdBn4M3(>   email varchar(255)
mYdBn4M3(> );
CREATE TABLE
mYdBn4M3=>
mYdBn4M3=> INSERT INTO employees (id, name, email) VALUES
mYdBn4M3->   ('1948', 'Gord McCance', 'gmccance@vandelayenterprises.com'),
mYdBn4M3->   ('7388', 'Chris Heigl', 'heigl@vandelayenterprises.com'),
mYdBn4M3->   ('4041', 'Sandy Jones', 'rjones@vandelayenterprises.com');
INSERT 0 3
mYdBn4M3=> \q
```

5. Test your PHP Heroku app with the following command:

```
$ heroku open
Opening php-non-facebook-example... done
```

Figure 13-6 shows the newly created PHP Heroku app up and running.

Employee List

Employee Id	Name	E-mail Address
1948	Gord McCance	gmccance@vandelayenterprises.com
7388	Chris Heigl	heigl@vandelayenterprises.com
4041	Sandy Jones	rjones@vandelayenterprises.com

FIGURE 13-6

If you run `heroku config`, you can see that no other config vars are added by Heroku besides the Heroku Postgres database connection strings.

Additional Considerations

Keep the following considerations in mind when writing or architecting PHP apps to be deployed to Heroku

➤ **Filesystem differences:** Make sure your app does not rely on any file being used after the current request has been completed — for instance, when uploading files from the user — because of the ephemeral nature of a dyno's filesystem.

➤ **Data stores:** Although this chapter uses Heroku Postgres as a data store, you can use any data store of your choice, and you can search the add-ons to find a cloud-based provider that can easily bolt on to your Heroku app. PHP and MySQL are commonly used together; and Heroku add-ons, ClearDB (`https://devcenter.heroku.com/articles/cleardb#using-cleardb-with-php`), or Xeround (`https://devcenter.heroku.com/articles/xeround`) can be used to bolt on a third-party MySQL database-as-a-service.

➤ **Session management:** PHP's default session management saves session information in an SQLite database which is stored locally as a flat file. This is unsuitable for a multi-dyno environment where a share-nothing architecture is used. To remedy this, you must use PHP's `session_set_save_handler()` to change the backing session storage to a central location, such as a backing database or Memcache data store (see `www.devshed.com/c/a/PHP/Storing-PHP-Sessions-in-a-Database` for instructions on how to do this).

➤ **Caching:** Information can be cached for quick retrieval using a solution such as the MemCachier add-on (`https://devcenter.heroku.com/articles/memcachier#php`) or IronCache (`https://devcenter.heroku.com/articles/iron_cache#php`).

➤ **Static assets:** Because of the 200MB maximum slug size, an app with a lot of static assets should store them outside of itself, in Amazon S3 or using Amazon CloudFront, for distributed asset storage. Apache is very good at serving static assets.

➤ **Config vars:** This chapter contains many examples of using config vars to manage environment variables, like `DATABASE_URL`. Use similar techniques for credential storage for backing third-party apps on which your app relies.

➤ **Web servers and containers:** Heroku automatically uses and configures Apache HTTP Server to serve up your PHP apps. However, you can use whatever web server you want, such as Nginx (see `https://github.com/iphoting/heroku-buildpack-php-tyler`), or build your own custom buildpack to use your choice of web server. You can use popular frameworks such as Symphony (setup instructions at `http://blog.pajap.com/?p=102`) or CakePHP (see the example at `http://zoombody.com/articles/deploy-cakephp-on-heroku`). Setting up other popular frameworks, such as Zend, should be done in a similar fashion. Note that Zend modules can be added without the whole framework (see `http://jonahlyn.heroku.com/blog/2011/04/06/using-zend-form-without-the-framework`). Ensure that the considerations in this section are kept in mind when configuring your framework to run on a scalable platform (e.g., keeping sessions out of memory or the local filesystem).

➤ **Managing dependencies:** Unlike most other languages, PHP apps on Heroku do not use a dependency manager by default. You can add your own, such as Composer (see the instructions and custom buildpack at `http://bergie.iki.fi/blog/using_composer_to_manage_dependencies_in_heroku_php_apps/`), to adhere to dependency isolation best practices in PHP development.

PHP developers typically use extensions, such as `XMLreader` and `Mcrypt`, which are added to PHP's run time during compilation. To see a full list of extensions pre-installed, go to `http://phpinfo.herokuapp.com`. You can add your own extensions by compiling the binaries needed on the Vulcan build server (see `https://devcenter.heroku.com/articles/buildpack-binaries` for instructions), put the extension's `.so` files in a folder called `ext`, and add a `php.ini` file to your root directory with the appropriate configuration, as directed in the extension's installation instructions. Alternatively, you can fork your own buildpack from Heroku's default PHP buildpack (`https://github.com/heroku/heroku-buildpack-php`) with whatever custom extensions you need (see the next chapter for more information on custom buildpacks).

➤ **E-mailing from your apps:** Use your own SMTP server (outside of Heroku) for sending e-mail in PHP apps with PHP's built-in `mail()` function by pointing it to your SMTP server:

```
ini_set ( "SMTP", "smtp.my-server-domain.com" );
```

Alternatively, you can use a Heroku add-on such as SendGrid (see the example at `http://docs.sendgrid.com/documentation/api/smtp-api/php-example/`) or another third-party service.

➤ **Logging:** The output of PHP and Apache's built-in logging can be sent to a sink server or third-party log manager. The popular Heroku log manager add-on Loggly can be plugged in to PHP for logging (see `http://wiki.loggly.com/phplogging` for instructions).

➤ **Relying on external programs:** An app should not rely on programs external to itself, such as using `exec()` or `shell_exec()` to run cURL. As a best practice for simplifying delivery, all libraries needed to run your application should be declared as dependencies.

➤ **Scaling up vs. scaling out:** Manage app memory efficiently, as failing to do so can cause memory to page if the 512 MB limit is exceeded. For simple profiling, you can use `get_memory_usage()` in your code to monitor memory usage in your logs. Memory profilers, such as the PHP Quick Profiler library, can easily be used with your apps; more robust solutions, such as XDebug (`http://xdebug.org`), which need to be compiled in with the PHP run time, take more work to set up (see the earlier bulleted item on managing dependencies for an outline of how to do this).

Keep your app's code base as lean as possible to ensure that scaling can be done quickly. See the earlier discussion on static assets for tips such as storing assets externally to reduce slug size. As a best practice to ensure that only necessary artifacts are included in the slug, it is recommended that you use GitHub's general Python `.gitignore` file or the one appropriate for your Python framework (see `https://github.com/github/gitignore` for some pre-built files) in all your projects.

➤ **Binding to ports:** Heroku's buildpack with automatically bind Apache to the PORT config var automatically set for your dyno. Other web servers should be configured similarly or bind manually in the code base using the port passed in through the config var.

➤ **Long-running processes:** Long-running processes should be run with a worker dyno in the background to avoid automatic connection closing upon timeout. Ported apps should be re-architected to use background processes for any third-party backing service used as a best practice for scalability. Heroku's PHP buildpack creates only a single dyno, which makes it challenging to create your own worker dynos running in the same app. You would have to create a separate app with a database-based job queuing system, as outlined in `http://stut.net/2009/05/29/php-job-queue`, but using a separate running process polling the job queue, instead of cron.

➤ **Shutting down gracefully:** Your app can be signaled at any time to shut down or restart. Therefore, it is important that you write logic into your app to set handlers for SIGTERM events and gracefully deal with the impending shutdown. As a best practice, try to complete any work that was not completed and respond to the web request, or put any work that is not complete back on a queue for a worker to pick up later. To capture a SIGTERM in PHP, you can use the `pcntl_signal()` function, following the example at `http://php.net/manual/en/function.pcntl-signal.php#refsect1-function .pcntl-signal-examples`.

➤ **Moving your domain:** Domains for PHP apps can be pointed in the same way as with any other apps, using DNS settings.

SUMMARY

This chapter explored how Heroku's polyglot nature can be leveraged to write apps in a number of different languages, enabling you to use the right tool for the job at hand. Python can be used to write apps on Heroku with popular and easy-to-use frameworks like Django. Node.js is an ideal language for taking advantage of Heroku's mass scalability and runs code quickly and with very efficient memory use.

Clojure is a JVM-based language that provides easy multithreading and concurrency, making it ideal for Heroku apps that are highly parallelizable. Scala also runs on the JVM and allows developers to write cleaner and more concise code in a language. Similarly, Groovy is also JVM-based and syntactically similar to Java, but also offers convention over coding to increase developer productivity. PHP development for non-Facebook apps is not officially supported by Heroku, but can be done nonetheless, allowing Heroku developers to use this highly popular language.

This chapter's examples used buildpacks that are built and supported by Heroku. The next chapter discusses how to use and write your own custom buildpacks for deploying apps on Heroku in almost any language you like.

14

Understanding Buildpacks

WHAT'S IN THIS CHAPTER?

➤ How buildpacks work

➤ Developing .NET applications on Heroku

➤ Developing Perl applications on Heroku

➤ Packaging binary buildpack dependencies

➤ Creating custom buildpacks

WROX.COM CODE DOWNLOADS FOR THIS CHAPTER

The wrox.com code downloads for this chapter are found at `www.wrox.com/remtitle .cgi?isbn=1118508998` on the Download Code tab. The code is in the Chapter 14 download and individually named according to the names throughout the chapter.

When the Cedar stack was first released, it ushered in a new era of polyglot development by enabling developers to run programs on Heroku, not just in Ruby, but also with a multitude of different languages. Instead of being designed with a set of popular languages in mind, Cedar was built to be language agnostic, with a buildpack used as a script to set up the run time for that language or framework on Heroku. Heroku provides a number of supported, open-source buildpacks, as shown in the examples in previous chapters. For a complete list, see `https://devcenter.heroku.com/articles/buildpacks#default-buildpacks`.

However, Heroku's creators realized that developers of less mainstream or esoteric languages would also want their programs to leverage Heroku's rapid scalability and increased developer productivity. Obviously, developing supported buildpacks in every language that exists is not a very scalable plan (or a good use of Heroku's resources). Therefore, they instead built in the capability to define and distribute your own custom buildpacks for nearly any language, framework, and application that will run on a Linux box.

This chapter first opens the hood to examine how buildpacks work. Next, you will look at how to use a couple of unsupported, third-party buildpacks to create .NET and Perl apps. You will then see an example demonstrating how to package binary assets in with your app for when you need to include dependencies that cannot be added with your dependency manager. Finally, you will learn how to create custom buildpacks for deploying any app you want to Heroku.

HOW BUILDPACKS WORK

When an app is pushed to Heroku, it produces a *slug*, a pre-packaged copy of an app after it has been processed by the buildpack. Slugs can then be quickly and efficiently placed and run on any dyno when starting, restarting, or scaling apps. The buildpack provides the recipe needed to prepare an app written in a specific language or framework to be run on a dyno. Typically, the scripts you must create for a buildpack automate a number of core functions in creating a run time for your language. Specifically, it handles the following:

➤ Detects whether the buildpack is appropriate for the app being pushed

➤ Signals the run time to run your program and install it (e.g., OpenJDK for Java apps)

➤ Retrieves and installs a dependency manager, if needed

➤ Runs your dependency manager, retrieving and installing dependent libraries in your code base

➤ Optionally auto-provisions a Heroku Postgres database if none already exists and your framework relies on a data store to work properly

➤ Injects your database configuration in the language or framework-specific location — for instance, replacing database.yml in Ruby apps to point to the DATABASE_URL configuration variable (config var)

➤ Builds and compiles your app's assets, if needed

➤ Installs Heroku-specific plugins, if needed (e.g., for logging on to Heroku or serving static assets)

Heroku provides a number of built-in buildpacks, but also allows you to define your own custom buildpack or use custom buildpacks that others have defined. Detractors might argue that using a custom buildpack locks the developer into the Heroku platform. Be that as it may, this buildpack process is being increasingly embraced by the development community. For example, ActiveState's Stackato PaaS service provides the capability to migrate to their platform using the same custom buildpack used on Heroku with no additional coding needed (www.activestate.com/stackato). Custom buildpacks can even be deployed locally or on another non-Heroku server using Mason (https://github.com/ddollar/mason). In other words, even the custom buildpack process does not lock the developer in, keeping apps deployed to Heroku fully portable.

Heroku provides support for programs written on languages and frameworks that are deployed using the supported buildpacks. For instance, if you are trying to install a library with a supported buildpack and it won't work, you can turn to Heroku support to help get it working. Clearly, it isn't possible for Heroku to support programs written in every language built with custom buildpacks. Realistically, how many LOLCODE experts exist in the world, let alone on the Heroku support team, specifically? However, Heroku provides support for the process of creating a buildpack if you do get stuck.

NOTE *For an up-to-date list of third-party buildpacks, see* https://devcenter
.heroku.com/articles/third-party-buildpacks.

Buildpacks typically consist of three core scripts:

➤ bin/detect: This script is used to determine whether the buildpack can be applied to build the current app.

➤ bin/compile: This script does the actual installation and build of the run time, download and installation of dependencies declared by the app, and the building of the app itself.

➤ bin/release: This script does the final setup, including provisioning any necessary add-ons, defining default config vars, and defining default process types for the app.

The following sections examine each of these components of buildpacks to explore what each script does.

bin/detect

The bin/detect script simply checks if the files it expects exist in the app that is being built. You would not want a buildpack for Ruby to run on a Java app! The bin/detect script is used as a failsafe to ensure that the buildpack is being applied to the appropriate application type.

The following is an example of bin/detect from Heroku's PHP buildpack (https://github.com/heroku/heroku-buildpack-php):

```
#!/usr/bin/env bash

if [ -f $1/index.php ]; then
    echo "PHP" && exit 0
else
    echo "no" && exit 1
fi
```

Pretty straightforward stuff here. The script simply looks for index.php in the root directory of the app (the first argument passed into the script, denoted by $1) and returns the human-readable name of the language and framework detected. It also returns zero on success, indicating that this buildpack is appropriate for the app pushed.

bin/compile

The bin/compile script is responsible for ensuring that the dyno is packaged with everything it needs to run apps on a dyno. The crucial element in running apps is the run time, which must be downloaded and installed. If you require a web server to run apps, where the web server is not embedded as a dependency, bin/compile must download, configure, and start the web server.

Your apps also may require other binaries to run, which also must be downloaded and configured here. Buildpacks that are specific to particular frameworks are also responsible for installing and configuring those frameworks. If your language must compile apps before they are run, `bin/compile` must also compile your apps. This often is done using a build manager, but a build manager is not strictly required if the app can be built without it.

Consider the `bin/compile` file from Heroku's PHP buildpack:

```bash
#!/usr/bin/env bash
# bin/compile <build-dir> <cache-dir>

# fail fast
set -e

# config
APACHE_VERSION="2.2.22"
APACHE_PATH="apache"
PHP_VERSION="5.3.10"
PHP_PATH="php"

BIN_DIR=$(dirname $0)
BUILD_DIR=$1
CACHE_DIR=$2
LP_DIR='cd $(dirname $0); cd ..; pwd'

# include .files when moving things around
shopt -s dotglob

cd $BUILD_DIR

# move app things to www
mkdir -p $CACHE_DIR/www
mv * $CACHE_DIR/www
mv $CACHE_DIR/www .

# keep Procfile
if [ -f www/Procfile ]; then
 mv www/Procfile .
fi

APACHE_URL="https://s3.amazonaws.com/php-lp/apache-$APACHE_VERSION.tar.gz"
echo "-----> Bundling Apache version $APACHE_VERSION"
curl --silent --max-time 60 --location "$APACHE_URL" | tar xz

PHP_URL="https://s3.amazonaws.com/php-lp/php-$PHP_VERSION.tar.gz"
echo "-----> Bundling PHP version $PHP_VERSION"
curl --silent --max-time 60 --location "$PHP_URL" | tar xz

# update config files
cp $LP_DIR/conf/httpd.conf $APACHE_PATH/conf
cp $LP_DIR/conf/php.ini php

# make php available on bin
mkdir -p bin
```

```
ln -s /app/php/bin/php bin/php

cat >>boot.sh <<EOF
for var in \'env|cut -f1 -d\'; do
 echo "PassEnv \$var" >> /app/apache/conf/httpd.conf;
done
touch /app/apache/logs/error_log
touch /app/apache/logs/access_log
tail -F /app/apache/logs/error_log &
tail -F /app/apache/logs/access_log &
export LD_LIBRARY_PATH=/app/php/ext
export PHP_INI_SCAN_DIR=/app/www
echo "Launching apache"
exec /app/apache/bin/httpd -DNO_DETACH
EOF

chmod +x boot.sh

# clean the cache
rm -rf $CACHE_DIR/*
```

Here you can see that in the `config` block, the versions are set. In the next block, the build directory is passed in with the first argument (`$1`, in this script), and the directory used to cache build artifacts is passed with the second argument (`$2` here.) Note that the caching directory stores files between builds, which speeds up subsequent builds. You then set up the app's code to the www directory you have made, and then download and uncompress both the Apache and PHP run times. These are remote, publicly available copies of the pre-compiled binaries for both apps that you have built on Heroku using Vulcan. (See the section "Packaging Binary Buildpack Dependencies" for more details about how to do this.)

Next, you add your default `httpd.conf` and `php.ini` configuration files (both sitting in the `conf` directory of the buildpack) that PHP relies upon, which are also part of our buildpack and copied to the correct location. You then ensure you can access the PHP run time in a directory on your system path by creating a soft link. Next, you make your system's environment variables available in PHP's configuration, and then add a couple of more environment variables and start up the Apache web server. Finally, you clean up anything remaining in the cache directory.

PHP differs from some other languages run on Heroku in that programs written on PHP are typically interpreted and not compiled (though it is possible to compile PHP code with a number of compiler options available), and no dependency manager is used. In many languages, a build manager is used to manage the build process and use the dependency manager to get libraries on which the app depends. For instance, Java uses Maven for both build automation and dependency management.

The following `bin/compile` file in the Java buildpack (`https://github.com/heroku/heroku-buildpack-java`) demonstrates what it looks like to use a build automation and dependency management tool:

```
#!/usr/bin/env bash
# bin/compile <build-dir> <cache-dir>

# fail fast
```

```
set -e

logger -p user.notice -t "slugc[$$]" "language_pack_java java_compile_start"

BIN_DIR=$(cd $(dirname $0); pwd) # absolute path
# parse args
BUILD_DIR=$1
CACHE_DIR=$2
LOGGER_FLAGS=""

curl --silent --location http://heroku-jvm-common.s3.amazonaws.com/jvm-buildpack-
common.tar.gz | tar xz
. bin/java

KEEP_M2_CACHE="true"

# create default system.properties for apps that had the jdk vendored in
if [ -f ${CACHE_DIR}/.jdk/vendor ] && [ ! -f ${BUILD_DIR}/system.properties ]; then
 echo "java.runtime.version=1.6" > ${BUILD_DIR}/system.properties
fi

if [ -f ${CACHE_DIR}/system.properties ] && [ ! -f ${BUILD_DIR}/system.properties ]
; then
 cp ${CACHE_DIR}/system.properties ${BUILD_DIR}/system.properties
fi

if [ ! -d $CACHE_DIR ]; then
 LOGGER_FLAGS="$LOGGER_FLAGS new_java_app"
  logger -p user.notice -t "slugc[$$]" "language_pack_java new_java_app"
  KEEP_M2_CACHE="false"
  if [ ! -f ${BUILD_DIR}/system.properties ]; then
   echo "java.runtime.version=1.6" > ${BUILD_DIR}/system.properties;
  fi
elif [ -f $CACHE_DIR/removeM2Cache ]; then
 KEEP_M2_CACHE="false"
fi

if [ "true" == $KEEP_M2_CACHE ]; then
 logger -p user.notice -t "slugc[$$]" "language_pack_java retain_m2_repo"
fi

#create the cache dir if it doesn't exist
mkdir -p $CACHE_DIR

# install JDK
if [ -f ${BUILD_DIR}/system.properties ]; then
 logger -p user.notice -t "slugc[$$]" "language_pack_java download_jdk"
  LOGGER_FLAGS="$LOGGER_FLAGS download_jdk"
  javaVersion=$(detect_java_version ${BUILD_DIR})
  echo -n "-----> Installing OpenJDK ${javaVersion}..."
  install_java ${BUILD_DIR} ${javaVersion}
  echo "done"
  cp ${BUILD_DIR}/system.properties ${CACHE_DIR}/
fi

# change to cache dir to install maven
```

```
cd $CACHE_DIR

# install maven with base repository
MAVEN_URL="http://s3.amazonaws.com/heroku-jvm-langpack-java/maven.tar.gz"

if [ ! -d .maven ]; then
 echo -n "-----> Installing Maven 3.0.3..."
  curl --silent --max-time 60 --location $MAVEN_URL | tar xz
  chmod +x .maven/bin/mvn
  echo " done"
fi

MAVEN_SETTINGS_URL="http://s3.amazonaws.com/heroku-jvm-langpack-java/settings.xml"

echo -n "-----> Installing settings.xml..."
if [ -f .m2/settings.xml ]; then
 rm .m2/settings.xml
fi
curl --silent --max-time 10 --location $MAVEN_SETTINGS_URL --output .m2/
settings.xml
echo " done"

# change to build dir to run maven
cd $BUILD_DIR

export MAVEN_OPTS="-Xmx512m"

# build app
BUILDCMD="$CACHE_DIR/.maven/bin/mvn -B -Duser.home=$BUILD_DIR
-Dmaven.repo.local=$CACHE_DIR/.m2/repository -s
$CACHE_DIR/.m2/settings.xml -DskipTests=true clean install"
echo "-----> executing $BUILDCMD"

$BUILDCMD 2>&1 | sed -u 's/^/        /'

if [ "${PIPESTATUS[*]}" != "0 0" ]; then
 echo " !     Failed to build app with Maven"
  exit 1
fi

# finalize cache
if [ "false" == $KEEP_M2_CACHE ]; then
 touch $CACHE_DIR/removeM2Cache
fi

#copy .m2 and .maven if needed
if [ "true" == $KEEP_M2_CACHE ]; then
 for DIR in ".m2" ".maven" ; do
   cp -r $CACHE_DIR/$DIR $DIR
  done
fi

logger -p user.notice -t "slugc[$$]" "language_pack_java java_compile_end $LOGGER_FLAGS"
```

Here you can see that you first get the common JVM buildpack, which bolts on functions similar to any language that runs on the JVM, using the `curl` command. You then build the `system .properties` file, which Java uses for its internal configuration, in the two blocks of code after `KEEP_M2_CACHE` is set. Next, the correct version of the JDK is vendored into the app in the block of code after the `install JDK` comment. After this point, the code differs from your PHP buildpack.

In the block of code following `MAVEN_URL` being set, you download and install Maven. The `settings.xml` file is then added, if you don't already have one, in the two blocks after that. The `settings.xml` file defines the settings that you will use for running Maven. The magic then happens in the code preceding the `build app` comment, where the Maven build script is run, which downloads and installs your dependencies, and assembles the app to be run.

bin/release

The last of the three core files required for buildpacks is the `bin/release` file. Unlike the other two files, which use scripts to accomplish their goals, this file is simply a YAML file that defines three important, but optional, pieces of configuration for Heroku apps built with your buildpack:

➤ `addons`: Specifies which add-ons need to be installed for running programs built with this language or framework. Often frameworks require a backing database to function properly, so a database can be procured here for your apps.

➤ `config_vars`: Defines default config vars you must set when creating an app.

➤ `default_process_types`: Delineates the standard process formation for apps that use this buildpack. Often, languages include a default web process pre-defined, sometimes along with other process types. Of course, other processes can be defined in the `Procfile`, and these can be overridden, if needed.

The following example shows a `bin/release` file in the Scala buildpack (`https://github.com/heroku/heroku-buildpack-scala`):

```
#!/usr/bin/env bash
# bin/release <build-dir>

BIN_DIR=$(cd $(dirname $0); pwd)
. $BIN_DIR/common
BUILD_DIR=$1

cat <<EOF
---
config_vars:
 PATH: .sbt_home/bin:/usr/local/bin:/usr/bin:/bin
 JAVA_OPTS: -Xmx384m -Xss512k -XX:+UseCompressedOops
 SBT_OPTS: -Xmx384m -Xss512k -XX:+UseCompressedOops
 REPO: /app/.sbt_home/.ivy2/cache
addons:
 heroku-postgresql:dev

EOF

if is_play $BUILD_DIR && [ ! -f $BUILD_DIR/Procfile ] ; then
```

```
cat <<EOF
default_process_types:
 web: target/start -Dhttp.port=\$PORT \$JAVA_OPTS
EOF
fi
```

This indicates that four default config vars are set: PATH, JAVA_OPTS, SBT_OPS, and REPO. You also need a backing database for Scala apps. This buildpack will automatically install a Heroku Postgres dev database because the addons section instructs Heroku to do so. Typically, you want to install only non-chargeable add-ons here to ensure that any developers who use your buildpack don't find unexpected charges on their Heroku bill.

Finally, you use the default_process_types to define your process formation. The most common process defined here is the web process. Oftentimes, other processes are defined here as well, one per line. Sometimes, no default processes are defined, requiring users to define their own Procfile to set up their process formation. Though you can add other files needed in your buildpack, only these three files are required for any buildpack to function correctly.

DEVELOPING .NET APPLICATIONS ON HEROKU

Heroku's dynos are essentially subvirtualized Linux machines, so .NET development on Heroku typically is seen as a nonstarter because of this OS dependency. However, the Mono framework provides a free, open-source, ECMA standards-compliant implementation of the .NET Framework's API. Pioneered by open-source advocate Miguel de Icaza, the Mono framework includes a C# compiler (implementing versions 1.0, 2.0, 3.0, and 4.0 of ECMA standards), a Mono run time (implementing .NET's Common Language Runtime, according to ECMA standards), a base class library (compatible with .NET Framework classes), and a Mono Class Library (extending the base class with functionality for common tasks, like working with ZIP files.)

Mono includes support for ASP.NET 1.2 and 2.0 development, though Web Parts and some other smaller features may not be fully implemented yet. ASP MVC 3 is also supported in Mono with a bit of additional legwork (www.mono-project.com/Release_Notes_Mono_2.10#ASP.NET_MVC3_ Support). Visual Basic.NET support should allow you to run and compile most Visual Basic 8 (Visual Studio 2005) apps using the Mono framework.

The following example demonstrates how to create a C# program that will run using the Mono and Nancy frameworks. Nancy is a lightweight framework, inspired by the Sinatra framework for Ruby. This example uses Ben Hall's Heroku custom buildpack (https://github.com/BenHall/ heroku-buildpack-mono) and example app (https://github.com/BenHall/nancy-demo- hosting-self). Ben originally posted this example on his blog, at blog.benhall.me.uk.

1. Clone Ben Hall's example app into a local directory:

```
$ mkdir dotnet-mono-nancy-example

$ git clone https://github.com/BenHall/nancy-demo-hosting-self.git
dotnet-mono-nancy-example/
Cloning into 'dotnet-mono-nancy-example'...
remote: Counting objects: 101, done.
```

```
remote: Compressing objects: 100% (46/46), done.
remote: Total 101 (delta 46), reused 97 (delta 42)
Receiving objects: 100% (101/101), 245.25 KiB, done.
Resolving deltas: 100% (46/46), done.

$ cd dotnet-mono-nancy-example/
```

2. In your app's directory, examine the main code in your sample app by opening `src/Program.cs` in your text editor:

```
namespace Nancy.Demo.Hosting.Self
{
    using System;
    using System.Diagnostics;

    using Nancy.Hosting.Self;

    class Program
    {
        static void Main()
        {
            var hostname = "deep-moon-1452";

            var port = System.Environment.GetEnvironmentVariable("PORT");
            var nancyHost = new NancyHost(new Uri("http://" + hostname +
                ".herokuapp.com:" + port), new Uri("http://0.0.0.0:" + port));
            nancyHost.Start();

            Console.WriteLine("Nancy now listening - navigating to http://" +
                hostname +".herokuapp.com:" + port +".");

            var line = Console.ReadLine();
            while(line != "quit") {
                line = Console.ReadLine();
            }
        }
    }
}
```

Here, you can see your main C# program logic. This simply binds to the hostname and port indicated. Although it is not a best practice to bind to a hostname, the Nancy framework requires it. Therefore, create a Heroku app so that you can update the default hostname:

```
$ heroku create --buildpack http://github.com/BenHall/heroku-buildpack-mono
dotnet-mono-nancy-example
Creating dotnet-mono-nancy-example... done, stack is cedar
BUILDPACK_URL=http://github.com/BenHall/heroku-buildpack-mono
http://dotnet-mono-nancy-example.herokuapp.com/ |
git@heroku.com:dotnet-mono-nancy-example.git
Git remote heroku added
```

Note that here is where you tell Heroku that you are using Ben Hall's custom buildpack to build this app.

3. Now that you have your app's hostname (in this case, `http://dotnet-mono-nancy-example.herokuapp.com`), you can alter the `src/Program.cs` file accordingly, replacing the line with `var hostname` to read as follows:

```
var hostname = System.Environment.GetEnvironmentVariable("HEROKU_APP_NAME");
```

You do this as a best practice so you can run your app in multiple environments — for instance, in QA and production environments, using config vars to indicate your hostname instead of a hardcoded string.

4. Commit the change and push the app to Heroku:

```
$ git commit -am "Initial commit"
[master bd178f4] Initial commit
 1 file changed, 1 insertion(+), 1 deletion(-)

$ git push heroku master
Counting objects: 105, done.
Delta compression using up to 4 threads.
Compressing objects: 100% (46/46), done.
Writing objects: 100% (105/105), 245.53 KiB | 85 KiB/s, done.
Total 105 (delta 49), reused 98 (delta 46)

-----> Heroku receiving push
-----> Fetching custom buildpack... cloning with git...done
-----> Mono app detected
-----> Fetching Mono binaries
...
-----> Vendoring mono 2.10.8
-----> building via /tmp/mono-VScH/bin/mono /tmp/mono-VScH/lib/mono/4.0/xbuild.exe
/tmp/build_25gvcjnhnkr7z/Nancy.Demo.Hosting.Self.sln
XBuild Engine Version 2.10.8.0
Mono, Version 2.10.8.0
Copyright (C) Marek Sieradzki 2005-2008, Novell 2008-2011.

Build started 09/03/2012 22:04:04.
_____
Project "/tmp/build_25gvcjnhnkr7z/Nancy.Demo.Hosting.Self.sln" (default target(s)):
...
Done building project "/tmp/build_25gvcjnhnkr7z/Nancy.Demo.Hosting.Self.sln".

Build succeeded.
        0 Warning(s)
        0 Error(s)

Time Elapsed 00:00:01.5914550
-----> Discovering process types
        Procfile declares types -> local, web
-----> Compiled slug size is 78.3MB
-----> Launching... done, v4
        http://dotnet-mono-nancy-example.herokuapp.com deployed to Heroku

To git@heroku.com:dotnet-mono-nancy-example.git
 * [new branch]      master -> master
```

First, Heroku fetches the custom buildpack, which contains the instructions needed to push the app. Once that is done, your custom buildpack is run, retrieving and building Mono. Mono is then used to compile your web app using `xbuild` (Mono's version of Microsoft's `msbuild` — similar to the `make` command for those in the Unix-based world). Lastly, your app is launched with the web and local processes defined in the app's `Procfile`.

5. Add your config var to indicate the app name — in this case, `"dotnet-mono-nancy-example"`:

```
$ heroku config:set HEROKU_APP_NAME="dotnet-mono-nancy-example"
Setting config vars and restarting dotnet-mono-nancy-example... done, v5
HEROKU_APP_NAME: dotnet-mono-nancy-example
```

6. Finally, test the app:

```
$ heroku open
Opening dotnet-mono-nancy-example... done
```

You should see a screen similar to Figure 14-1, showing your .NET app on the Nancy framework that you are running on Heroku using a custom buildpack.

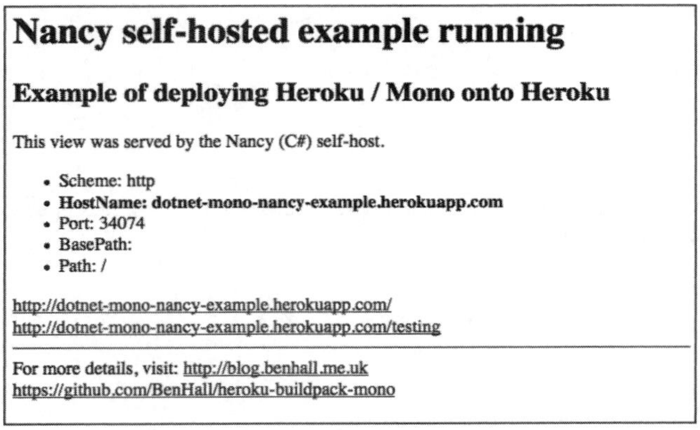

Nancy self-hosted example running

Example of deploying Heroku / Mono onto Heroku

This view was served by the Nancy (C#) self-host.

- Scheme: http
- HostName: **dotnet-mono-nancy-example.herokuapp.com**
- Port: 34074
- BasePath:
- Path: /

http://dotnet-mono-nancy-example.herokuapp.com/
http://dotnet-mono-nancy-example.herokuapp.com/testing

For more details, visit: http://blog.benhall.me.uk
https://github.com/BenHall/heroku-buildpack-mono

FIGURE 14-1

DEVELOPING PERL APPLICATIONS ON HEROKU

Created by Larry Wall in the late 1980s, Perl's roots are a combination of the best of C, AWK, sed, and shell scripting, and it was originally intended mostly for manipulating text. However, Perl has evolved into a flexible and versatile scripting language used for everything from web apps to systems programming. Its robust collection of modules also enables developers to easily add functionality to their apps. The popular Catalyst and Dancer frameworks have also made developing web apps with Perl easy and fast.

Often when we talk about PHP and Python, the Perl language is mentioned in the same breath. However, unlike PHP and Python, Perl does not have a supported Heroku buildpack. Luckily, active

Perl community developer Tatsuhiko Miyagawa has created one. Miyagawa's buildpack can run any Perl Web Server Gateway Interface (PSGI) web app and uses Starman, the efficient and high-performance Plack web server, to run Perl apps. You can use a `cpanfile`, a dependency manager that used the CPAN repository, or the more commonly used `Makefile.PL` and `Build.PL` files, to declare your app's dependencies. You will use the CPAN dependency manager in the example in this section.

You are going to create a Perl app on Heroku using a custom buildpack (code file: `ch14-perl-custom-buildpack-example.zip`). You will revisit the employee directory app that you have developed throughout this book using different languages. Follow these steps to develop your Perl app on Heroku:

1. Create a file called `app.psgi` with the following Perl code:

```perl
#!/usr/bin/perl

use DBI;

my $app = sub {

    # Connect to Heroku Postgres DB
    my($user, $password, $host, $port, $name) =
        $ENV{"DATABASE_URL"} =~ m/postgres:\/\/(.+?):(.+?)\@(.+?):(\d+?)\/(.*?)$/;
    my $dbh = DBI->connect("DBI:Pg:dbname=$name;host=$host", $user, $password,
        {'RaiseError' => 1});

    # Execute SELECT SQL query
    my $sth = $dbh->prepare("SELECT * FROM employees");
    $sth->execute();

    # Loop through result records
    while(my $ref = $sth->fetchrow_hashref()) {
        $result_string .= "<tr>";
        $result_string .= "<td>$ref->{'id'}</td>";
        $result_string .= "<td>$ref->{'name'}</td>";
        $result_string .= "<td>$ref->{'email'}</td>";
        $result_string .= "</tr>";
    }

    $dbh->disconnect();

    return [200, ['Content-Type' => 'text/html'], ["
        <head>
            <title>Employee List</title>
        </head>

        <body>
            <h1>Employee List</h1>

            <table>
                <tr>
                    <th>Employee ID</th>
                    <th>Name</th>
                    <th>E-mail Address</th>
```

```
            </tr>
    " . $result_string . "
            </table>
         </body>
     </html>"]];
}
```

The block of code below the `Connect to Heroku Postgres DB` comment will parse your `DATABASE_URL` config var with a regular expression to pull out the elements that your Perl Database Interface (DBI) driver needs to connect to a Postgres database. You do your database query in the block of code below the `Execute SELECT SQL query` comment. The block of code preceding the `Loop through result records` comment does just that: loops through each result row and prepares your output for them. You clean up and close your DB connection with `dbh->disconnect()`. Finally, you produce the output: the header and footer with your result string sandwiched in the middle.

2. To declare the dependencies for your app, you will create a `cpanfile`, which is also a Miyagawa creation (see `https://github.com/miyagawa/cpanfile`):

```
requires 'DBI',      '1.622';
requires 'DBD::Pg', '2.19.3';
```

You only need to declare dependencies for accessing the database — in this case, `DBI` and `DBD::Pg`. `DBI` is Perl's standard database access interface, similar to ActiveRecord in Ruby. `DBD::Pg` is the Postgres-specific database driver.

3. Initialize your repository and create your Heroku app:

```
$ git init
Initialized empty Git repository in /Users/ckemp/Documents/Sites/test-perl/.git/

$ heroku create --buildpack http://github.com/miyagawa/heroku-buildpack-perl.git
perl-buildpack-example
Creating perl-buildpack-example... done, stack is cedar
BUILDPACK_URL=http://github.com/miyagawa/heroku-buildpack-perl.git
http://perl-buildpack-example.herokuapp.com/ | git@heroku.com:perl-buildpack-
example.git
Git remote heroku added
```

Much like in the .NET app you created, you simply specify the buildpack you want to use when creating your app. In this case, you use Miyagawa's Perl buildpack for the app and point Heroku to the Git repository for it.

4. Push your Perl app to Heroku:

```
$ git add .

$ git commit -am "Initial commit"
[master (root-commit) 13007a1] Initial commit
 2 files changed, 49 insertions(+)
 create mode 100644 app.psgi
 create mode 100644 cpanfile

$ git push heroku master
```

```
Counting objects: 4, done.
Delta compression using up to 4 threads.
Compressing objects: 100% (4/4), done.
Writing objects: 100% (4/4), 856 bytes, done.
Total 4 (delta 0), reused 0 (delta 0)

-----> Heroku receiving push
-----> Fetching custom buildpack... cloning with git...done
-----> Perl/PSGI app detected
-----> Bootstrapping cpanm
       Successfully installed JSON-PP-2.27200
       Successfully installed CPAN-Meta-YAML-0.008
...
       Successfully installed App-cpanminus-1.5017
       12 distributions installed
-----> Installing dependencies
       Successfully installed DBI-1.622
       Successfully installed DBD-Pg-2.19.3
       2 distributions installed
-----> Installing Starman
       Successfully installed ExtUtils-MakeMaker-6.62 (upgraded from 6.55_02)
       Successfully installed Test-Requires-0.06
...
       Successfully installed Starman-0.3001
       38 distributions installed
-----> Discovering process types
       Procfile declares types -> (none)
       Default types for Perl/PSGI -> web
-----> Compiled slug size is 3.4MB
-----> Launching... done, v4
       http://perl-buildpack-example.herokuapp.com deployed to Heroku

To git@heroku.com:perl-buildpack-example.git
 * [new branch]      master -> master
```

Here you can see that after fetching your custom buildpack, you first detect your PSGI-compliant Perl app by looking for an app.psgi in the root directory. Next, you retrieve and install your dependency manager, cpanm. Once this is installed, cpanfile is read, and then you fetch and install the dependencies for your app. Next, you download and build the Starman web server, and a default web process is added and launched. The default process uses the following command:

```
web: perl -Mlib=./local/lib/perl5 ./local/bin/starman --preload-app --port \$PORT
```

5. Add your Heroku Postgres database, creating your table and filling it with some test data:

```
$ heroku addons:add heroku-postgresql:dev
Adding heroku-postgresql:dev on perl-buildpack-example... done, v5 (free)
Attached as HEROKU_POSTGRESQL_JADE
Database has been created and is available
Use 'heroku addons:docs heroku-postgresql:dev' to view documentation.

$ heroku pg:promote HEROKU_POSTGRESQL_JADE_URL
```

```
Promoting HEROKU_POSTGRESQL_JADE to DATABASE_URL... done

$ heroku pg:psql
psql (9.1.4, server 9.1.5)
SSL connection (cipher: DHE-RSA-AES256-SHA, bits: 256)
Type "help" for help.

mYd4T4b453N4m3=> create table employees (
mYd4T4b453N4m3(>    id    bigint,
mYd4T4b453N4m3(>    name  varchar(100),
mYd4T4b453N4m3(>    email varchar(255)
mYd4T4b453N4m3(> );
CREATE TABLE
mYd4T4b453N4m3=>
mYd4T4b453N4m3=> INSERT INTO employees (id, name, email) VALUES
mYd4T4b453N4m3->    ('5634', 'Justin Sit', 'jsit@vandelayenterprises.com'),
mYd4T4b453N4m3->    ('8086', 'Mike Brosseau', 'mbrosseau@vandelayenterprises.com'),
mYd4T4b453N4m3->    ('1007', 'David Majetic', 'dmajetic@vandelayenterprises.com');
INSERT 0 3
mYd4T4b453N4m3=> \q
```

6. Test the app:

    ```
    $ heroku open
    Opening perl-buildpack-example... done
    ```

As shown in Figure 14-2, the Perl app is now
successfully running on Heroku, built and
deployed with a custom buildpack.

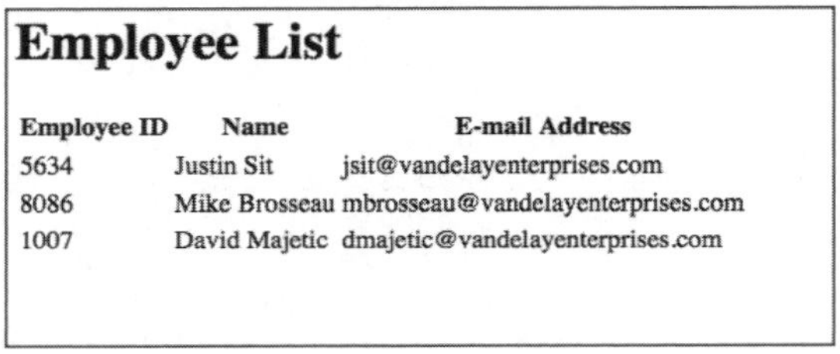

Employee List

Employee ID	Name	E-mail Address
5634	Justin Sit	jsit@vandelayenterprises.com
8086	Mike Brosseau	mbrosseau@vandelayenterprises.com
1007	David Majetic	dmajetic@vandelayenterprises.com

FIGURE 14-2

PACKAGING BINARY BUILDPACK DEPENDENCIES

Custom buildpacks can be used not only to support running apps in new languages on Heroku, but
also to add binary dependencies to your app. We have stated previously that in terms of dependency
management best practices, you should not rely on dependencies to the app's code not explicitly
defined in your dependency manager (such as shelling out to run cURL.) However, if you do not
have the capability to add this as a dependency by including the source code as a library in your app
(for instance, through a dependency manager), you can package binary assets that have been pre-
compiled on Heroku's servers with your app.

This section looks at an example demonstrating how to include the binary package dependencies
with your buildpack. This could include other programs, such as cURL, on which your app relies.
Most of the time, however, you will simply build any binaries you need with your app, including the
run time, build manager, and dependency manager, in the same way.

1. Install the Vulcan build server gem locally, which you will use to create your binaries in the
    cloud:

    ```
    $ sudo gem install vulcan
    Password:
     !     Heroku recommends using the Heroku Toolbelt to install the CLI.
     !     Download it from: https://toolbelt.heroku.com
    ```

```
Please run 'vulcan update' to update your build server.
Successfully installed excon-0.16.2
Successfully installed heroku-api-0.3.4
Successfully installed netrc-0.7.7
...
12 gems installed
Installing ri documentation for excon-0.16.2...
Installing ri documentation for heroku-api-0.3.4...
...
```

2. Create your Vulcan build server:

```
$ mkdir vulcan-curl

$ cd vulcan-curl/

$ vulcan create vulcan-kemp
Creating vulcan-kemp... done, stack is cedar
http://vulcan-kemp.herokuapp.com/ | git@heroku.com:vulcan-kemp.git
Initialized empty Git repository in /private/var/folders/sx/
0lvgjtds1qn6k3cx8j78clcc0000gn/T/d20120911-10072-2s65xm/.git/
Counting objects: 883, done.
Delta compression using up to 4 threads.
Compressing objects: 100% (803/803), done.
Writing objects: 100% (883/883), 1014.76 KiB | 30 KiB/s, done.
Total 883 (delta 81), reused 0 (delta 0)

-----> Heroku receiving push
-----> Node.js app detected
-----> Resolving engine versions
       Using Node.js version: 0.6.20
       Using npm version: 1.1.4
-----> Fetching Node.js binaries
-----> Vendoring node into slug
-----> Installing dependencies with npm
...
       Dependencies installed
-----> Building runtime environment
-----> Discovering process types
       Procfile declares types -> web
-----> Compiled slug size is 4.1MB
-----> Launching... done, v3
       http://vulcan-kemp.herokuapp.com deployed to Heroku

To git@heroku.com:vulcan-kemp.git
 * [new branch]      master -> master
```

In the preceding code, Vulcan actually creates a Node.js app that you will use as your build server. Creating a Vulcan server also creates a hidden file on your local computer that contains the information needed for the tool to do future builds:

```
$ cat ~/.vulcan
---
:host: vulcan-kemp.herokuapp.com
:app: vulcan-kemp
:secret: mY53cR3tP455pHr453
```

This specifies your host, the app name, and a secret key that is used when you access your build server. This is stored locally because you don't need to create a new build server for every build you do; you only need to create one, which you can use for each subsequent build.

If you need to update your build server later (for instance, if you run `gem update vulcan`), you can do so using the `vulcan update` command:

```
$ vulcan update
Initialized empty Git repository in /private/var/folders/sx/
0lvgjtds1qn6k3cx8j78c1cc0000gn/T/d20120912-11228-qsle9r/.git/
Counting objects: 883, done.
Delta compression using up to 4 threads.
Compressing objects: 100% (803/803), done.
Writing objects: 100% (883/883), 1014.76 KiB | 28 KiB/s, done.
Total 883 (delta 81), reused 0 (delta 0)

-----> Heroku receiving push
-----> Node.js app detected
...
-----> Building runtime environment
-----> Discovering process types
       Procfile declares types -> web
-----> Compiled slug size is 4.1MB
-----> Launching... done, v6
       http://vulcan-kemp.herokuapp.com deployed to Heroku

To git@heroku.com:vulcan-kemp.git
 + 4848b8e...f143417 master -> master (forced update)
```

3. Get the cURL source code and uncompress it:

```
$ curl -O http://curl.haxx.se/download/curl-7.27.0.tar.gz
  % Total    % Received % Xferd  Average Speed   Time    Time     Time  Current
                                 Dload  Upload   Total   Spent    Left  Speed
100 3080k  100 3080k    0     0   255k      0  0:00:12 0:00:12 --:--:--  439k

$ tar zxvf curl-7.27.0.tar.gz
x curl-7.27.0/
x curl-7.27.0/config.guess
x curl-7.27.0/mkinstalldirs
x curl-7.27.0/Makefile.am
x curl-7.27.0/Android.mk
x curl-7.27.0/config.sub
x curl-7.27.0/COPYING
x curl-7.27.0/configure.ac
x curl-7.27.0/missing
x curl-7.27.0/Makefile.msvc.names
x curl-7.27.0/Makefile
...
```

4. Run the following commands to build your app's binaries on the Vulcan server:

```
$ cd curl-7.27.0

$ vulcan build
Packaging local directory... done
Uploading source package... >> Downloading build artifacts to: /tmp/curl-7.27.tgz
    (available at http://vulcan-kemp.herokuapp.com/output/47e1d1b3-3edf-4104-8209-
6793a5968b71)

$ tar tf /tmp/curl-7.27.tgz
bin/
bin/curl
bin/curl-config
include/
include/curl/
include/curl/typecheck-gcc.h
include/curl/easy.h
...
```

Here you can see that your source code in the current working directory is uploaded to the Vulcan build server, the code is compiled, and Vulcan returns the resulting tar with the binaries output to /tmp/curl-7.27.tgz. Vulcan's default command to compile your program is the typical configure then make install. You can override this behaviour with your own custom command using the -c flag.

5. Now that your assets are compiled, you must put the resulting tarball in an accessible location on the web, typically Amazon Simple Storage Service (Amazon S3) or something similar. When doing the build in your custom buildpack, you must fetch and uncompress these assets to an appropriate location. As a convention, the vendor subdirectory in your build directory is a good place to put these files.

6. Create a bin/compile file with the following code:

```
echo "-----> Vendoring cURL binary"
mkdir -p $CACHE_DIR/curl-7.27
cd $CACHE_DIR/curl-7.27

curl -s -O -m 120 http://professional-heroku-programming.s3.amazonaws.com/curl-7.27.tgz
tar zxf curl-7.27.tgz
rm -f curl-7.27.tgz

cp $CACHE_DIR/curl-7.27
mkdir -p $BUILD_DIR/curl-7.27
cp $CACHE_DIR/curl-7.27/curl $BUILD_DIR/vendor/curl-7.27
```

Having created a directory for the download of your binaries, you then use the curl command to get the cURL binary from where you uploaded it in Amazon S3 (ironic, isn't it?). You then unpack it and copy the binary to the vendor subdirectory in your build directory.

7. In bin/compile, set the PATH environment variable to point to this directory with the following lines to ensure it is available on the command line:

```
PATH=$BUILD_DIR/curl-7.27:$PATH
```

That completes the steps to create a binary dependency for your app. This example provided a high-level look at how you can use a custom buildpack to include such binary dependencies in your app. In the next section, you'll take a closer look at the full process of creating a custom buildpack.

CREATING CUSTOM BUILDPACKS

One of Heroku's greatest strengths is its ability to use buildpacks to run nearly any language or framework you want, as long as it will run on Ubuntu 10.04. This not only enables you to create buildpacks for esoteric or obscure languages for which no official buildpack is available, but also provides complete flexibility to customize the runtime environment for apps you develop. For instance, if you want particular versions of the stack for your app to run on, perhaps experimental versions not supported by existing buildpacks, you can customize your own buildpack to do this.

When I was young, my Uncle Ron gave me my first computer, a Tandy TRS-80. Unlike modern computers that have operating systems and graphical user interfaces, users were greeted with a BASIC prompt where they could start writing programs or load one from the tape drive (yes, for the younger folk, you read that correctly). Like many other developers, the first programming language that I learned and wrote programs on was BASIC.

In this section's example, you will make a program written in BASIC run on Heroku by creating a custom buildpack. First, you will build the runtime binaries on Vulcan. Then, you will create the scripts for your custom buildpack. Finally, you will create a BASIC app that will be deployed to Heroku with your custom buildpack.

Building the Blassic Binary on Vulcan

You first need to create the binary for your BASIC run time. You do this in a similar fashion to creating your external binary in the previous section, using the following steps. Basically, you need to get your BASIC interpreter compiled on your build server so that you can vendor it in using your buildpack.

1. Download your run time, the open-source Blassic BASIC interpreter:

```
$ curl -O ftp://62.93.32.21/pub/gentoo/source/distfiles/blassic-0.10.2.tgz
  % Total    % Received % Xferd  Average Speed   Time    Time     Time  Current
                                 Dload  Upload   Total   Spent    Left  Speed
100  353k  100  353k    0     0  81279      0  0:00:04 0:00:04 --:--:-- 87491

$ tar zxvf blassic-0.10.2.tgz
x blassic-0.10.2/
x blassic-0.10.2/README
x blassic-0.10.2/acinclude.m4
x blassic-0.10.2/configure.ac
x blassic-0.10.2/aclocal.m4
x blassic-0.10.2/Makefile.am
x blassic-0.10.2/Makefile.in
x blassic-0.10.2/blassic.spec.in
x blassic-0.10.2/configure
...
```

2. Build the Blassic binary on Heroku to ensure that this run time will work with your buildpack:

```
$ cd blassic-0.10.2

$ vulcan build -v
Packaging local directory... done
Uploading source package... done
Building with: ./configure --prefix /app/vendor/blassic-0.10 && make install
checking build system type... x86_64-unknown-linux-gnu
checking host system type... x86_64-unknown-linux-gnu
checking for version number in ./version.cpp... got 0.10.2
...
configure: creating ./config.status
config.status: creating Makefile
config.status: creating blassic.spec
config.status: executing depfiles commands
g++ -g -O2  \
        -o gencharset \
        gencharset.cpp
make  install-am
make[1]: Entering directory '/tmp/d20120912-2-12y9u9e/input'
...
g++  -g -O2  -o blassic  blassic-charset_default.o blassic-charset_cpc.o blassic-
charset_spectrum.o blassic-charset_msx.o blassic-blassic.o blassic-codeline.o
blassic-cursor.o blassic-dim.o blassic-directory.o blassic-dynamic.o blassic-edit.o
blassic-element.o blassic-error.o blassic-file.o blassic-fileconsole.o
blassic-filepopen.o blassic-fileprinter.o blassic-filesocket.o blassic-filewindow.o
blassic-function.o blassic-graphics.o blassic-key.o blassic-keyword.o blassic-mbf.o
blassic-memory.o blassic-program.o blassic-regexp.o blassic-runner.o
blassic-runnerline.o blassic-runnerline_impl.o blassic-runnerline_instructions.o
blassic-runnerline_print.o blassic-showerror.o blassic-socket.o blassic-sysvar.o
blassic-token.o blassic-trace.o blassic-using.o blassic-var.o blassic-version.o
-lSM -lICE -lX11  -lncurses -ldl
make[2]: Entering directory '/tmp/d20120912-2-12y9u9e/input'
test -z "/app/vendor/blassic-0.10/bin" || mkdir -p -- "/app/vendor/blassic-0.10/bin"
  /usr/bin/install -c 'blassic' '/app/vendor/blassic-0.10/bin/blassic'
test -z "/app/vendor/blassic-0.10/share/blassic/examples" || mkdir -p
-- "/app/vendor/blassic-0.10/share/blassic/examples"
 /usr/bin/install -c -m 644 '4raya.bas'
'/app/vendor/blassic-0.10/share/blassic/examples/4raya.bas'
 /usr/bin/install -c -m 644 'allkeywords.blc'
'/app/vendor/blassic-0.10/share/blassic/examples/allkeywords.blc'
 /usr/bin/install -c -m 644 'anime.bas'
'/app/vendor/blassic-0.10/share/blassic/examples/anime.bas'
...
make[2]: Leaving directory '/tmp/d20120912-2-12y9u9e/input'
make[1]: Leaving directory '/tmp/d20120912-2-12y9u9e/input'
>> Downloading build artifacts to: /tmp/blassic-0.10.tgz
   (available at http://vulcan-kemp.herokuapp.com/output/431c7687-acc5-4efe-95cf-
ed91df0ef714)
```

Note that you didn't have to create another build server because you already have one. Recall that you need only a single build server, not one per app. In the preceding code, your local directory is bundled and uploaded to your build server. You then start the build process, using the standard commands `configure` and `make install`. Different commands are also acceptable, such as something like `vulcan build -v -c ./setup.sh` if your run time requires you to run the `setup.sh` script instead of using `make`. This example uses the `-v` flag to provide verbose output, so you know exactly what's going on.

You can also use the `-n` flag to name the library something other than the name of the current directory (in this case, `blassic-0.10`) After the build is done, Vulcan typically looks in the `/app/vendor/<name>` directory on your build server to find the compiled artifacts for your run time to return. If you want to use a different directory, the `-p` flag can be added to specify another location. Typically, the output of the build is sent to `/tmp/<name>.tgz`, but you can use the `-o` flag to output this file to another location to which Vulcan has permission to write. The `-d` flag defines any dependencies that should be added during the default `make` command, if other dependent libraries are needed to compile your program.

3. Examine the resulting tarball containing your binaries, which have been compiled on the Heroku build server, to ensure that the Vulcan has built your binaries:

```
$ tar tf /tmp/blassic-0.10.tgz
bin/
bin/blassic
share/
share/blassic/
share/blassic/examples/
share/blassic/examples/graph.bas
share/blassic/examples/deepsea.bas
...
```

As you can see, your BASIC run time is available in `bin/blassic` inside your compressed file.

4. Put this somewhere publicly accessible so that when your buildpack is used, it can download this file for use. Upload your file to Amazon S3 by going to `http://aws.amazon.com/account/`. Select My Account ⇨ Console from the menu, and then select the AWS Management Console from the drop-down menu. After signing in, select Amazon S3 from the list of services. You can create a new bucket or use an existing one. Then upload your file into a bucket — in this case, the `/tmp/blassic-0.10.tgz` file that your build server output (see Figure 14-3).

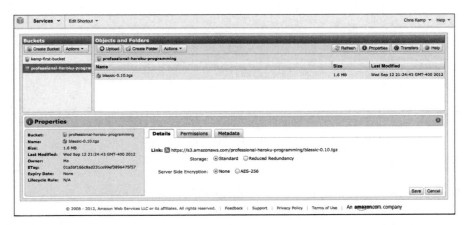

FIGURE 14-3

You also must ensure that this file is publicly available by clicking on the file and selecting Actions ⇨ Make Public. This is very important; otherwise, your buildpack will not be able to access it. Now that your binaries are built and in a place that is accessible to your buildpack, the next step is to create the buildpack itself.

> **NOTE** *Though the example uses Amazon S3, you can store the file wherever you like, as long as it is publicly available in a place where your buildpack can access it.*

Creating the Build Scripts

Now that you have built the Blassic binary needed to run your app, you have to write the three scripts required for running your buildpack: `bin/detect`, `bin/compile`, and `bin/release` (code file: ch14-heroku-buildpack-basic.zip).

1. Create the `bin/detect` file and add the following code:

```sh
#!/bin/sh

# this pack is valid for apps with app.bas in the root
if [ -f $1/app.bas ]; then
    echo "BASIC"
    exit 0
else
    exit 1
fi
```

This script will verify that any BASIC app that is using this buildpack to run has the `app.bas` file in the root directory.

2. Create the file `bin/compile`, adding the following code:

```sh
#!/bin/sh
# usage: bin/compile <build-dir> <cache-dir>

set -e

indent() {
    sed -u 's/^/       /'
}

BUILD_DIR=$1
CACHE_DIR=$2

VERSION=0.10
FILE_NAME=blassic-$VERSION.tgz
DOWNLOAD_URL=http://professional-heroku-programming.s3.amazonaws.com/$FILE_NAME

echo "-----> Using Blassic version $VERSION"
```

```
(
    set -e

    # Check if Blassic is already cached
    test -d $CACHE_DIR/blassic-$VERSION/bin && exit

    mkdir -p $CACHE_DIR/blassic-$VERSION
    cd $CACHE_DIR/blassic-$VERSION

    echo "-----> Fetching Blassic binaries"
    curl -s -O -m 120 $DOWNLOAD_URL | indent
    tar zxf $FILE_NAME
    rm -f $FILE_NAME
)

# create default Procfile
if [ ! -r $BUILD_DIR/Procfile ]; then
    echo " No Procfile found; defaulting to \"web: ./blassic app.bas\"."
    echo "web: ./blassic app.bas" > $BUILD_DIR/Procfile
fi

# make runtime available
cp $CACHE_DIR/blassic-$VERSION/bin/blassic $BUILD_DIR

# clean the cache
rm -rf $CACHE_DIR/*
```

The `indent()` function is used by convention to ensure that any output for your program is indented so that it lines up with the headings denoted by "----->" to highlight where error messages and output belong. The two variables that are passed into the `bin/compile` script, `BUILD_DIR` and `CACHE_DIR`, are loaded into more human-readable variables.

You then set variables, `VERSION`, `FILE_NAME`, and `DOWNLOAD_URL`, for your script. This is not required, as you can simply hardcode these where you need them, but doing so makes it easier to upgrade your buildpack with subsequent releases of your run time — for instance, to simply change the version number in one place instead of hunting for it in your script and changing it multiple times. The `DOWNLOAD_URL` variable points to the Blassic binary you created with Vulcan and uploaded to Amazon S3.

The first `echo` command is used as a best practice to indicate in your output which version of the run time is being used. This should be done for any apps that you are using, including dependency managers and other programs you rely upon. The `test -d` command checks whether a version of the runtime binary is already available in the cache directory, as this directory will be cached across builds.

If the runtime binary is not found, the directory for it is created with `mkdir`. The `curl` command is used to get the runtime binaries that you created with your build server. Notice that you pipe your output to the `indent()` function. Though cURL is in silent mode, it is a best practice to do this for any program that might provide error output that would be useful to debug what went wrong with your buildpack. Other commands, such as `cd` and `mkdir`, are less likely to produce errors, so you don't need to use `indent()` with them.

The block of code under the `create default Procfile` comment checks for a `Procfile` defined by the user in the root directory. If one is not found, you create a default `Procfile` defining your default processes. This block of code is unnecessary in this context because you will define a default process in `bin/release`. This simply demonstrates that if no web processes are defined there, or complex logic is needed to define the `Procfile`, it can be done in `bin/compile` as part of the app's build process instead.

The `cp` command copies the `bin/blassic` binary file used as your run time into your build directory. This ensures that it is packaged with the slug you create when you push the app. Oftentimes, this is also put in a subdirectory of the build directory, especially if more than one file needs to be used for your run time. It is a good idea to add this directory to the `PATH` environment variable, such as in this example where your binaries are in the `bin` subdirectory of the build directory:

```
PATH=${BUILD_DIR}/bin:$PATH
```

Finally, the `rm` command at the end of the script cleans up the `cache` directory to ensure that you don't clutter it up between builds. It is important to ensure that this directory isn't filled up, as it is stored with the Git repository and needs to be downloaded each time an app using this buildpack is deployed. If your app's deploys are taking a very long time, it may be because this directory isn't being cleaned up properly between builds and the resulting clutter is being packaged and transferred in your slug, slowing down the process as a result.

3. Create the `bin/release` file, adding this code:

```
#!/bin/sh

BUILD_DIR=$1

cat << EOF
---
addons:
config_vars:
      PATH: local/bin:/usr/local/bin:/usr/bin:/bin
default_process_types:
      web: ./blassic app.bas
EOF
```

The preceding shows a fairly simple example of a `bin/release` file. You do not need any add-ons for your program to work, so you leave that configuration section empty after `addons`. In the `config_vars` section, you set the default `PATH` for your dynos. The `default_process_types` section defines your default processes, which in this case simply run the `app.bas` file that you looked for in `bin/detect` with the Blassic interpreter binary that you built in `bin/compile`.

Pushing Your Buildpack to a Public Git Repository

Now that you have created your binaries and buildpack scripts, you need to make your buildpack available for Heroku to use to push apps by putting in a Git repository. In this case, you will add this to a public Git repository, as you want to enable others to use your great BASIC buildpack.

1. Go to Github's website (`https://github.com/`) and log in.

2. Click the Create a New Repo button at the top of the screen.

3. Create a unique repository name — in this case, "heroku-buildpack-basic."

   You can optionally add a description and specify whether you want this repository to be publicly available. (Private Github accounts require a subscription.)

   > **NOTE** *By convention, the repository is called* `heroku-buildpack-<name>`, *where* `<name>` *is the name of the language or specific framework for which the buildpack is used to deploy apps.*

4. Click the Create Repository button to make the new repository for your custom buildpack (see Figure 14-4).

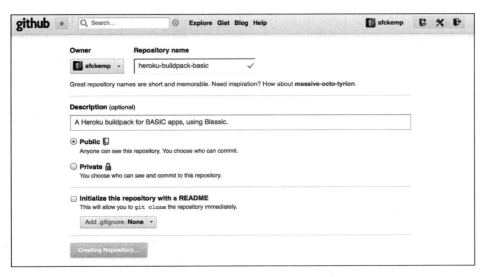

FIGURE 14-4

5. Push your buildpack to Github:

```
$ touch README.md

$ git init
Initialized empty Git repository in /Users/ckemp/Documents/Sites/heroku-buildpack-basic/
.git/

$ git add .

$ git commit -m "Initial commit"
[master (root-commit) 907936f] Initial commit
 3 files changed, 58 insertions(+)
 create mode 100644 README.md
 create mode 100755 bin/compile
 create mode 100755 bin/detect
 create mode 100755 bin/release

$ git remote add origin git@github.com:sfckemp/heroku-buildpack-basic.git

$ git push -u origin master
Counting objects: 7, done.
Delta compression using up to 4 threads.
Compressing objects: 100% (6/6), done.
Writing objects: 100% (7/7), 1.00 KiB, done.
Total 7 (delta 0), reused 0 (delta 0)
To git@github.com:sfckemp/heroku-buildpack-basic.git
 * [new branch]      master -> master
Branch master set up to track remote branch master from origin.
```

Here you have created a blank README.md (required for pushing to Github), which you can later edit to add instructions on using your buildpack. You then initialize, commit, and push your code to Github in a somewhat similar manner to the way you push code to Heroku, without the additional steps to actually do the build.

Creating and Deploying Your Application to Heroku

Your custom buildpack is now built and available in a public Git repository. The next step is to create a BASIC program to test the buildpack you created. Once you have created your BASIC app, you will push it to Heroku using your custom buildpack.

1. Complying with the requirement in your buildpack, you will create an app called app.bas that contains the code for your program (code file: app.bas):

```
rem app.bas

print "This is my first BASIC program running on Heroku.  Watch me count!"; chr$(10);

for i = 1 to 10
        print "Counting "; i; chr$(10);
next

print "Phew! That was tiring. I am done counting now."; chr$(10);
```

This simple program just counts to ten, using BASIC. Note that you only display a message with the first and last `print` commands. You include `chr$(10)` at the end of each line because this is the ASCII code for line breaks in UNIX-based systems. You iterate through a `for` loop, incrementing the `i` variable on each iteration and outputting the value.

> **NOTE** *Most programs for which no web server is packaged with the binaries and launched as part of the web process listen on the port defined by the* `$PORT` *variable. For simplicity's sake, this example just outputs some text to the logs, making your buildpack of limited usefulness for writing web-based apps. However, if you find a web server written in BASIC (they are out there, though it is surely not an easy task to write one!), you could write BASIC web apps on Heroku.*

2. Push the BASIC app you have created to Heroku using the custom buildpack you created:

```
$ git init
Initialized empty Git repository in /Users/ckemp/Documents/Sites/basic-example/.git/

$ heroku create basic-example --buildpack https://github.com/sfckemp/heroku-buildpack-basic
Creating basic-example... done, stack is cedar
BUILDPACK_URL=https://github.com/sfckemp/heroku-buildpack-basic
http://basic-example.herokuapp.com/ | git@heroku.com:basic-example.git
Git remote heroku added

$ git add .

$ git commit -am "Initial commit"
[master (root-commit) cd264e8] Initial commit
 1 file changed, 9 insertions(+)
 create mode 100644 app.bas

$ git push heroku master
Counting objects: 18, done.
Delta compression using up to 4 threads.
Compressing objects: 100% (12/12), done.
Writing objects: 100% (18/18), 1.46 KiB, done.
Total 18 (delta 5), reused 0 (delta 0)

-----> Heroku receiving push
-----> Fetching custom buildpack... cloning with git...done
-----> BASIC app detected
-----> Using Blassic version 0.10
-----> Fetching Blassic binaries
-----> Discovering process types
       Procfile declares types -> (none)
       Default types for BASIC -> web
-----> Compiled slug size is 1.6MB
```

```
-----> Launching... done, v4
       http://basic-example.herokuapp.com deployed to Heroku

To git@heroku.com:basic-example.git
 * [new branch]        master -> master
```

Much like the earlier custom buildpacks you used, when you run `heroku create`, you point it to your custom buildpack's Git repository on Github. When you push to Heroku, it successfully fetches the custom buildpack. When `bin/detect` is run, your `app.bas` file is found and a success message is returned. The output from `bin/compile` tells you that the Blassic binaries have been fetched and installed. You then launch the web process that is defined in `bin/release`.

3. Examine the logs to see the output of your program:

```
$ heroku logs
2012-09-15T15:54:48+00:00 heroku[slugc]: Slug compilation started
2012-09-15T15:54:52+00:00 heroku[api]: Add PATH config by ckemp@salesforce.com
2012-09-15T15:54:52+00:00 heroku[api]: Release v3 created by ckemp@salesforce.com
2012-09-15T15:54:52+00:00 heroku[api]: Deploy cdb576b by ckemp@salesforce.com
2012-09-15T15:54:52+00:00 heroku[api]: Release v4 created by ckemp@salesforce.com
2012-09-15T15:54:53+00:00 heroku[slugc]: Slug compilation finished
2012-09-15T15:54:56+00:00 heroku[web.1]: Starting process with command
'./blassic app.bas'
2012-09-15T15:54:56+00:00 app[web.1]: This is my first BASIC program running on Heroku.
Watch me count!
2012-09-15T15:54:56+00:00 app[web.1]: Counting 1
2012-09-15T15:54:56+00:00 app[web.1]: Counting 2
2012-09-15T15:54:56+00:00 app[web.1]: Counting 3
2012-09-15T15:54:56+00:00 app[web.1]: Counting 4
2012-09-15T15:54:56+00:00 app[web.1]: Counting 5
2012-09-15T15:54:56+00:00 app[web.1]: Counting 6
2012-09-15T15:54:56+00:00 app[web.1]: Counting 7
2012-09-15T15:54:56+00:00 app[web.1]: Counting 8
2012-09-15T15:54:56+00:00 app[web.1]: Counting 9
2012-09-15T15:54:56+00:00 app[web.1]: Counting 10
2012-09-15T15:54:56+00:00 app[web.1]: Phew! That was tiring. I am done counting now.
2012-09-15T15:54:57+00:00 heroku[web.1]: Process exited with status 0
2012-09-15T15:54:57+00:00 heroku[web.1]: State changed from starting to crashed
2012-09-15T15:54:57+00:00 heroku[web.1]: State changed from crashed to starting
2012-09-15T15:54:59+00:00 heroku[web.1]: Starting process with command
'./blassic app.bas'
...
```

This shows your release and slug compilation, along with the output of your BASIC program. You can also see that Heroku thinks that your app has crashed after it finishes and exits. It really hasn't crashed, but Heroku expects that any process running on it will stay running (such as a web server), so Heroku tries to restart the process as part of its erosion resistance feature.

4. Examine your app's `config vars` to see which ones have been created for you automatically:

```
$ heroku config
=== basic-example Config Vars
BUILDPACK_URL: https://github.com/sfckemp/heroku-buildpack-basic
PATH:          local/bin:/usr/local/bin:/usr/bin:/bin
```

Your `BUILDPACK_URL` is added as part of Heroku's process of using a custom buildpack to deploy an app. The `PATH` variable shown here is the one that you defined earlier in `bin/release`.

That completes the example demonstrating how to create a custom buildpack from scratch and then use it to deploy a sample app.

> **NOTE** *If you create your own custom buildpack (in a more useful language than our example, hopefully) and want to share it with the world, have it listed on Heroku's Custom Buildpack page at* `https://devcenter.heroku.com/articles/third-party-buildpacks` *by notifying Heroku at* `buildpacks@heroku.com`.

SUMMARY

In this chapter, we first explained how custom buildpacks work by examining the purpose and structure of the three required files: `bin/detect`, `bin/compile`, and `bin/release`. .NET web apps that use the Mono framework to run on Linux can be deployed to Heroku using a custom buildpack. The popular and useful language Perl can be used to write Heroku apps, also using a custom buildpack to deploy. Sometimes, apps you deploy to Heroku rely on a binary app that cannot be included as a dependency. Custom buildpacks can include binary files that your app requires, by compiling them on Vulcan, Heroku's build server.

You can create your own custom buildpacks to deploy pretty much any app to Heroku that will run on Ubuntu 10.04, Heroku's operating system of choice. To create a custom buildpack, you must first build the runtime binaries on the Vulcan build server and make them publicly available for the custom buildpack to download. You must then create the buildpack scripts and upload them to a public Git repository. After these preliminary steps are complete, you can deploy apps to Heroku using your custom buildpack.

In the next chapter, we will explore how Heroku can be used to create highly scalable mobile apps, either using an HTML5 front end or as a back end for mobile apps.

PART V
Creating a New Generation of Heroku Applications

15

Building Mobile Applications with Heroku

WHAT'S IN THIS CHAPTER?

➤ Understanding mobile development architectures

➤ Writing an HTML5 mobile application

➤ Using toolkits and add-ons for mobile application development

WROX.COM CODE DOWNLOADS FOR THIS CHAPTER

The wrox.com code downloads for this chapter are found at `www.wrox.com/remtitle .cgi?isbn=1118508998` on the Download Code tab. The code is in the Chapter 15 download and individually named according to the names throughout the chapter.

In previous chapters, you saw examples demonstrating how to write programs in pretty much any language or framework under the sun that will run on a Linux system, and how to deploy them to Heroku. However, we haven't talked about the different types of apps you can deploy with Heroku. In the decade following the year 2000, smartphones started to become ubiquitous. Later that decade, with the release of Apple's iPad, tablet computers became all the rage. These changes represented a paradigm shift in the way both consumers and businesses access applications. The traditional desktop or laptop method of delivering apps waned as users increasingly demanded that apps be accessible anywhere and on any device.

Traditionally, many consumers would have both a personal mobile phone and a work phone, often a BlackBerry or similar device. When Apple's iPhone came along, consumers no longer wanted to carry two devices that served the same purpose, and the era of "bring your own device" was ushered into the corporate world. This presented significant headaches for IT departments in managing these devices within their security and compliance frameworks. It also changed the way enterprise apps were delivered. The old model of installing software on a computer made way for a new generation of mobile-optimized apps that enabled easy use of the device's built-in peripherals (camera, GPS, etc.) and easy access to information for those in the field.

This chapter discusses how mobile apps can be made to leverage the Heroku platform. First you will get an overview of the architectural decisions that have to be made when considering how to deliver mobile apps, and you will get a crash course in common architectures for mobile development. After looking at how Heroku fits in, you will create an HTML5 mobile app using a Heroku back end. Finally, you will look at some popular add-ons for Heroku and learn how to leverage them to make mobile development on Heroku even faster and easier.

UNDERSTANDING MOBILE DEVELOPMENT ARCHITECTURES

Mobile application development represents a revolution in how apps can be delivered, but it also presents unique architectural challenges. Several delivery methods must be considered, each of which has its own merits and drawbacks in certain use cases. There are three main types of mobile architectures:

➤ Native

➤ HTML5

➤ Hybrid

Before you can understand where Heroku fits in, you must understand the advantages and disadvantages of each in order to make the correct design decisions. After looking at these models, you will learn how to use a central data repository for your apps to "phone home" and see how Heroku is integrated with this repository.

Native Mobile Applications

Native mobile apps are developed and delivered with device-specific languages and tools. For instance, if you are developing native apps for iOS devices, such as the iPhone and iPad, you must write your app in Objective-C using the Xcode development platform. If you are developing native apps for Android devices, you have to write your app in Java using the plugin for Eclipse. With native apps, you are restricted to these development platforms.

Typically, choosing this option severely limits your development flexibility with respect to languages and development tools, and limits the code created to a single device. This means, for example, that you must write and maintain three different code bases if you want to write native apps for iOS, Android, and BlackBerry devices. This does not allow for easy portability of code, and forces you to choose the devices on which your app will work.

On the one hand, this is sometimes okay — for instance, in a business that standardizes on one particular type of mobile device — but it makes determining which devices to support more difficult, as changing supported devices later typically requires software to be rewritten. On the other hand, native apps can be used to create far more robust apps than those that can be created with other architectures. Because development is done using APIs that are closely tied to the device and its operating system, this generally means that the developer has full use of all the peripherals and facilities included with the device.

For instance, almost all modern mobile devices include a camera and global positioning system (GPS.) This enables new apps to take pictures inside an app and tag them with the location from which the picture was sent, using both device capabilities as part of the app. Devices often also include an encrypted data store that is protected by a keychain of app-specific certificates, providing a higher level of security that makes native apps appropriate for enterprise use, where such greater levels of safekeeping are typically required.

Native apps can also leverage the user interface (UI) elements of the device. For instance, multi-touch gestures can be detected easily only using a native app. Gestures such as pinching and spreading can be used to make a UI extremely intuitive and easy to use. The UI capabilities of other mobile development architectures can make an app seem more like a web page than a full-fledged app. Intuitive UIs can make a big difference in terms of user adoption of a mobile app, by maximizing the user's overall experience when interfacing with the app.

Native mobile app development also provides access to facilities that are built into the operating system. For instance, native apps can often access the contact list on a device, which can be useful when you want an app to e-mail or call someone without requiring the user to reenter contact information already loaded in the device. In addition, the device's app-management software, such as Apple's App Store, makes notifying users of updates and pushing them easy, although installing updates is still a somewhat manual process for users. For certain apps, functionality like this is a necessity.

Native mobile apps are also the highest performing apps. If complex graphics or 3D rendering is needed — for instance, when making mobile games — this may make a native architecture your only choice. If you are simply creating a web app that displays some information and allows input of forms, building a native app probably won't make a noticeable difference in performance compared to the alternatives. For CPU-intensive operations, it isn't always clear whether it is better to do the computation on the device (which, it can be safely assumed, will not be extremely fast) or offload it elsewhere (such as on a server somewhere), depending on the use case.

Finally, one of the most important considerations in choosing your architecture is the availability of resources to develop apps for that particular architecture. Because native apps require knowledge of very esoteric tools and languages, staffing projects for mobile app development can often be difficult and very expensive. The scarcity of highly specialized developers allows them to demand greater compensation than a generalist Ruby or Java developer, whose skills are far more readily available. Requiring resources with specialized skills also increases risk to the project and your business. What if your rock star iOS developer leaves for another job in the middle of your project? How easily or quickly can he or she be replaced without affecting timelines?

Overall, native mobile apps offer the richest ability to deliver high performance apps that leverage the device's built-in capabilities with a rich UI. However, you have to decide whether these benefits outweigh the locked-in nature of the toolset and language used to develop the platform, which limits development to a particular set of devices and skills, and requires developing and maintaining multiple versions of an app's code base for different types of devices. However, in some scenarios this trade-off is well worth it to create apps with a rich UI, secure local data storage for offline apps, or high-performance apps. Fully native mobile apps cannot be created on Heroku, but they can leverage the capability to interface with a central data repository deployed to Heroku using APIs. We discuss this in more detail in the section "Using a Central Data Repository for Mobile Applications."

HTML5 Mobile Applications

HTML5 mobile apps are delivered through the web and accessed using a mobile device's browser. Standards-based technologies are often used to deliver these apps, including HTML, CSS, and JavaScript. Because of these standards, developers can write apps once and run them on an assortment of mobile devices, instead of maintaining multiple, device-specific code bases. These apps can be written in virtually any language and framework, with whatever development toolset is preferred. Moreover, these web-based apps can be written and hosted anywhere web apps can be delivered, including on Heroku. However, because HTML5 apps are delivered through the browser, they are not available on devices' app stores, as are native apps, making marketing and distribution more difficult.

The primary drawback to writing HTML5 apps is the inability to use the device's built-in peripherals and facilities, as native apps can. Developers cannot easily leverage the device's camera or the contact list built into the device's operating system, which significantly limits what apps written with HTML5 can do. Delivering alerts natively through the device with the app alone becomes impossible. Multi-touch gestures cannot be captured with HTML5 yet, making intuitive and robust UIs more difficult to deliver than with native apps. However, mobile UI frameworks, such as jQuery Mobile and jQMobile, make developing apps for multiple screen sizes that look and feel more like native apps much easier. Responsive design techniques are used to make an app's UI scale up and down according to the screen real estate available on the device used to access it.

The delivery of HTML5 apps through the web also presents its own sets of challenges and benefits when architecting them. First, the user typically must be online to access the app (at least the first time). Local caching mechanisms can be used for basic offline storage, but these techniques do not generally offer enterprise-grade security levels for storing sensitive information compared with native offline storage. Second, the organization that owns the data has no mechanism to revoke it, as it would with a native app. On the other hand, this web-based delivery mechanism also means that updates are propagated instantly when accessed online, reducing the need to support and debug multiple versions of an app or go through a complex and sometimes time-consuming process to deploy new versions of an app to multiple app stores.

The performance of HTML5 apps is a function of three factors: the web server(s) from which they are served, the connection over which the apps and their data are delivered, and the rendering engine of the web browser on the device. Typically, this is perfectly acceptable for most apps, but graphics-intensive apps and 3D games may not yet be ready for HTML5 delivery. When standards for delivering these types of graphics-heavy apps, such as WebGL, are more ubiquitous and readily supported in all browsers, this is likely to change.

Developing apps that require a central repository for information is also much quicker and less complex. Though it is not always the case, the HTML5 app and back-end server reside in the same code base. This means that you don't need to maintain multiple, device-specific code bases along with a separate code base for a central data repository — nor do you need to write or maintain APIs in order for both to communicate with one another. Cross-domain origin issues also disappear if you use the same domain for both. This simplifies your app's architecture and typically makes delivery quicker as a result.

Overall, using a fully HTML5-based architecture is suitable for apps for which using built-in peripherals or functionality is not needed, multi-touch gestures or high-performance graphics are not used, and high levels of security for offline access of data is not required. In return for these compromises, a write-once, run-anywhere approach can be taken for apps, using the language and toolset of the developer's choice. This reduced complexity and added flexibility makes developing apps faster and cheaper, makes application architectures less complex, and reduces staffing risks associated with developing apps with esoteric languages and development tools.

Hybrid Mobile Applications

Though many compromises are made in developing either native or HTML5 apps, hybrid apps provide a middle ground, providing some of the best of both worlds, while presenting a new set of challenges. Hybrid apps simply use a lightweight native application container that provides an interface to some of the device's peripherals and built-in functionality. This also enables the app to be launched like any other native app on the device, instead of through a browser. However, behind the scenes, an embedded browser is used to deliver the web app on the device. The UIWebView class is used in iOS devices and android.webkit.WebView class in Android devices, which may not behave the same way as other browsers, making debugging difficult and frustrating at times.

Hybrid apps offer the same flexibility in terms of language and toolset as HTML5 apps. There are also readily available containers for hybrid apps, such as PhoneGap, which provide a cross-device interface for using a single code base to access native functionality, such as using the device's camera or built-in contact list. This platform delivers multiple, device-specific apps that can be made available on each device's app store. The app can be delivered entirely through the web, updates can be made instantly, and the core app can be hosted on your choice of provider, including Heroku. Alternatively, you can write the app using HTML and a JavaScript API, whereby the code is translated and packaged with the device-specific apps, providing offline access. This architecture can communicate with a central data repository using APIs that communicate with a mobile back-end server — for instance, one deployed on Heroku.

However, of the three mobile architectures, hybrid apps are probably the slowest performing. Including a native wrapper adds another layer, which makes these apps typically much slower than native apps. Delivery through the web also slows performance over native apps, but the wrapper can make it possible to deliver alerts to users natively through their devices — and you can now leverage more secure, device-level offline storage, which you could not do with HTML5 apps. This is typically very important to enterprise developers, who have more stringent security requirements.

A hybrid mobile architecture tends to best suit apps where performance is not of paramount concern, but access to device peripherals and features, such as the camera and secure, offline storage, is necessary. It is not always obvious whether this represents a significant enough advantage over an HTML5 or native approach, but you can use these guidelines to make the best choice. Each of these different delivery methods offers its own merits and drawbacks in certain situations and certain apps, which must be considered during the initial architectural design.

Using a Central Data Repository for Mobile Applications

So far, we've talked mostly about how the app will be delivered and not much about where data will be kept. Unless you are creating a completely standalone app, you will need a backing central repository, or *back end*, to store and share information. For instance, if you are creating a native or hybrid mobile app that may be installed across devices, you need a place to put your data in a central repository that can be accessed by all devices. If you are creating an HTML5 or hybrid app, this central repository may even be the same repository the app itself is delivered from.

Heroku is also a perfect choice for a mobile back end because of its scalability, flexibility, and the lack of maintenance required. Consumer-facing mobile apps often have very unpredictable and spiky traffic patterns. If your app is featured in the App Store or climbs the download charts, this quickly accelerates the load on your mobile app's back end. Heroku makes scaling up to meet this unexpected demand fast and easy, without any perceived downtime for end users during application upgrades. In addition, scaling down later, once traffic subsides, is just as easy and quick. The elastic nature of Heroku makes it very well suited as the back end for consumer-facing mobile apps.

Similarly, Heroku apps are polyglot, enabling them to be written in whatever language is best suited for the task. For instance, if you are writing an HTML5 app, you may want to use Ruby on Rails or Spring Roo to quickly and easily create the scaffolding for your app with minimal coding. For a back end for native apps that need to communicate via an API, you might use Node.js, as it is a very lightweight server and can handle many connections at once, making it an ideal fit for a mobile app's central repository. You don't have to choose a single stack for your app or manage multiple stacks; you can choose the best in breed for each component of your overall architecture.

For example, Figure 15-1 provides an example of a hybrid mobile app running on mobile devices using PhoneGap, using a Heroku app as a back end. The mobile app uses offline storage for making changes to the database when the app is not connected to the Internet. Using the Heroku back end's REST API, the mobile app is able to synchronize these changes when connected to the Internet.

One of the most popular picture-sharing apps on the web, PicCollage, uses a different architecture, using Heroku as a back end for native applications. This app enables users to take pictures with their device and share them with others using the app. For tight integration with the device's camera and the need to use multi-touch gestures to provide a user-friendly UI, a native app made the most sense. However, the mechanism used to share the images between users (which are stored on Amazon S3) is built on top of Heroku for its robust and rapid scalability.

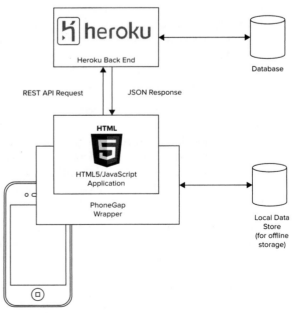

FIGURE 15-1

For example, Figure 15-2 shows an example of a native app that uses Heroku as a back end. Like in the sample hybrid architecture, offline storage is used for making changes to the database when the app is not connected to the Internet. The Heroku back end's REST API is used to synchronize the application's changes when connected to the Internet.

Even for more complex architectures, Heroku is a good fit to serve as a central mediator for information. For instance, FlightCaster uses Heroku to deliver an app that predicts flight delays based on historical performance of similar flights. Heroku is being used as a mobile back end for their apps as well as the front end for visitors to their website using a browser. This back end uses a massive cluster of Amazon EC2 servers to do the complex number crunching needed to analyze huge amounts of flight data and process the algorithms used to make predictions. This information is then fed back into a data store that the Heroku app can access and deliver to end users.

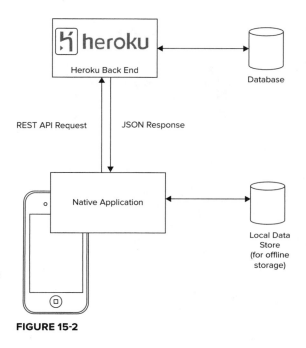

FIGURE 15-2

The one place where Heroku may not be as good a fit as a mobile back end is for some apps for which WebSockets is needed. At the time of this book's writing, Heroku does not support WebSockets, which is often needed for real-time streaming of information by keeping a socket open for long periods of time. Often, this is done in apps, such as for online gaming. Heroku will close idled connections, making streaming more challenging. Alternatives, such as using CometD or the PubNub add-on for broadcast notifications, should be explored. (PubNub is discussed later in this chapter, in the "Using Toolkits and Add-Ons for Mobile Application Development" section.)

As you have seen, using Heroku for a central repository for mobile apps is an excellent fit and can provide developers and architects with many benefits with little downside. This approach can be used with virtually any type of architecture that requires a back end, which is needed for most modern apps. Next, we will look at an example of an HTML5 mobile app with a back-end server running on Heroku to demonstrate a typical mobile application architecture.

WRITING AN HTML5 MOBILE APPLICATION

In this section you are going to write a mobile app using HTML5. You will reprise your employee list app, but you will make this app mobile optimized. The basic online operations will look something like Figure 15-3.

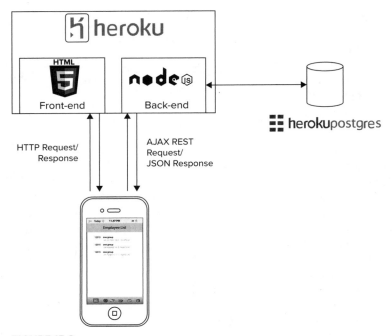

FIGURE 15-3

The user makes a GET request using AJAX from the HTML5 UI (code file: ch15-html5-mobile-front-end-example.zip) to the Node.js back-end app on Heroku (code file: ch15-html5-mobile-back-end-example.zip), via REST, to get a list of all the records. This will return a JSON representation of the records and their contents. The HTML5 app will then parse the JSON response and display the resulting records on the mobile screen.

Creating the Back End

Start by creating a Node.js back end for the app, as follows:

1. Create a new directory and add a file called web.js to it:

```
// web.js

var express = require('express');

var app = express.createServer(express.logger());

app.get(
    '/', function(request, response) {

        var pg = require('pg');

        // Connect to the DB
        pg.connect(
```

```
            process.env.DATABASE_URL, function(err, client) {

        if (err) {
            // Output error to console if can't connect
            console.log(err);

        } else {

            // Get all employees
            client.query(
                'SELECT id, name, email FROM employees',
                function(err, result) {

                    // Return cross-origin JSON response
                    response.writeHead(200, {
                        'Content-Type': 'application/json',
                        'Access-Control-Allow-Origin': '*'
                    });

                    response.write(JSON.stringify(result));
                    response.end();
                }
            );
        }
    }
    )
    }
);

// Initiate web server
var port = process.env.PORT || 5000;
app.listen(
    port, function() {
        console.log("Node.js server listening on " + port);
}
```

By setting the express and app variables, you include your libraries and initialize a server using the Express framework. The app.get() function indicates that the enclosed block of code will be a handler for GET requests to the root URL. The pg variable is defined to initialize your Postgres database library, and pg.connect() is used to create your database connection. If there is an error, you output the error to the log with console.log(). The client.query() function is used to query the Heroku Postgres database that you will use for data storage and to retrieve all the employees.

Next, JSON.stringify() packages the database result set as JSON, and response .writeHead() passes in the Access-Control-Allow-Origin HTTP header. This header is used to allow cross-domain JSON requests. Normally, AJAX requests made to and from a different domain are subject to the same-origin policy and disallowed by the browser. Adding this will allow your front-end site (e.g., http://html5-mobile-example.herokuapp.com) to access your Node.js back end on a different domain (e.g., http://html5-mobile-backend-example.herokuapp.com). Finally, app.listen() sets up the app to listen to the correct port for requests.

2. Define a `package.json` file in the same directory, defining your app's dependencies:

```
{
    "name": "nodedotjs-sample",
    "version": "1.0.0",
    "dependencies": {
        "express": "2.5.x",
        "pg": "0.8.2"
    },
    "engines": {
        "node": "0.8.x",
        "npm": "1.1.x"
    }
}
```

3. Include a `Procfile` to tell Heroku how to run the app:

```
web: node web.js
```

4. Create, commit, and push the app to Heroku:

```
$ git init
Initialized empty Git repository in /Users/ckemp/Documents/Sites/
html5-mobile-backend-example/.git/

$ heroku create html5-mobile-backend-example
Creating html5-mobile-backend-example... done, stack is cedar
http://html5-mobile-backend-example.herokuapp.com/ |
git@heroku.com:html5-mobile-backend-example.git
Git remote heroku added

$ git add .

$ git commit -m "Initial commit"
[master (root-commit) 7c84f39] Initial commit
 5 files changed, 72 insertions(+)
 create mode 100644 .DS_Store
 create mode 100644 Procfile
 create mode 100644 insert.sql
 create mode 100644 package.json
 create mode 100644 web.js

$ git push heroku master
Counting objects: 7, done.
Delta compression using up to 4 threads.
Compressing objects: 100% (6/6), done.
Writing objects: 100% (7/7), 1.39 KiB, done.
Total 7 (delta 0), reused 0 (delta 0)

-----> Heroku receiving push
-----> Removing .DS_Store files
-----> Node.js app detected
-----> Resolving engine versions
       Using Node.js version: 0.8.8
       Using npm version: 1.1.49
-----> Fetching Node.js binaries
-----> Vendoring node into slug
```

```
-----> Installing dependencies with npm
...
       Dependencies installed
-----> Building runtime environment
-----> Discovering process types
       Procfile declares types -> web
-----> Compiled slug size: 6.1MB
-----> Launching... done, v3
       http://html5-mobile-backend-example.herokuapp.com deployed to Heroku

To git@heroku.com:html5-mobile-backend-example.git
 * [new branch]      master -> master
```

5. Add a Heroku Postgres database to the app:

    ```
    $ heroku addons:add heroku-postgresql:dev
    Adding heroku-postgresql:dev on html5-mobile-backend-example... done, v4 (free)
    Attached as HEROKU_POSTGRESQL_CYAN_URL
    Database has been created and is available
    Use `heroku addons:docs heroku-postgresql:dev` to view documentation.

    $ heroku pg:promote HEROKU_POSTGRESQL_CYAN
    Promoting HEROKU_POSTGRESQL_CYAN to DATABASE_URL... done

    $ heroku pg:psql
    psql (9.1.4, server 9.1.5)
    SSL connection (cipher: DHE-RSA-AES256-SHA, bits: 256)
    Type "help" for help.

    mYD4t4B453n4m3=> create table employees (
    mYD4t4B453n4m3(>     id    bigint,
    mYD4t4B453n4m3(>     name  varchar(100),
    mYD4t4B453n4m3(>     email varchar(255)
    mYD4t4B453n4m3(> );
    CREATE TABLE
    mYD4t4B453n4m3=>
    mYD4t4B453n4m3=> INSERT INTO employees (id, name, email) VALUES
    mYD4t4B453n4m3->     ('1026', 'Brad Gyger', 'gyges@vandelayenterprises.com'),
    mYD4t4B453n4m3->     ('9913', 'Mike Pyle', 'mpyle@vandelayenterprises.com'),
    mYD4t4B453n4m3->     ('7000', 'Ryan Huber', 'rhuber@vandelayenterprises.com');
    INSERT 0 3
    mYD4t4B453n4m3=> \q
    ```

    Now you should be ready to test the mobile app's back end.

6. Run the following command:

    ```
    $ heroku open
    Opening html5-mobile-backend-example... done
    ```

    When your browser opens your URL, you can see the JSON representation of the response, which looks something like this:

    ```
    {
        "rows":[
            {
                "id":    1026,
                "name":  "Brad Gyger",
    ```

```
                "email":   "gyges@vandelayenterprises.com"
        },{
            "id":      9913,
            "name":    "Mike Pyle",
            "email":   "mpyle@vandelayenterprises.com"
        },{
            "id":      7000,
            "name":    "Ryan Huber",
            "email":   "rhuber@vandelayenterprises.com"
        }
    ],
    "command":   "SELECT",
    "rowCount":  3,
    "oid":       null
}
```

Now that you have set up the back end for your mobile app, you have to set up your front end.

Creating the Front End

To create the front end, this example uses Tiggzi, a visual mobile UI builder that uses HTML, jQuery Mobile, and PhoneGap to create both HTML5 and hybrid apps. You will use Tiggzi to quickly and easily create a front end for your mobile app that will call your REST-based back-end service to get the list of employees and display them.

1. To get started, create a Tiggzi account by going to `http://tiggzi.com/home` and clicking the Sign Up link. Enter the required information (see Figure 15-4).

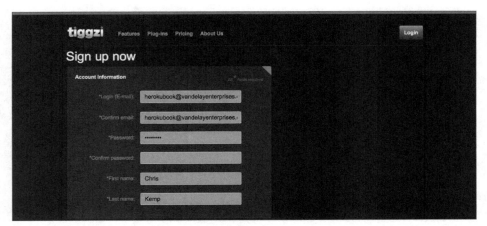

FIGURE 15-4

After signing up, you will be automatically logged in and prompted to create your first app (see Figure 15-5).

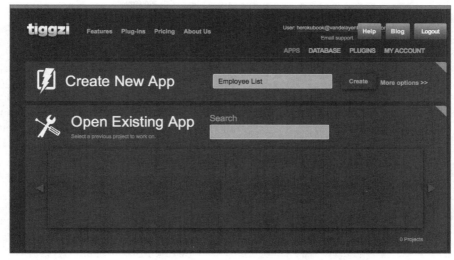

FIGURE 15-5

2. Call your app **Employee List** and then click the Create button. The mobile app design editor will appear, as shown in Figure 15-6.

On the left side is the Control Panel, which enables you to browse the elements in your current project (Project tab), to see the outline of all the elements in your project (Outline tab), and to add widgets to your app using drag-and-drop (Palette tab).

On the right side are the MobileScreen Properties, with the configurable properties of whatever element is currently in focus (Properties tab) and a list of events that trigger actions (Events tab).

The middle section of the screen is the design canvas, a mobile phone outline showing a configurable preview of what your mobile app will look like.

FIGURE 15-6

3. To get started with the designer, on the right side of the screen, under Properties, uncheck Show Footer and click the More Themes link. Change "Start screen" to "mobilescreen1," change "Theme" to "jQuery Mobile," and change "Swatch" to "D (White)." This will set up the basics for your app so that it looks like a native iOS app.

4. At the top of the phone in the center of the screen is a block with the word "Caption." This is the app's header. If you click on this, you should see an orange outline around the element on the designer. Note that the properties (on the right side of the screen) have changed to match those of this element type. Change the text here by changing the Text property to Employee List. When you press Enter, you can see that the WYSIWYG design editor reflects the change (see Figure 15-7).

FIGURE 15-7

5. Add a Grid element to show each employee's data. Grid elements are used to iterate over lists of items. In this case, the Grid element will iterate over the list of employees. To add a Grid element to the app, click the Palette tab on the Control Panel. You can see all sorts of different elements that you can add to your web app, including buttons, text areas, date pickers, and sliders. As shown in Figure 15-8, if you scroll down, you will find the Grid component. Drag and drop this component onto the design canvas, right underneath the header.

FIGURE 15-8

6. On the right side, under the Properties tab, change the Rows value from 1 to 2 to add a second row for your information, and change the Name value to **outputGrid**.

7. Add your Employee ID text by adding a Label element, dragging and dropping it in the top-left box in the grid. Make the following changes to the properties of this Label (see Figure 15-9):

➤ Text value to **[ID]** (a placeholder until you connect to the REST API)

➤ Name value to **employeeID**

➤ Face to **Helvetica**

➤ Color/Size to **13**

➤ Centered alignment

FIGURE 15-9

8. Drag and drop another Label in the top-right box of the grid, and make the following changes to the Label's properties:

➤ Text value to **[Employee Name]**

➤ Name value to **employeeName**

➤ Face to **Helvetica**

➤ Color/Size to **13**

9. The last element to add is for the e-mail addresses. Drag and drop an element of type Link to the bottom-right box, and make the following changes to the Link element's properties:

> ➤ Text value to [**E-mail Address**]

> ➤ Text value to **employeeEmail**

> ➤ Margin to **0 0 8 0**

> ➤ Face to **Helvetica**

> ➤ Color/Size to **12**

> ➤ Unbold

> ➤ Italicize

You now have the basic design for your app, which should look something like Figure 15-10.

FIGURE 15-10

10. The next thing you need to do is connect the mobile front end you are creating in Tiggzi to the REST API that you created with your Node.js back end running on Heroku. Select the Services collapsible section under the Palette tab. You should see Rest Service, which you can drag and drop onto the screen (not just anywhere on the canvas) to add the connector for your REST web service. The pop-up shown in Figure 15-11 should appear.

FIGURE 15-11

11. Click the Add New button to configure Tiggzi to connect to your web service. The REST Service Properties dialog will appear, as shown in Figure 15-12. Set the following values:

> ➤ Name to **EmployeeListService**

> ➤ URL to whatever the URL is to your Heroku back end Node.js app — in this
> example, `http://html5-mobile-backend-example.herokuapp.com/`. (The
> trailing slash is important here.)

> ➤ Method to **get**

> ➤ Data Type to **json**

12. Test the connection by clicking on
the Response Parameters collapsible
section. Click the Test Connection
button near the bottom to test out your
REST API call. In the Test Connection
pop-up, you can see your request
parameters (none are defined here) and
click the Test button to test your web
service. If you have done everything
correctly so far, you should see a "Test
Successful" message, with the result
of your web service displayed in the
"Response" section of the window (see
Figure 15-13).

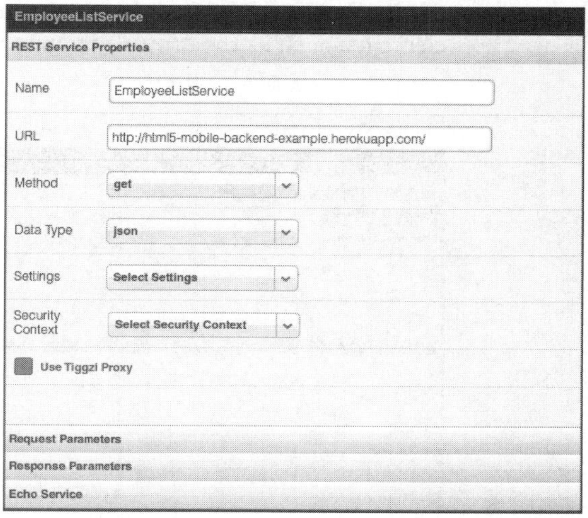

FIGURE 15-12

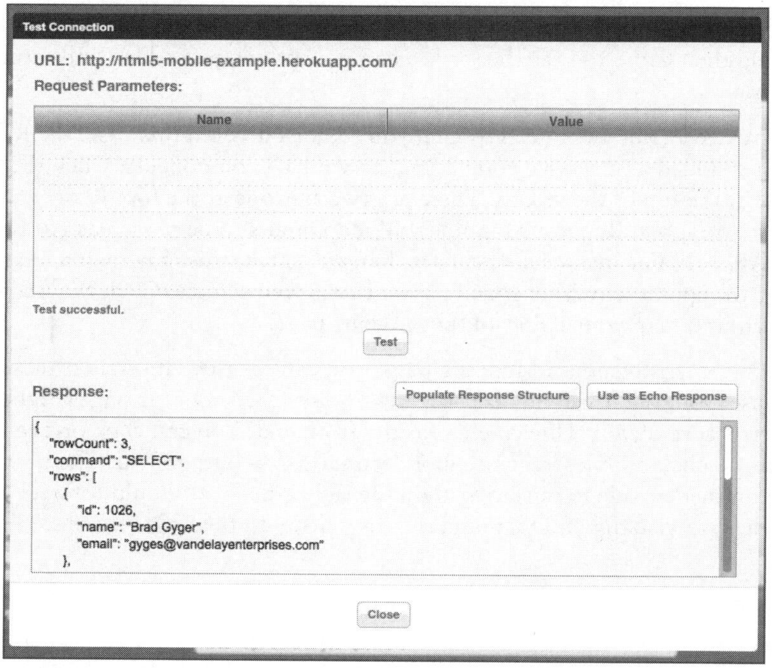

FIGURE 15-13

13. The last step in setting up your connection is clicking the Populate Response Structure button on this screen. This will take the response returned from the web service and create a scaffold that you can use to map elements in the REST response to UI elements in your mobile app. When you click the Close button, you can see that the Response Parameters section is now populated with the structure of your REST web service, including nested elements, such as the "rows" array with each employee's data (see Figure 15-14).

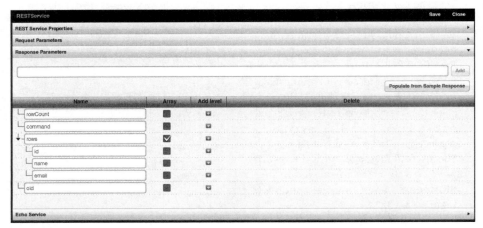

FIGURE 15-14

14. Click Save and then Close to save the service component you just added and return to the design screen.

15. On the design screen, you next need to map your data source (in this case, the REST web service you just added as a service component) to your UI components. Click the Data Mapping tab at the top of the screen. There are two buttons at the top: Request Mapping and Response Mapping. Request Mapping will map inputs to be passed as parameters to your REST API call. For instance, if you are doing a search, this may map a Text UI element on your page to input a search term and pass it to the web service. Click the Response Mapping button to map your REST output to your page.

16. On the left side of the Response Mapping page, you can see the data structure from your REST response from the back end, as shown in Figure 15-15. On the page's right side, you can see the structure of your UI elements for the front end. You can click on the arrows to expand them, so click mobilescreen1 ➪ mobilecontainer ➪ outputGrid. Then, drag and drop rows[] on the left side to outputGrid on the right side. You should now see a line connecting the two visually and mapping the rows array to the Grid element.

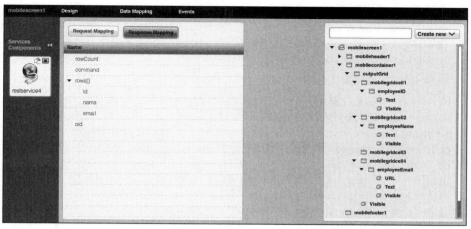

FIGURE 15-15

17. Expand "rows[]" on the left by clicking on the arrow. You can see the id, name, and email values from your REST service. Drag "id" on the left over "mobilegridcell1," and it will expand, revealing "employeeID." When you drag over "employeeID," you will see its two properties, Text and Visible, representing the text that will appear on the Label element and a Boolean indicating whether this element should be shown or not, respectively.

18. Map "name" to mobilegridcell2 ⇨ employeeName ⇨ Text, and "email" to mobilegridcell3 ⇨ employeeEmail ⇨ Text and URL. Your mapping should now look something like Figure 15-16.

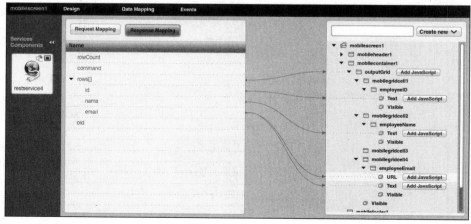

FIGURE 15-16

19. You also want the URL for your link to properly link to an e-mail address, so click the Add JavaScript button beside URL. This enables you to modify the value using custom JavaScript. In the pop-up, enter the following:

```
return 'mailto:' + value;
```

20. Now that your data mapping is set up, the last step is to invoke the service. This can be done in a number of ways (e.g., clicking a button) but here you want your employee list web service to be called when you load the page. Click the Design tab at the top of the page, and then click "mobilescreen1" in the Outline tab of the Control Panel on the left side. Following Figure 15-17, on the MobileScreen properties on the right side, click the Add Event drop-down and choose Load. In the Add Action drop-down that appears, select Invoke Service and choose the service component you created earlier.

FIGURE 15-17

21. You are done designing your app's UI and ready to test. To start, click Save in the top-left corner in the menu bar to save your Tiggzi project. You can test Tiggzi projects in a few different ways: through your browser or computer, by e-mailing a link to your mobile device, or via an iOS or Android test app. If you click the arrow beside Test, you can see all the delivery options, along with QR codes that can be used to open the link used to test (see Figure 15-18).

FIGURE 15-18

22. Click the Launch in Web Browser button. A preview of your mobile app appears, as shown in Figure 15-19.

FIGURE 15-19

You can interact with the app, preview it in both portrait and landscape perspectives, and see the site in a number of popular resolutions in the Mobile Preview screen. You can see that the app works properly, getting the values from the REST service and showing them on your mobile app. Close the preview pop-up browser window and you're ready to deploy the app.

23. Back on the Tiggzi designer screen, when you click the Export button, you see that you can deploy your app in a few different ways (see Figure 15-20). You can create hybrid apps for Android, iOS, and Windows Phone platforms, as well as create a native HTML5 app (in Other Platforms) that works across all devices of any kind. This enables you to create your app once and deploy it to the web or to multiple mobile app stores.

FIGURE 15-20

> **NOTE** *For more information on the process of getting your app on your device as a hybrid app that can be published on the mobile app store of your choice (e.g., Apple App Store, Google Play Market, etc.), see* `http://help.gotiggr` `.com/documentation/exporting.`

24. Click the HTML/CSS/JS link beside Other Platforms and download the HTML5 source code, unzipping it to a new local directory and renaming `index.html` so that Heroku will use the PHP buildpack later:

```
$ unzip ~/Downloads/project_50361.zip
Archive:  /Users/ckemp/Downloads/project_50361.zip
  inflating: files/resources/image/grad_white_5px.png
  inflating: files/resources/image/arrow_right_disabled.png
...
  inflating: files/views/assets/css/general+css5.css
  inflating: files/views/assets/css/general+css6.css
  inflating: files/views/assets/image/no-image.jpg

$ mv index.html index.php
```

25. Create a Heroku app for your front end and deploy it to Heroku:

```
$ git init
Initialized empty Git repository in /Users/ckemp/Documents/Sites/html5-mobile-example/
.git/
cK-MacBook-Air:html5-mobile-example ckemp$ heroku create html5-mobile-example
Creating html5-mobile-example... done, stack is cedar
http://html5-mobile-example.herokuapp.com/ | git@heroku.com:html5-mobile-example.git
Git remote heroku added

$ git add .

$ git commit -am "Initial commit"
[master (root-commit) 53e41b7] Initial commit
 227 files changed, 36648 insertions(+)
 create mode 100644 descriptor.txt
 create mode 100644 files/resources/css/base.css
 create mode 100644 files/resources/css/mobilebase.css
 create mode 100644 files/resources/image/addthis/addthis.png
...

$ git push heroku master
Counting objects: 242, done.
Delta compression using up to 4 threads.
Compressing objects: 100% (237/237), done.
Writing objects: 100% (242/242), 511.61 KiB | 40 KiB/s, done.
Total 242 (delta 43), reused 0 (delta 0)

-----> Heroku receiving push
-----> PHP app detected
-----> Bundling Apache version 2.2.22
```

```
-----> Bundling PHP version 5.3.10
-----> Discovering process types
       Procfile declares types -> (none)
       Default types for PHP   -> web
-----> Compiled slug size: 10.0MB
-----> Launching... done, v3
       http://html5-mobile-example.herokuapp.com deployed to Heroku

To git@heroku.com:html5-mobile-example.git
 * [new branch]      master -> master
```

Here, you can see that your app is detected as a PHP app, and that the Apache web server is used to serve up your HTML5 front end. To test the app properly, access it via a mobile browser. Figure 15-21 shows the app in iPhone's Safari browser.

Congratulations! Your mobile app is running with a back end written in Node.js, with both the front end and back end running on Heroku. You could even add this to your home screen so that it looks like any other app by clicking the third icon to the right at the bottom and going to Add to Home Screen.

FIGURE 15-21

> **NOTE** *For more information on customizing the icon that will be added to your home screen, see* http://taylor.fausak.me/2012/03/27/ios-web-app-icons-and-startup-images/. *Android uses the same conventions as the iOS examples given.*

USING TOOLKITS AND ADD-ONS FOR MOBILE APPLICATION DEVELOPMENT

You have seen how you can create a back end for a mobile app using Heroku; but Heroku's add-on ecosystem provides developers with a number of tools that can be used to make mobile development easier. StackMob and Parse provide a mobile back end as a service (BaaS). RhoConnect can handle offline synchronization of data between your mobile app and any back-end database; and PubNub and BoxCar provide push messaging services to make your mobile apps real-time. The following sections describe each of these add-ons and how they can help you develop mobile apps quickly and easily.

StackMob

StackMob is the original mobile BaaS provider. It is often referred to as *Heroku for Mobile* because of the simplicity and productivity gains that it offers mobile developers and its easy scalability. StackMob facilitates many of the common tasks that need to be done when developing mobile apps.

For instance, user management and authentication is taken care of by StackMob, including single sign-on capabilities with OAuth and hooks to use popular identity providers such as Facebook and Twitter. Mobile developers no longer have to write their own capabilities for these functions, or collect and bolt on the libraries that perform these functions to their code base.

StackMob also makes creating a back end for your app a snap. As you saw in the earlier example, creating a back end for your app often includes creating a database, writing an app to interface with your database, and exposing APIs with which your front end can communicate. With StackMob you can create your schema and relationships without having to use a database, and even update your schema at run time if a new field is detected after your front end app is updated, for maximum flexibility. This data store also supports geospatial functionality for creating apps that can find nearby locations; and your database can be automatically exposed as REST APIs to use with your front end app.

Push notifications are also commonly needed for mobile apps, as they give mobile app users the capability to receive alerts in real time natively, through their devices. This could be in the form of badges (like the counter on the e-mail app that tells you how many messages you have in your inbox), sounds, and alerts (the detailed pop-ups that let you know that something has happened). StackMob can deliver these alerts to specific devices or all registered devices, making notification delivery painless.

StackMob also provides a plethora of other useful features for mobile app developers. You can use sandbox and production environments with StackMob and manage the two environment separately. One of the more useful features StackMob provides is analytics for your app. This enables you to monitor performance, API usage, and keep on top of errors that users are experiencing, for quality control.

StackMob also enables you to create native mobile apps using their SDK, so you can leverage StackMob's functionality in native iOS or Android apps; and these SDKs are open source, enabling you to tinker with them (see `https://github.com/stackmob`). StackMob support can be added to any Ruby app (Node.js support is planned) and the plans available differ in the level of API calls, push notifications, and analytics retention periods. The highest level also includes a second production API and backup for your Amazon S3 buckets (where user-generated content can be uploaded) as well. In short, StackMob provides a useful suite to simplify mobile back end development.

> **NOTE** *To install this add-on, see* `https://addons.heroku.com/stackmob` *for a list of plans. An example of StackMob in action can be found at* `https://devcenter.heroku.com/articles/stackmob`. *More in-depth information can be found at the StackMob Dev Center at* `https://developer.stackmob.com/`.

Parse

Parse is a direct competitor of StackMob, and offers a similar value proposition. Parse provides similar user management functionality to StackMob, with social network integration. It also enables you to easily create a back-end database exposed through a REST API in a similar fashion, also with geospatial support built in. Push notification capabilities are also built in to Parse, and SDKs are available for creating native mobile apps. Both operate very similarly at a high level, but there are a few key differences.

Overall, Parse offers easier offline event handling functionality, built into their native SDK. For instance, when you want to save a new record, you can use Parse's saveEventually function, which simply waits until later and retries when the app is online. You can do this in StackMob but you have to write the logic in a handler when the error occurs while sending the request to the back end.

Parse also provides more robust capabilities for file uploading with your mobile device. Both Parse and StackMob require you to use a data storage service, like Amazon S3, to store file uploads. However, Parse's PFFile object wraps this with convenience functions that make storing and retrieving files easier for developers. Parse's plans also come with S3 storage included, providing more tight integration than StackMob with your storage.

Though we have discussed Parse's strengths over StackMob, there are a few shortcomings as well. Parse's Native SDK is not open source, as is StackMob's. For those who are concerned about the portability of their app or the ability to extend and customize the SDK, this should be kept in mind. Nor does Parse provide analytics, as StackMob does, leaving developers on their own to add this to their app. Without distinctly separated environments for sandbox and production, this may not fit well with enterprise software development life-cycle requirements. Overall, Parse appears to be a solution that is easier to learn and use, but StackMob provides some features that may appeal more to enterprise users.

> **NOTE** *Parse is currently in private beta. For instructions on installing and implementing Parse, see* https://devcenter.heroku.com/articles/parse. *For in-depth documentation, see* https://www.parse.com/docs/index.

RhoConnect

RhoConnect is part of the RhoMobile Suite, Motorola's cross-device mobile development platform, which provides an enterprise-grade mobile offline synchronization solution — for instance, if you are writing a smartphone app that you need to synchronize with a back-end server to provide data offline, which later updates once a connection is restored. RhoConnect is an excellent solution for simplifying this typically complex, code-heavy workflow, ensuring that data on the device is current and that only incremental changes are sent (not the entire data set each time.) RhoConnect can be synchronized to multiple data sources, including Enterprise Resource Planning (ERP) or Customer Relationship Management (CRM) systems, to facilitate access to enterprise system data anywhere and on any device. Synchronization happens in the background, providing an excellent user experience for your mobile app users. A sample architecture is shown in Figure 15-22.

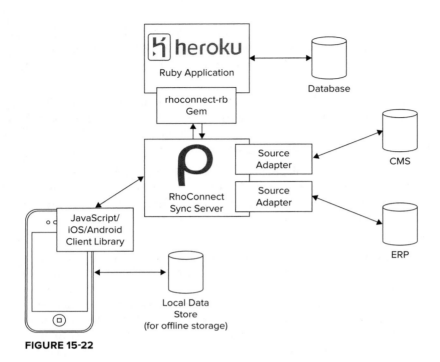

FIGURE 15-22

Server plugins can be added to your Heroku app, which provides a NoSQL-based synchronization server to incrementally update information as changes are made on devices and the server. This synchronization server provides authentication and source adapters to synchronize the server with back-end databases. This can be used to mobilize data without code from proprietary apps such as Salesforce.com, Microsoft Dynamics, and Oracle On-Demand. You can also write your own source adapter using the provided template to connect to most any back-end data store, if a source adapter is not already available.

RhoConnect can be added as an add-on to a Ruby-based back-end Heroku app and expose a REST interface to connect with your mobile front end. The RhoConnect client can be added to your iOS or Android app using the provided code, or you can simply use a JavaScript client to connect with apps built with frameworks such as PhoneGap. You can even add fields to your mobile apps without having to push new versions of the mobile app, saving time spent managing upgrade cycles. It is very well suited for apps that need to expose information from an enterprise back-end system to mobile devices or to simply act as a synchronization system for whatever data store you are using.

> **NOTE** *A list of RhoConnect add-on plans can be found at* https://addons
> .heroku.com/rhoconnect. *Installation and setup documentation can be found*
> *on the Heroku Dev Center, at* https://devcenter.heroku.com/articles/
> rhoconnect. *More in-depth documentation, including source adapter and client*
> *references, is available on Motorola's RhoMobile Development Community site,*
> *at* http://docs.rhomobile.com/rhoconnect/introduction.

PubNub

Often when you are creating mobile apps, updates need to happen in real time. For instance, if you are writing an app that provides stock ticker updates, the price of the stock needs to change in real time as the back-end server gets the latest stock price. Because Heroku does not currently support WebSockets, the connection will time out. PubNub offers a broadcast solution whereby bidirectional information can be sent to implement a publisher/subscriber pattern, enabling updates to be sent and received in real time.

Note that this is different from StackMob's messaging service, which can push device-specific alerts. PubNub does not push device alerts, it only acts as an open connection between your back end and web clients for information to be sent and received. What you do with the message is up to you. PubNub's add-on can be provisioned for your back end, and pricing is based on the volume of messages broadcasted. PubNub offers APIs for JavaScript, Objective-C, Java, PhoneGap, Ruby, PHP, Python, Perl, and .NET, amongst others, to provide real-time messaging for your mobile apps.

> **NOTE** *Add-on plans for PubNub can be found at* `https://addons.heroku.com/pubnub`. *The Heroku Dev Center article shows sample code for publishing and subscribing at* `https://devcenter.heroku.com/articles/pubnub`. *More in-depth documentation is available via the PubNub Dev Center at* `www.pubnub.com/devcenter`.

BoxCar

BoxCar offers real-time alerts via push notifications for users who have installed their iOS or Mac-based apps. For those familiar with the Growl notification system often used in Mac OS X apps, BoxCar offers a similar solution for web and mobile apps. The BoxCar add-on can be bolted on to Heroku-based back ends to provide a publish/subscribe model that can be used to broadcast messages to all, or a subset of, users. This message is sent to user devices for those who have signed up and installed the BoxCar app and provides alerts or banners similar to those delivered through a native app. This differs from PubNub in that the alerts come from the device itself, rather than providing a push/pull only when the web app is open.

> **NOTE** *BoxCar is currently in private beta. Installation instructions and sample code can be found on Heroku's Dev Center, at* `https://devcenter.heroku.com/articles/boxcar`. *The BoxCar API documentation is available at* `http://boxcar.io/help/api/providers`.

SUMMARY

In this chapter we explored how Heroku can be used to create mobile apps. Developers can choose from one of three types of mobile architectures: native, HTML5, and hybrid. Native apps can use all the device's features but are more difficult and time consuming to code and maintain. HTML5 apps are device and platform agnostic and easier to create, but cannot use the device's peripherals or access information offline securely. Hybrid apps use a lightweight native container to make building apps as easy as HTML5, while providing access to device peripherals and features, including offline storage.

Heroku can be used for creating and deploying HTML5 apps or as a back end for hybrid and native applications. The rapidly scalable nature of Heroku makes it an excellent fit as a central repository in mobile back ends to store and share information. Though any language can be used for a mobile back end, Node.js is exceptionally well suited because of its lightweight footprint and ability to handle many concurrent connections. Tiggzi provides an excellent tool for rapidly creating mobile front-end apps using point and click that can be deployed as HTML5 or hybrid apps.

In the next chapter, we explore how to create socially connected apps using Heroku.

16

Building Social Applications with Heroku

WHAT'S IN THIS CHAPTER?

➤ Writing Facebook applications with PHP

➤ Making Heroku applications social with the Chatter API

WROX.COM CODE DOWNLOADS FOR THIS CHAPTER

The wrox.com code downloads for this chapter are found at www.wrox.com/remtitle
.cgi?isbn=1118508998 on the Download Code tab. The code is in the Chapter 16 download
and individually named according to the names throughout the chapter.

In the previous chapter we talked about the paradigm shift in application development toward
mobile apps that are accessible anywhere, on any device. Around the same time as the mobile
revolution, a paradigm shift was happening in the consumer world, with Myspace and
Facebook creating groundbreaking apps that model social connections between users. This
gave users a conduit to easily share information and connect with others online, regardless of
location or time zone. This social revolution peaked during the Arab Spring, when dissidents
of oppressive governments in the Middle East rose up against their overlords, organizing social
revolution through these social networks.

It wasn't long after the rise of social and mobile apps in the consumer space that this paradigm
shift made its way to the business world. Businesses were already using social tools, such as
instant messaging and products like Microsoft SharePoint, as document repositories that
enabled collaboration. Salesforce.com's release of Chatter, a social network targeted for the
enterprise, in 2010 represented a move to make a company's users socially connected without
setting up the silos of information used with traditional social tools such as instant messaging
and e-mail. Enterprise-grade security and privacy enable a business to embrace these tools

over their consumer-grade brethren. This new generation of enterprise apps focused on social networking allows for easier sharing and collaboration among employees.

This chapter explores how to make social apps with Heroku. First you will look at an example of a socially engaging Facebook app built with PHP and hosted on Heroku. You will then learn how you can make any app social using Database.com and the Chatter API. These examples demonstrate how you can use apps to connect socially in public with Facebook and collaborate with others in your organization privately with social apps built on Heroku.

WRITING FACEBOOK APPLICATIONS WITH PHP

Today's business-to-consumer (B2C) businesses are looking for new and innovative ways to engage with their customers. Marketing departments are turning more often to social media to connect with their customers and increase brand awareness by building apps on Facebook. One such app, created by a holiday resort, enables users to create a photo album of their vacation by choosing a theme for their photo album, uploading photos, and sharing their creation with Facebook friends using Facebook's Graph API.

Heroku is well suited for these socially connected apps. As you are likely well aware, interesting and novel apps gain popularity quickly through social sharing. If one user shares his or her vacation experience using a Facebook app, others in that individual's group of friends will see the new photo album and want to create their own, and in turn share those with their social circle. This viral growth can create very spiky traffic patterns for these apps. Heroku's rapid and elastic scalability enables you to meet demand in this unpredictable environment with minimal effort. Moreover, because developers can quickly create apps with zero maintenance required, marketers can experiment with a portfolio of socially engaging apps with minimal sunk and ongoing costs, instead of putting all their eggs in one basket by choosing a single app to develop and hoping it becomes a hit.

Facebook allows you to create an app that will appear on your company's or your personal Facebook page. Facebook apps are created using a *Canvas Page*, which is simply an iFrame that points to the URL of your app running elsewhere and which defines its logic and behavior. This Canvas acts as a container for your app and enables you to access the Graph API to provide a customized experience for specific users and access objects within the context of that user from Facebook (e.g., their friends, photos, notifications, and events).

In this section's example, you will create a simple Facebook Canvas-based app hosted on Heroku (code file: `ch16-facebook-canvas-php-example.zip`). The app will be used to collect entries for a contest in which participants' information is collected in a Heroku Postgres database. These entries can be used later in a drawing for a prize.

Creating a Facebook Canvas Application

The first thing you need to do is create a Facebook Canvas app in Facebook. This will create a generic template that demonstrates how to do basic functions of Facebook Canvas apps, like logging in, displaying user-specific information, and showing which of the user's friends have previously used the app. If you do not already have a Facebook account, you will need to sign up for an account at `http://www.facebook.com/r.php` before starting.

1. To get started, go to the Facebook Developers page (`https://developers.facebook.com/apps`).

2. Click Create New App in the top-right corner of the screen. In the Create New App dialog, add a unique name for the app and check "Yes, I would like free web hosting provided by Heroku," as shown in Figure 16-1.

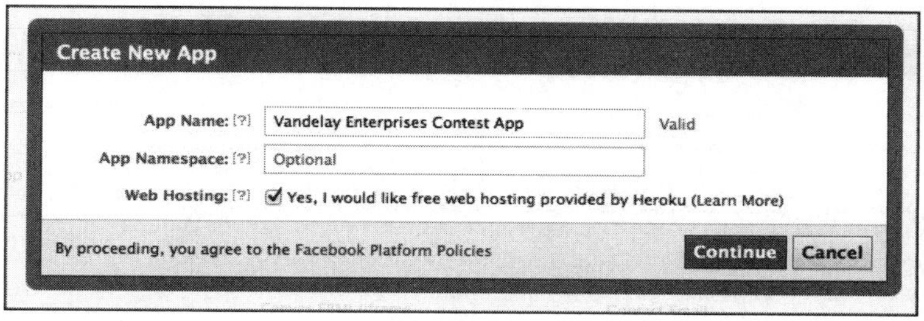

FIGURE 16-1

> **NOTE** *Heroku is currently the only hosting partner for Facebook apps, after going through the rigorous certification process to ensure the security, reliability, and scalability that Facebook demands for such a partnership.*

Facebook sets up an app with your unique name, and generates an App ID and an App Secret, as shown in Figure 16-2. These two values are important because they are used by your Heroku app to interface securely with this particular app. Although you could host your Facebook anywhere on the public web, you want to put your app on Heroku.

FIGURE 16-2

3. Scroll down and click the Get One link beside Hosting URL. You are presented with a pop-up displaying the available certified hosting providers—a pretty easy choice in this case, as Figure 16-3 demonstrates. Click Next.

4. In the "Host your site with Heroku" dialog, choose which environment you want to use to create your app—in this case, PHP. Enter your e-mail address, which corresponds to the e-mail address you use for your Heroku account, and click the Create button (see Figure 16-4).

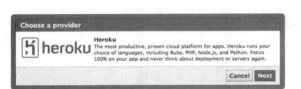

FIGURE 16-3

FIGURE 16-4

NOTE *If you don't already have a Heroku account associated with that e-mail address, Heroku will automatically set one up for you.*

As shown in Figure 16-5, Facebook opens another dialog showing the template app it has automatically set up with the language of your choice.

FIGURE 16-5

5. Click the Log In button and give the template application permissions to see some of your information, by clicking the Allow button. A "welcome" page appears, as shown in Figure 16-6.

FIGURE 16-6

Unfortunately, Lauren is a bit of a loner and doesn't have any Facebook friends yet; but you will probably see a bunch of friends, some of your recent photos, and things you like, and other friends who are using this app (probably none yet). These examples of accessing the Facebook Graph API are baked into the Facebook application template that is provided when you create a new app, and they can be easily leveraged to add this functionality to your app.

6. Go back to the previous window and click the Apps tab and then the Edit Settings link. You will see that Facebook also set up a Canvas URL for you, as shown in Figure 16-7.

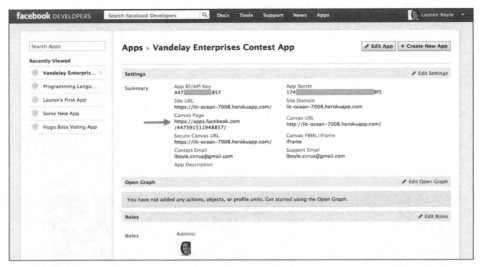

FIGURE 16-7

This is the URL that you can use to access your app within the Facebook Canvas. It will be in the form `https://apps.facebook.com/<Facebook App ID>/`. If you visit this URL, you will see your app framed within a Canvas container, as shown in Figure 16-8.

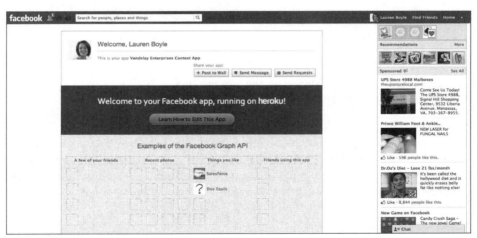

FIGURE 16-8

Writing the Contest App Code

You have created a Facebook Canvas, with the template application running successfully. Next, you need to replace this with an app where logged in Facebook users can check a box to agree to the contest rules and click a button to enter the contest. This app will use Facebook's Graph API to retrieve the user's personal info, including his or her name and e-mail address.

1. Go to the command line and get a local copy of the template code that was created for you:

```
$ git clone git@heroku.com:lit-ocean-7008.git -o heroku facebook-canvas-php-example
Cloning into 'facebook-canvas-php-example'...
remote: Counting objects: 180, done.
remote: Compressing objects: 100% (112/112), done.
remote: Total 180 (delta 82), reused 132 (delta 62)
Receiving objects: 100% (180/180), 137.91 KiB, done.
Resolving deltas: 100% (82/82), done.
```

This command clones the code to your local machine. The -o flag tells Git that you want to use the remote name "heroku" (as in git push heroku master) instead of the default "origin" remote name. The last part of the command is optional; you can use it to create a directory name of your choice, rather than the app name by default (in this case, "lit-ocean-7008").

2. Take a look at the app's config vars to verify that your Facebook credentials have been automatically added:

```
$ cd facebook-canvas-php-example/

$ heroku config
=== lit-ocean-7008 Config Vars
FACEBOOK_APP_ID: 123456789012345
FACEBOOK_SECRET: mYf4C3b00K4pPl1C4t10n53Cr3Tk3Y
```

Note that as part of the process of creating your app, when you chose your application provider and language of choice, the config vars to connect this app to the Facebook API were automatically added.

This directory contains a few key files. The AppInfo.php file defines an AppInfo class that you can use to access handy functions, such as appID() to get the Facebook Application ID, appSecret() to get the Facebook App Secret Key, and getUrl() to return the URL of the app. The utils.php file provides the helper functions idx(), for returning a value in an array or a default value if it doesn't exist, and he(), which simplifies PHP's htmlentities() function, used to convert user input to escaped characters (useful for preventing cross-site scripting attacks or SQL injection). The channel.html file is used to improve loading speed in some older browsers and should be left as it is. Finally, of course, index.php is the main page for your Facebook app.

3. Replace index.php with the following code:

```php
<?php

// Provides access to app specific values such as your app id and app secret.
// Defined in 'AppInfo.php'
require_once('AppInfo.php');

// Enforce https on production
if (substr(AppInfo::getUrl(), 0, 8) != 'https://' &&
    $_SERVER['REMOTE_ADDR'] != '127.0.0.1') {
    header('Location: https://'. $_SERVER['HTTP_HOST'] .
    $_SERVER['REQUEST_URI']);
    exit();
```

```php
}

// This provides access to helper functions defined in 'utils.php'
require_once('utils.php');

require_once('sdk/src/facebook.php');

$facebook = new Facebook(array(
    'appId'  => AppInfo::appID(),
    'secret' => AppInfo::appSecret(),
    'sharedSession' => true,
    'trustForwarded' => true,
));

$user_id = $facebook->getUser();
if ($user_id) {
    try {
        // Fetch the viewer's basic information
        $basic = $facebook->api('/me');
    } catch (FacebookApiException $e) {
        // If the call fails we check if we still have a user. The user will be
        // cleared if the error is because of an invalid accesstoken
        if (!$facebook->getUser()) {
            header('Location: '. AppInfo::getUrl($_SERVER['REQUEST_URI']));
            exit();
        }
    }
}

?>
<!DOCTYPE html>
<html xmlns:fb="http://ogp.me/ns/fb#" lang="en">
    <head>
        <meta charset="utf-8" />
        <meta name="viewport" content="width=device-width, initial-scale=1.0,
            maximum-scale=2.0, user-scalable=yes" />

        <title><?php echo he($app_name); ?></title>
        <link rel="stylesheet" href="stylesheets/screen.css" media="Screen"
            type="text/css" />
        <link rel="stylesheet" href="stylesheets/mobile.css" media="handheld,
            only screen and (max-width: 480px), only screen and
            (max-device-width: 480px)" type="text/css" />

        <style type="text/css">
            #guides div {
                margin-bottom: 20px;
            }

            #error {
                border:         1px solid red;
padding:            15px;
background-color: #FFE6E6;
                color:          red;
font-weight:        bold;
}
```

```
        </style>

        <!--[if IEMobile]>
        <link rel="stylesheet" href="mobile.css" media="screen"
            type="text/css" />
        <![endif]-->

        <!-- These are Open Graph tags.  They add meta data to your  -->
        <!-- site that facebook uses when your content is shared  -->
        <!-- over facebook.  You should fill these tags in with  -->
        <!-- your data.  To learn more about Open Graph, visit  -->
        <!-- 'https://developers.facebook.com/docs/opengraph/'  -->
        <meta property="og:title" content="<?php echo he($app_name); ?>" />
        <meta property="og:type" content="website" />
        <meta property="og:url" content="<?php echo AppInfo::getUrl(); ?>" />
        <meta property="og:image" content="<?php echo
            AppInfo::getUrl('/logo.png'); ?>" />
        <meta property="og:site_name" content="<?php echo he($app_name); ?>" />
        <meta property="og:description"
            content="Vandelay Enterprises Facebook Contest" />
        <meta property="fb:app_id" content="<?php echo AppInfo::appID(); ?>" />

        <script type="text/javascript"
            src="/javascript/jquery-1.7.1.min.js"></script>

        <script type="text/javascript">
            function logResponse(response) {
                if (console && console.log) {
                    console.log('The response was', response);
                }
            }

            $(function() {
                // Set up so we handle click on the buttons
                $('#postToWall').click(function() {
                    FB.ui(
                        {
                            method: 'feed',
                            link: $(this).attr('data-url'),
                            name: 'Vandelay Enterprises Facebook Contest',
                            description: 'I just entered the Vandelay ' +
                            'Enterprises Facebook Contest.  You should too!'
                        }, function (response) {
                            // If response is null the user canceled the dialog
                            if (response != null) {
                                logResponse(response);
                            }
                        }
                    );
                });

                $('#sendToFriends').click(function() {
                    FB.ui(
                        {
                            method: 'send',
                            link: $(this).attr('data-url'),
```

```
                              name: 'Vandelay Enterprises Facebook Contest',
                              description: 'Hey buddy.  I just entered the ' +
                                  'Vandelay Enterprises Facebook Contest.  ' +
                                  'You should too!'
                      }, function (response) {
                          // If response is null the user canceled the dialog
                          if (response != null) {
                              logResponse(response);
                          }
                      }
                  );
              });
          });
      </script>

      <!--[if IE]>
      <script type="text/javascript">
          var tags = ['header', 'section'];
          while(tags.length)
              document.createElement(tags.pop());
      </script>
      <![endif]-->
  </head>

  <body>
      <div id="fb-root"></div>
      <script type="text/javascript">
          window.fbAsyncInit = function() {
              FB.init({
                  appId      : '<?php echo AppInfo::appID(); ?>', // App ID
                  channelUrl :
                      '//<?php echo $_SERVER["HTTP_HOST"]; ?>/channel.html',
                      // Channel File
                  status     : true, // check login status
                  cookie     : true,
                      // enable cookies to allow the server to access the
                      // session
                  xfbml      : true // parse XFBML
              });

              // Listen to the auth.login which will be called when the user
              // logs in using the Login button
              FB.Event.subscribe('auth.login', function(response) {
                  // We want to reload the page now so PHP can read the cookie
                  // that the Javascript SDK sat. But we don't want to use
                  // window.location.reload() because if this is in a canvas
                  // there was a post made to this page and a reload will
                  // trigger a message to the user asking if they want to send
                  // data again.
                  window.location = window.location;
              });

              FB.Canvas.setAutoGrow();
```

```
                };

                // Load the SDK Asynchronously
                (function(d, s, id) {
                    var js, fjs = d.getElementsByTagName(s)[0];
                    if (d.getElementById(id)) return;
                    js = d.createElement(s); js.id = id;
                    js.src = "//connect.facebook.net/en_US/all.js";
                    fjs.parentNode.insertBefore(js, fjs);
                } (document, 'script', 'facebook-jssdk'));
            </script>

            <header class="clearfix">
                <div>
                    <h1>Vandelay Enterprises Facebook Contest</h1>
                </div>
            </header>

            <section id="guides" class="clearfix">
<?php

    // Check that user is logged in and that we can get basic FB info for user
    if (isset($basic)) {

    // Creates the connection string for our Postgres DB using DATABASE_URL
    extract(parse_url($_ENV["DATABASE_URL"]));
    $pg_conn = "user=$user password=$pass host=$host port=$port " .
        "dbname=" . substr($path, 1) . " sslmode=require";
    $db = pg_connect($pg_conn);

    // Check if user ID is already in DB entries table
    $result = pg_query($db, "SELECT * FROM entries WHERE fb_id = '" .
        pg_escape_string($basic['id']) . "' LIMIT 1;");

    if (pg_num_rows($result) != 0) {
?>

            <div>
                Sorry, <?php echo he(idx($basic, 'first_name')); ?>, but you
                have already entered this contest.  There is a maximum of one
                entry per person.
            </div>
<?php
        } else {
            // Check that form was submitted and user has agreed to rules
            if (isset($_POST["submit"]) and isset($_POST["agreed"]) and
                $_POST["agreed"] == 'yes') {

                // Insert new entry in the DB
                $result = pg_query($db, "INSERT INTO entries (fb_id, " .
                    "first_name, last_name, date_of_birth, gender, email, " .
                    "created) VALUES ('" .
                    pg_escape_string($basic['id']) . "', '" .
                    pg_escape_string($basic['first_name']) . "', '" .
                    pg_escape_string($basic['last_name']) . "', '" .
                    pg_escape_string($basic['birthday']) . "', '" .
                    pg_escape_string($basic['gender']) . "', '" .
                    pg_escape_string($basic['email']) .
```

```
                              "', clock_timestamp());");

                          if ($result != null) {
?>
                  <div>
                      Thanks, <?php echo he(idx($basic, 'first_name')); ?>!  Your
                      entry for the contest has been <b>successfully recorded</b>.  We
                      will let you know shortly if you have won.
                  </div>

                  <div>
                  <p>Why not <b>share this contest</b> with your friends?</p>
                      <span>
                          <a href="#" class="facebook-button" id="postToWall"
                              data-url="<?php echo AppInfo::getUrl(); ?>">
                              <span class="plus">Post to Wall</span>
                          </a>
                      </span>
                      <span>
                          <a href="#" class="facebook-button speech-bubble"
                              id="sendToFriends" data-url="<?php
                              echo AppInfo::getUrl(); ?>">
                              <span class="speech-bubble">Send Message</span>
                          </a>
                      </span>
                  </div>

<?php
                      } else {
?>

                  <div>
                      Whoops!  Something went wrong and your entry could not be saved
                      Please come back and try again later.
                  </div>

<?php
                      }
                  } else {
                      // Form was submitted, but rules were not agreed to
                      if (isset($_POST["submit"]) and (!isset($_POST["agreed"]) or
                          $_POST["agreed"] != 'yes')) {
?>
                  <div id="error">
                      You must agree to the official rules in order to enter the
                      contest.
                  </div>
<?php
                      }
                      // Display home page for app if logged in
?>
                  <div>Hi, <?php echo he(idx($basic, 'first_name')); ?>!</div>

                  <div>
                      <form method="post" id="myform" name="myform"
                          style="margin: 0px;">
```

```
                                 <input type="hidden" name="submit" value="submit" />

                                 <div>
                                     We are running a contest where you can win some really,
                                     really neat prizes. All you have to do to enter, is
                                     <b>check off the checkbox below</b>, indicating that
                                     you have read the rules.
                                 </div>

                                 <div>
                                     Don't worry, we won't spam you.  We only need your
                                     e-mail address to contact you if you win.  For details,
                                     see our <a class="privacy" href="#"
                                     onclick="javascript:alert('Privacy Policy:\n\nBlah, ' +
                                     'blah, blah...');">Privacy Policy</a>.
                                 </div>

                                 <div>
                                     <input type="checkbox" name="agreed" value="yes" /> I
                                     have read and agree to the <a class="rules" href="#"
                                     onclick="javascript:alert('Contest Rules:\n\nBlah, ' +
                                         'blah, blah...');">official rules</a>.
                                 </div>

                                 <div>
                                     <input type="submit" name="btn-submit"
                                         value="Enter the Contest" />
                                 </div>
                             </form>
                         </div>
<?php
                     }
                 }
         } else {
             // Could not get FB user info, they must not be logged in
?>
                         <div>
                             To enter the contest, you must first log in to the
                             application.
                         </div>

                         <div class="fb-login-button" data-scope="user_birthday,email"></div>
<?php
         }
?>
             </section>
             <br /><br />
         </body>
</html>
```

Phew! That's a lot of code. Let's analyze what all this does. First, the lines under the comment "Enforce https on production" verify that you are using HTTPS for the app, as Facebook requires that apps must be accessed via a secure connection. The Facebook SDK is used to set the parameters for your app in `$facebook` and stores the information for the currently logged in user with `$basic`, using the Facebook Graph API. The `<meta property="og:XXX" content="YYY" />` lines are used to include meta tags for OpenGraph. (See `https://developers.facebook.com/docs/opengraph/` for more details about this.)

The `$('#postToWall').click()` and `$('#sendToFriends').click()` define JavaScript functions that enable posting to the user's wall and sending a message to friends using the app, respectively. Next, authentication for your app occurs using the `FB.init()` JavaScript function that interacts with the Facebook API. In the first block of PHP code, you confirm that `$basic` is filled with the user's basic information to ensure that the user is logged in to the app. If so, the code directly after confirms that the currently logged in user hasn't already entered the contest.

If the user has not entered the contest already, check whether the user has submitted the form on the main page and checked the checkbox indicating agreement to the contest rules. If so, you must save the record in the Heroku Postgres database using `pg_query()` to do the SQL `INSERT`. The HTML elements with class `facebookButton` use HTML to display the buttons for posting to your wall or sending a message to friends through this app.

If the user has submitted the form but not checked off the box, the lines after the comment "Form was submitted, but rules were not agreed to" will display an error message for the user. The HTML after the comment "Display home page for app if logged in" defines the UI for the main page. Finally, the HTML element with class "fb-login-button" will display a Login button for users who try to access your app without first logging in and being authorized. This also sets the scope for the information this Facebook Canvas app will have access to, in addition to your basic information (e.g. name, user ID, etc.), inside the `data-scope` attribute. In this case, your app has access to the user's birthday address and e-mail address.

Deploying the Application to Heroku

You have created a Facebook Canvas app and have edited the template to define the logic for your app. You now have to deploy your Facebook app to Heroku.

1. Commit your app and push it to Heroku (you've cloned your app already, so your Git repository is initialized; therefore, you can skip that step here):

```
$ git commit -am "Initial commit"
[master f0a6742] Initial commit
 1 file changed, 338 insertions(+), 384 deletions(-)
 rewrite index.php (95%)

$ git push heroku master
Counting objects: 5, done.
Delta compression using up to 4 threads.
Compressing objects: 100% (3/3), done.
Writing objects: 100% (3/3), 4.18 KiB, done.
Total 3 (delta 1), reused 0 (delta 0)

-----> Heroku receiving push
-----> Git submodules detected, installing
       Submodule 'sdk' (https://github.com/facebook/facebook-php-sdk.git) registered
       for path 'sdk'
```

```
          Initialized empty Git repository in /tmp/build_rysapv6cw1n2/sdk/.git/
          Submodule path 'sdk': checked out '98f2be163c96a51166354e467b95dd38aa4b0a19'
-----> PHP app detected
-----> Bundling Apache version 2.2.22
-----> Bundling PHP version 5.3.10
-----> Discovering process types
          Procfile declares types -> (none)
          Default types for PHP   -> web
-----> Compiled slug size: 9.7MB
-----> Launching... done, v4
          http://lit-ocean-7008.herokuapp.com deployed to Heroku

To git@heroku.com:lit-ocean-7008.git
   5b0f7da..f0a6742  master -> master
```

Notice that when you do your push, a submodule called `sdk` is checked out and installed in
your slug. Git submodules enable you to include the contents of another Git repository in your
Git repository automatically, without having to copy and paste the code. In this case, you are
including the Facebook PHP SDK (`https://github.com/facebook/facebook-php-sdk`),
which ensures that you are using the latest and greatest copy of this code in your
Facebook app.

> **NOTE** *For more information on Git submodules, see* `http://git-scm.com/book/`
> `en/Git-Tools-Submodules`.

2. Create the table in the database for storing your contest entries:

```
$ heroku addons:add heroku-postgresql:dev
Adding heroku-postgresql:dev on lit-ocean-7008... done, v5 (free)
Attached as HEROKU_POSTGRESQL_WHITE_URL
Database has been created and is available
Use `heroku addons:docs heroku-postgresql:dev` to view documentation.

$ heroku pg:promote HEROKU_POSTGRESQL_WHITE
Promoting HEROKU_POSTGRESQL_WHITE to DATABASE_URL... done

$ heroku pg:psql
psql (9.1.4, server 9.1.5)
SSL connection (cipher: DHE-RSA-AES256-SHA, bits: 256)
Type "help" for help.

mYd4T4b453N4m3=> create table entries (
mYd4T4b453N4m3(>     id            serial,
mYd4T4b453N4m3(>     fb_id         varchar(255),
mYd4T4b453N4m3(>     first_name    varchar(255),
mYd4T4b453N4m3(>     last_name     varchar(255),
mYd4T4b453N4m3(>     date_of_birth varchar(255),
mYd4T4b453N4m3(>     gender        varchar(255),
mYd4T4b453N4m3(>     email         varchar(255),
mYd4T4b453N4m3(>     created       timestamp
mYd4T4b453N4m3(> );
```

```
NOTICE:  CREATE TABLE will create implicit sequence "entries_id_seq" for serial column
"entries.id"
CREATE TABLE
mYd4T4b453N4m3=> \q
```

3. Before visiting the app, remove access to it so that you can log in again and give the app the proper permissions. Go to your Facebook news feed, click the down arrow in the top-right corner, and choose Privacy Settings. Click Edit Settings beside Ads, Apps and Websites. Then click Edit Settings beside Apps You Use. Hover over your app and click the X on the right to remove the app.

4. Now that you are starting from a clean slate, visit your Facebook app's URL (remember, it looks like `https://apps.facebook.com/<Facebook App ID>/`), which should look similar to what is shown in Figure 16-9.

FIGURE 16-9

5. Click the Log In button. A pop-up will appear, asking you to authorize the app to access certain personal information (see Figure 16-10). Click the "Log in with Facebook" button.

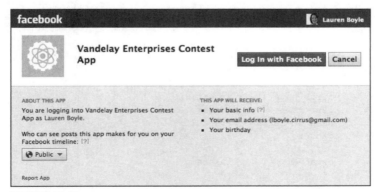

FIGURE 16-10

After you are authorized, you can see the main page of your app, as shown in Figure 16-11.

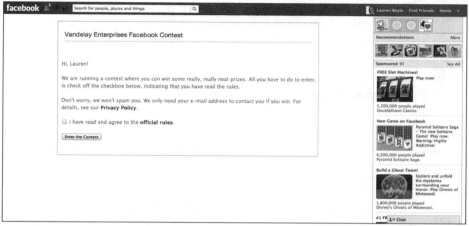

FIGURE 16-11

6. Check the "I have read and agree to the official rules" checkbox, and then click the Enter the Contest button.

As shown in Figure 16-12, you can now use the buttons at the bottom of the screen to share this app with your Facebook friends.

FIGURE 16-12

Figure 16-13 shows the dialog that appears after clicking the Post to Wall button.

FIGURE 16-13

After filling in a personalized message and clicking the Share button, a post is added to your Timeline (see Figure 16-14).

FIGURE 16-14

7. Run the following command to verify that the user's contest entry was recorded in your database:

```
$ heroku pg:psql
psql (9.1.4, server 9.1.5)
SSL connection (cipher: DHE-RSA-AES256-SHA, bits: 256)
Type "help" for help.

mYd4T4b453N4m3=>
SELECT id, first_name, last_name, date_of_birth, gender, email FROM entries;
 id | first_name | last_name | date_of_birth | gender |         email
----+------------+-----------+---------------+--------+------------------------
  1 | Lauren     | Boyle     | 03/14/1972    | female | lboyle.cirrus@gmail.com (1 row)

mYd4T4b453N4m3=> \q
```

Looks good! You can see that you have recorded all of your visitor's information successfully. If you go back to your app's original URL and try to enter the contest again, you will not be allowed (see Figure 16-15).

FIGURE 16-15

You have created your first Facebook Canvas app hosted on Facebook and using PHP. You could now scale your app up and down very easily. For example, if you ran an advertisement for the app and were flooded with traffic, you could scale up to meet this demand and then scale down once it subsides. In the next section, you'll learn how to make an app social within your organization, using the Salesforce.com Chatter API.

MAKING HEROKU APPLICATIONS SOCIAL WITH THE CHATTER API

The previous section described how you can make a social app on Facebook with Heroku to engage with the general public. However, a fast-growing trend is the creation of apps that are social but private to an organization. You can leverage Database.com and its Chatter API to make any app social. The Chatter API includes a plethora of built-in functionality that you can utilize with apps that need to be made social. For instance, the Chatter API includes news feeds, posts, comments on posts, likes, the capability to follow records (to get updates in your news feed), groups, file sharing, and private messages. In addition, authentication is built in to Database.com with OAuth or delegated authentication, and you can leverage Salesforce's powerful permissions and sharing system, all of which makes Database.com a real time-saver for writing social apps.

Any app you make and run on Heroku can easily be made social simply by adding the Chatter API. For instance, making a front end for an app on Heroku that accesses a back-end database, like an ERP or other legacy system, provides an excellent opportunity to modernize the app to make this siloed data social. Even if the data is going to live in another system, you can use shadow records in Database.com to correspond to the records in the outside system for the purpose of isolating Chatter on a particular record and following particular records.

In order to create shadow records, every time you create a record in the third-party system, you must also create a corresponding record in Database.com. This lightweight record simply points back to the ID of the record in the third-party system and holds the discussions that happen on that record. This means you don't need to make any changes to the third-party system in order to make it social.

It can be difficult to make changes on some types of legacy systems, so this example creates a social app without altering the original database. For your example app, you are going to make a Ruby on Rails app running on a Heroku Postgres database social using the Chatter API (code file: ch16-social-chatter-example.zip).

Creating a Shadow Object in Database.com

The first step in creating your social app is to create your shadow object in Database.com. You will create a new Database.com object with a field that will correspond to an ID in your Heroku Postgres object representing a shipment. You then need to turn on Chatter for this object and create a Remote Access entry to enable OAuth for your Heroku app to access Salesforce's REST API.

1. Log in to your Database.com account.

> **NOTE** *We will assume that you have signed up for a Database.com account, as described in Chapter 9, "Using Database.com as a Data Store for Your Heroku Applications." If not, go to* https://database.secure.force.com/en/signup/ *to sign up now. The account is free.*

2. Select App Setup ➪ Create ➪ Objects, and then click the New Custom Object button. On the New Custom Object dialog, shown in Figure 16-16, enter **Shipment Chatter** in the Label field; **Shipments Chatter** in the Plural Label field; **ShipmentChatter** in the Object Name field; **Shipment ID** in the Record Name field; and **Text** in the Data Type field. This last field is the one that will correspond to the ID of the record in the legacy database.

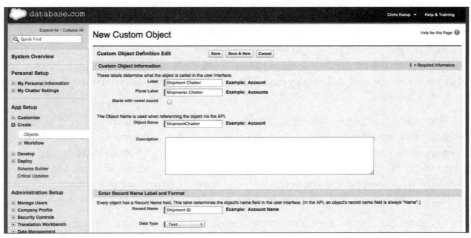

FIGURE 16-16

If your new shadow object is set up correctly, it should resemble Figure 16-17.

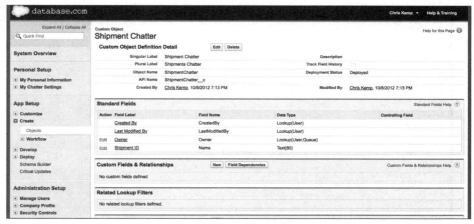

FIGURE 16-17

3. Because Chatter is not automatically enabled for your new object, select App Setup ⇨ Customize ⇨ Chatter ⇨ Feed Tracking. Click the Shipment Chatter option in the Object list, check off Enable Feed Tracking, and then click the Save button (see Figure 16-18).

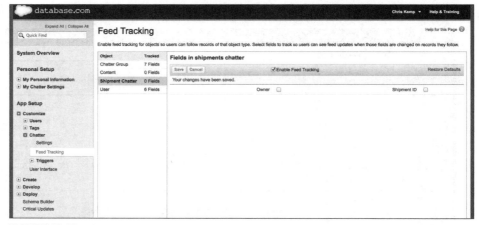

FIGURE 16-18

Now that Database.com is set up for your shadow object, you have to set up OAuth authentication for your app.

4. Select App Setup ⇨ Develop ⇨ Remote Access, and then click the New button. On the Remote Access dialog, shown in Figure 16-19, enter **My Heroku App** in the Application field and set the Contact Email to your e-mail address. Enter **https://<your app name> .herokuapp.com/auth/salesforce/callback** in the Callback Email field. This represents the URL that will be called by OAuth once the user has logged in and approved access for your app. Scroll to the bottom of the screen and click the Save button.

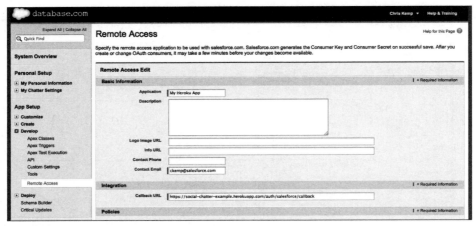

FIGURE 16-19

5. After you have saved the record, your new Remote Access settings appear. On this dialog, you can get the OAuth Consumer Key and Consumer Secret that you need for authentication with your app. Click on Click to Reveal beside Consumer Secret, and your Consumer Secret will appear, as shown in Figure 16-20.

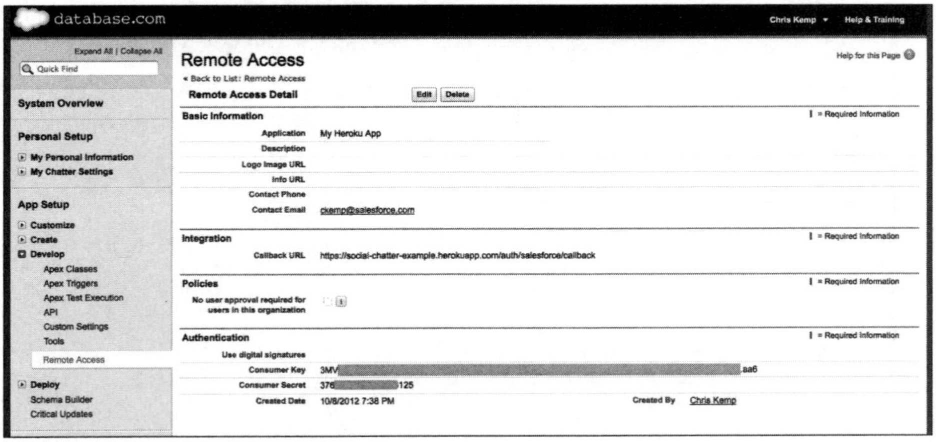

FIGURE 16-20

Be sure to make note of the values for Consumer Key and Consumer Secret for later. You will need to add these as config vars to your Heroku app so that you can use OAuth to access the Salesforce.com API.

6. Now that your shadow object and authentication for Database.com is set up, create a Ruby on Rails app:

```
$ rails new social-chatter-example
      create
      create  README.rdoc
      create  Rakefile
      create  config.ru
...
      create  vendor/plugins/.gitkeep
      run  bundle install
Fetching gem metadata from https://rubygems.org/........
Using rake (0.9.2.2)
Using i18n (0.6.1)
...
Using sqlite3 (1.3.6)
Using uglifier (1.3.0)
Your bundle is complete! Use 'bundle show [gemname]' to see where a bundled gem is
installed.
```

7. Create the scaffolding for your Rails app:

```
$ cd social-chatter-example/

$ rails generate scaffold Shipment id:integer shipped:boolean shipment_date:date
      invoke  active_record
      create  db/migrate/20121009022914_create_shipments.rb
      create  app/models/shipment.rb
...
      invoke  scss
      create  app/assets/stylesheets/scaffolds.css.scss
```

8. Now that the app has been created, you need to set it up to use OAuth. Open `config/application.rb` and add the following lines of code:

```
module SocialChatterExample
    class Application < Rails::Application

    VARS=%w(TOKEN_ENCRYPTION_KEY CONSUMER_KEY CONSUMER_SECRET)
    VARS.keep_if{|var| ENV[var].nil? || ENV[var].empty?}

    fail "Environment Variables required: #{VARS.join(',')}" if(!VARS.empty?)

    require "base64"
    require "databasedotcom-oauth2"

    config.middleware.use Databasedotcom::OAuth2::WebServerFlow,
    "token_encryption_key" =>
        Base64.strict_decode64(ENV['TOKEN_ENCRYPTION_KEY']),
    "endpoints" => {
        "login.salesforce.com" => {
            "key" => ENV['CONSUMER_KEY'],
            "secret" => ENV['CONSUMER_SECRET']
        }
```

```
        }

        config.force_ssl = true

        # etc...
```

9. Replace `app/controllers/shipments_controller.rb` with the following code:

```ruby
require 'httparty'

class ShipmentsController < ApplicationController
    include Databasedotcom::OAuth2::Helpers
    include HTTParty

    before_filter :init

    def init
        @authenticated = authenticated?

        if authenticated?
            @me = me

            # Set up URL and headers for REST calls
            @root_url = client.instance_url + "/services/data/v" +
                client.version
            @options = {
                :headers => {
                    'Authorization' => "OAuth #{client.oauth_token}",
                    'Content-Type' => "application/json",
                    'X-PrettyPrint' => "1"
                }
            }
        end
    end

    def logout
        client.logout if authenticated?
    end

    def post
        # Create JSON for REST request
        options = @options
        options.merge!(
            :body => {
                :body => {
                    :messageSegments => [
                        {
                            :type => "Text",
                            :text => params[:content]
                        }
                    ]
                }
            }.to_json
        )

        # Do REST request
```

```ruby
    response = HTTParty.post(@root_url + "/chatter/feeds/record/" +
        params[:parent_id] + "/feed-items", options)
end

# GET /shipments
# GET /shipments.json
def index

    @shipments = Shipment.all

    respond_to do |format|
        format.html # index.html.erb
        format.json { render json: @shipments }
    end
end

# GET /shipments/1
# GET /shipments/1.json
def show
    # Get shipment from Postgres DB
    @shipment = Shipment.find(params[:id])

    # Get shadow object from database.com
    @shadow_obj = client.query("SELECT Id, Name FROM " +
        "ShipmentChatter__c WHERE Name = \'" << params[:id] << "\'")
    @id = @shadow_obj[0].Id

    # Get Chatter feed for shadow object
    @feed = client.query("SELECT Body, InsertedById FROM " +
        "FeedItem WHERE ParentId = \'" + @id +  "\' ORDER BY CreatedDate")

    # Get User list for identifying Chatter post user
    @user_list = Hash.new()
    raw_user_list = client.query("SELECT Id, Name FROM User")
    raw_user_list.each do |user|
        @user_list[user.Id] = user.Name
    end

    respond_to do |format|
        format.html # show.html.erb
        format.json { render json: @shipment }
    end
end

# GET /shipments/new
# GET /shipments/new.json
def new
    @shipment = Shipment.new

    respond_to do |format|
        format.html # new.html.erb
        format.json { render json: @shipment }
    end
```

```ruby
  end

  # GET /shipments/1/edit
  def edit
      @shipment = Shipment.find(params[:id])
  end

  # POST /shipments
  # POST /shipments.json
  def create
      # Save shipment in Postgres DB
      @shipment = Shipment.new(params[:shipment])

      respond_to do |format|
          if @shipment.save

              # Create JSON for REST request
              options = @options
              options.merge!(
                  :body => {
                      :Name => @shipment.id
                  }.to_json
              )

              # Do REST request
              response = HTTParty.post(@root_url +
                  "/sobjects/ShipmentChatter__c", options)

              format.html { redirect_to @shipment, notice:
                  'Shipment was successfully created.' }
              format.json { render json: @shipment, status: :created,
                  location: @shipment }
          else
              format.html { render action: "new" }
              format.json { render json: @shipment.errors,
                  status: :unprocessable_entity }
          end
      end
  end

  # PUT /shipments/1
  # PUT /shipments/1.json
  def update
      @shipment = Shipment.find(params[:id])

      respond_to do |format|
          if @shipment.update_attributes(params[:shipment])
              format.html { redirect_to @shipment,
                  notice: 'Shipment was successfully updated.' }
              format.json { head :no_content }
          else
              format.html { render action: "edit" }
              format.json { render json: @shipment.errors,
                  status: :unprocessable_entity }
          end
      end
```

```
    end

    # DELETE /shipments/1
    # DELETE /shipments/1.json
    def destroy
        @shipment = Shipment.find(params[:id])
        @shipment.destroy

        respond_to do |format|
            format.html { redirect_to shipments_url }
            format.json { head :no_content }
        end
    end
end
```

First, notice that at the beginning of the `ShipmentsController` class you include your two key libraries: HTTParty (to make the REST requests) and the Database.com OAuth gem. The `init` function determines whether the user is logged in and, if so, constructs the REST API URL and headers. The `logout` function is used to log out of the app. The `post` method constructs the REST request for the Chatter API. Then the API call itself is made using `HTTParty.post()`.

The `index` method is used to get a list of all the shipments in the Heroku Postgres database for the main page. You select a specific Shipment record in the `show` method, using `Shipment.find()` to retrieve the record's details. You must also get the shadow object using `client.query()`, and use the Database.com's record ID that you get from that query to retrieve the Chatter feed in the subsequent `client.query()` call. The block under the comment "Get User list for identifying Chatter post user" gets a list of all the users and their IDs in a hash table to identify the owner of each post.

The `new` function is used to create a new `Shipment` object, while the `edit` function retrieves a record for editing by selecting it from the database. In the `create` function, you create a new Shipment record in the Heroku Postgres database using `Shipment.new()`; and if that is successful, you construct the REST request to create a shadow record in Database.com with the `options` variable. You make the request using `HTTParty.post()` and display the appropriate output with `format.html` and `format.json`.

As the name implies, the `update` method is used to update an existing Shipment record. Note that it's a good idea here to ensure that your ID isn't changed in Heroku Postgres; otherwise, it will become out of synchronization with the ID stored in your shadow object. Therefore, you would update your shadow record at the same time. We will leave that as an exercise for the reader. Finally, the `destroy` method is used to delete records in the database. You should probably also delete your shadow record in Database.com here to keep things clean across the two systems.

Note that the previous section demonstrated two very different ways to interact with Database.com. You used the client's `query()` function to execute SOQL queries on Database.com to get the records you need. You also saw how, alternatively, you can use the REST API to interface with Database.com instead. Either approach is fine; it's just a matter of preference.

10. Change `app/views/shipments/show.html.erb` to show your Chatter Feed for that record in your view:

```
<p id="notice"><%= notice %></p>

<p>
    <b>Id:</b>
    <%= @shipment.id %>
</p>

<p>
    <b>Shipped:</b>
    <%= @shipment.shipped %>
</p>

<p>
    <b>Shipment date:</b>
    <%= @shipment.shipment_date %>
</p>

<h3>Chatter:</h3>

<% @feed.each do |f| %>
    <b><%= @user_list[f.InsertedById] %>:</b> <%= f.Body %><br />
<% end %>

<form action="/post" method="post">
    <input name="parent_id" type="hidden" value="<%= @id %>" />
    <input name="content" type="text"/>
    <%= csrf_meta_tag %>
    <input value="Post" type="submit"/>
</form>

<%= link_to 'Edit', edit_shipment_path(@shipment) %> |
<%= link_to 'Back', shipments_path %>
```

Here, you can see that the code loops through each of your Chatter feed items, showing each along with the user who made the Chatter post. Then you add a form with a text input for creating new posts.

11. Replace `app/views/shipments/index.html.erb` with a view that includes your login information, like this one:

```
<h1>Listing shipments</h1>

<table>
    <tr>
        <th>Id</th>
        <th>Shipped</th>
        <th>Shipment date</th>
        <th></th>
        <th></th>
        <th></th>
```

```
        </tr>
<% @shipments.each do |shipment| %>
    <tr>
        <td><%= shipment.id %></td>
        <td><%= shipment.shipped %></td>
        <td><%= shipment.shipment_date %></td>
        <td><%= link_to 'Show', shipment %></td>
        <td><%= link_to 'Edit', edit_shipment_path(shipment) %></td>
        <td><%= link_to 'Destroy', shipment, method: :delete, data:
            { confirm: 'Are you sure?' } %></td>
    </tr>
<% end %>
</table>

<p><% if @authenticated%>
    You're logged in as <%= @me.username%>. Click <a href="/logout">here</a> to
    logout.

<%= yield %>

<% elsif%>
    You're not logged in. Click <a href="/auth/salesforce">here</a> to login.
<% end%></p>


<%= link_to 'New Shipment', new_shipment_path %>
```

Here you can see that an `if` statement checks whether you are authenticated, displaying the username if the user is logged in or a link if they are not logged in.

12. Add the file `app/views/shipments/post.html.erb`, which you will show when you successfully add a new Chatter post:

```
<h1>Post Successful</h1>
<p>You have posted successfully.</p>
<%= link_to 'Back', shipments_path %>
```

13. Add the file `app/views/shipments/logout.html.erb`, to be used as a simple view indicating that you have successfully logged out:

```
<h1>Logout Successful</h1>
<p>You have logged out successfully.</p>
<%= link_to 'Back', shipments_path %>
```

14. Add the following lines to define the correct routes for your app in `config/routes.rb`:

```
root :to => 'shipments#index'
match "logout" => "shipments#logout"
match "post" => "shipments#post"
match "*rest" => "shipments#index"
```

15. Remove your default home page:

```
$ rm public/index.html
```

16. In `config/environments/production.rb`, replace the line:

```
config.assets.compile = false
```

with the following:

```
config.assets.compile = true
```

This ensures that you precompile the static assets needed for your app.

17. Open the `Gemfile` and replace the line:

```
gem 'sqlite3'
```

with these lines:

```
gem 'pg'
gem 'databasedotcom'
gem 'databasedotcom-oauth2'
gem 'httparty'
```

Here, you add the libraries for your Postgres database: for accessing records with Database .com, for using OAuth to authenticate with Database.com, and HTTParty to make REST calls, respectively.

18. Install the following libraries with Bundler:

```
$ bundle install
Using rake (0.9.2.2)
Using i18n (0.6.1)
Using multi_json (1.3.6)
...
Using uglifier (1.3.0)
Your bundle is complete! Use `bundle show [gemname]` to see where a bundled gem is
installed.
```

Your code is ready; just a couple of more steps before testing your app.

19. Initialize your repository, create and push your app to Heroku, and migrate your database:

```
$ git init
Initialized empty Git repository in /Users/ckemp/Documents/Sites/social-chatter-example/
.git/

$ heroku create social-chatter-example
Creating social-chatter-example... done, stack is cedar
http://social-chatter-example.herokuapp.com/ | git@heroku.com:social-chatter-example.
git
Git remote heroku added

$ git add .

$ git commit -am "Initial commit"
[master (root-commit) 88a5226] Initial commit
 54 files changed, 1447 insertions(+)
 create mode 100644 .gitignore
```

```
 create mode 100644 Gemfile
 create mode 100644 Gemfile.lock
...
 create mode 100644 vendor/assets/stylesheets/.gitkeep
 create mode 100644 vendor/plugins/.gitkeep

$ git push heroku master
Counting objects: 96, done.
Delta compression using up to 4 threads.
Compressing objects: 100% (86/86), done.
Writing objects: 100% (96/96), 30.96 KiB, done.
Total 96 (delta 8), reused 0 (delta 0)

-----> Heroku receiving push
-----> Ruby/Rails app detected
-----> Installing dependencies using Bundler version 1.2.1
        Running: bundle install --without development:test --path vendor/bundle
        --binstubs bin/ --deployment
        Fetching gem metadata from https://rubygems.org/.......
        Fetching gem metadata from https://rubygems.org/..
        Installing rake (0.9.2.2)
        Installing i18n (0.6.1)
...

        Installing sass-rails (3.2.5)
        Installing uglifier (1.3.0)
        Your bundle is complete! It was installed into ./vendor/bundle
        Post-install message from rdoc:
        Depending on your version of ruby, you may need to install ruby rdoc/ri data:
        <= 1.8.6 : unsupported
        = 1.8.7 : gem install rdoc-data; rdoc-data --install
        = 1.9.1 : gem install rdoc-data; rdoc-data --install
        >= 1.9.2 : nothing to do! Yay!
        Post-install message from httparty:
        When you HTTParty, you must party hard!
        Cleaning up the bundler cache.
-----> Writing config/database.yml to read from DATABASE_URL
-----> Rails plugin injection
        Injecting rails_log_stdout
        Injecting rails3_serve_static_assets
-----> Discovering process types
        Procfile declares types        -> (none)
        Default types for Ruby/Rails -> console, rake, web, worker
-----> Compiled slug size: 9.0MB
-----> Launching... done, v2
        http://social-chatter-example.herokuapp.com deployed to Heroku

To git@heroku.com:social-chatter-example.git
 * [new branch]        master -> master

$ heroku run rake db:migrate
Running `rake db:migrate` attached to terminal... up, run.1
Connecting to database specified by DATABASE_URL
Migrating to CreateShipments (20121009022914)
==  CreateShipments: migrating ================================================
-- create_table(:shipments)
NOTICE:  CREATE TABLE will create implicit sequence "shipments_id_seq" for serial column
```

```
"shipments.id"
NOTICE:  CREATE TABLE / PRIMARY KEY will create implicit index "shipments_pkey" for
table "shipments"
   -> 0.0692s
==  CreateShipments: migrated (0.0693s) =========================================
```

20. Next, you need to create a random token to be used by OAuth for encryption. Create this with OpenSSL by issuing the following command:

```
$ ruby -ropenssl -rbase64 -e "puts Base64.strict_encode64
(OpenSSL::Random.random_bytes(16).to_str)"
mYr4Nd0MlYg3N3r4t3dT0k3N==
```

21. Add this token, along with the settings you noted earlier from the Remote Access screen in Database.com, to the config vars for your Heroku app:

```
$ heroku config:set CONSUMER_KEY=tH15l5mYc0N5uM3r.K3y
CONSUMER_SECRET=1234567890123456789 TOKEN_ENCRYPTION_KEY=mYr4Nd0MlYg3N3r4t3dT0k3N==
Setting config vars and restarting social-chatter-example... done, v3
CONSUMER_KEY:           tH15l5mYc0N5uM3r.K3y
CONSUMER_SECRET:        1234567890123456789
TOKEN_ENCRYPTION_KEY:   mYr4Nd0MlYg3N3r4t3dT0k3N==
```

22. Test the app:

```
$ heroku open
Opening social-chatter-example... done
```

Figure 16-21 shows the home page (that was automatically redirected to HTTPS), which indicates that you have not yet logged in and need to do so.

> **Listing shipments**
>
> **Id Shipped Shipment date**
>
> You're not logged in. Click here to login.
>
> New Shipment

FIGURE 16-21

23. Use OAuth to log in with your Database .com credentials, as shown in Figure 16-22.

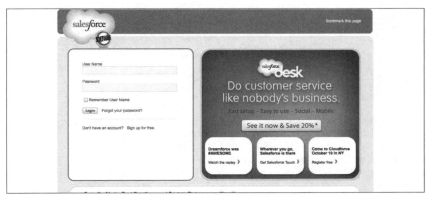

FIGURE 16-22

24. You are asked to grant permission for this app to access your information and data (see Figure 16-23). Click Allow.

You are then redirected back to your app. As shown in Figure 16-24, you are now logged in to Database.com.

FIGURE 16-23

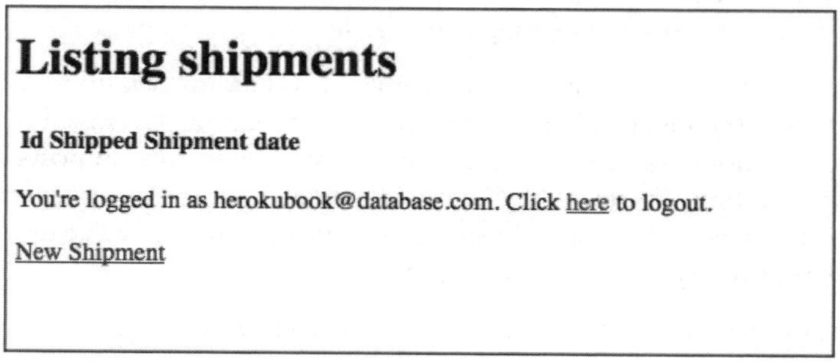

Listing shipments

Id Shipped Shipment date

You're logged in as herokubook@database.com. Click here to logout.

New Shipment

FIGURE 16-24

25. Enter a numeric ID, leave Shipped unchecked, and choose a date in the future. Click the New Shipment link to create a new Shipment record (see Figure 16-25).

26. Add a Chatter post to the record by entering **When is this going to ship?** in the available text field, and then clicking Post (see Figure 16-26).

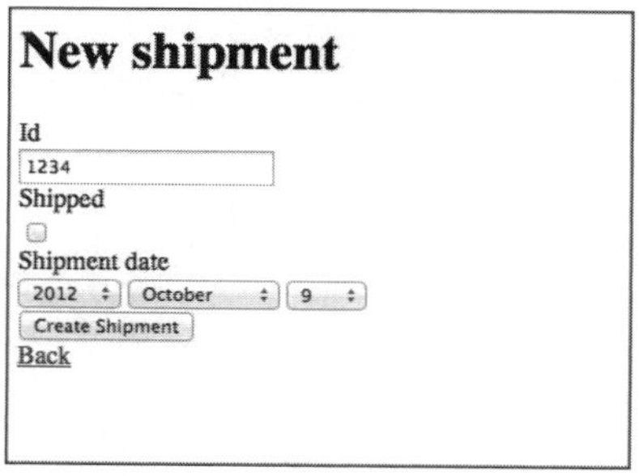

FIGURE 16-25

FIGURE 16-26

When you navigate back to your record, you will see the new post, as shown in Figure 16-27.

Congratulations! You have successfully made your Postgres-backed app social with Database.com and the Chatter API. We leave it as an exercise for the reader to create a news feed on the index page containing all of the Chatter for your records.

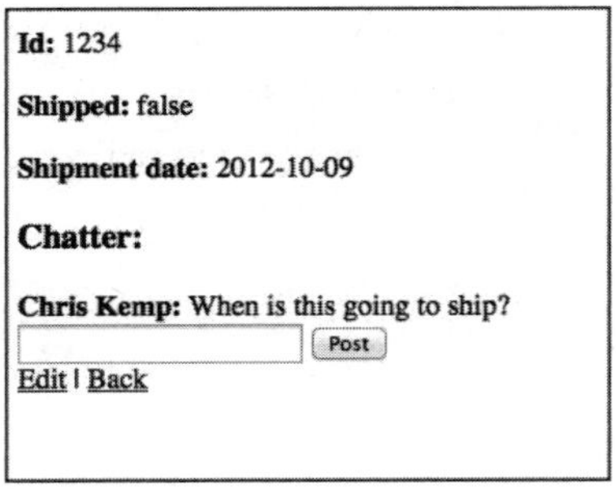

Id: 1234

Shipped: false

Shipment date: 2012-10-09

Chatter:

Chris Kemp: When is this going to ship?

Post

Edit | Back

FIGURE 16-27

SUMMARY

In this chapter, you learned how Heroku is used to create both public and private social apps. The viral nature of public social apps makes Heroku an excellent fit because of its rapid scalability. With the marked improvements in developer productivity, Heroku allows systems of innovation, like social apps, to be developed quickly, and allows organizations to experiment with many innovative ideas.

To create a Facebook app on Heroku, you must first create a Facebook Canvas app. Facebook Canvas apps give you access to the Facebook Graph API, which allows you to do things such as see a visitor's user information, who a visitor is friends with, and which of your visitor's friends have accessed your app. Heroku is the only official hosting provider for Facebook apps.

Social apps can be private to your organization, helping members collaborate on internal data in a secure environment. Database.com includes the Chatter API, which can be leveraged to make data social by adding social functionality like news feeds, posts, and comments on posts to your apps. Shadow objects are used to link Chatter API feeds to a back-end database, like Heroku Postgres. This allows you to make your apps social using a feed as a service like Chatter, rather than reinventing the wheel by writing your own social functionality.

Now that you have created apps that are both mobile and social, you can see how Heroku can be used to create the new generation of apps.

APPENDIX

Additional Resources

This appendix describes several useful websites that will help you as a Heroku developer. Some sites provide additional content that is useful for continued learning. Other sites offer a community of Heroku developers and experts with whom those new to the platform can interact. Some are simply sites that Heroku developers should be aware of to keep track of changes and updates to the ever-improving Heroku platform.

THE HEROKU WEBSITE

www.heroku.com

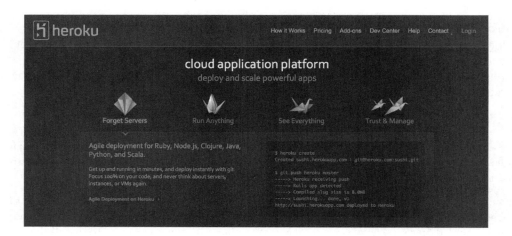

If you have gotten this far in the book, you have already been to this site many times. It's your first stop for logging in to Heroku and provides important information. Want to find out about Heroku's pricing? Check out the pricing page (www.heroku.com/pricing#0-0). To find out how to contact the folks at Heroku, see the contact information page (www.heroku.com/contact).

Now that you're a Heroku expert and realize how awesome Heroku really is, perhaps you would like to work there. For information on working at Heroku and a list of available positions, check out the jobs page (`http://jobs.heroku.com/`). Want to dive deeper into Heroku's legal or privacy policies? There are legal (`http://policy.heroku.com/promise`) and privacy (`http://policy.heroku.com/privacy`) policy pages there, too.

THE HEROKU DEV CENTER

`https://devcenter.heroku.com/`

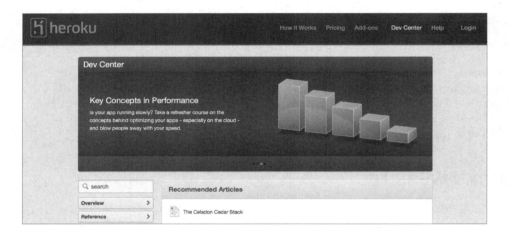

The Heroku Dev Center is your one-stop shop for all things Heroku. Whenever you need a reference for a particular command, APIs, or the tools you can use for building Heroku apps, the reference section is the place to be. You can also find a number of useful tutorials for different languages, frameworks, and types of apps (e.g., Facebook, mobile, etc.). In-depth language-specific information is also available.

For administrative information, including FAQs on billing, see `https://devcenter.heroku.com/categories/billing`; for support information, see `https://devcenter.heroku.com/categories/support`). You can also find numerous articles about the various add-ons available for Heroku. For instance, if you are interested in getting started with a particular add-on, chances are good that the add-on publisher has already published Heroku-specific instructions here.

You can also search the vast amounts of information here to find the answers you need. Instead of going to the Heroku Dev Center page every time you want to look something up, you can use the OpenSearch-enabled Heroku Dev Center search engine plugin for your browser. To install the Dev Center plugin (compatible with most modern versions of Firefox, IE, and Chrome), go to the Mycroft Project site at `http://mycroft.mozdev.org/search-engines.html?name=heroku`.

Now that you're an expert, why not contribute a Dev Center article for the community? Several open topics (`https://devcenter.heroku.com/articles/open-topics`) are waiting for experts to contribute their knowledge. There is also a style guide (`https://devcenter.heroku.com/articles/writing`) available to coach you along in writing your first article.

PROFESSIONAL HEROKU PROGRAMMING'S GITHUB REPOSITORY

https://github.com/ProfessionalHerokuProgramming

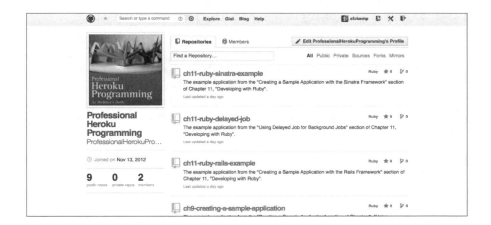

The code examples in this book are available for download at www.wrox.com/remtitle .cgi?isbn=1118508998, with the file name containing the code for each example indicated before each example. However, some prefer to use GitHub, which allows you to leverage the `heroku git:clone` command to get a local copy of the code quickly and easily. The authors of this book provide this GitHub repository as a convenience for readers to work with the example code.

LOG A TICKET WITH HEROKU SUPPORT

https://help.heroku.com/tickets/new

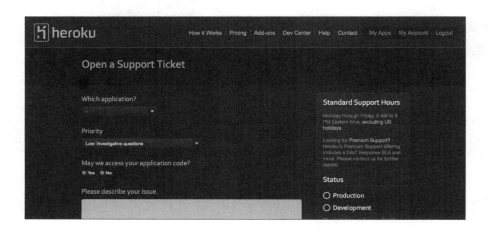

Sometimes you may run into a problem for which you can't find the answer. (Continue reading this appendix for a number of places you can look first.) Other times, something on Heroku may not work as you expect. Fortunately, Heroku's technical support team offers free real-time support 6:00 a.m. to 6:00 p.m. Pacific Time, Monday to Friday (excluding U.S. holidays). Either you can e-mail the support team using the `support@heroku.com` address (assuming you have access to send the e-mail to them from the account associated with your Heroku account), or you can log a ticket on the support site at `https://help.heroku.com/tickets/new`.

You can check Heroku's support policy at `http://policy.heroku.com/support` to see what sort of issues the support team can help with. If you are looking for a higher level of service — for instance, with 24x7 ticketed and phone support around the clock, an assigned technical account manager for one-on-one, expert consultation, and direct access to members of Heroku's technical staff, among other benefits — either visit `http://go.heroku.com/critical/` or contact your Salesforce.com account manager to discuss package options. This level of service is highly recommended for any business-critical apps that you are running on Heroku.

HEROKU NINJA

www.herokuninja.com

Heroku Ninja is the personal site of Chris Kemp, one of the co-authors of this book. There is a blog on the Heroku Ninja site where you can get information about this book, including corrections, announcements and updates on future editions, and links to resources and articles that Chris thinks are cool. If you have read this book, you are definitely going to want to visit here regularly to keep up to date.

HEROKU JAVA

http://java.heroku.com/

The Heroku Java site is the starting place for any Java developer who wants to learn more about Java on Heroku. Note that most of the links here are the same as those to the general Heroku site with a couple of key differences. First, there are convenient links to blog posts, events, and Twitter tweets of interest to Java developers. Second, and most important, there are the very useful Create App buttons.

These are the very same templates that you can use with the Eclipse plugin to quickly create Java apps on Heroku. When you click the Get Started button, Heroku will clone the template into a new Heroku app and display instructions outlining how to get started with either Eclipse or the command-line interface.

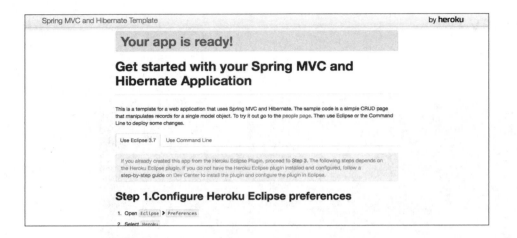

STACK OVERFLOW

`http://stackoverflow.com/questions/tagged/heroku`

At some point in your Heroku programming career, you will run into a problem that you can't solve yourself. If you search the question online, chances are good that the answer will show up in the results from a question on Stack Overflow, the free Q&A site meant for, and run by, programmers of all languages to help with development-related questions. The people who drop in here eat curly braces for lunch, so don't be afraid to throw down some code when asking (or answering!) a question.

Indeed, as you move forward in your path to becoming a Heroku expert, this is also a great place to give back to the community by answering other developers' questions on Heroku. There is a Heroku tag that you can filter on to view only Heroku-related questions (`http://stackoverflow.com/questions/tagged/Heroku`). You can filter further to find questions with combinations of tags aligned to your area of expertise (e.g., Heroku + Java or Heroku + Ruby). Either way, your participation builds a reputation score based on the quantity and quality of your questions and answers. As you build your score, you also unlock certain privileges (`http://stackoverflow.com/privileges`).

HEROKU COMMUNITY GOOGLE GROUP

```
https://groups.google.com/forum/?fromgroups#!forum/heroku
```

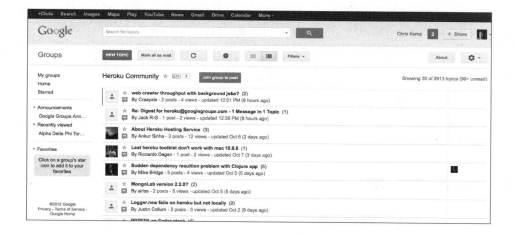

Google Groups are just what the name implies — groups in which to have discussions. They are similar to message boards but have a very familiar interface that could only be Google. You can also be e-mailed when people post, get combined updates (25 posts per e-mail), and receive daily summaries of activities on groups. The Heroku Google Group is one of the unofficial support channels (along with the IRC channel and Twitter) that some members of the Heroku team occasionally visit to answer questions.

HEROKU IRC CHANNEL

```
#heroku on Freenode
```

For those who prefer real-time conversations, Heroku has an Internet Relay Chat (IRC) channel. This enables you to tap into the expertise on the channel to ask questions, engage in dialogue, share best practices, and generally geek out about the awesomeness of Heroku among peers. You can access the IRC channel using either a client or the web. mIRC is a popular client for Windows (`www.mirc.com/`) and Adium is a popular Mac OS X client (`www.adium.im/`). You can access Freenode through the web at `http://webchat.freenode.net/`. The IRC channel is an unofficial support channel on which members of the Heroku team sometimes lurk to chat with members of the community and answer their questions.

HEROKU'S TWITTER ACCOUNTS

```
https://twitter.com/heroku
```

Want to get the latest news on Heroku, 140 characters at a time? Then you should definitely follow Heroku's official Twitter account, `@heroku`. With 17,000 followers and growing, this account will help keep you abreast with important announcements and interesting news and articles of interest to Heroku users. There are several Twitter accounts related to Heroku:

- `@herokustatus`: This provides real-time news and updates about issues and outages on the Heroku platform.

- `@HerokuChangelog`: Alerts users to any additions and changes made to the Heroku platform. This is a must-follow for any Heroku power user who wants to keep on top of changes, feature additions, and deprecations.

- `@HerokuDevCenter`: Keep your Heroku knowledge up to date by staying on top of new articles in the Heroku Dev Center.

- `@HerokuPostgres`: Learn about what's new with Heroku's database-as-a-service offering and Postgres in general with the official Heroku Postgres group's Twitter account.

- `@HerokuAddons`: Use this to stay informed about the latest additions to the Add-ons ecosystem as well as interact with the Add-ons team and receive quick status updates.

- `@HerokuVibe`: Want to see what it's like to work at Heroku? Live and breathe the awesome culture of employees at Heroku, also known as *Herokai*.

- `@bgyger`: This is the Twitter account for Brad Gyger, co-author of this book.

- `@herokuninja`: This is the Twitter account for Chris Kemp, the other author of this book.

Also, be sure to follow key members of the Heroku team at `https://twitter.com/i/#!/heroku/crew`.

If you don't check Twitter very often or prefer to get important alerts via e-mail, you can use a service like Feed My Inbox (`www.feedmyinbox.com/`) to have tweets from Heroku's accounts e-mailed to you.

HEROKU'S OFFICIAL BLOG

`http://blog.heroku.com/`

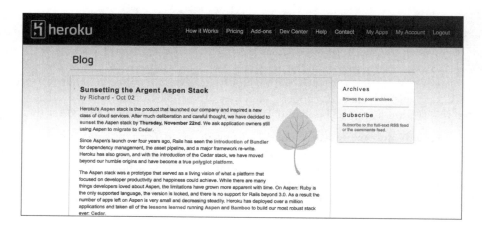

The Heroku Blog is required reading for every Heroku developer. It is mostly announcements that are discussed in far more detail than the Facebook or Twitter pages provide. (How in depth can you be with only 140 characters?) There is also an interactive component to blog posts, with a Disqus forum built in to enable comments, and tags at the bottom of each post that enable searching similar posts.

If you are new to the Heroku Blog and want to see a history of topics previously discussed, you can also browse the blog's archives (`http://blog.heroku.com/archives`), which extend all the way back to the kick-off post made in October 2007 (`http://blog.heroku.com/archives/2007/10/30/the_big_kickoff/`.) If you prefer to consume this feed with your favourite RSS reader, you can subscribe to it at `http://feeds2.feedburner.com/heroku`.

HEROKU NEWS

`http://news.heroku.com/`

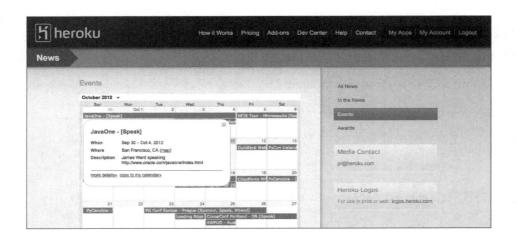

Heroku News is a site dedicated to keeping you up to date with what is new in the world of Heroku. Most of the news here is PR-based, such as press releases, awards that Heroku has won (`http://news.heroku.com/awards`), and articles in which Heroku has been featured or mentioned (`http://news.heroku.com/in_the_news`). Not found here are all the cool new features and announcements that typically excite developers; Heroku's official blog or some of the other avenues featured in this section (e.g., Facebook and Twitter) will probably be more useful for that.

The part of this site that will most interest developers is the events page (`http://news.heroku.com/events`), which lists all the local events that Heroku is sponsoring or events where members of the Heroku team are speaking at, across the world. If you use Google Calendar, you can also synchronize this information with it to stay informed about all upcoming events. They offer a great way to meet with other Heroku users and members of the Heroku team.

HEROKU ON FACEBOOK

https://www.facebook.com/Heroku

Heroku's official Facebook page contains interesting links, useful tidbits, product announcements, discussions, and photos of the folks at Heroku doing crazy fun things. In addition, if you want to find out what is being served for lunch at Heroku's offices, check out the link to the Starving Samurai Tumblr blog (http://starving-samurai-42.tumblr.com/). Haven't you always wanted to "Like" Heroku so all your friends know how awesome it is?

HEROKU STATUS

https://status.heroku.com/
http://status.addons.heroku.com/

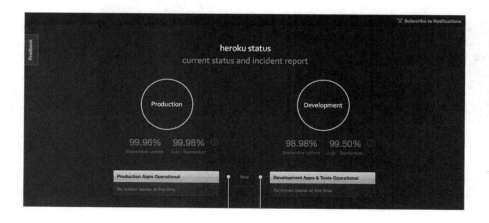

The Heroku Status site provides real-time updates regarding incidents on the Heroku platform. Green circles indicate that all is currently well; yellow circles indicate intermittent issues; and red circles indicate a major disruption in service. These rings change colour in real time as updates are received from the Heroku command center using the Pusher add-on.

A timeline along each side shows a history of incidents that affect the normal operation of dynos, Heroku Postgres databases, HTTP caching, routing, or other platform components. Each incident can be clicked on to see a detailed report about that incident. Recent uptime statistics for the platform are shown here as well, providing operational transparency and accountability.

Using the link in the top-right corner, you can also subscribe to notifications through a variety of methods, including e-mail, SMS, and RSS feeds. If anything seems to be going wrong on Heroku, this is the first place you want to check to find out what's going on and track the issue until it is resolved.

The Heroku Addon Provider Status site (`http://status.addons .heroku.com/`) provides a dashboard-style summary of all current providers, including those whose service is up and available or seeing issues. Also here is a link to the various Twitter accounts for each provider.

HEROKU POSTGRES

> `https://postgres.heroku.com/`

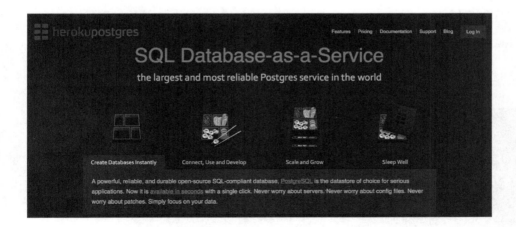

Heroku's popular data as a service (DaaS) has its own dedicated site although, much like the Java site, most of the links are the same as heroku.com. This site includes information about key features, such as forking, following, multi-ingress, and automated health checks, along with some important videos demonstrating key features in action.

The site also contains information about the Heroku Postgres plans offered (`https://postgres`
`.heroku.com/pricing`) and what each one includes.

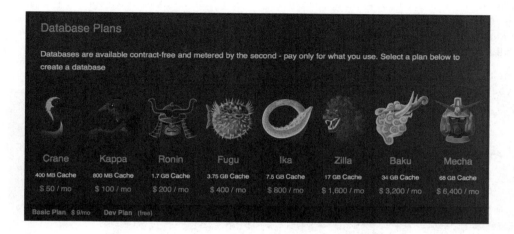

You can keep on top of the latest Heroku Postgres news by visiting the Heroku Postgres Blog
(`https://postgres.heroku.com/blog`) on this site as well. It is also available via RSS feed
at `https://postgres.heroku.com/blog/rss` if you prefer to consume the information that way.
Previous posts are archived at `https://postgres.heroku.com/blog/past`.

HEROKU ADD-ONS

`https://addons.heroku.com/`

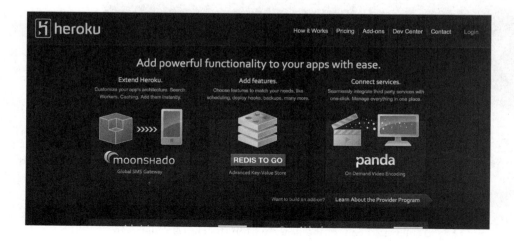

Chapter 6, "Working with Add-Ons," was devoted to the Heroku add-on ecosystem. By now, you've probably already visited the Heroku Add-ons site. It is recommended that all Heroku developers familiarize themselves with the add-ons available there. Each generally available add-on includes a full description of what the add-on does, a list of all the plans, and a link to add a specific plan to your app. Most add-ons also have a Docs link in the top-right corner that links to associated documentation for that add-on in the Dev Center, or you may find links in the description to documentation on the add-on provider's website.

Also available is a changelog for add-on apps at `https://addons.heroku.com/changelog`. This will alert you when new apps are available or beta apps become generally available. You can also add `https://addons.heroku.com/changelog.rss` to your RSS reader to consume this as a feed.

HEROKU ADD-ON PROVIDER SITE

`https://addons.heroku.com/provider`

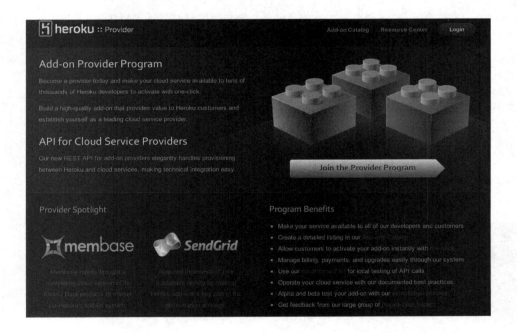

In the "Creating Add-Ons" section of Chapter 6, we briefly reviewed the process to create add-ons on Heroku and curate a service that can be made available via the Heroku ecosystem. The Provider site provides all the details for both the business and technical details of the Heroku Add-on Provider Program.

Visit the Provider Resource Center to walk through the steps to join the program, create and connect your service, and then start generating usage within the Heroku platform.

DATABASE.COM USER GUIDE

http://docs.database.com/dbcom/en-us/db_help/index.htm

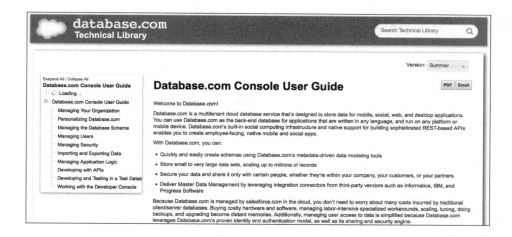

Chapter 9, "Using Database.com as a Data Store for Your Heroku Applications," described how to use Database.com as a backing data store for your apps. A full discussion of setting up and maintaining your Database.com environment was beyond the scope of the chapter, however. For numerous helpful links and videos, simply click Help & Training when you are logged in to Database.com; and the user guide provides more detailed information about many topics that will be very useful to Database.com users.

For instance, you will need to set up your organization (http://docs.database.com/dbcom/en-us/db_help/dbcom_help_managing_your_organization.htm), which includes tasks such as setting up your company's time zone, currencies, and locales, and monitoring usage (especially API usage, as your Heroku app is using this). You will also learn here how to manage users within your environment (http://docs.database.com/dbcom/en-us/db_help/dbcom_help_managing_users.htm) and add a layer of security to your database so only specified users can see certain records (http://docs.database.com/dbcom/en-us/db_help/dbcom_help_managing_security.htm). Instructions on loading data into and extracting data out of your Database.com database are also available here (http://docs.database.com/dbcom/en-us/db_help/dbcom_help_importing_and_exporting_data.htm).

Advanced topics include adding advanced logic to your data layer (http://docs.database.com/dbcom/en-us/db_help/dbcom_help_managing_application_logic.htm), such as to add an Apex trigger that executes when records are inserted or updated. You may also want to set up a separate Database.com database, called a *sandbox*, for testing (http://docs.database.com/dbcom/en-us/db_help/dbcom_help_developing_and_testing_in_a_sandbox_organization.htm), which contains a subset of your production data. Finally, if things don't work as expected, perhaps with something such as triggers, you can use the Developer Console to debug problems (http://docs.database.com/dbcom/en-us/db_help/dbcom_help_working_with_the_developer_console.htm).

To learn about support options, such as ticket-based support, or to get pricing information if you are hitting the limits of your free account, simply go to the Database.com site and click on Pricing (`www.database.com/en/pricing`).

DEVELOPER FORCE INTEGRATION

`http://wiki.developerforce.com/page/Integration`

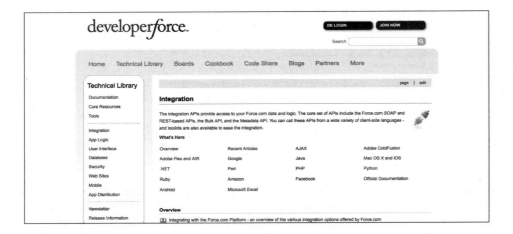

If you are looking for a language-specific toolkit and information on integrating with Database .com, either standalone or as a part of your company's Salesforce environment, the Developer Force Integration page is the first place you should go. A couple of examples in this book used the `databasedotcom` gem (`https://rubygems.org/gems/databasedotcom`) to do integrations with Ruby, but many other libraries and toolkits can be used to integrate with Database.com with your language of choice.

If you are developing a Java app there are many different methods to integrate it (`http://wiki .developerforce.com/page/Integration#Java`) with the Force.com Web Services Connector, Apache Axis, or JAX-WS. Perl apps can use the Perl Toolkit or the Perl CPAN DBD Salesforce module to integrate (`http://wiki.developerforce.com/page/Integration#Perl`). PHP developers can use the Force.com Toolkit for PHP or the Bulk API client, depending on which API is best (`http://wiki.developerforce.com/page/Integration#PHP`). Also available are a few different toolkits that can be used for Python integration (`http://wiki.developerforce.com/ page/Integration#Python`). Alternatively, you can simply use the documentation here to interface with the REST API with just about any language under the sun.

Regardless of the language you are developing with or the use case you have for moving information in and out of Database.com, numerous integration methods and tools can be used. This is also a one-stop shop for documentation on each of the APIs available (`http://wiki.developerforce .com/page/Web_Services_API#Official_Documentation`), along with a handy print-out cheat sheet (`https://na1.salesforce.com/help/doc/en/salesforce_api_developer_cheatsheet.pdf`).

FORCE.COM DISCUSSION BOARDS

```
http://boards.developerforce.com/t5/Developer-Boards-for-Force-com/ct-p/developers
```

If you are developing an app that integrates with Database.com and can't find your answer in the Database.com user guide, you can tap the Force.com Discussion Boards to get help from the Force.com developer community. Of particular interest to those developing social apps will be the Chatter and Chatter API Development board (`http://boards.developerforce.com/t5/Chatter-and-Chatter-API/bd-p/chatter`). If you are building out a database schema, the Schema Development board (`http://boards.developerforce.com/t5/Schema-Development/bd-p/schema`) will be very useful. If you get stuck while writing triggers, the Apex Development board (`http://boards.developerforce.com/t5/Apex-Code-Development/bd-p/apex`) is the place to go for answers.

If you integrating Database.com with a Java app, the Java Development board (`http://boards.developerforce.com/t5/Java-Development/bd-p/JAVA_development`) is a great place to discuss this. If you are building an app on Heroku with Perl, PHP, Python, or Ruby, the Perl, PHP, Python, and Ruby Development board (`http://boards.developerforce.com/t5/Perl-PHP-Python-Ruby-Development/bd-p/PerlDevelopment`) is the place to go for language-specific integration questions. The APIs and Integration board (`http://boards.developerforce.com/t5/APIs-and-Integration/bd-p/integration`) is more of a general forum for any type of integration.

HEROKU'S GITHUB SITE

```
https://github.com/heroku
```

Curious about the inner workings of some of the tools, such as the Heroku command-line interface? Want to see how the supported buildpacks work behind the scenes? Want to check out some sample apps that the folks at Heroku have developed? Heroku's Github site is the place to look for all this and much, much more.

Heroku takes a very open approach to development, open sourcing most of the tools, plugins, and buildpacks that are used by the Heroku platform. Pretty much everything except the core Heroku kernel is available here. Heroku also encourages members of the community to make improvements and fix bugs they find. Feel free to fork a repository you see in there and submit your merge request to contribute, making the Heroku platform better for everyone.

HEROKU API DOCUMENTATION

```
https://api-docs.heroku.com/
```

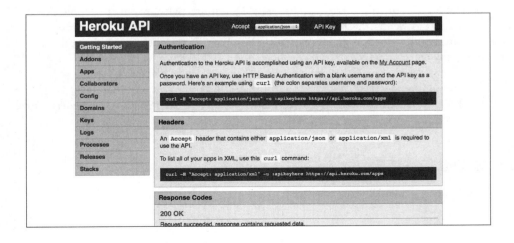

Heroku has an open API to its control layer. Heroku tools such as the command-line interface and the Eclipse plugin, which aid in performing tasks such as installing add-ons to apps, scaling processes, and viewing a list of releases for an app, use this API. Third-party organizations have also leveraged this API to build things such as mobile apps that can be used to interface with your Heroku apps through your smartphone or tablet. Others have built out auto-scaling tools that can monitor your apps logs and intelligently scale up or down.

How you use the Heroku API is up to you. Because Heroku's API is open, they provide a powerful way to tune your apps and do so automatically. However, with great power comes great responsibility. If you scale up an app automatically and it uses a lot of dynos, resulting in a huge bill at the end of the month, you are still on the hook for these costs. Proceed cautiously when using the API, as you are responsible for your actions, even if they are automated.

HEROKU PARTNERS

```
https://partners.heroku.com/
```

Even after you become a Heroku expert, sometimes there aren't enough hours in the day to do everything you want to do. Everyone needs some help sometimes. If you're looking for an agency or contractor to help design and/or develop an app on Heroku, the Partner site is the place to go to find the right partner for your project.

On the Heroku Partner site, you can find a partner using a variety of criteria. For example, you can use the interactive map on the home page if you prefer to use someone local. Perhaps you're looking for specific expertise (e.g., a Ruby or Java shop), or maybe you just want training for your developers or specialized skills in building mobile apps. It may also be that you want to find a partner that fits a certain budget level for a project. On the Heroku Partner site, you can search by development language, skill, location, or billing rate to find the perfect partner.

You can also become a partner and leverage the expertise you learned in this book to earn praise and profit. Visit `https://partners.heroku.com/program` for more information on how to apply to become an official Heroku partner.

HEROKU BETA PROGRAM SIGN-UP

`https://beta.heroku.com/signup`

Before new features are released to the general public, they are available through the Heroku Beta program. They typically go through two stages: a private beta program available only to select users, and a public beta whose features are available to all but should be used with production apps with caution. Heroku screens users for the private beta program, looking for a focused group that can provide useful feedback to make the features better before they become generally available.

If you want to apply, you must go to the Heroku Beta Sign-up page and indicate why you would be a good beta tester, perhaps listing your excellent communication skills and other beta programs that you have participated in and how you contributed. You can also indicate which program(s) you want to join if you have heard about specific features to which you would like early access. Shortly after submitting your app, you should receive an activation e-mail.

HEROKU SUCCESS STORIES

`http://success.heroku.com/`

Want to hear about the cool things that other Heroku customers are doing? Look no further than the Heroku Success site. Here, each story highlights a particular organization and an app that they are using Heroku to run. Each story lists the number of dynos that the client typically uses, what type of data stores it uses, what Heroku Postgres database plan they use (if they are using one), and highlights a few of the key add-ons that they are using to run their app.

Stories here come from organizations of all shapes and sizes. Some are success stories of agencies that have built cool Heroku apps for other companies, such as ALLDAYEVERYDAY (`http://success.heroku.com/ade`), a full-service creative agency that has built apps for well-known brands like Ann Taylor and Dos Equis; and Milyoni (`http://success.heroku.com/milyoni`), which built an e-commerce site for Warner Brothers where up to 25 million Facebook users rent and watch movies on Facebook, using Facebook credits.

Other stories focus on interesting use cases for Heroku, such as SCVNGR (`http://success.heroku.com/scvngr`), which is using Heroku as a mobile back end; or PageLever (`http://success.heroku.com/pagelever`), which uses Heroku via API calls from Facebook to provide an analytics platform for your brand's social media presence. For nearly any use case you are looking for, someone has probably done it already and posted the success story on Heroku's Success Stories site.

HEROKU ON VIMEO

`http://vimeo.com/heroku`

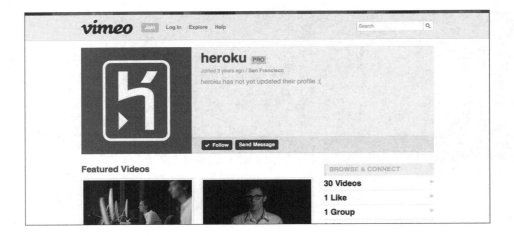

Heroku archives a number of interesting videos on Vimeo, a popular video-sharing site. Most of the videos on this site are case studies, similar to those found on the Success Stories site but in an easier to consume format. There are also some instructional videos, such as on Facebook/Heroku integration (`http://vimeo.com/29082940`), and a number of workshop videos, featuring both internal and guest speakers, such as Twilio (`http://vimeo.com/13770489`).

You can also find other neat videos here that are not use cases or instructional in nature. For instance, if you want to find out what it's like to work at Heroku, check out the video at `http://vimeo.com/33429172`; or perhaps you want to learn about the Heroku Customer Advisors and how they help make the Heroku platform better (`http://vimeo.com/33431113`). There's a lot of interesting videos here to keep you occupied for hours.

HEROKU WAZA

`http://waza.heroku.com/`

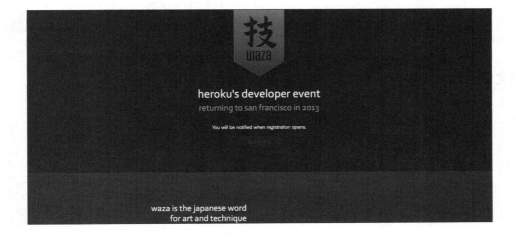

Waza is Heroku's conference for developers — a place to get together, share best practices, and hear a lot of very smart people orate on their subject of expertise. It was held for the first time at Yoshi's Jazz Club and Japanese restaurant in San Francisco on January 12, 2012, and quickly proved itself to be no ordinary developer event. As one attendee said, "Waza is like Burning Man for nerds!" It is also free.

If you want to check out the sessions from the 2012 conference, they are available on Vimeo at `http://vimeo.com/groups/waza2012`. You can also view photos of the event on Flickr at www `.flickr.com/groups/2080225@N23/pool/with/7874588512/#photo_7874588512`. If you want to be notified when detailed information about upcoming events is available, click the Notify Me button on the site's home page.

THE TWELVE-FACTOR APP

`www.12factor.net/`

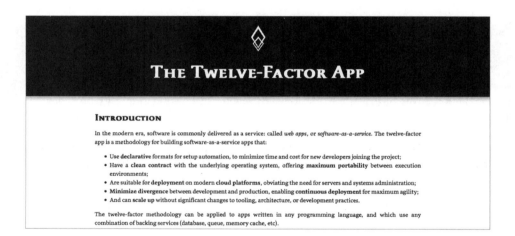

Chapter 2, "Architectural Considerations," discussed the Twelve-Factor App, which is Adam Wiggins' manifesto outlining a best practice methodology for building web apps for maximum scalability and portability. We would be remiss not to mention this site again while outlining important additional resources, simply because it is such an important work for every developer to read and internalize. Even if you have already read this material, you may want to review it again.

Many of the patterns demonstrated and discussed throughout this book are outlined here, such as treating backing services as attached resources (`www.12factor.net/backing-services`); and keeping production and development environments as similar as possible (`www.12factor.net/dev-prod-parity`). Now that you have seen what Heroku can do and how it does it, this site will help you understand why Heroku was designed as it was by exposing the blueprint that made it happen.

JAMES WARD'S BLOG

`www.jamesward.com/`

Many Heroku experts have a blog, but the standout blog among them is definitely James Ward's. James previously held the role of Principal Developer Evangelist at Heroku and is a true coder at heart. He is constantly exploring new and exciting frameworks, holding interesting talks at events across the world, and discussing best practices for making Heroku apps. His blog is heavy on code samples and tutorials and pushes the envelope in terms of what can be done on Heroku. His focus is heavily biased towards Java, Play, and Scala, and is a must-read for Heroku developers of JVM-based languages.

INDEX